PRAISE FOR
THE TV BRAND BU

'*The TV Brand Builders* is an outstanding and in-depth examination of the craft of television marketing, full of insight, perspective and anecdotes into what really works and why. It is sure to become a must-read for all those wanting to understand what's important in today's rapidly evolving TV landscape. Bryant and Mawer combine their many years of experience to provide the reader with an entertaining and easily read journey into how to build a TV brand.'

Jeremy Darroch, CEO, Sky plc

'Rich in anecdote, example and insight, this is an encyclopedic survey of the crucial role marketing plays in great content finding audiences. It is an essential handbook for anyone looking to build content brands in a transmedia age.'

Wayne Garvie, Chief Creative Officer,
International Production, Sony Pictures Television

'Two of the field's top talents draw a road map of the best routes to brand just about any kind of television content. In the process, Bryant and Mawer entertain and inform you with a wealth of case studies, peppered with amusing anecdotes and assessments by a host of industry insiders. Written in an engaging style, this book is a must-read for its concise history of the evolution of television branding from in-house afterthought to a booming, and often entrepreneurial, industry sector.'

Jennifer Gillan, Professor, English and Media Studies, Bentley University, and
author of *Television Brandcasting: The return of the content–promotion hybrid*

'*The TV Brand Builders* manages to be both a weighty tome of real insight into the industry today, and a fun and gossipy read. Great case studies abound across the US market and it proves a valuable book for anyone wrestling with the challenge of finding and keeping viewers.'

Dave Howe, President, Strategy and Commercial Growth,
NBCUniversal Cable Entertainment

'As entertainment marketing continues to evolve, we must adapt to thrive in this new dynamic landscape. Bryant and Mawer are true visionaries in our industry. *The TV Brand Builders* gives all brand marketers, regardless of expertise, the insights needed to drive not only viewership but, more importantly, the deep emotional bonds that are the underpinning of the world's most valuable entertainment brands.'

Steve Kazanjian, President and CEO, PromaxBDA

'*The TV Brand Builders* is a gift to students and media industry scholars seeking to understand the fast-moving world of television marketing. Brimming with insights, and written with verve, the book offers a compelling and clear-sighted account of TV promotion from leading practitioners in the field. Bryant and Mawer bring all their experience to bear in demonstrating the creativity and skill of TV brand building. A must-read for anyone interested in promotional screen culture.'

Paul Grainge, Professor of Film and Television Studies, The University of Nottingham, and co-author of *Promotional Screen Industries*

'*The TV Brand Builders* is comprehensive, well-researched and insightful – the definitive guide for anyone looking to build their career in entertainment marketing.'

Walter Levitt, EVP, Chief Marketing Officer, Comedy Central

'I don't think I have ever read a more comprehensive account of the craft of marketing in television. There are many inspiring examples within an increasingly complex industry, which makes this book really valuable, as it describes the landscape so entirely. Armed with it, perhaps the TV marketing and branding fraternity can bring simplicity, joy and fun to communications despite that complexity.'

Martin Lambie-Nairn, founder, Lambie-Nairn, and author of *Brand Identity for Television: With knobs on*

'Was it ever true in TV that "if you build it, they will come"? It's certainly not so anymore in our exciting multi-screen, on-demand, dynamic industry. The art and science of TV marketing was never so vital, nor so full of possibility. But there are good reasons why it's still one of the most dysfunctional marketing jobs around, as frustrating as it is rewarding.

'This book, written by two people who have practised what they preach for many years at the heart of some of the most iconic TV marketing campaigns, is an absolute gold mine of best practice case studies, insider anecdotes and wise counsel. It covers every aspect of marketing TV, from channels to programmes, and from genres to sub-audiences. If you're trying to unpick your "timeless principles" from your "seismic changes" as you nobly serve audiences, producers and broadcasters, you'd be dotty not to have this book at your side.'

Tess Alps, Chair, Thinkbox

'A fascinating piece of television history that shows how marketers moved from being the monkeys to the organ grinders of the broadcasting world, this book will be enjoyed by broadcasting professionals as well as those who just love watching TV. The authors take us into the much maligned and misunderstood world of TV marketing, showing how this art will become evermore important as we move further into a multi-platform, on-demand age.'

Lorraine Heggessey, Advisor, Channel 4 Growth Fund, and former Controller, BBC One

'Fragmented, segmented, bundled, unbundled, TV marketing today apes 3D chess. Thoroughly researched and wonderfully compiled, this book transmits a clear picture of advertising and marketing's special role.'

Tim Lefroy, Chief Executive, Advertising Association

ANDY BRYANT
CHARLIE MAWER

THE TV BRAND BUILDERS

How to win audiences and influence viewers

KoganPage

LONDON PHILADELPHIA NEW DELHI

All views expressed are those of the authors, and do not represent the views of Ericsson Broadcast & Media Services.

First published in Great Britain and the United States in 2016 by Kogan Page Limited

2nd Floor, 45 Gee Street
London EC1V 3RS
United Kingdom
www.koganpage.com

1518 Walnut Street, Suite 900
Philadelphia PA 19102
USA

4737/23 Ansari Road
Daryaganj
New Delhi 110002
India

© Andy Bryant and Charlie Mawer, 2016

The right of Andy Bryant and Charlie Mawer to be identified as the authors of this work has been asserted by them in accordance with the Copyright, Designs and Patents Act 1988.

ISBN   978 0 7494 7668 7
E-ISBN   978 0 7494 7670 0

British Library Cataloguing-in-Publication Data

A CIP record for this book is available from the British Library.

Library of Congress Cataloging-in-Publication Data

Names: Bryant, Andy, author. | Mawer, Charlie, author.
Title: The TV brand builders : how to win audiences and influence viewers /
    Andy Bryant, Charlie Mawer.
Description: London ; Philadelphia : Kogan Page, 2016. | Includes
    bibliographical references and index.
Identifiers: LCCN 2015050760 (print) | LCCN 2016007539 (ebook) | ISBN
    9780749476687 (paperback) | ISBN 9780749476700 (ebook)
Subjects: LCSH: Television broadcasting--Marketing. | Television
    programs--Marketing. | Branding (Marketing) | BISAC: BUSINESS & ECONOMICS
    / Advertising & Promotion. | BUSINESS & ECONOMICS / Marketing / General. |
    BUSINESS & ECONOMICS / Industries / Media & Communications Industries.
Classification: LCC HE8689.7.M37 B79 2016 (print) | LCC HE8689.7.M37 (ebook)
    | DDC 384.55068/8--dc23
LC record available at http://lccn.loc.gov/2015050760

Typeset by Graphicraft Limited, Hong Kong
Print production managed by Jellyfish
Printed and bound by CPI Group (UK) Ltd, Croydon, CR0 4YY

CONTENTS

Acknowledgements xii

Introduction 1

PART ONE: THE CONTEXT 9

1 | **Marketing in the world of television** 11

The invisible pyramid 11
Marketers as content makers 13
Keeping a distance 14
Too many cooks? 15
The Tao of TV marketing 16
Three sides of a triangle 18
When it all comes together 20
Notes 24

PART TWO: BUILDING TV CHANNEL BRANDS 27

2 | **What's the point of a TV channel brand?** 29

Predictions of doom 29
The Unknown Prince Charles 30
Going on safari 31
Jam decisions 32
Detectives, wrestlers and dogs 33
What's in a line? 35
Blue skies and fruit bowls 37
Ingredients of success 39
Cloudier skies 39
Notes 41

3 | **Relaunching a TV channel: waving a flag on the horizon** 43

Share wars 43
Virgin Atlantic, Chicken McNuggets or Pampers? 44

The invisible channel 46
Flags, lighthouses and shipping lanes 47
Two little questions 48
A better version of Steve 50
'Doing a Dave' 52
Spreading the wit 53
Law and order 54
Pawnshops and tow trucks 55
An oasis of fun 56
X marks the spot 58
Vorsprung Durch Characters 60
Updating a classic 62
Flag wavers 62
Notes 63

4 The 800lb gorillas: building a big broadcast brand 67

The big three 67
In the frame 68
Clocks and globes 69
Circle time 70
Shouting to the blue summer sky 73
'You're going to reap just what you sow' 75
A brand in poor health 78
A rallying cry 79
Good enough is not enough 83
The big brand builders 84
Notes 84

5 The risk takers: building a TV channel brand with attitude 87

A revolution 87
A body with arms 91
Dipping a toe 92
Brain, heart and gut 94
A fearless network 97
The risk takers 98
Notes 98

6 | Idents: giving a channel a personality 101

Puzzles and blocks   101
Packaging with a purpose   102
The 2s   106
Killing 'boring'   110
Setting the blocks free   112
The origin story   114
An enduring role   116
Notes   116

PART THREE: BUILDING AND PROMOTING TV PROGRAMME BRANDS 119

7 | Marketing drama: glimpsing the future, unravelling the helix and speed dating 121

Why it matters so much   121
Speed dating   122
Emotional engagement   123
Down the lens   123
Universal themes   126
Glimpsing the future   128
The three-act structure   130
Music and rhythm   132
Finding a voice   132
Divide and conquer   134
Will it work on a pencil case?   136
Returning in the fall   139
Notes   143

8 | Timing and other secrets: a guide to promoting TV comedy 147

The hardest part   147
Crimes against comedy   148
This time next year we'll be millionaires   149
Deconstruct and reconstruct   152
Officially very funny   154
The secret...   157

If you work in marketing, kill yourself   157
Taking the marketing on the road   159
Go out on a laugh   160
Notes   161

9   Selling the news   163

Editorial balance versus marketing reductiveness   163
Choppers, dopplers and boots on the ground   164
The fight to be first   165
Moving a mountain   167
Anchorman   168
Closer to the people   169
Making people care   169
Re-creating the News   172
The biggest stories sell themselves   172
Future challenges   173
Notes   176

10   Promoting entertainment shows: scrubbing the shiny floors   179

Pressure in the spotlight   179
Lasting brands   180
The great survivor   182
Creating an event   182
The phone lines are open now   184
Hosts or format? You decide   185
Sociable. Shareable   189
Taking the show on the road   190
Putting on the party frock   191
Notes   192

11   Documentaries and reality: stories and storytellers   195

Why we watch what we watch   195
Programmes visible from space   197
Creating factual stars   200
Child labour   202
What type of storyteller are you?   203
Seasons and stunts   205
Shark Week   206
Treat it like a thriller   207

Scoring the thriller   208
Future focus   209
Notes   210

**12   Faster, higher, stronger, longer:
the hyperbolic world of TV sports promotion**   213

More important than life and death   213
Understanding a sports fan   215
Knowing the tribes   216
Seeing the funny side   218
Not giving it 110 per cent   220
In tune with the nation   221
Animation to avoid elimination   222
A successful campaign   223
The big ones   225
Shared memories   228
Putting the talent upfront   229
A P McCoy clings on   230
Bumping and grinding   230
'The Game Never Ends'   231
Notes   232

13   Marketing to children: nailing jelly to a moving train   235

Stories and characters   235
Involve me and I'll understand   236
Kids on screen   236
Playing along at home   237
Tracking down kids away from TV   239
The inventors of mash-up   241
An ever-changing audience   242
All the way through childhood   242
Keeping the worlds apart   243
Talking to the grown-ups   244
Kids versus Parents   245
Past and future generations   245
Rebels with a cause   246
Merchandise as marketing   247
A trusted friend   247
Showing character   248
Rewarding the viewers   249
Notes   251

PART FOUR: BUILDING BRANDS IN THE AGE OF ONLINE TV   253

14   Storyworlds: blurring the lines between content and marketing   255

A 'fatal' fall   255
Oceanic 815, The Serial Huntress and Bicycle Girl   256
Is it content or is it marketing?   258
Building early: the launch of *Defiance*   259
Creating immersive experiences   261
Developing characters: 'Let's Go To The Mall'   264
Sending 'love letters' to the audience   265
Keeping the storyworld alive   269
Taking the story into the real world   271
So where next?   273
Notes   274

15   Social media: from viewers to fans to friends   279

Two essential truths   279
The water cooler on steroids   280
Word of mouth amplified   281
It's all about the fans   281
A gas in your system   283
Before, during and after   284
Between the tent poles   286
Big data   288
Launching with social   288
Building a following   289
Being the first   291
Being responsive   295
Forging new bonds   295
Keep it in perspective   297
Notes   298

16   The future of TV marketing: seismic change, timeless principles   301

The enduring power of hits   301
Long live TV channel brands   303
The evolution of curatorial TV brands   304

Assertive producer brands   306
Fewer, bigger, better   307
Building an on-demand brand   308
The rise of usage-based promotion   311
Getting personal   312
A hybrid future   315
Our manifesto redux...   317
Notes   317

About the authors   321
Index   323

A bonus chapter, 'TV channel design in a multiscreen world', is available at the following url. (Please scroll to the bottom of the page and complete the form to access it.)

www.koganpage.com/TheTVBrandBuilders

ACKNOWLEDGEMENTS

When we set out to write a book about global best practice in TV marketing we knew that the project would stand or fall on the quality and breadth of our contributors. By the time we hit our deadline we had interviewed 50 leading practitioners from eight countries. They invited us to their offices, they met us in hotel lobbies, bars and coffee shops or they accepted conference calls across multiple time zones. They offered their encouragement and were unfailingly generous with their time, even when (in the manner of the TV detective Columbo) we kept returning to ask 'just one more thing'. In the process we learned so much more than we could ever have written from our own experiences and secondary research. So, first and foremost, we need to say a huge thank you to our TV Brand Builders:

ABC (Australia): Diana Costantini
AMC (USA): Linda Schupack
BBC (UK): Philip Almond, Justin Bairamian, Jane Lingham
Bravo/Oxygen (USA): Ellen Stone, Adam Zeller
CANAL+ (France): Olivier Schaack
CANAL+ (Spain): Germán Sela Orbe
CBS (USA): Beth Haiken
Channel 4 (UK): David Abraham, John Allison, Chris Bovill, Dan Brooke, James Walker
Comedy Central (USA): Walter Levitt
Discovery Networks (UK): Robin Garnett
Discovery Networks (Denmark): Carsten Lakner
DreamWorks (International): Jennifer Lawlor
ESPN (USA): Aaron Taylor (until 2015)
Fox (International): Liz Dolan
Fox (USA): Robin Benty
FX Networks (USA): Stephanie Gibbons, John Varvi
HBO (USA): Sabrina Caluori, Chris Spencer (until 2015)
Hulu (USA): Jenny Wall
ITV (UK): Clare Phillips, Tony Pipes, Rufus Radcliffe
Lee Hunt LLC (USA): Lee Hunt
loyalkaspar (USA): Daniel Dörnemann, David Herbruck
NBCUniversal (International): Marco Giusti, Lee Raftery
PromaxBDA (USA): Steve Kazanjian
Sky (UK): Robert Tansey
Sparkler (UK): Magnus Willis
Stun Creative (USA): Michael Vamosy
Syfy (USA): Michael Engleman (until 2015)

Trailer Park (USA): Rick Eiserman
truTV (USA): Puja Vohra
UKTV (UK): Simon Michaelides, Steve North
United Senses (Germany): Markus Schmidt
USA Network (USA): Jason Holzman, Alexandra Shapiro
Viacom (International): Kerry Taylor
Vice Media (USA): Rafael Sandor
Yle (Finland): Riikka Takila

(Please note that all titles and companies were correct at the time of writing.)

From the list above, our thanks go to two people in particular. As well as giving us insightful interviews themselves, Lee Hunt and Steve Kazanjian provided the keys to ensuring that our research covered a lot of ground in the US. Lee supported us from day one and opened the doors to some of our first interviews, which gave us confidence that we could make the whole project happen. Steve picked up the baton towards the end of the process and made introductions that helped us gather some vital contributions. Without the help of Lee and Steve this book would have been narrowly Euro-centric.

Alongside our interviewees we're also very grateful to the people in their organizations who helped us so diligently and cheerfully in responding to our e-mails, setting up meetings, nagging their bosses, securing permissions and supplying rights-cleared images. As a result of their efforts we ended up with enough material to fill three books and were left with the problem of what to leave on the cutting room floor. We started to write a list to thank everyone by name but once it exceeded 100 we realized that wouldn't be practical (and also realized what a task this had turned into). However, we would like to say a special thank you to Helen Prangnell at Channel 4, Jo Pitman at ITV and our colleague Uzma Painchun, who all put in a lot of effort beyond the call to help us secure key images without which the book would have looked a bit naked.

We set out to make this book as representative as possible. Despite television being, for understandable reasons, an IP-obsessed industry, almost everyone we approached was happy to share their thinking and their creative work and just a tiny minority weren't allowed to play. So, if you wonder why we didn't include network x, entertainment company y or campaign z... well, we tried.

We are indebted to our good friends from the Department of Culture, Film and Media at the University of Nottingham, Paul Grainge and Cathy Johnson, who encouraged us to believe there could be a gap in the market for this book, and to Andy Milligan, who supported us with huge amounts of practical advice. Andy guided us on how to write a half-decent proposal, it was thanks to his introduction that we found Kogan Page, and he was there for us as a 'phone a friend' throughout the journey. Quite simply, this book wouldn't exist without his help.

Talking of Kogan Page, we'd like to thank the team there who guided these first-time authors patiently through the process. Jasmin Naim believed in the project from the beginning, Philippa Fiszzon produced it skilfully and our thanks in particular go to Jenny Volich, our brilliant commissioning editor, who supported us indefatigably every step of the way.

The creative directors, designers, creatives, producers, production coordinators, researchers, account handlers and strategic planners who have been vital to us at Red Bee are numerous, and to single any individuals out here would be impossible. Occasionally we have credited people alongside particular pieces of work, but that is not to elevate them or their achievements above all the many other talented individuals whose work has been consistently of industry-leading class. They have been collectively – and deservedly – the most consistently awarded and genuinely nice people you could hope to spend years in the trenches with.

We must also acknowledge our clients, particularly the marketing department of the BBC, without whom much of the work described in the book would not have been commissioned. Again, far too many to mention individually, but for every bold creative decision and standout piece of promotional work, there had to be a bold marketer to sign it off, and we salute them.

It is important also to thank the craftspeople who over the years have made all our work exponentially better. For the last time, too many to list, but we will single out Thomas Ioannou, editor extraordinaire, who has modestly been the making of many creative careers. His eye and ear should be preserved in the BFI.

Our special thanks go to colleagues who helped to make the book possible to write in ways they may not even realize: Aileen Madden and Lisa Matchett, for putting up with us rambling about the project on long flights and train journeys and for offering wise advice and encouragement at the right times; Mandy Combes, Laura Gould and (for much of the time) Michelle Marks, for keeping the business on the rails in case our attention ever momentarily strayed. Thanks also to Thorsten Sauer, Elena Galkina, Stella Medlicott and Malin Allard for their support throughout the venture.

PERSONAL ACKNOWLEDGEMENTS FROM ANDY

I want to thank my mum and dad, who always encouraged me to write a book. Well, it took me this long to write half a book, but it's a start...

And there are not enough thanks for my wife Julia, whose achievements in recent years make this little project seem insignificant by comparison. Without her patience and understanding *The TV Brand Builders* could never have been written.

PERSONAL ACKNOWLEDGEMENTS FROM CHARLIE

I would like to thank my parents, whose disapproval of television in my early life was only matched by their enthusiasm for developing creativity and originality of thought. Hopefully demonstrating the latter has made up for a career in the former.

Thanks to Sue, Kit and Jem who have put up with a lot of writing over the years, much of which has still to find an audience.

Finally for Ceri Evans, who sadly passed away while I was writing this book. My first mentor, he stood behind me at a drinks party in an early month at the BBC whispering: 'Don't get sucked in.' Well sorry Ceri, I didn't listen to you on that point, but I listened to you on so much else. This book is really for you.

AB
For J, C & D

CM
For S, K & J

INTRODUCTION

*The puzzle, Grasshopper, that is to find a way
so that others may see you.*

MASTER PO, *KUNG FU*[1]

– LATE TO THE PARTY –

In one of those rare moments when an impending office move forces you to explore the darkest recesses of an old filing cabinet, we found a tattered, spiral-bound BBC report dated 1993. It was titled 'Up The Junction' – a song title from British new-wave band Squeeze applied to the TV industry term for the content between two TV programmes. A cross-discipline group had worked for months to answer the following question: 'In the future environment of a multichannel culture, how can BBC Presentation make use of its airtime between programmes to fulfil its vision?'[2] (For historical context, 'Presentation' was the BBC department responsible for, amongst other things, the junctions, including the announcers and promotional trailers. The predecessors of our own company, the department was spun off by the BBC as a commercial business and, later, sold.)

One of the key conclusions of the report was that BBC Television should 'appoint a marketing director'. This was 1993, remember. Can you imagine a company like Procter & Gamble (P&G), General Motors or Coca-Cola leaving it until the early 1990s to decide that marketing might be a useful skill to have around the place?

In the past, marketing in TV organizations had not enjoyed a high profile. Talented writers and producers (or, as they have come to be known in drama, showrunners) were the creative people in TV. They had the ideas, they attracted the talent, they made the shows. Commissioners and channel controllers used their creative judgement to back the right programmes and construct TV schedules that would pull in big audiences and keep them watching. At a time when there were very few channels to choose from, they did not have to try too hard to do that. Marketing, as ITV's group marketing and research director, Rufus Radcliffe, put it to us, was seen as nothing more than the 'mugs and T-shirts department'.[3]

But look at the top tables of some of the world's leading TV organizations today and you will find advertising and marketing people running the show. In the United States, at NBCUniversal alone there are currently three presidents of major channels with marketing backgrounds: Chris McCumber

(USA Network), who had been an agency creative director before a 10-year stint running USA Network's marketing; Dave Howe (Syfy and Chiller), who ran the BBC's in-house on-air creative division in London for many years; and Adam Stotsky (Esquire Network and E! Entertainment), who had a long marketing career at Discovery Communications and NBCUniversal, having started out at leading ad agency Fallon.

In the UK the picture is even more striking. David Abraham spent his early career as an account man in highly creative ad agencies before moving seamlessly into TV, first at Discovery Networks, then UKTV as chief executive officer (CEO) and, since 2010, at Channel 4 in the same role. His predecessor, Andy Duncan, had been marketing director at the BBC following a long career at Unilever, where he was responsible for brands including Flora and I Can't Believe It's Not Butter (look out for mentions of 'yellow fats' in Chapter 1). ITV's CEO, Adam Crozier, had been the youngest-ever board member of the legendary ad agency Saatchi & Saatchi, and BBC Worldwide is currently being led by Tim Davie, also a former BBC director of marketing, who was described somewhat dismissively by the *Telegraph* as 'the man who turned Concorde and the *Daily Mirror* blue', following an earlier role in the relaunching of Pepsi-Cola.[4] Davie even ran the BBC for a few months in 2012–13 as acting director-general in the wake of the Jimmy Savile affair: perhaps the ultimate symbol of the rise in status of marketing and brand building in the television industry.

– THE BATTLE FOR EYEBALLS –

So what happened? How did these talented and successful leaders graduate from 'mugs and T-shirts' to positions of such power and influence in television? What led to the ascendency of the TV Brand Builders?

To answer that question it is important to understand the seismic changes that have happened in the TV industry, globally, over the past 25 years or so. To summarize a complex and fascinating story, there have been two major transitions. The first started in earnest in the early 1990s when, as the BBC's Up The Junction working party recognized, the combination of digital technology and deregulation led to a rapid increase in the number of TV channels. It is hard to imagine, for example, that as recently as 1990 there were fewer than 10 nationally available channels for people to watch in the UK. The second transition is happening right now, as further technological innovation from the likes of Apple, Google and Roku, coupled with the entrepreneurial ambition of new players such as Netflix, Amazon and Hulu, is bringing viewers an even greater level of choice and control in their TV watching. All of this has meant one big thing. Competition. Intense and relentless competition for (to use the industry's somewhat vulgar term) 'eyeballs'. And with that competition has come a dramatic increase in the importance and influence of marketing and brand building. In the words of director of BBC Creative, Justin Bairamian:

> Marketing is really beginning to gain traction in broadcasting because there is so much proliferation. In the old days you didn't need marketing at the BBC. You had three channels and people sat and watched them.[5]

The proliferation that Justin refers to has fuelled one of the most dynamic and valuable sectors in the global economy.[6] Market-size calculations vary but Deloitte estimates total worldwide revenues from television advertising and subscription at over £260 billion and PwC predicts that TV advertising alone will generate revenue of over $200 billion globally by 2019.[7] (For the avoidance of doubt, when we say 'TV' we don't just mean the traditional device in the corner of the living room but all forms of on-screen video content.) TV dramas can have budgets of tens of millions of pounds per series and the US TV production industry, worth $35 billion, is growing at a healthy rate.[8] Major shows from *Game of Thrones* to *Downton Abbey*, from *EastEnders* to *House of Cards*, are reviewed in national media, dissected in blogs and tweets and debated passionately by viewers and fans. Their stars have become some of the biggest celebrities of our time.

But TV shows like this do not magically appear in our lives, fully formed and with established fan bases. They do not go from the first cut of a pilot episode to worldwide fame without the skill and talent of marketers in helping them to reach potential viewers. So how do these shows find an audience? How does marketing work in television? How are the great TV brands built?

– A NEW GOLDEN AGE –

Marketing has become a vital cog in the global TV machine. TV marketers within broadcasting, their in-house creative teams, specialist entertainment marketing agencies and even some of the major generalist ad agencies are collaborating to create distinctively positioned TV channels. They are attracting audiences to shows with engaging campaigns, harnessing social media to create a permanent sense of buzz and excitement amongst TV superfans and, increasingly, influencing the narrative of the shows themselves.

As one of our interviewees, Linda Schupack, executive vice president (EVP) of marketing at AMC Networks, said recently when talking to her alma mater Yale's School of Management: 'I am very privileged to be working in what many have called the new golden age of television.'[9] That phrase captures exactly how we both feel about the roles we have been lucky enough to enjoy in the TV marketing world. When we first started talking about this project, we felt sure that the topic would be well documented by many leading practitioners and industry commentators. We found that, to our surprise, the available literature on the subject beyond a small number of niche academic texts was very limited, so we decided to attempt to write a book ourselves about the role of marketing and brand building in this new golden age. We have been fortunate to work with some of television's most talented characters on a number of high-profile promotional campaigns and channel rebrands all over the world. However, a book relying on our personal experiences would not have captured the scope of marketing and creative innovation that has been happening globally in response to the recent dizzying changes in the industry. For that reason we set out to interview the world's best TV brand builders and draw on their wisdom and their most successful case studies. By the time we reached our publishing deadline we had managed to talk to a total of 50 of the TV marketing industry's leading figures, primarily in the influential US market and our home territory of the UK, but also taking in contributions from France, Germany, Spain, Denmark, Finland and Australia.

As we will go on to describe, around every corner there are challenges facing us all and each day seems to bring a new headline like this one:

A 'media meltdown'? Disney remark on TV viewing sends industry into tailspin[10]

That article from the *Los Angeles Times* describing a panicky dumping of media stocks by investors, sparked by a profit warning from Walt Disney Co due to reduced numbers of consumers subscribing to TV packages, was typical of the frequent scare stories about cord-cutting viewers, the inexorable rise of stand-alone TV programme brands and the death of TV as we know it. Senior industry executives, prompted by a speech by the influential CEO of FX Networks, John Landgraf, have even been debating recently whether there is simply too much good TV.[11]

Despite all that, amongst all our interviewees there was a unanimous belief in some timeless principles of brand building, the enduring role of distinctive curatorial TV channel brands, the importance of skilful promotion to attract audiences, and the exciting opportunities presented by new technology and distribution platforms. We found a strong consensus that marketing will have a major influence over the ways in which the TV industry will evolve and thrive over the coming years.

– A DEER ON THE WINDSHIELD –

The world's best TV marketers have a realistic appreciation of where they fit in the ecology of TV. One of our most charismatic contributors was FX Networks's marketing chief Stephanie Gibbons. When interviewed by the TV promotion and design journal *Promax Daily Brief* immediately following her team's award in 2015 as North America's Marketing Team of the Year for the fifth consecutive time, Stephanie said:

> We know that this consumes our very existence but, to other people, it's a gnat on a windshield in a place they may never drive. If we actually have a chance to make contact we want what hits your windshield to be bigger than a deer and to pull you off the side of the road and make you experience a different kind of consciousness.[12]

Selecting examples and case studies of TV brand building to talk about in the book has been a real challenge and there are many, many others we wish we had room to include, but throughout the process we have always looked for work that lives up to Stephanie's windshield-hitting benchmark.

Here's a brief trailer for the way we have scheduled all our material. We start in Part 1 by examining the main characteristics of marketing within the TV industry and the significant ways in which it differs from other sectors. Part 2 focuses on TV network and channel brands: how they are built, how they are positioned for success and why they will stay relevant in the future. In Part 3 we turn to the promotion of individual genres and programmes: the craft of the TV trailer maker and how the battle for audience share is won. Part 4 looks at a number of ways in which the expertise of TV market-ers is evolving to embrace transmedia storytelling, the powerful potential of social media and new forms of creativity learned from the digital world. We conclude with a bit of crystal-ball gazing to consider what the future holds for the marketing of television.

As we will see, one of the most fundamental roles of marketing in TV is navigation: simply helping viewers to find their way. In that spirit, each chapter ends with a print equivalent of a credit squeeze (those mini-promotional trailers we see increasingly in small windows within the closing credits of a TV show): we have included short 'next' and 'later' summaries to help you find the sections of the book that you are most interested in. And to reflect the way in which television is moving towards an on-demand, viewer-controlled world, we fully expect you to fast forward or rewind to the bits you most want to read.

Some of the material we cover is drawn from our own personal experi-ences in the TV industry and it is important here to register a big caveat. Throughout the book, when we use the words 'we' or 'our' we are generally referring to the collective efforts of many of our colleagues, past and present. Although we had a bit to do with some of the examples we describe – and in a few cases our personal involvement was extensive – on many occasions we talk about the insightful strategic thinking, creative ingenuity and craft excellence of others, to which our contribution was sometimes tangential at best. The full list of credits is too long to record accurately with no accidental omissions, but we have tried to include the most significant namechecks in the body of the text and/or the acknowledgements section.

– HOW STORIES FIND AN AUDIENCE –

Whether we are talking about promoting dramas, sport or news, exploring ways to build a TV channel identity or demonstrating how best to use social media, we hope you will find a constant theme shining through: the fundamental need for good storytelling. At this point, for the first and last time, one of us feels it is appropriate for the other to receive a personal credit. Back in 2005, when our business became fully independent from its former ownership by the BBC, we relaunched our own brand with a short manifesto written by Charlie Mawer:

STORIES SHAPE THE WORLD

Whether fact or fiction, we use stories to educate, inspire and entertain each other. All broadcast content is a form of storytelling, but without our unique skills those stories would not reach an audience. In the digital landscape it will be harder and harder for stories to find their audiences, without our ability to navigate, connect and make accessible.

Stories are the most important thing in the world. Without stories, we wouldn't be human beings at all.

Bringing stories and people together.[13]

While we like to think that the contribution of TV marketers to our industry is greater than the commissioning of 'mugs and T-shirts', we know our place. We are here to support the work of gifted creators such as Ryan Murphy, Matthew Weiner, Steven Moffat, Matt Groening and Jim Brooks. When we do our jobs well, we help their brilliant stories to find an audience. That's the role of the TV Brand Builders.

SPOILER ALERT

This book assumes a lot of knowledge of a great many TV shows and their plot points. If you don't yet know, for example, the back story of Sister Jude in *American Horror Story: Asylum*, what Don did in the final season of *Mad Men*, who became the most hated character in *Game of Thrones*, or what happened to the Trotters after they became millionaires, proceed with caution.

NEXT	LATER
★ The invisible hierarchy of television.	★ When Monk met Johnny Smith.
★ The 'colouring in' department.	★ Horseferry and Chadwick.
★ Interview with Iceland's minister for fisheries.	★ Moving a mountain in Tibet.
★ The Tao of TV marketing.	
★ From 'consumers' to 'the audience'.	
★ Good + cheap + fast.	

NOTES

1 *Kung Fu: The Well* (1973) season two, episode 16, ABC, 27 September

2 Red Bee Media (1993) Internal Document, 25 May

3 Rufus Radcliffe, group marketing and research director, ITV, interview, 14 April 2015

4 Mills, D (2005) [accessed 4 September 2015] It's Win-Win for BBC Marketing Man, *Telegraph*, 8 March [Online] http://www.telegraph.co.uk/finance/2907420/Its-win-win-for-BBC-marketing-man.html

5 Justin Bairamian, director of BBC Creative, interview, 22 July 2015

6 Deloitte (2015) [accessed 18 March 2016] Short Form Video: A Future, But Not The Future, Of Television [Online] http://www2.deloitte.com/global/en/pages/technology-media-and-telecommunications/articles/tmt-pred-short-form-video.html

7 PwC (2015) [accessed 2 November 2015] TV Advertising At a Glance [Online Video] http://www.pwc.com/gx/en/industries/entertainment-media/outlook/segment-insights/tv-advertising.html

8 Ibis World (2015) [accessed 4 September 2015] Television Production in the US: Market Research Report [online] http://www.ibisworld.com/industry/default.aspx?indid=1246

9 Yale School of Management (2014) [accessed 4 September 2015] An Interview With Linda Schupack, Executive Vice President of Marketing at AMC Networks, March 11 [Online] http://som.yale.edu/interview-linda-schupack-evp-marketing-amc-networks

10 James, M (2015) [accessed 4 September 2015] A 'Media Meltdown'? Disney Remark On TV Viewing Sends Industry Into Tailspin, *Los Angeles Times*, 7 August. http://www.latimes.com/entertainment/envelope/cotown/la-et-ct-media-stocks-20150807-story.html#page=1

11 Koblin, J (2015) [accessed 2 November 2015] Soul-Searching In TV Land Over The Challenges Of A New Golden Age, *New York Times*, 30 August [Online] http://www.nytimes.com/2015/08/31/business/fx-chief-ignites-soul-searching-about-the-boom-in-scripted-tv.html?_r=0

12 Sanders, J (2015) [accessed 4 September 2015] FX Networks Wins 2015 PromaxBDA In-House Marketing Team Of The Year, 1 June [Online] http://brief.promaxbda.org/content/2015-promaxbda-in-house-marketing-team-of-the-year-fx-networks

13 Mawer, C (2005) [accessed 4 September 2015] Stories Shape the World (Original Manifesto), Quotes Pullman, P (2015) *IMDB* [Online] http://m.imdb.com/name/nm1099514/quotes

PART ONE

THE CONTEXT

CHAPTER ONE

MARKETING IN THE WORLD OF TELEVISION

*We're creative. We're gonna sit at our desks typing
while the walls fall down around us. Because we're the least important,
most important thing there is.*

DON DRAPER, *MAD MEN*[1]

– THE INVISIBLE PYRAMID –

Marketing came late to the TV party. Take the BBC, for example. As we described in our Introduction, it was not until 1993 that the organization contemplated hiring a marketing director. Prior to that, there had been no one with a marketing title employed. There were people performing promotional functions, certainly, but rather more of the 'informing people what was on' variety than 'persuading them to watch'. The people responsible for making promotional trailers were the same people driving the transmission desks on alternate weeks, keeping the channels on air.

Indeed, the first meetings in the UK of the industry body PromaxBDA (the 'global community of professionals passionately engaged in the marketing and promotion of television and video content'[2]) in the late 1980s and early 1990s were gatherings of a disparate assortment of designers and presentation operators from the ITV regional companies, the BBC nations and a nascent Channel 4. Not a marketer in sight. In the United States, by contrast, the trade association was, from the start, a highly professional outfit, representing networks, cable channels and affiliate broadcasters. In all parts of the world, though, for decades marketing sat several layers below the top table in TV organizations. Referring back to the BBC's 1993 Up The Junction report that we mentioned in the Introduction, it concluded somewhat hopefully:

> We believe the case for a marketing director of BBC Television is self-evident. However... it is vital that the power vested in such an individual is sufficient to enable him [sic] both to formulate and implement marketing

policy, and that the work of his [sic] department will both influence and impact the work of other departments within BBC Television.[3]

(As an aside, the male bias in this statement is awkwardly outdated in light of the large number of talented and high-achieving female marketers now occupying senior positions in television, some of whom we have interviewed for our research.)

The BBC working party's recognition that marketing without influence would not lead to an improvement in the use of the airtime between programmes was no doubt based on an astute acknowledgement of the power structure of the organization. In our BBC days we were once in the room when the conclusions of a report commissioned by the then director-general were presented, with the aim of fostering better cross-functional working relationships. Titled 'BBC Unwritten Rules', the study was based on internal interviews by an expert in corporate culture. It revealed that, in contrast with the 'official' hierarchical organization structure (within which the director of marketing, communications and audiences sat on the BBC's executive board), the true pecking order was based on a pyramid topped by a creative elite (the star on-air talent: entertainment presenters, chat show hosts, news anchors and comedy acts, for example). Star talent was followed by senior managers, then those who actually made the programmes. Marketing was ranked firmly below the programme makers in a group labelled 'programme support', along with technical, studio and post-production people. In the eyes of the programme makers, this was the 'back office'. So, exaggerating only slightly for effect, the influence of a marketing head of one of the world's largest and most respected broadcasting organizations was relegated below that of a junior programme researcher.

ITV's Rufus Radcliffe helps to explain why this situation existed:

Marketing did not used to play an important role in TV companies... In years gone by you could rely on viewers turning up night after night as regular as clockwork. All that has now changed. TV companies need to be brand-centric and audience obsessed.[4]

A similar picture could be seen in the United States, with the dominance of the traditional TV networks not being challenged until the rapid growth of cable and the launch of the Fox network in the 1980s, resulting in the relative lack of importance of marketing compared with other industries. As the writers of the helpful handbook *Branding TV*, Walter McDowell and Alan Batten, confirm:

The late arrival of brand management to American television was due primarily to a lack of competition. For over three decades, the competitive arena for commercial television was restricted to three major players: ABC, CBS and NBC... With a captive national audience... viewer choices were restricted to a handful of media brands.[5]

It is little wonder, then, that marketing professionals used to a place at the centre of a brand's universe can find their entry into broadcasting a jolt. Liz Dolan, now chief marketing officer of Fox International Channels, was formerly a senior marketer at Nike working alongside founder Phil Knight:

> My first observation coming into the television business was that I couldn't believe how separate product and marketing were. It still doesn't make any sense. At Nike, as the head of marketing I was in charge of how all the products and the marketing came together to be one brand. I remember Phil Knight said to me, 'We are a marketing company and our number one marketing tool is our products.' That's true in television too, but people don't operate their companies like that. Programme making is elevated... and then they dump it onto marketing.[6]

– MARKETERS AS CONTENT MAKERS –

It is no surprise, then, that TV people beyond marketing and in-house creative services departments tend not to see promotional output as 'content' in its own right. In fact, the BBC Presentation Department we mentioned in our Introduction once made programmes... real, actual programmes. It had been responsible for announcers who, until the 1960s, were seen by viewers on screen. Two small studios were built at BBC Television Centre for this purpose. Once in-vision announcements were discontinued, a new subdivision was created – Presentation (Programmes) – to produce original content for the BBC from those studios. Productions included the rock music show *The Old Grey Whistle Test* and a movie review show called, initially, *Film 73*, which was presented for over 25 years by Barry Norman and has lived on, fronted by Jonathan Ross and, today, Claudia Winkleman.

Although that practice was discontinued, running a team responsible for creating and producing around 95 per cent of the BBC's on-air promotional trailers we once calculated that, if we were a BBC programme-making department, we would be the third biggest measured by hours of output per year – behind news and sport but well ahead of other genres including drama and comedy. In the words of Jane Lingham, the BBC's brand director:

> People forget that marketing is content. In the broadcast industry, marketing can sometimes be dismissed as the 'colouring in' department... particularly amongst people who spend their day making long-form programmes. They often don't think of marketing as content in the same way as what *they* produce – but whilst obviously different, marketing *is* content, and actually if you add up all the airtime that we (in marketing) need to fill on a daily basis it amounts to an awful lot.[7]

TV marketing people are generally under no illusions about the purpose of the content they create. It is there to serve a need, to support other content. It is a symbiotic relationship. Our job is, to coin a phrase, to win audiences and influence viewers. But just occasionally an audience member is moved to write an unsolicited message of appreciation of our work, like this tweet from the opinionated TV critic and columnist Caitlin Moran:

> **Who does all the trailers for *EastEnders*? They're amazing. Can they do ALL of *EastEnders*, please?[8]**

The campaign that moved Caitlin Moran to take to Twitter: EastEnders *'There's A Killer Amongst Them'*   Source: *Reproduced by permission of BBC*

– KEEPING A DISTANCE –

Given the traditional disregard for the craft of TV promotional content amongst 'proper' programme makers – themselves highly creative people – it is inevitable that when the first part of a project they have been working on for years is going to be reduced by a trailer maker into a 30-second snippet they will have a strong view on what it should contain.

(Incidentally the title for this job varies across countries and companies, with versions including promo producer, editor and creative. From now on we will stick with the grammatically dubious but standard advertising industry term, creative.)

To help explain why programme creators invariably make the worst promotional trailers for their own content, the following comments from filmmaker Michael LaPointe (writing about movie trailers) hit the nail on the head. His firm advice is that neither the director nor the editor should make the trailer, and he recommends that a different editor do the job:

> They have something much better than you, the director, and your editor have, they will start the project with objectivity. You, as the director, may have some very passionate, specific reasons for making the movie, and probably have a certain few scenes, or themes that really resonate with you. These however, may in fact, not resonate with the audience.[9]

Regularly when making trailers for *Panorama* (a fast-turnaround BBC current-affairs show), the producer would say something like: 'The really great thing is we've got the first interview with the minister for fisheries from Iceland... no one else has got this guy, that's your trailer right there.' You would be thinking: 'Okay, this is an extraordinary programme about, let's say, the decline of the British fish-and-chip shop. The way I am going to put 5 million bums on seats is not through that interview.'

Similarly, drama and comedy programme makers will feel pressures from their proximity to the talent – for example, to give equal screen time to ensemble casts. Only the distance of a professional marketing creative can lead to the sort of ruthless decisions needed to hone a single-minded and compelling marketing campaign.

– TOO MANY COOKS? –

The quest for a focused promotional message is made more difficult in television by the sheer number of people who insist on being involved. With any typical brand there are always stakeholders. But they are usually, for example, the sales director or the people who run the factory. Interested parties with opinions, sure, but usually self-aware enough to defer to the marketing and advertising people for the really big decisions. In TV everyone not only has an opinion but, as a creative person, feels qualified to make it: production teams who may have spent two years painstakingly crafting a drama; commissioners who made the decision to fund the show in the first place; heads of genres; channel controllers (often with production backgrounds) who have responsibility for every second of output on their channel; frequently CEOs or directors-general too. And, in most cases, people with a deep understanding of television, of audiences and of creativity. All prone to adding notes.

For one international entertainment format that we won't name, 37 scripts were written and presented to the following cast of opinions: two executives from the channel's commissioning team; the executive producer from the host broadcaster; two executive producers from the production company and format rights holder; the (let's say) four star performers, their agents and management; and the channel controller. Oh, yes, and then the three levels of marketers working on the project. It is little wonder that those voices all had profound views on everything, from the overall positioning of the show, to how close it should be to a trailer that ran in another territory, or the choice of music that might feature, or the prominence and role of the talent. It is also little wonder to any veteran of the advertising trenches that, at the end of the process, the script number that got made was... yes, you guessed it, the first one that our team had presented.

ITV's Rufus Radcliffe emphasizes the fact that to be a successful marketer in television you have to be diplomatic, empathetic and be respectful of the creative instincts of producers and commissioners:

> We work with big personalities with strong views. The ability to get on with people, building trust and relationships is vital.[10]

He goes on to stress the need for TV marketers to 'market themselves': prove their value and adopt a good 'bedside manner' when dealing with the people who make and commission the programmes:

> You have to be incredibly mindful of what you are doing here. Someone may have been working on a project for one year or two years and it has been a hugely important part of their lives and you are turning that into inevitably quite a reductive marketing campaign because you have to encapsulate what they are doing into an audience 'sell'. You have to listen, take on board what people think, be adaptable, collegiate and empathetic. At the same time you need to be determined and strong about what you think the right solution is. If you're not all those things then you're going to come unstuck.[11]

– THE TAO OF TV MARKETING –

At the risk of being deemed pretentious this early in the book, we have found through experience that the secret of not coming unstuck is to be found in Taoism. To get out of one's own way.

In most other sectors, marketers and advertising people are trained to use deep research insight, ingenious strategic planning and lateral creative thinking to capture the essence of a brand or product in an original creative idea that will command attention and elicit a response amongst consumers. Brands in relatively low-interest categories need the addition of an advertising-led idea to position them against the competition, to make them distinctive, to give them a personality.

Marketing in television requires a different approach. Simon Michaelides, a classically trained marketer (P&G, PepsiCo) who is now the commercial director of multichannel broadcaster UKTV, explains it like this:

> At the heart of a piece of entertainment there is already a compelling creative idea. And that is the thing that traditional ad agencies really

struggle with because they are used to being asked to give personality and engagement and a level of dynamism to largely boring products. So if you work in commoditized categories – classically the yellow fats category – it's a tub of yellow fat, it's in desperate need of a creative idea, but in our world you don't need that because there is a really compelling idea at the heart of it already, and... advertising agencies struggle with that because... they just don't understand how to amplify an existing idea as opposed to overlaying it with a new idea.[12]

(We're not sure why the yellow fats category seems to symbolize the antithesis of TV content for our interviewees, but Simon was not the only senior UK television marketer to mention it, as we will see.)

Many people in charge of marketing in TV organizations, running broadcasters' in-house creative units or working in entertainment marketing agencies the world over are refugees from traditional blue-chip marketing departments or creative agencies, as we both were. We have all had to train ourselves to apply the basic principles of marketing, brand building and advertising to a world in which our subject is content that is already inherently interesting and entertaining. Getting out of our own way means respecting that and understanding how best to apply original creative thinking to amplify rather than overshadow the content. As the BBC's Jane Lingham (early career: advertising) says:

Sometimes, people (and agencies) who are not used to working with media brands overengineer their creative ideas for them and end up overwhelming the content. There is a really fine balance when you are marketing a media brand... you need to ensure there is enough of an idea in the creative to provide a narrative, but within that you need to allow the content to come through and speak for itself. If you've got something like *Doctor Who* or *Luther* or *Strictly Come Dancing*, why would you hide that brilliant content behind another (imagined) creative concept? The point of marketing is to provide the right platform on which the programmes themselves can shine.[13]

What this does not mean, though, is lazily compiling a few clips from every programme and expecting that alone to inform and engage viewers. In the competitive environment we have described, original creativity is vital to capture the essence of a piece of TV content in the most persuasive way. Many of the case studies we go on to talk about demonstrate this point. Robert Tansey (early career: advertising, and now in charge of marketing at the UK's biggest pay-TV broadcaster, Sky) emphasizes the importance of achieving the right balance with every campaign:

You have to be very careful with the level of concept you put between the content and the audience because the material that you have to play with is so utterly brilliant in and of itself. However, just showing the content back to people doesn't necessarily work in the long term. But any advertising agency's instinct is 'right, let's do a metaphor' or 'let's put a high concept on it', which can often diminish the power of the content... So the challenge is how do you take [TV] material and stitch it together with a bit of an insight or an observation or a narrative to give it a broader context... Unlike other clients, you've got the stuff.[14]

For UKTV's Simon Michaelides, one of the keys to this is a timeless advertising discipline: a clear brief with a simple message at its heart:

I think the single most prominent weakness of... broadcast marketing is what I call 'bat signal marketing'. You throw the signal up into the sky, you tell people that the show exists, but you don't actually tell anyone anything about it and you expect people to come. In an increasingly competitive world... where viewing is essentially discretionary and on demand for the viewer, you've got to tell them what's in it for them, you've got to tell them why, which is why... in all our briefs we (have) 'the hook'... What is it about this show that will interest and engage them? Why should they care? What is going to make them come and watch this versus something else at 9 pm on Tuesday?[15]

For guidance on how to do this well, TV marketers could do worse than follow the advice of advertising guru Paul Feldwick in his short but brilliant book *The Anatomy of Humbug*. Commenting on the fact that ad agency people have been trained to think exclusively about the idea of a proposition in a creative brief, Feldwick writes:

We could often more usefully think in terms of the 'story'... Stories are generally far better at getting and keeping our attention, involving us emotionally, and lodging material in our memory... Journalists instinctively search for the 'story' – there is no reason that we in advertising should not do the same.[16]

Writing a good creative brief for a TV marketing campaign is less about the pursuit of a stripped-down 'unique selling proposition' (although clarity is still important). It is more about rooting out the story: why will this content be interesting? Why will viewers find it relevant? Why will it be worth spending time with? To do this we find it hugely helpful to stop thinking about people as 'consumers' and instead consider them as 'the audience'. To think like programme makers, not traditional marketers.

– THREE SIDES OF A TRIANGLE –

The biggest enemy of this disciplined approach is the need for speed. A familiar trope in ad agency creative departments, which typically plays out when a world-weary creative director shares the benefit of his or her experience with an eager young account handler, is to draw a triangle with a word at each point: good; cheap; quick. The CD's party piece is to announce, triumphantly: 'You can only have two, so which two would you like?' The point is that achieving advertising of high quality does not always have to cost the earth, but can take time. If high executional standards are demanded in a short space of time, the accepted wisdom goes, this can only be achieved by throwing money at the problem. Cheap + fast = poor-quality work.

Except in TV marketing.

Lee Raftery, EVP of marketing and communications at NBCUniversal (with a background at Birds Eye Walls and, later, Hasbro), explains why:

> In FMCG (fast-moving consumer goods) you have a specific product that you're launching and for which you've developed a campaign. You work very hard, often for a long time, and then 'bang' it's out there and it's a fixed-view window. In television the product itself is constantly evolving and changing around you. Your brand is pumping out 24/7 and perceptions of it are constantly changing and evolving. With a car brand, for example, you launch your new model and the perceptions are fixed for two or three years. But for a channel brand, we are show-to-show, day-to-day and hour-by-hour.[17]

Lee goes on to say:

> Internationally 'day-and-date' launches, aligned to US premieres, are becoming more common and that's compressing our campaigns.[18]

('Day-and-date' is an increasingly familiar phenomenon amongst international TV organizations in particular, in which a new show or new season of a hit show is launched globally on the same day, even sometimes at the same hour – despite time differences across continents – to create a sense of event and make piracy more difficult.)

In our ad agency days we both remember working for a full year on a single TV commercial: one of us for a global car brand, involving innumerable rounds of concept testing in research; the other for a confectionery brand that had so many differences of opinion about how it should be positioned that not a single frame of TV advertising was produced for it in that 12-month period. The biggest contrast we both noticed when we switched to the world of TV marketing was the exhilarating speed at which it moves and the sheer number of projects and campaigns that get turned around in the space of weeks, sometimes days. Rick Eiserman, CEO of leading US entertainment agency Trailer Park, describes a similar feeling of invigoration when he first stepped into the agency after several years in the comparatively sedate environment of a big traditional advertising group:

Even my first visit to the agency, the speed at which they work, the quality of the creative that is being created in a very short period of time, that constant competing for every job, burning it every day, the craftsmanship from a design standpoint. It was an efficiency and a quality and a speed unlike anything I had seen in the brand world, and while it is very much the way of working in the world of entertainment marketing it was night and day from what I'd come from. So I found an agency that didn't have conference rooms because they didn't wait four days to come up with a creative brief to get started on a project, they started immediately.[19]

So, good + cheap + fast is what we aspire to in the TV marketing world. The need to promote a large number of programmes, with schedules prone to frequent changes and revisions to briefs at short notice, means that the best entertainment marketing agencies and in-house creative groups have had to cultivate a way of working that is agile, fluid and cost-effective. Quality does not have to mean a lavishly executed, high-concept film (although there is an important role for these, as we will see). It can mean simply a clever choice of music track, an ingenious piece of editing or an unexpectedly fresh graphic treatment: whatever it takes to present the content in a way that will capture attention, appeal to viewers and, if possible, make a contribution to the overall channel brand too. The dynamic nature of TV content makes this latter task a constant challenge.

Rick Eiserman describes the potential downsides of working at speed across a large and ever-changing range of content:

We still have the tendency in the world of entertainment marketing to think 'we'll know it when we see it' and some of that... lack of depth creates a lot of waste... too much left on the cutting-room floor.[20]

Justin Bairamian, director of BBC Creative, agrees. What can suffer in this environment compared with other sectors is, he says: 'long-term thinking, discipline, consistency, sticking to a campaign'. He continues:

The good marketers I have seen operate [at the BBC] get the right balance between going with the flow – because it is a fast-moving fluid business – but actually sticking to the core principles of what marketing is about, which is a deep understanding of the audience and a deep understanding of how to build the brand, and those principles apply in broadcasting as much as they do anywhere.[21]

– WHEN IT ALL COMES TOGETHER –

Marketing is at its best in television when programme makers recognize the value of the core principles (as outlined above by Justin Bairamian) or, better still, are intuitive marketers themselves. Having talked earlier in this chapter about the perceived low status of marketing amongst content creators, there have always been notable exceptions: those who recognize that it is inherently a different discipline from their own and are hugely open to original external thought on how to promote their shows. Mal Young and John Yorke, two successive BBC controllers of continuing drama series, responsible for showrunning all the key pillars of the flagship channel's schedule, were both happy to let their programmes be promoted with lateral and original creative approaches. Mal Young used to defend the glossy advertising for *EastEnders*, when high-concept trailers were filmed on 35 millimetre film, compared with the fast-turnaround beta-tape feel of the actual show. He believed that it gave a 'halo effect' to the show itself, convincing people that it had higher production values than perhaps was the case.

Liz Dolan of Fox remarks that many showrunners now have an instinct for marketing in their DNA:

> Look at *Glee, Scream Queens, American Horror Story* – Ryan Murphy, he sees the key art before he sees the show. He is on top of everything and has a very holistic view of how to get people to pay attention.[22]

(The term 'key art' refers to a single iconic image that captures the essence of a TV show in a promotional campaign.)

Ryan Murphy has certainly presided over some remarkable print campaigns. The 'loser sign forehead shots' that introduced the cast of *Glee*, the sewn-up body parts from *Nip/Tuck*, the 'snake mouths' and conjoined faces of *American Horror Story*... we will expand on this in Chapter 7 when we explore FX Networks's approach to drama promotion and the exceptionally close collaboration between Murphy and the marketing team.

Linda Schupack, EVP of marketing at AMC (home of *Mad Men* and *Breaking Bad*), considers the bond between showrunner and marketer to be pivotal:

> We feel very lucky and privileged to have close relationships with the showrunners and I think that is what sets our marketing apart. At the beginning of any series and any season of a series we are having conversations with the showrunners to understand from their perspective what is the vision of the show, or what is the vision and the larger theme of a particular season. Those conversations are somewhat wide-ranging in the sense that sometimes we are just talking about general themes and that sends us in a different direction. Or sometimes we are talking about iconic images from a season that may or may not have been shot yet, but the showrunners are directing us to these images that they feel represent that season in a particularly compelling way.[23]

In the most creative TV organizations this way of working is embedded in the culture. We will see in later chapters how this can lead to outstanding

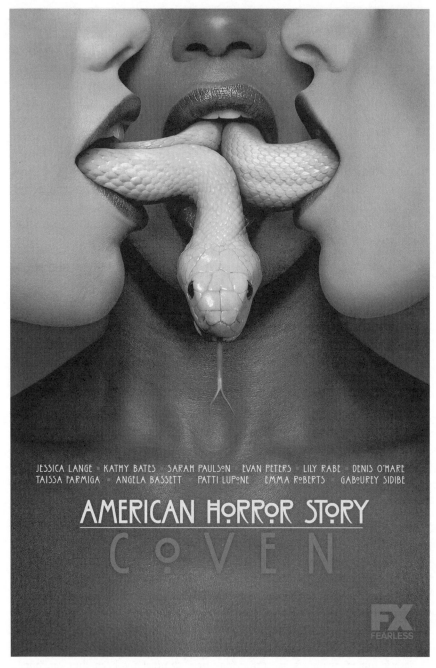

Striking key art for a Ryan Murphy drama – FX Networks's American Horror Story: Coven   *Source: Reproduced by permission of FX Networks, LLC*

results and nowhere more so than at UK broadcaster Channel 4. Here, the marketing team and in-house creative 'agency', branded 4Creative, are highly respected internally, as CEO David Abraham explains:

> I have never been at a broadcaster where the commissioners are more excited to see what the marketing team do with their editorial decisions and I constantly get feedback from them: 'Have you seen this amazing campaign?' It is coming from the programming people, which I haven't seen in any other organization. Often it is, 'Well, the marketing people have gone off and done their poster, it's got nothing to do with the programme, they've just been indulgent creatively,' whereas here they are sitting in the cafe together, they are talking to each other and then the 4Creative guys come up with their great work. I cannot entirely explain how that culture has evolved but it has evolved and it is one of our great strengths.[24]

The ultimate outcome of this very close collaboration is for marketers to have an influence on the narrative development of a show itself. It is certainly not the end goal, but sometimes excellent marketing can play a bigger role. Another leading Los Angeles-based agency living 'at the intersection of advertising and entertainment' is Stun Creative. Michael Vamosy, chief creative officer, worked for several years at Fox and cites an example from those days of collaborating with *Lost* co-creator J J Abrams on the sci-fi series *Fringe*:

> J J Abrams was very creative, totally open. They took the stuff we did to advertise the show and they brought it into the show, embedded it into the show and made it part of the show. We did an on-air spot that they turned into an episode, and that's the beauty of what television can do as opposed to what movies can do. TV has an opportunity to have the marketing influence the direction of how that show can develop over the course of a couple of weeks or a couple of years, so it's a real opportunity to be part of the bigger brand and the bigger storytelling if you can help shape and shift that series.[25]

When TV marketers have this level of influence, they do not belong on the bottom rung of an invisible hierarchy but in a place close to the heart of a broadcaster's output. In the following chapters of the book we bring to life many examples of this influence at work on highly creative and award-winning promotional campaigns across a range of TV genres, from drama to comedy, from factual entertainment to news and current affairs, but first we look at ways in which distinctive channel brands are created. In the words of Rufus Radcliffe:

> Marketing is on a journey within media organizations now from a sort of support function towards the end of the creative process through to

something that has to be much more upstream, as the basic fundamentals of branding that have been playing out in so many industries for so long have to play out here now. And that is why marketing in TV and marketing in media... is about to go into an incredibly fascinating period, and anyone lucky enough to work in it should not forget that...

Adding, with a flourish: '... because we could be marketing yellow fats'.[26]

NEXT
★ *The Unknown Prince Charles.*
★ Audience safaris.
★ The jam display paradox.
★ 'Characters Welcome'.
★ A 'fruit bowl' in every scene.
★ The success of *Mr Robot*.

LATER
★ *Hardcore Pawn.*
★ Dodgeball with One Direction.
★ A stretch three-wheeler.

NOTES

1 *Mad Men*, 'Blowing Smoke' (2010) season four, episode 12, AMC, 10 October
2 PromaxBDA (2015) [accessed 4 September 2015] PromaxBDA – Create What's Next [online] https://www.promaxbda.org/
3 Red Bee Media (1993) Internal Document, 25 May
4 Rufus Radcliffe, group marketing and research director, ITV, interview 14 April 2015
5 McDowell, W and Batten, A (2005) *Branding TV: Principles and practices*, Focal Press, Burlington, MA
6 Liz Dolan, chief marketing officer, Fox International Channels, interview 11 June 2015
7 Jane Lingham, director, BBC Brand, interview 29 July 2015
8 Moran, C (2014) [accessed 4 September 2015] Who does all the trailers for EastEnders? They're amazing. Can they do ALL of EastEnders, please? [Twitter] 28 April [Online] https://twitter.com/caitlinmoran/status/460848057094250496
9 LaPointe, M (2013) [accessed 4 September 2015] The Structure Of The Trailer, *Filmcourage*, 27 May [Online] http://filmcourage.com/content/the-structure-of-the-trailer-by-filmmaker-michael-lapointe
10 Rufus Radcliffe, group marketing and research director, ITV, interview, 14 April 2015
11 Rufus Radcliffe, group marketing and research director, ITV, interview, 14 April 2015
12 Simon Michaelides, executive board, commercial director, UKTV, interview 13 May 2015

13 Jane Lingham, director, BBC Brand, interview, 29 July 2015

14 Robert Tansey, brand director, content products, Sky, interview, 26 June 2015

15 Simon Michaelides, executive board, commercial director, UKTV, interview 13 May 2015

16 Feldwick, P (2015) *The Anatomy of Humbug: How to think differently about advertising*, Matador, Kibworth Beauchamp

17 Lee Raftery, executive vice president of marketing and communications, NBCUniversal International, interview 08 May 2015

18 Lee Raftery, executive vice president of marketing and communications, NBCUniversal International, interview 08 May 2015

19 Rick Eiserman, CEO, Trailer Park, interview 30 June 2015

20 Rick Eiserman, CEO, Trailer Park, interview 30 June 2015

21 Justin Bairamian, director of BBC Creative, interview 22 July 2015

22 Liz Dolan, chief marketing officer, Fox International Channels, interview 11 June 2015

23 Linda Schupack, executive vice president of marketing, AMC, interview 11 June 2015

24 David Abraham, CEO, Channel 4, interview 26 June 2015

25 Michael Vamosy, chief creative officer, Stun Creative, interview 10 June 2015

26 Rufus Radcliffe, group marketing and research director, ITV, interview, 14 April 2015

PART TWO

BUILDING TV CHANNEL BRANDS

CHAPTER TWO

WHAT'S THE POINT OF A TV CHANNEL BRAND?

Hey, Alex – You know the really great thing about television?
If something important happens, anywhere in the world, night or day...
you can always change the channel.

'REVEREND JIM' IGNATOWSKI, *TAXI*[1]

– PREDICTIONS OF DOOM –

Enter the terms 'future of TV' or 'future of channels' into your favourite browser's search bar and you're likely to be confronted by a set of blog posts and opinion pieces predicting the imminent demise of channels. For example, research conducted by the technology company Cisco, amongst industry experts, recorded that:

> 100 per cent of the experts agree with the expectation that TV channels will go away in the future. Instead of TV channels, viewers will use customized on-demand media streams (personalized TV portals), which provide them with unlimited access to programmes and content.[2]

Online technology site MakeUseOf concurs:

> Like the pager, cassette tapes and fax machines, the very notion of the TV channel is becoming obsolete.[3]

That same post drew on a piece from *The Economist* revealing the fear that lurks in the hearts of TV 'suits' everywhere:

> Television executives already share horror stories about how their children have asked them what a 'channel' is.[4]

So is the game up for TV channels? Should we draw a line under this section of the book and fast forward to the chapters about the marketing of programmes? Is that all we will have left of TV marketing in a fast-approaching world of streaming services, on-demand players and apps?

But wait. Glance at the websites of the major global media corporations – the six giants who still control over 90 per cent of US media – or their major television networks, and you will see that they all, in one form or another, celebrate the strength of their TV channel brands.

Take Viacom, for example. Virtually the first word you will see on its corporate website is brands. How does Viacom define 'brands'? Primarily as TV channels (alongside the movie studio Paramount). This is how Viacom Media Networks is described on its website:

> It is... among the most vibrant, diverse and culturally relevant collection of brands in media and entertainment. MTV is the cultural home of the millennial generation. Nickelodeon is the number one brand for kids. Comedy Central is the number one brand in comedy.[5]

All three are famous and distinctive TV channels.

Turner talks about: 'More than 100 branded channels in some 30 languages in more than 200 countries', including TNT ('Television's destination for drama'), Cartoon Network and Adult Swim.[6] Fox International? 'Our brands'.[7] NBCUniversal? Again, a TV business organized by brands, including: 'E! Entertainment ("The only global, multiplatform brand for all things pop culture") and Oxygen Media ("A multiplatform entertainment brand that targets young, multicultural women").'[8] The picture is similar for Disney and CBS: they may use different words ('properties' and 'portfolio' respectively) but they, too, describe their TV businesses according to channel brands.

Who is right? Are 'Big TV' executives ignoring the wisdom of their children, who don't see the point of a television channel? Are they clinging on to the outdated concept of a continuous stream of TV programmes broken up by advertising and promotional airtime purely because their business models depend on it? Or are predictions of a technology-enabled, content-on-demand, channel-free world (frequently from people whose businesses would profit from such an outcome) ignoring basic and timeless human needs that a well-constructed, well-marketed TV channel serves? Let's consider whether television channels do, still, have a purpose and, more specifically, whether the role of TV marketing in creating them and building them is still important.

– *THE UNKNOWN PRINCE CHARLES* –

Keen to explore the influence of channel brands on viewers' expectations of programmes, we commissioned a research project. We invented some TV programme titles and asked 5,000 viewers what conclusions they would draw from two alternative descriptions of the fictional programmes.

The results were revealing. For example, 62 per cent of people thought that a programme called *Save Me* on BBC Two would be a hard-hitting documentary about single mothers failing to cope. However, the same programme title on Sky 1 was expected by 80 per cent of respondents to be a reality show with former celebrities pleading for a career revival; 77 per cent thought *The Unknown Prince Charles* on BBC Four would be an informative documentary about his role and achievements, whereas 53 per cent anticipated the same programme title on ITV1 (since simplified as 'ITV') to be an exposé by former girlfriends and servants. In our survey, 71 per cent of people agreed that the TV channel a programme is shown on affects their expectation of the programme. The results of this research on fictional programmes were not surprising to us. Channel brands with strong identities, even the well-established generalist terrestrial channels in the UK, are likely to influence the type of programming we expect to find on them. We explore this more fully in the next two chapters when we look at 'flag' and 'frame' channels. But, in an increasingly on-demand world, do we still *need* channels as a conduit to the programmes we want to watch?

– GOING ON SAFARI –

Another research study, this time commissioned by the BBC and conducted by Illuminas, helps us to answer that question. Sharing the findings in 2014 at a Thinkbox event (Thinkbox is the marketing body for commercial TV in the UK), Margo Swadley, the BBC's former head of audiences, television, explained that one of the project's initial hypotheses was that channel brands are not important any more (or at least, much less important). Key to the research methodology was that conclusions were not drawn simply from how respondents said they made TV viewing decisions but how they were observed to have made those decisions in their 'natural habitats' (well, Illuminas did label this form of research 'audience safaris'), as well as via the completion of media consumption diaries. One of the main findings of the study was that channel brands are still frequently used as a cue to likely programme quality. Familiar channels also serve as signposts for content and simplify the browse process: 50 per cent of viewers were found to pay most attention to channels they like/tend to watch. According to Swadley:

> So you are looking for programmes but you are subconsciously filtering through places where you think you are going to find content that you like. Familiar channels serve as a signpost, so (they) play quite a considerable role.[9]

Perhaps more significant than the raw findings of the Illuminas research were the approach and the interpretation of results, which were based on behavioural economics. As anyone familiar with the UK ad agency scene over the past few years will well know, behavioural economics was adopted with puppyish enthusiasm by the industry at a time when the charismatic

Rory Sutherland was president of the Institute of Practitioners in Advertising. Sutherland's mission was to help the advertising industry to explain, perhaps truly for the first time, why it works the way it does. Writing in the *Telegraph* in 2010, Laurence Green, then chairman of ad agency Fallon, summed up what he described as a 'quiet revolution' in advertising thinking:

> At its broadest, behavioural economics reminds us of the 'status quo bias' that keeps most markets stable (because we crave the familiar, and are adverse to the potential loss that attaches to a 'new' decision) and the 'heuristics', or rules of thumb, that we use to aid decision making.
>
> Brands, of course, are the ultimate heuristic: mental shortcuts that make potentially complex decisions simple for consumers. They speak to the 'cognitive miser' in all of us.[10]

Returning to the BBC's research with Illuminas, Margo Swadley explains why these unconscious mental shortcuts help us in our choice of viewing:

> So, essentially, we are not all, in our decision making, making a pros and cons list and weighing up every choice and making a rational decision. That's got to be true, especially in television. It's your leisure time. You don't sit and choose and think very carefully about what you're doing.[11]

TV channel brands are not the only heuristics we use to guide us on what to watch, as we will see later, but they still play a very important role. The bold vision of Cisco's industry experts, which is that they will be replaced by 'customized on-demand media streams' with 'unlimited access to programmes and content', seems to ignore the fact that human beings do not like to have to work too hard when in relaxation mode: in this semi-focused state we crave quick and intuitive ways to help us make choices.

– JAM DECISIONS –

As with many other topics in this canter through the diverse world of TV marketing, what we're touching on in a couple of short paragraphs here is covered in much more depth by academics far more qualified than we are. For example, the US psychologist Barry Schwartz wrote an influential book on how choice overload creates anxiety and paralysis for consumers, appropriately titled *The Paradox of Choice: Why more is less*. Schwartz refers to a number of studies, with subjects ranging from gourmet chocolates to retirement plans, suggesting that a higher number of options discourages people from making decisions.[12] The example we have quoted many times to our clients is the sampling of exotic jams and basically it goes like this: a gourmet food store set up a display of 24 varieties of these jams and offered tasting samples. On one occasion all 24 were available to taste, but on another consumers could taste just six varieties. The number of people tasting was roughly the same, yet when it came to purchase there was a vast difference between the two samples: only 3 per cent of shoppers faced with 24 varieties to taste actually bought a jar, while amongst those who had the lower number to try, 30 per cent went on to buy: 10 times more.

In our world, a clearly positioned TV channel brand acts a bit like the jam display with just six varieties to sample. There may be a much wider and more diverse range available, but by acting as a curatorial filter the channel simplifies the decision-making process and provides shortcuts.

There are several examples we could draw on to illustrate this, but in this chapter we want to focus on a US cable network that has stood out in recent years for the enduring clarity of its brand positioning: USA Network. It is a great case study to get us started and a helpful benchmark against which to compare and contrast the approaches of the other channels and networks we are going to look at in the next four chapters. We should emphasize that the impact of new technology and new TV content platforms will undoubtedly have a huge influence on how channel brands behave in the future, and where they fit in the ecology of television. In fact, USA Network's positioning and identity are in the process of being refreshed to maintain its relevance in a fast-changing market. We will share more thoughts in Chapter 16 on how we think channel brands will evolve. However, the USA Network case illustrates some of the key principles of successful media brand positioning and marketing that we believe will remain relevant long into the future.

– DETECTIVES, WRESTLERS AND DOGS –

At the risk of perhaps stretching the jam metaphor way too far, in the giant exotic fruit preserves warehouse that is the US TV market, one channel has, over more than 10 years, stood out due to its inspired and consistent marketing, which has simplified viewer choice and given the channel a razor-sharp market positioning (with a truly impressive commercial performance as an outcome). With a big sign above its 'display' reading 'Characters Welcome', USA Network has made sense of its (sometimes disparate) programming, maintained a brand filter for the commissioning of new shows and, ultimately, raised the marketing stakes amongst its competitors, who have responded with varying degrees of success.

In 2005, USA Network, owned by NBCUniversal, was a successful but middle-of-the-road and uninspiring basic cable channel with a brand problem. Despite two popular original drama series, *Monk* and *The Dead Zone*, their proximity to diverse programming such as dog shows, tennis coverage and World Wrestling Entertainment did not add up to a clear brand proposition. Chris McCumber, then USA Network's EVP of marketing, digital and brand strategy (and now its president), described the issue:

Even though people loved *Monk* and *Dead Zone*, some people didn't know they aired on USA [Network], and if they had any perception of the USA brand it was fairly negative. They were seeing it as a second-choice network.[13]

Research commissioned by the USA Network team at the time confirmed the problem:

Despite ratings success, the USA brand is unfocused, undifferentiated and homogeneous.[14]

A trusted advisor to McCumber and the USA Network team has been Lee Hunt, a highly respected consultant with recognized expertise in TV strategy and audience management. (Lee's annual presentations on 'New Best Practices' at the PromaxBDA entertainment marketing and promotion conferences around the world are always standing-room only and have influenced a generation of TV marketers.) He encapsulates the challenges facing media brands in four simple paradoxes:

1 Media brands need the reach of a general entertainment channel but the focus of a niche network.
2 Media brands are different things to different people at different times on different platforms but they must stand for one thing.
3 Media brands must expand and contract yet be clearly defined.
4 Media brands must be fresh and evolve but be consistent and reliable.[15]

Lee's original positioning overview for USA Network, a pithy document running to just two pages, highlighted ways in which general entertainment networks on cable were positioning themselves as niche channels. Some settled for demographic niches (eg Lifetime: Television for Women). Some were based on programme genre niches (eg TNT: We Know Drama). But a different approach was needed by USA Network. Lee described the potential of 'characters' as an ownable territory:

Even though every general entertainment channel has characters...
and drama, *and* comedy... it's all about staking a claim.
'Characters' is a powerful positioning to own.
Television is and will always be a personality-driven medium.
And USA [Network] shows have lots of interesting and diverse characters.
    Serious detectives. Obsessive-compulsive detectives. Clairvoyant children.
    Reluctant psychics. Tennis stars. Wrestling stars. Dog stars.
But since diverse characters are a part of any general entertainment channel, what makes ours different?
It's what we do with them.[16]

The 'what we do with them' turned out to be one of the biggest recent success stories of US TV marketing. The USA Network team took two pivotal decisions, the first of which revolved around the channel logo. Research confirmed that the channel's name was still one of its most powerful assets but its 'old postage stamp logo' featuring a stylized American flag was 'generic', 'cold' and 'impersonal'.[17] The flag was ditched and a new logo introduced. The second big, and related, decision was to think less about USA as a place and more as 'a rich, vital and welcoming collection of people'.[18] By doing this, USA Network could be positioned as a warm and inclusive destination in which the characters of the USA – both the characters in the channel's programmes and the real characters of the nation – could be celebrated. A new tagline captured the essence of this new brand proposition: Characters Welcome.

The 'old postage stamp' and the logo that replaced it
Source: Reproduced by permission of NBCUniversal Media, LLC

– WHAT'S IN A LINE? –

Taglines – those short, succinct phrases that sit at the end of virtually every TV commercial or print ad to encapsulate the brand proposition in a memorable form – have been, perhaps surprisingly, less familiar in the TV industry than other sectors, say packaged goods, for example. Early US TV taglines dating back to the 1950s and 1960s generally tended to be calls to action (eg 'Have the Time of Your Life with NBC' or 'Turn On the Excitement' for ABC) and even the iconic 'I Want My MTV' from the early 1980s was more a campaign line to encourage America's youth to 'call your cable company' than a true positioning statement. With lines like 'Must See TV' for NBC in the 1990s and 'It's Not TV. It's HBO' from 1996, positioning lines became more familiar in US television, while our creation of 'The Home of Witty Banter' for Dave was a landmark moment in the UK (as we expand on in Chapter 3).

Creating a brand identity for a TV channel used to be purely an exercise in graphic design to bring order to its visual elements, but in today's über-competitive environment that is nowhere near enough. 'Identity' these days does not just mean a channel's visual appearance – its look and feel, its logo, its on-screen presentation (OSP) system – but the way the channel presents itself to its viewers (and prospective viewers) across every touchpoint: the tone and strategic relevance of its on-air promotional content; its off-air advertising; its online and social media presence; its PR strategy; its internal communications; even the way in which marketing influences the commissioning and scheduling of the programmes themselves. Corralling all these elements under a coherent and holistic banner is made a whole lot easier when you can capture the channel's positioning in a distinctive and relevant tagline, but it is a tough creative challenge. Characters Welcome proved to be a very potent brand property for USA Network. In the words of Alexandra Shapiro, EVP of marketing and digital:

> The key was it wasn't just a tagline, it was a philosophy that informed both the way we operate internally and with our partners... it informed... our on-air environment, our programming strategy, our development.[19]

By applying Characters Welcome as a brand filter with remarkable discipline and focus for nearly 10 years, the USA team managed to achieve a high level of consistency across all elements of the marketing mix. An important factor was the new visual appearance of the brand. According to Alexandra:

> There was a very specific look and feel that became unique to USA, from almost day one, that we didn't deviate from. We evolved it but it was a natural evolution, it was a modern aesthetic... There was an incredibly identifiable look and feel to USA and that happened in our on-air graphics, in our animations, in our print, in our promos.[20]

A key feature of the brand's visual identity was the use of negative space: a term used by designers to describe the white space around or between the elements of an image, often to form an integral part of the image itself. A classic example is WWF's panda logo. USA Network's new logo, to replace the 'postage stamp' flag, used negative space to form the S between the U and the A, and this distinctive look was carried through to all other elements of the channel's presentation, on- and off-screen, with the signature use of bold cut-out images of USA's lead characters, typically on plain white or pale blue backgrounds.

After a major multimedia launch campaign, the USA Network marketing team worked hard to add meaning to Characters Welcome by combining characters from their leading shows in promotional films. A typical example set at the 'American Detectives Association' featured two members from the original USA stable: the obsessive-compulsive Monk colliding with *The Dead Zone*'s Johnny Smith, who can look into people's past and future just by touching them. Keen to avoid physical contact, Monk asks if Smith can discover anything just by being 'in the immediate vicinity' or 'hovering nearby'.[21] Another example combined characters from *White Collar*, a police procedural drama, and one of USA Network's still popular wrestling shows. These are described by NBCUniversal's marketing team as 'talent spots': not traditional promotional trailers urging us to watch a specific show on

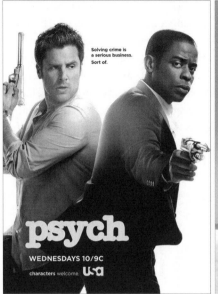 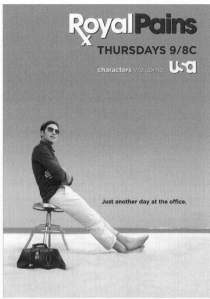

White space and blue skies: key art for USA Network shows Psych *and* Royal Pains
Source: Reproduced by permission of NBCUniversal Media, LLC

a specific day at a specific time but short interstitial films to reinforce USA Network's 'characters' proposition and nourish its brand personality.

– BLUE SKIES AND FRUIT BOWLS –

On the subject of that brand personality, words that have become familiar in association with USA Network are 'blue sky', 'quirky' and 'optimistic' (as well as 'character-driven', of course). These evolved quickly from merely a tone of voice for marketing communications to an effective filter for making programming decisions. At a time when rival networks were going darker and edgier, USA Network took the view that blue skies – both figuratively and literally – would give their characters broad appeal. By taking decisions such as moving *Burn Notice* to Miami from its original setting of New Jersey, or commissioning shows set in aspirational locations like The Hamptons (*Royal Pains*), USA applied the Characters Welcome brand personality as a guiding principle for the whole channel.

Commenting on this approach in a piece titled 'The Happy-Time Network', Amy Chozick, writing in the *Wall Street Journal*, asserted that:

> USA [Network] is so specific about the look and feel of its shows that it tells producers to make sure there is a 'fruit bowl' in each potentially drab scene. This is metaphor: it could literally mean a bowl of fruit or, more often, a splash of colour.[22]

Innovative marketing initiatives also helped USA Network to establish Characters Welcome as a highly distinctive and engaging brand property. Perhaps the first social networking site from a TV brand, www.showusyourcharacter.com, described by Alexandra Shapiro in 2015 as 'in essence, a precursor to Facebook',[23] invited viewers to upload pictures of, and facts about, themselves and to find like-minded fans. USA Network set out to build a welcoming fan-based community beyond the shows on the channel themselves and, in an era before social media had such a huge impact on TV marketing (as we will see), activity like this was truly ahead of its time.

'A precursor to Facebook': www.showusyourcharacter.com
Source: Reproduced by permission of NBCUniversal Media, LLC

Other elements included Character Approved (in which innovative real-life characters from a range of fields were awarded USA Network's 'seal of approval'), Characters Unite (an award-winning social action campaign), and the Character Project (a photography book and film series).

Jason Holzman, SVP, brand creative, summed up for us the key ingredients of Characters Welcome's success:

> When you take a very powerful brand positioning, tagline, strategy and marry that with programming that is very reflective of that positioning, that's when you hit the home run. And that's what I think has been particularly successful about Characters Welcome. It was a real marriage between a very authentic and powerful brand positioning and tagline that resonated with consumers along with a programming strategy that came very specifically out of that brand strategy and positioning. The two of those things together were really what made Characters Welcome particularly effective.[24]

– INGREDIENTS OF SUCCESS –

A 'home run' it most definitely was. Characters Welcome quickly became the most recognizable tagline in the US cable TV market, with exceptionally high levels of brand attribution to USA Network. Within 18 months of the relaunch, in July 2005, USA Network became the number one cable network in the United States and after nine straight years of leadership it ended 2014 as the most-watched general entertainment channel.[25] Alexandra Shapiro explains the key ingredients of this success story:

> After we relaunched the brand... every time we have launched a new show it has often been the number one new series of the year, so it gave us clear focus and an incredible marketing platform. Because we were so consistent with the brand, more than any other network people tended to watch 2+ shows, because they understood and knew what they could expect from USA [Network]. Also, since the relaunch we increased our profitability by over 200 per cent over a decade, and that's a testament to the power of this brand and our ability to be very focused in terms of what we choose to do and choose not to do.[26]

– CLOUDIER SKIES –

Despite the exceptional longevity of USA Network's success, clearly the competitive environment for TV channels is very different now compared with 2005. Just as we talked with Alexandra and Jason about the Characters Welcome case study, they shared with us the reasons why they were in the process of evolving the brand positioning. In late 2014 entertainment news outlets began reporting that USA Network was set to move away from 'blue skies' programming towards darker, edgier shows. The launch of *Dig*, a conspiracy drama 'event' set in contemporary Jerusalem, pointed the way, but it was the success of another new drama, *Mr Robot*, that really foreshadowed a significant shift in marketing strategy for the network. Josef Adalian, writing for Vulture.com, posed the question of a cable channel that he described as previously reliant on 'the video equivalent of beach reading':

> How in *Monk*'s name did a show so complex, twisted – and critically acclaimed – end up on USA Network? *Mr Robot* may be TV's most beautifully byzantine mystery-thriller since the first season of *Lost*, a show that encourages its audience to debate subtext and obsess over detail. It's all very much off-brand for USA, and as execs at the network see it, that is exactly the point.[27]

Mr Robot is a psychological thriller about a security engineer with a complex personality (anxiety, depression) who becomes a cyber-vigilante on a mission to take down one of the world's largest corporations. The USA Network team took a bold approach to the marketing launch. Viewing the pilot episode gave them the confidence not just to order a second series before a single episode had aired (a rare event in US television) but to mount a launch campaign more like a theatrical movie release than a typical new TV drama. The show was previewed on every available non-linear platform, resulting in more than 3 million people viewing at least part of the pilot before its first linear transmission.[28] *Mr Robot* played a big part in making USA Network the number one cable entertainment network in the summer of 2015 amongst the key 18–49 demographic group.[29] USA's Jason Holzman made it clear to us that the repositioning of the network has been driven to a large extent by the goal of reaching that audience, which is now made up to an increasing extent by millennials. However, the solution has not been to race towards copycat edgy and challenging dramas (of the kind, for example, that we look at in Chapter 5 with FX Networks). Jason describes the tone of USA Network's new breed of programming like this:

> We think our white space is what we call 'silver linings'. Very much not blue skies, because that feels completely out of step with the reality that people are experiencing now, not dark skies because: a) that's not true to who we are; and b) we don't want to be the last person to join the parade of dark, nihilistic programming.[30]

At the time of writing, while the evolution in USA Network's programme strategy was already very apparent, the network had not moved away from its Characters Welcome tagline. Hinting at an imminent change, though, Jason also stressed the extent to which the property of 'characters' built up over a decade of distinctive and consistent marketing would continue to serve as the foundation for USA Network's positioning:

> The word 'characters' may not be in our tagline but as a brand we're not ceding that territory of characters because what we continue to look for and what I think will continue to be a differentiating criterion for us in the marketplace is that we create and look for shows that have distinctive and memorable characters at the core. It's about the character first and then finding interesting worlds and non-derivative premises. *Mr Robot* is a great example of that. At the core of that show is an incredibly distinct and memorable and unique and never-seen-before character... That DNA will continue to be part of our brand because ultimately that is what is at the core of the best stories of all time.[31]

To echo Jason's words, consistency is at the core of the best TV channel brands of all time. The difficult trick is identifying when it is time to evolve, or to move towards a more radical reinvention. In Chapter 3 we look at three channels that took a dramatic change of direction to give them a much stronger competitive edge in the battle for audience share.

NEXT

★ Virgin Atlantic, Chicken McNuggets or Pampers?

★ Flags, lighthouses and shipping lanes.

★ Two little questions.

★ 'The Home of Witty Banter'.

★ An oasis of fun.

★ 80% Saint, 20% Sinner.

LATER

★ 'Where angels feared to tread'.

★ Man jumps out of window.

★ Stinson Breast Reduction and Linson Breast Lawsuit.

NOTES

1 *Taxi*, (1978) Paramount Television, American Broadcasting Corporation, 12 September

2 Puopolo, S (2009) [accessed 8 July 2015] The Future Of Television: Why You Won't Recognise Your Television Just A Few Years From Now, *IPTV Magazine* [Online] http://www.iptvmagazine.com/IPTVMagazine_Article_The_Future_of_Television.html

3 Pot, J (2015) [accessed 8 July 2015] TV Channels Are Dead: Why Sling Isn't The Future Of Sports TV (Online) http://www.makeuseof.com/tag/tv-channels-dead-sling-isnt-future-sports-tv/

4 The Economist (2014) [accessed 8 July 2015] Switching Channels: More Signs That The TV Business Is Set For A Profound Upheaval, *The Economist* [Online] 25 October, http://www.economist.com/news/business/21627662-more-signs-tv-business-set-profound-upheaval-switching-channels

5 Viacom, 2015 [accessed 8 July 2015] Viacom Brands [Online' http://www.viacom.com/brands/pages/default.aspx

6 Turner Broadcasting System (2015) [accessed 8 July 2015] Brands: We Are Where You Are [Online] http://www.turner.com

7 Fox International (2014) [accessed 8 July 2015] FX [Online] http://foxinternationalchannels.com/brands/fx

8 NBC Universal (2015) [accessed 8 July 2015] E! [Online] http://www.nbcuniversal.com/business/e-entertainment

9 Thinkbox (2015) [accessed 8 July 2015] TV Futures: Viewers, Advertisers And Technology [Online] http://thinkboxlive.tv/2014/20mar/

10 Green, L (2010) [accessed 8 July 2015] Rory Sutherland's Quiet Behavioural Revolution Gives The Status Quo Bias A Nudge, *Telegraph*, 25 September [Online] http://www.telegraph.co.uk/finance/newsbysector/mediatechnologyandtelecoms/media/8023044/Rory-Sutherlands-quiet-behavioural-revolution-gives-the-status-quo-bias-a-nudge-think-tank.html

11 Thinkbox (2015) [accessed 8 July 2015] TV Futures: Viewers, Advertisers And Technology [Online] http://thinkboxlive.tv/2014/20mar/

12 Schwartz, B (2005) *The Paradox of Choice: Why more is less*, HarperCollins Perennial, London

13 Hampp, A (2010) [accessed 8 July 2015] How USA Network Built 'Character' ratings, *Advertising Age*, 17 May [Online] http://adage.com/article/cmo-interviews/usa-network-built-character-ratings/143844/

14 Mad Logic Research, conducted for USA Network,14 September 2004

15 Hunt, L (2010) Lee Hunt's New Best Practices, Promax BDA Conference, 24 June, Los Angeles

16 Hunt, L (2005) Channel Positioning Overview, USA Network, Summer

17 Alexandra Shapiro, executive vice president, marketing and digital, USA Network, interview 26 May 2015

18 USA Network (2013) Cable and Telecommunications Associations for Marketing awards paper

19 Alexandra Shapiro, executive vice president, marketing and digital, USA Network, interview 26 May 2015

20 Alexandra Shapiro, executive vice president, marketing and digital, USA Network, interview 26 May 2015

21 Bjossigudjons (2011) [accessed 2 November 2015] *The Dead Zone/Monk* promo, American Detective Association [Online] https://www.youtube.com/watch?v=ws-1iF8gUaY

22 Chozick, A (2011) [accessed 8 July 2015] The Happy-Time Network, *Wall Street Journal*, 22 April [Online] http://www.wsj.com/articles/SB100014240527 4870391600457627103335367848 2

23 Alexandra Shapiro, executive vice president, marketing and digital, USA Network, interview 26 May 2015

24 Jason Holzman, senior vice president, brand creative, USA Network, interview 26 May 2015

25 USA Network (2014) [accessed 2 November 2015] USA Network Continues Unprecedented Ratings Streak with 9th Consecutive Year as #1 in Cable Total Viewers, Press Release, 18 December [Online] http://www.thefutoncritic.com/ratings/2014/12/18/usa-network-continues-unprecedented-ratings-streak-with-9th-consecutive-year-as-number-1-in-cable-in-total-viewers-745311/20141218usa01/

26 Alexandra Shapiro, executive vice president, marketing and digital, USA Network, interview 26 May 2015

27 Adalian, J (2015) [accessed 2 November 2015] How Did A Show Like Mr Robot End Up On USA? *Vulture*, 27 August [Online] http://www.vulture.com/2015/08/mr-robot-how-did-it-end-up-on-usa.html#

28 Adalian, J (2015) [accessed 2 November 2015] How Did A Show Like Mr Robot End Up On USA? *Vulture*, 27 August [Online] http://www.vulture.com/2015/08/mr-robot-how-did-it-end-up-on-usa.html#

29 Lynch, J (2015) [accessed 2 November 2015] How USA's Mr Robot Hacked The Problem Of Summer TV, *Ad Week*, 6 September [Online] http://www.adweek.com/news/television/how-usa-s-mr-robot-hacked-problem-summer-tv-166735

30 Jason Holzman, senior vice president, brand creative, USA Network, interview 29 September 2015

31 Jason Holzman, senior vice president, brand creative, USA Network, interview 29 September 2015

CHAPTER THREE

RELAUNCHING A TV CHANNEL

Waving a flag on the horizon

Hello, and welcome to Never Mind The Buzzcocks. *If you're watching on BBC Two, hello, and if you're watching on Dave +1 in the year 2020, Hangchangchangchangquaa Hanggangwannahaaaa.*

FRANKIE BOYLE, *NEVER MIND THE BUZZCOCKS*[1]

– SHARE WARS –

Imagine a market in which 497 new brands were launched in the space of 20 years: a 12,525 per cent increase. That would make the jam display we talked about in the previous chapter look like a shelf in a food store behind the Iron Curtain during a Cold War winter shortage. Yet that's what had happened to the television market in the UK over roughly a 20-year period between the late 1980s and late 2000s.[2]

In that insanely competitive arena, UKTV (an independent British multi-channel broadcaster) relaunched a channel with a name that initially raised eyebrows across the TV industry yet went on to become the UK's number one non-terrestrial channel, with the highest spontaneous awareness and a market share that has nearly trebled (+271 per cent) since launch.[3]

Looking at the television market in other countries, the specific statistics and data periods may change but the general picture is similar: a fiercely competitive environment with a growing number of players (big and global, smaller and local) vying for a higher audience share, leading to an abundance of choice for the viewer. In this world, it is relatively easy to know when a TV channel needs to be reinvented but much more difficult to execute it in a way that has a significant commercial impact. In this chapter we look at three very different channel relaunches: the story of a TV channel in the UK called Dave; the radical transformation of Court TV, a US cable channel that once relied largely on live trial coverage; and the rebrand of NBCUniversal's global entertainment channel, which had to work in 103 countries and 16 languages. We want to set the context by considering the different ways that channel brands are named and organized in this (okay, let's say it just one last time) oversupplied market.

– VIRGIN ATLANTIC, CHICKEN McNUGGETS OR PAMPERS? –

Although television is different from most other markets in so many ways (as we saw in Chapter 1), when we look at brand architecture we can see that it follows a fairly classic pattern. Possibly the most useful tool for TV marketers to apply to the way that brand portfolios are organized is the Brand Relationship Spectrum developed by David Aaker and Erich Joachimsthaler in 2000.[4]

According to Aaker and Joachimsthaler (to simplify a more detailed model), this spans three broad categories of brand portfolio: what they call a branded house, a group of endorsed brands and a house of brands. In a branded house strategy, an overall master brand has a dominant role across multiple offerings. A classic example is Virgin: Virgin Money, Virgin Trains, Virgin Media, Virgin Atlantic and so on. Endorsed brands are linked to some form of organizational master brand but act more independently. An example would be Polo by Ralph Lauren. A subset of endorsed brands is what Aaker and Joachimsthaler call a linked name, like Big Mac or Chicken McNuggets. By contrast, a house of brands is made up of an independent group of stand-alone brands, each with an individual presence in its specific market sector. P&G is cited as a perfect example: over 80 major brands in its 'house', including Ariel, Pampers and Duracell, largely with little link to the P&G brand or each other.[5]

Applying this model to television and looking at some of the biggest players in the major markets, we can see examples across the whole Brand Relationship Spectrum.

The CANAL+ portfolio in France conforms to the classic branded house model: a uniform brand architecture in which a number of descriptive channel names are linked together under a dominant CANAL+ master brand. To a large extent, the BBC, ITV and Sky portfolios in the UK also fit this model, and in Chapter 4 we come back to these network brands.

Channels in the UK such as E4 and More4 are the equivalent in the TV world of Chicken McNuggets: endorsed brands with linked names (although, as we will see in Chapter 5, the marketing team at Channel 4 very much sees its brand portfolio grouped together as a single coherent and distinctive offering). Aaker and Joachimsthaler say that you might lean more towards

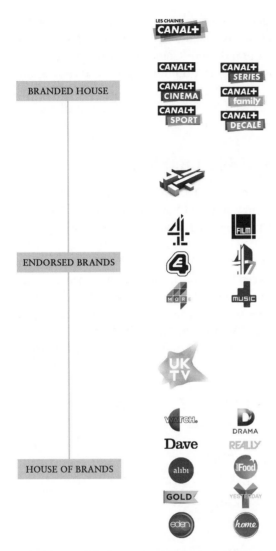

A highly simplified version of Aaker and Joachimsthaler's Brand Relationship Spectrum illustrated by three TV networks: CANAL+ (France), Channel 4 (UK) and UKTV (UK) Source: CANAL+ logos reproduced by permission of CANAL+. Channel 4 logos © Channel 4 Television. UKTV logos reproduced by permission of UKTV Media Limited

a house of brands if there is a compelling need for a separate brand, for example to avoid an unhelpful association with a parent brand or more easily to present a new, different offering.

Looking at the US TV market, all the models can be seen, although the house of brands approach seems most prevalent. Going back to NBCUniversal, its line-up of cable channels features stand-alone brands such as E!, Syfy, Bravo, Oxygen and, of course, USA Network. However, it also has branded house elements, including CNBC and NBC Sports Network. Viacom is a house of brands with Comedy Central, Nickelodeon and MTV. Fox is a mixed bag, acting as a branded house with Fox Sports and Fox Crime, using the FX Networks portfolio as endorsed brands and behaving like a house of brands with National Geographic and Channel V. There is no single, standard model for success.

– THE INVISIBLE CHANNEL –

Returning to UKTV, in just 18 months it transformed its whole channel portfolio from an underperforming branded house to a house of (very distinctive) brands, and this bold and unprecedented move was spearheaded by a TV channel named Dave.

By early 2007, UKTV had a portfolio of 10 channels and seven '+1' channels. At that time a joint venture between BBC Worldwide and Virgin Media, it had successfully pursued a strategy of broadening its range of genre-based channels to create increased opportunities to exploit its access to BBC archive programmes. However, growth in UKTV's viewing figures had started to plateau and competition was getting tougher, so radical solutions were called for.

How the UKTV network looked in its branded house days.
Source: Reproduced by permission of UKTV Media Limited

One key move was not so much a result of inspired marketing thinking but a strategic change in distribution. UKTV's analysis concluded that a key audience for delivering significant increases in advertising revenue was, in demographic terms, men in the social groups labelled ABC1, aged 16–44 years. Fortunately, UKTV already had a channel with the potential to attract bigger audiences from this group if it could be added to the UK's free-to-air digital terrestrial TV platform Freeview alongside its existing presence in pay TV. Unfortunately, it was a channel with no visibility, no brand personality and no clear role in people's lives: uktvG2.

We always tend to think of Dave as a new channel, but the truth is that it was actually the result of a relaunch. The unloved channel that languished with a market share of just 0.761 per cent and 2 per cent spontaneous awareness, and the channel that went on to add 8 million new viewers in six months and become the UK's Medium of the Year, were, technically, one and the same.[6] uktvG2 already existed in UKTV's portfolio, with a healthy schedule of popular BBC archive programmes such as *Top Gear*, *Have I Got News For You*, *QI*, *Mock the Week* and *Never Mind the Buzzcocks*. Simply adding uktvG2 to Freeview would automatically increase its audience, but not enough to achieve UKTV's five-year ambition: to become the UK's number one digital channel for men aged 16–44.

UKTV considered whether to follow the lead of other digital channels at the time, such as Virgin1, Sky One and the UK version of FX, by investing in a single, high-profile programme commission or acquisition and then promoting it heavily to bring in new viewers. The cost was prohibitive and, anyway, viewing data had shown how hard it was to turn one showpiece programme into sustained audience growth. The task facing uktvG2 was clearly a brand challenge.

– FLAGS, LIGHTHOUSES AND SHIPPING LANES –

Magnus Willis, co-founder of the insight and strategy consultancy Sparkler, is one of the best thinkers and researchers we have worked with in the TV world, and we have been influenced by his concept of 'flag channels' and 'frame channels'. Talking in particular about channels that have to get noticed from the outer reaches of the programme guide (which, incidentally, uktvG2 didn't have to: it enjoyed the luxury of a slot on the first page of the Sky guide, making its invisibility to viewers all the more remarkable), Willis explained where his 'flag channel' metaphor came from:

> What you need to do is to create brands that are disruptive in terms of their behaviour but are pin-sharp in terms of their offer... The analogy I always had in my head was: if you're standing on a plain, there are things that are nearby that you can see because you have been looking at them for a while, you kind of understand them. Meanwhile there are things in the distance that you can't even contemplate because they are so far away. Therefore, what is the best way to get people to see things that are far away? That's where the whole flag thing came from... On the horizon, you are basically going to have to put a stake in the ground with a flag on top of it and you have to wave your flag like a maniac to get people to go there.[7]

UKTV's commercial director, Simon Michaelides, uses a different metaphor to describe essentially the same thing. He talks about lighthouses and shipping lanes, and it is worth setting the context with a brief mention of Adam

Morgan and his 'Lighthouse Identity' concept. Founder of the strategic brand consultancy eatbigfish, a business based on his influential book *Eating The Big Fish*, which examined the shared qualities of brands that challenge the conventional wisdom of the categories in which they compete and take on the market leaders, Morgan describes what he means by 'Lighthouse Identity':

> Success as a challenger comes through developing a very clear sense of who or what you are as a brand/business and why – and then projecting that identity intensely, consistently and saliently to the point where, like a lighthouse, consumers notice you (and know where you stand) even if they are not looking for you... Challenger brands do not attempt to navigate by the consumer. Instead, they invite the consumer to navigate by them.[8]

Thinking about how this concept can be applied most successfully to the TV market, to take account of the greater diversity of a TV channel's 'product' compared with other brands cited by Morgan, such as Audi, Virgin Atlantic and MAC cosmetics, Simon Michaelides adds a shipping lane to the lighthouse:

> I have stolen shamelessly from Adam Morgan. Imagine our brand is the lighthouse. You define it, you build it on a rock that is immovable and then you broadcast your promise to the world in the form of the light. So you shine the beam of light out, you shine it right down the centre of the shipping lane, it's the truest, safest path. The problem is, if the ships then represent our content, they all leave port and they fan out across the shipping lane. Now, some go right down the centre of the shipping lane, in the light, they are bang on brand, they are brand defining. Others may be one or two degrees off. They are still on brand, they are still within the shipping lane, but perhaps not so brand defining. Others stray perilously close to the edge or even outside, and risk becoming a problem.[9]

Simon's key point is that TV content is dynamic. It is much more fluid than, say, the current range of Audi models or the end-to-end experience of flying with Virgin Atlantic. A successful TV brand needs to have a clear editorial positioning that unites and makes sense of what can often be a diverse range of programmes. A TV brand that sets out to challenge the established market leaders – as UKTV did in attempting to claim the highest share amongst men aged 16–44 despite Sky Sports 1's access to Premiership football rights for the (now comparatively modest) investment of £669 million[10] – needs to have a very clear, distinctive and compelling brand promise at its heart.

– TWO LITTLE QUESTIONS –

If you enter the term 'brand positioning' in the search bar and then click on images, you can find a wide range of shapes and diagrams all claiming to be the definitive positioning model. You will find Venn diagrams with varying numbers of overlapping circles, X and Y axes, concentric circles, pyramids and multiple boxes. In our experience many marketers have a habit of overcomplicating things. The model we tend to use is elegantly simple: so simple, in fact, that in checking our sources we could not establish whether it was originally set out in a learned academic tome – in which case apologies for the absence of a credit – or simply evolved as a way of working in our team with no known source. We ask two very simple questions of a TV channel:

1 What does the audience want?
2 What can we uniquely provide?

To expand on that, what is our audience insight? Can we clearly identify and describe a core target group for the channel? And then: what is our content offering? Is there a way to present it to viewers that is compelling and deliverable? Is it something we can imply that the audience will only find on our channel: this particular mix of content, presented in the way only we present it?

To be successful, a TV channel brand promise doesn't have to apply to 100 per cent of the content, 100 per cent of the time. It doesn't need to be an all-embracing definition of absolutely everything on the channel. As we saw in Chapter 2, USA Network continued to attract large audiences to World Wrestling Entertainment and tennis coverage, while establishing its Characters Welcome proposition primarily to encapsulate the essence of its core drama content.

One of the best quotes we have read on this subject was not referring to the subject of marketing at all, but came from management guru Peter Drucker talking about the art of leadership through times of transition:

> Leading change is about aligning people's strengths so that their weaknesses become irrelevant.[11]

To apply Drucker's comments to the purpose at hand, it can also be said that transforming a TV channel brand is about aligning its strengths so that its weaknesses become irrelevant. The key thing is to identify the strengths of the content, find the commonalities, seek out the connective tissue and package that as a coherent promise to the audience, so that the weaknesses (or inconsistencies) in some parts of the schedule are overridden.

Research commissioned by UKTV back in 2007 revealed that, despite uktvG2's fairly broad range of programmes, what lay at the heart of its content was 'intelligent, irreverent humour'.[12] The real breakthrough, though, came from an understanding of the role that the channel's core programmes had in the lives of men aged 16–44. For fans of uktvG2 (yes, despite its non-existent brand identity, it did have a core of loyal viewers), the channel almost played the role of a surrogate wise-cracking mate. To answer the two key brand proposition questions from our original creative brief for the new brand identity:

What does the audience want? They're blokes who appreciate wit and intelligence and something a bit subversive that gives them social currency. They've got partners, families and careers – lots going on. They need an entertainment channel that allows them to retreat into a world that is just for them. They go out with their mates a couple of times a month, even once a week, but meanwhile our brand offers a little bit of male camaraderie and stimulation every day.

What can we uniquely provide? It's a faithful mate they can rely on for a bit of a laugh. Alternative, smart, funny and quick witted. Like being down at the pub with the funniest, smartest version of your own mates. Imagine your local pub with Paul Merton, Jeremy Clarkson and Johnny Vegas as barflies.[13]

As we saw with USA Network, capturing the proposition in the form of a distinctive and evocative tagline gave us a rich and fertile creative platform:

The Home of Witty Banter

Defined by *Urban Dictionary* as an 'inherently English' term to describe 'activities or chat that is playful, intelligent and original' (and coming years before the contemporary derivative #bantz became such a familiar hashtag on Twitter),[14] banter (of the witty kind) perfectly captured the camaraderie and intelligent teasing remarks that characterized uktvG2's most popular shows. The proposition, which became the tagline, also suggested that the channel was an accessible physical place where its male target audience could come and hang out. This became a springboard for creative development of the brand identity.

– A BETTER VERSION OF STEVE –

Before a new identity could be created, the channel needed a new name. At the time, as we have seen, UKTV's portfolio was very much a branded house, but it was highly doubtful whether the UKTV brand was then strong enough to meet the criteria suggested by Aaker and Joachimsthaler, which they summed up as:

Most fundamentally, does the master brand make the product more appealing in the eyes of the consumer?[15]

Rather than attempt to create a more distinctive 'flag channel' with a descriptive name like 'UKTV Banter', the UKTV team decided that a completely new, stand-alone name was needed. Even before our team had cracked the proposition and tagline, Steve North (currently general manager of UKTV's entertainment channels, one of the few people who has lived through the whole Dave saga from the beginning) was grabbing colleagues for impromptu naming workshops. Steve takes up the story:

> I remember running brainstorm after brainstorm... just taking a section of people (for) half an hour... and we got, I don't know, 500 names... Somebody in the room said Dave at one point and I couldn't tell you who, but it was written on the board. I remember in the room saying 'that's quite fun but we can't really do that...' We liked it but we dismissed it because you can't call a TV channel Dave, it just wouldn't be done, it's madness.[16]

However, once The Home of Witty Banter was in the bag, further research led UKTV to question whether the idea of a male Christian name was quite so silly after all. Steve recalls one research group in which a respondent was first heard talking about uktvG2 as a surrogate friend and, so:

> If it's a friend, can you give it a name? Is there a way in which it makes sense?[17]

After a quantitative research study commissioned from YouGov (a company known more for its political polls than data on which name would be best for a TV channel: Dave, Matthew or Kevin?), North found himself in the office of UKTV's newly arrived CEO, David Abraham (who has since gone on to lead Channel 4), making the case for renaming uktvG2 as Dave. The name already had comedy associations through the likes of David Mitchell and David Baddiel, it was relatively classless (from Cameron to Beckham), and free from regional or age biases – in short, a completely universal name. There was only one small hitch: it just happened to be the new CEO's name too. As Steve recalls:

> He instantly loved the idea of giving it a name, but was slightly against calling it Dave, for obvious reasons. 'Everyone's going to think that I have come in, I have been here for three months and I have named a channel after myself.'[18]

David Abraham suggested that the name Steve might work equally well, but was eventually convinced by a UKTV colleague who explained that 'Dave is just a better version of Steve', a judgement with which Steve (North) reluctantly concurred to get the final green light for the relaunch.

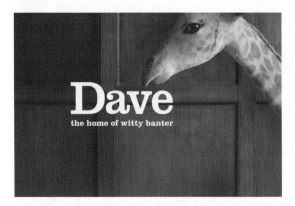

Oak panelling and stuffed animals: the world of a TV channel called Dave
Source: Reproduced by permission of UKTV Media Limited

– 'DOING A DAVE' –

Under the characteristically quirky creative direction of Kevin Hill and Ruth Shabi, a 'World of Dave' was devised: a gentlemen's club with a twist, full of visual ephemera such as ornate gilt frames, flock wallpaper and stuffed animals. Dave was launched in October 2007 with a campaign in which a relatively modest investment in outdoor advertising was boosted by a huge level of PR coverage generating 93 million opportunities to see and hear about Dave on the day of the launch, soon followed by 22 Facebook groups set up in spontaneous appreciation.[19]

The results were immediately staggering. We have mentioned some of the statistics already, but the most convincing 'before and after' story was the audience-share impact in pay-TV homes: a 71 per cent increase amongst UKTV's bullseye target of ABC1 men aged 18–44 over less than six months following the relaunch.[20] Remember that in pay-TV homes the only elements of the channel that had changed were the name and brand identity. All UKTV's other key audience measures moved in the right direction too and in less than six months Dave achieved its ambition to become the number one non-terrestrial TV channel amongst men aged 16–44 – well, at least it had drawn level with the formidable live football-driven Sky Sports 1.

Over the following two years or so, Dave became the definitive case study of TV channel transformation in the UK,[21] due in no small part to the demonstrable additional profit it generated for UKTV, with a return on marketing investment of nearly 3:1.[22] We lost count of the number of executives from other networks who came to us politely enquiring whether we could 'do a Dave' for them too, in many cases failing to understand the fact that the very essence of a 'Lighthouse Identity' is that it is unique and unrepeatable.

– SPREADING THE WIT –

The Dave brand continued to serve UKTV well for several years but by 2011 the market-share growth curve began to dip for the first time and UKTV's increased levels of ambition for the channel in terms of new programmes (both acquisitions from the United States and new original commissions) led to a re-examination of all aspects of the brand identity. Two elements in particular needed to be refreshed. The channel's distinctive visual appearance with its flock wallpaper and gilt frames had become so strongly associated with well-established BBC programmes such as *Have I Got News For You* that when UKTV tried to launch a completely new show, the audience tended to assume that it, too, was a BBC repeat, just one they were less familiar with. This, along with the line The Home of Witty Banter, were felt to have become constraining factors over time. Using a pub metaphor, UKTV's marketing team explains:

> Dave was at risk of only being seen as a pub, the Dave Arms if you will... Even though it contained some of the most entertaining people you knew, they did have a tendency to tell similar stories and also repeat themselves. If you were after a newer, fresher experience you may be tempted to go somewhere else.[23]

The brand proposition evolved into Dave Adds Wit To Your World, a broader and more flexible expression of the promise of witty banter that was no longer anchored to a physical 'home' – the Dave mansion house. Simon Michaelides of UKTV describes the rationale:

> The formula for success for broadcast brands is recognizing that every single touchpoint that the viewer has with the brand... must deliver an experience that embodies that brand promise or that editorial proposition, so (in the case of Dave) it doesn't matter whether that is the packaging or the on-screen presentation or whether that is the marketing communication or whether it is the content itself, it must all deliver that witty banter.[24]

Our team led by Jane Fielder developed a new visual identity for the channel's on-screen communication, based on the simple concept of a highly flexible 'blank slate'.[25]

This, combined with the new mantra that Dave adds wit to the world in a multitude of different ways (including a vastly increased volume of social media content), has liberated and broadened the channel's personality to embrace a much wider scope of programming. Talking about two quite different US acquisitions, Simon sums this up:

> It's that editorial proposition and that tone of voice that allows us to hold arguably disparate content together. So it doesn't matter whether we're talking about *Suits* or *Storage Hunters*... one a New York law drama, the other a show about people making anonymous bids for storage

containers... what we say about the show may differ but the way we talk about the show and the way we stamp our personality on it is the consistent glue that holds them together.[26]

Dave adding topical wit to the world with a flexible on-screen blank slate
Source: Reproduced by permission of UKTV Media Limited

This latest expression of the Dave promise of 'witty banter' has allowed UKTV to broaden the range of programmes in the channel's 'shipping lane'. A show does not have to be inherently witty so long as the way that the channel talks about it during promotional airtime and advertising is consistent with Dave's sharp and subversive personality. The net result has been a recent return to audience share growth, leading to the +271 per cent stat we mentioned at the beginning of this chapter and the highest level of spontaneous awareness amongst all non-terrestrial entertainment channels in the UK.[27]

– LAW AND ORDER –

When strategic consultant and researcher Magnus Willis talked about his flag channel concept he was thinking in particular about channels that most people don't visit very often: those in the lower reaches of the TV programme guide. With uktvG2 the basic ingredients – the programme schedule and electronic programme guide (EPG) position – were already in place. In contrast to this, one of the most dramatic relaunch stories we have come across recently involved taking a channel whose target audience was not even aware of it, and completely transforming both its brand positioning and programming over a period of just a few short months, including the launch of no fewer than 18 new shows.

Court TV started life as a new US cable network back in 1991. Prompted initially by the opportunity for live television coverage of a high-profile trial involving the rape and attempted murder of a jogger in Central Park, entrepreneurial lawyer and journalist Steven Brill saw a gap in the market for a channel that would 'substitute real law for *L.A. Law*'.[28] As more US states allowed cameras into their courthouses more frequently, Court TV began to build a loyal audience and for over 16 years covered prominent cases involving well-known characters such as Jeffrey Dahmer, Rodney King and, in particular, O J Simpson. However, in pursuit of a more advertiser-friendly audience, the channel (part of the Turner Broadcasting portfolio) started to move away from wall-to-wall live trial coverage to what it described as 'programming with real people in exciting real-life situations'. To reflect that shift, on 1 January 2008 the name of the channel was changed from Court TV to truTV. According to Turner at the time, truTV would join its sister networks TNT, TBS and TCM in 'establishing itself as a solid, identifiable brand, paving the way for continued growth'.[29]

– PAWNSHOPS AND TOW TRUCKS –

Over the years that followed, truTV continued to attract healthy audiences to its diet of 'caught on camera' programmes, typical of which was *Hardcore Pawn*, a reality show featuring a family-run pawnshop in Detroit. Although popular with certain types of viewers, programming like this is accused of being downscale and derivative. *Hardcore Pawn* itself bore an uncanny resemblance to History Channel's successful *Pawn Stars*, a problem highlighted by *Ad Age*:

> At one time the 500-channel cable universe promised a show for every niche; indeed entire networks for many niches. What cable viewers instead got is not an infinite variety of anything, unless you consider the infinite (well, 19) offerings in the pawnshop 'genre' that have hit the dial since *Pawn Stars* made its debut on History Channel.[30]

It hasn't just been pawnshops: in recent years the basic cable TV landscape has been littered with copycat reality shows on subjects as diverse as hoarders, weddings, real estate, dangerous jobs, swamp scavengers and even cupcakes. truTV was more guilty than most of this tendency to replicate popular reality formats, prompting one TV blogger to write a post with the headline: TruTV is King of the Road with Four Tow-Truck Shows.[31]

As *Ad Age* observed:

> The copies rarely exceed the original, and they just wear out the format faster. What's worse, the networks' own brands start to blur together in a world of sameness.[32]

The recruitment of a new president and head of programming in 2013, Chris Linn (who had a track record of success with unscripted programmes at MTV, including *Jersey Shore*), signalled a recognition by Turner that the 'identifiable brand' promised when the channel was renamed had become too strongly identified with a genre of conflict-driven programming that, while still delivering viewers in large numbers, was less popular with advertisers. Puja Vohra, EVP of marketing and digital at truTV, describes the problem:

> A lot of these shows were not brand defining. They were a bit outrageous, quite downscale, conflict-driven, very staged... it was as if despite its name, truTV was the most fake TV. You had to keep upping the ante of the situations to get bigger and bigger eyeballs, and this kind of content was very hard to monetize.[33]

Puja goes on to explain that, compared with the other 'very upscale, very shiny... very advertiser-friendly and... aspirational brands' in the Turner house of brands – channels such as TBS, TNT and Cartoon Network, to say nothing of the iconic news channel CNN – truTV was a little bit of an anomaly. However, the size of its viewer ratings meant that, in her words, the network 'just couldn't get off the crack':

> To produce shows that attract millions of people to tune in is no easy feat in this day and age, so the fact it was able to do that inexpensively incentivized truTV to keep doing it.[34]

– AN OASIS OF FUN –

Under the bold leadership of Chris Linn, the management, programming, sales and marketing teams at truTV united in making a far-reaching decision with the goal of attracting a more premium audience to the network and increasing advertising revenue. They knew that this would result in a significant decline in viewers, in the short term at least, but felt that only a radical overhaul of the channel's programme strategy, positioning, marketing and brand identity would wean truTV off its dependence on conflict-driven docuseries. One existing show acted as a beacon for the new strategy. Around a year after Linn joined the network, he told the *Hollywood Reporter*:

> One of the biggest things that I wanted to address when I came to the channel was the derivative nature of the content... *Impractical Jokers* was the one outlier on the network. That was sort of the canary in the coal mine.[35]

Puja Vohra underlines the symbolic importance of *Impractical Jokers* to the reinvention of truTV:

> It is a show about four best friends who pull pranks on each other and embarrass themselves publicly. It's extremely funny, very authentic,

not staged, not fake... It's now in its fourth season and continues to do extremely well for us. It has a very rabid fan base... That was the impetus for us to start to think about developing more programmes that could generate that kind of passionate, positive response and loyalty without requiring viewers to spend hours and hours catching up on storylines. Easy entry points and very shareable... that's our sweet spot.[36]

The 18 new shows we mentioned earlier in the chapter were introduced to the schedule in quick succession, in a spirit of experimentation and continual learning, all rooted in a new positioning inspired by *Impractical Jokers*: 'a fun ride for grown-ups'. Consistent with the channel's name, reality shows were still very much in evidence, but it was a new breed of reality: lighter, more entertaining and, in the words of the tagline created for the relaunch in October 2014: Way More Fun.

The essence of the new truTV brand is captured beautifully by Michael Vamosy, chief creative officer of Los Angeles-based entertainment marketing agency Stun, while working on a campaign to launch a new show commissioned for the autumn of 2015, *Santa's In the Barn*:

A reality show to find the next, biggest, best Santa Claus, it sounds ridiculous, and yes it is, but it's so much fun. It's about goodwill, the essence of Santa Claus, it's not *The Real Housewives of the North Pole*, there's no conflict with these guys, they're competing to be the best Santa Claus. Santa Claus would not screw over another Santa Claus to become Santa Claus, he just wouldn't.[37]

Contrasting the truTV relaunch with the transformation of uktvG2 to Dave, the biggest difference was the radical change in programme strategy, as Puja Vohra emphasizes:

Often rebrands can be very cosmetic. Rebrands often mean you change or tweak the logo, you change the tagline, you maybe add one new show, but everything else stays the same. But here at truTV, it was a total overhaul. We completely turned over the schedule.[38]

A vibrant new brand identity was created by US entertainment branding agency loyalkaspar (and, no, we don't know where the name comes from either: one day we must ask them). They created the Way More Fun line along with a refreshed logo, an on-screen presentation system and multiplatform identity bursting with colour and energy, to bring to life the 'fun ride for grown-ups' positioning. Daniel Dörnemann, executive creative director, agrees with Puja that superficial graphic tweaking would not have been enough to relaunch the network effectively:

It wasn't like 'let's put a fresh coat of paint on it and tell people we're a different network' when we didn't change the menu... going from an

Italian restaurant to a Spanish restaurant and you're not going to change the menu a year later, this is still Italian food, right? And this is where I think branding and programme content need to deliver equally.[39]

What we love most about the truTV rebrand is the way it has pivoted so wholeheartedly, not once but twice: first from its live courtroom roots to a successful breed of reality shows, and second towards the white space it identified to become, in Puja's words, 'an oasis of fun' in a landscape of darker, more dramatic programming.[40] As the trade press has been quick to point out, the decline in viewing expected by the truTV team certainly happened and time will tell whether their bold strategy will pay off in the long term. In the early months, though, Puja summed up the impact of the relaunch on truTV's audience profile (an audience previously so unfamiliar with the channel that truTV ran a social media campaign with the hashtag #HaveUFoundtruTV to respond directly to Twitter conversation amongst viewers who didn't know where it was, as we describe in Chapter 15):

> The metric we use the most to measure success or growth has been the change in our audience. We have pretty clear data to show that the average age of our viewers has come down (from) 45 years old to 37 in eight months; our viewership's median income has gone from the high $40,000 range to the high $50,000 range, again in eight months; and our A/B county concentration and education levels have both improved. So we have built a strong solid core with this audience – the right people are watching us now – and this is very hard to do. It can take a very long time to change brand perceptions.[41]

– X MARKS THE SPOT –

The two channel relaunch stories we have explored so far, despite their individual challenges, had the advantage of being limited to a single country. The task of channel brand reinvention becomes exponentially harder when the positioning and identity need to work equally well in over 100 countries in over 15 different languages.

One of the joys of our business, which can sometimes lead us astray, is the continual drive towards new thinking and new concepts. TV marketers can be reluctant to learn from ideas that have worked elsewhere, for example for a sister channel in another part of the world. However, in the summer of 2012, we were sent a pitch brief that resembled a treasure map with a big X labelled 'dig here'. We would be spared the usual strategic contortions we put ourselves through during a competitive pitch process, striving for the perfect channel positioning. The marketing team at Universal Channel was convinced that if 'characters' could work for USA Network it would help to give NBCUniversal's flagship general entertainment channel in all territories outside the United States a simple and cohesive global proposition for the first time. Their conclusion could not have been more clear:

> Characters are Universal. They're the heart of great stories with unique personalities that drive compelling entertainment.[42]

This deceptively simple brief, based as it was on USA Network's (then) seven years of success with 'characters', belied the complexity of the channel's marketing challenges. It is fair to say that Universal Channel had experienced something of a chequered past. For example, in Latin America it had been rebranded from USA Network back in 2004, but in some markets (including the UK and Australia) it was a rebadged version of Hallmark Channel, which NBCUniversal had acquired in 2010. This was not a recipe for brand consistency. Universal Channel reached over 80 million subscribers in 103 countries but there was no consistency of programming across territories and no consistent launch dates for its key programmes internationally.[43] So, for example, you could watch *House* and *The Mentalist* on Universal in the UK, but not in Australia or Poland. In the UK viewers had reached season 14 of *Law & Order: SVU*, whereas in Latin America they were still in season eight. Awareness of Universal Channel was pretty low and viewers in different countries had different perceptions. Soon after NBCUniversal had been acquired by Comcast, Lee Raftery took on responsibility for Universal Channel's marketing:

> Our biggest channel was just not in a good shape; the whole brand needed a complete overhaul. There was no agreement on what Universal Channel was – even internally. To my dismay, you would look at the channel in one part of the world and it was unrecognizable to the next. While it shared the same name, it often didn't have the same graphics package and there was very little consistency.[44]

In a decisive move to resolve these issues, NBCUniversal gathered their equivalent of (to use an analogy from *The Godfather*) 'the heads of the five families' for a pivotal brand workshop: 48 hours with 36 key stakeholders from 19 countries. Cat-herding duties were entrusted to strategic consultant Lee Hunt, with the stated aim of achieving alignment on a positioning for Universal Channel that would be simple, obvious, intuitive and emotional. The group decided that 'characters' should be the X on the treasure map, but not in the form of a direct facsimile of USA Network. This was a rebrand that had to work in 103 countries, remember, and to be translatable into 16 languages. There was general agreement that Characters Welcome could not be successfully grafted onto Universal Channel and that USA Network's relentless blue-skied optimism would jar with non-US audiences (particularly, according to Lee Raftery, amongst 'us cynical Europeans').[45] In our experience, although the adrenalin rush of a competitive pitch with a tight deadline often produces fresh and interesting creative thinking, it is rare for the original pitch work to end up on the client's channel. Universal Channel was a classic example. Having won the pitch (for the record, from an original long-list of 25 agencies on both sides of the Atlantic; one of our better days in the office), we set about working in collaboration with NBCUniversal's marketing team to crack the problem, and we felt that everything would flow once we had nailed the tagline.

– VORSPRUNG DURCH CHARACTERS –

The importance of a new tagline to Universal Channel was summed up by one of our key collaborators in the creative development process, NBCUniversal's Marco Giusti:

> Prior to this, if you had asked anybody 'What is Universal Channel about – and what does it stand for?' I don't think they would have been able to give you a straight answer – even internally, even people on the channel. So getting that clarified was hugely important. We knew where we were coming from. And we wanted a rallying cry that we could hang everything around. The tagline was of core importance. It became very much the essential part of our brand; it was the one thing that brought it all together.[46]

The line that brought everything together was this: 100% Characters.

Having been given, in 'characters', such a fertile property to work with, a line that would capture the essence of Universal Channel and allow us to tick off every requirement of the brief remained elusive during the early stages of creative development. Once we had 100% Characters, we knew we had a line that would not only be relevant and understandable globally but would give us a platform for two vital ingredients of the brand's identity: a strategic linking device for Universal Channel's inconsistent programming, and a visual device that would enable us to thread the proposition throughout all elements of the channel's on-screen presentation.

In our early development work we had explored the potential of 'percentages' to capture the fact that the characters in Universal Channel's shows were diverse, but always somewhat complex and never bland or predictable. Doctor Gregory House, Hugh Laurie's diagnostic medic in the eponymous drama, is a misanthropic maverick yet goes to great lengths to solve puzzling medical cases. He despises weaknesses in others, yet is himself addicted to painkillers. He is 60% Brilliant, 40% Broken, and 100% a Character. Alicia Florrick, lead character of *The Good Wife*, returns to her legal career after her state's attorney husband is jailed following a sex scandal. She strives to be that 'good wife' and mother of two while being a successful litigator and dealing with her own romantic diversions. She is 80% Saint,

20% Sinner, and 100% a Character. Jonny Lee Miller's Sherlock Holmes in the contemporary US version of Conan Doyle's stories, *Elementary*, is an eccentric former drug addict: 92% Genius Detective, 8% Socially Defective, 100% a Character.

Our planning team spotted a particularly interesting point about these complex characters: although on the surface shows like *House* have extremely tight and predictable formulas for individual episodes, a fact underlined by numerous parody sites,[47] the slow revealing of the sometimes contradictory facets of their characters is also what keeps you watching them for 24 episodes over seven or more series. Hence, our sweet spot was also aligned with a key potential business driver.

In pursuit of a holistic new identity for Universal Channel we found a way to visualize this 'percentages' concept and link it inextricably with the channel's logo. We created a circular 'dial' that could be colour-coded to denote the contrasting traits of each character, with triangular 'nicks' marking the percentage points. This would prove to be highly versatile in linking many elements of the global marketing mix, from the end boards of promotional trailers to print advertising, from Universal Channel's website to social media, from conceptual idents to launch party invitations. The device would give teams in different territories a lot of flexibility in applying the concept to the characters in their specific programme schedules. Crucially, it gave all of the markets a way of unifying the 'key art' that they received from the 'producing' studios and owning the content in a distinctive way.

100% Characters in Universal Channel's on-screen presentation in multiple languages.   Source: Reproduced by permission of NBCUniversal International

– UPDATING A CLASSIC –

A further breakthrough was the realization that, as all elements of the new identity were coming together, the existing Universal Channel logo didn't fit. Based on the classic Universal globe – so familiar to so many as a symbol of Universal Pictures since its earliest versions in the 1920s – the NBCUniversal International marketing team felt it was too reminiscent of the movie studio and theme parks and did not reflect the new positioning of the channel. They wanted something that had a link to the Universal heritage but that was essentially fresh and new.[48] By giving us licence to remove the landmass and to create a more contemporary version of its recognizable outer ring, we were able to integrate our triangular 'percentage nick' device into the logo itself, which integrated the updated logo seamlessly into a holistic new identity and on-screen presentation.[49]

Before and after: the evolution of the Universal Channel logo
Source: Reproduced by permission of NBCUniversal International

The combination of the new positioning, updated logo and refreshed visual identity across all touchpoints certainly had a positive effect on Universal Channel's performance. After the first 12 months, the channel had seen a 17 per cent increase in viewers across its key global markets.[50]

– FLAG WAVERS –

The three channel relaunch stories we have explored in this chapter all differ in terms of their geographical territories, their audiences, their programme strategies and the creative execution of their marketing, but they all illustrate the flag channel concept. Whether they interrogated their existing programming until it confessed to its strengths or (as in the case of truTV) completely overhauled the shows on the network, all three channels demonstrated a deep understanding of their target audiences, identified what they can uniquely provide, developed clear brand promises and then created bold and distinctive brand identities. As all our interviewees have stressed, in a savagely competitive market this has been no mean feat. The broader the scope of the programmes in the 'shipping lane', the harder the task. General entertainment channels are the most difficult of all. In the words of NBCUniversal International's Lee Raftery:

> General entertainment is an enormous challenge. Give me an E! or a Syfy or a DIVA any day. Much easier! General entertainment is the hardest of the lot because you have to be broad enough to accommodate any kind of programming while trying to convey a personality. Having now gone through it with Universal Channel, I look at all general entertainment rebrands and think 'that's really tough – and hats off to anybody who successfully completes them'.[51]

NEXT

★ 'Frame' channels.

★ The Bat's Wings.

★ Those swimming hippos.

★ For all the moments we share.

★ 'The Heart of Popular Culture'.

★ 'Believe In Better'.

LATER

★ 'Good luck gays on Gay Mountain'.

★ The universal truth of fandom.

★ 'We're all gonna die'.

NOTES

1 *Never Mind the Buzzcocks* (2011) series 24, episode 12, BBC Two, 3 January

2 Yelin, H, Wise, J, Phillips, C, Willis, M, Boston, E, Chandler, L, Hales, L, Jordon, J, Goldman, S and Ali, S, Institute of Practitioners in Advertising, Gold, IPA Effectiveness Awards 2008

3 UKTV (2015) Dave: More than Just a Name, Marketing Society Excellence Awards, June,

4 Aaker, D and Joachimsthaler, E (2000) The brand relationship spectrum: the key to the brand architecture challenge, *California Management Review*, 42 (4), pp 8–23

5 Aaker, D and Joachimsthaler, E (2000) The brand relationship spectrum: the key to the brand architecture challenge, *California Management Review*, 42 (4), pp 8–23

6 UKTV (2015) Dave: More than Just a Name, Marketing Society Excellence Awards, June

7 Magnus Willis, founding partner and joint chairman, Sparkler, interview, 27 May 2015

8 Morgan, A (2014) [accessed 27 July 2015] Eating The Big Fish: How Challenger Brands Can Compete Against Brand Leaders [Online] http://eatbigfish.com/wp-content/uploads/2014/09/Eating-the-Big-Fish-Sample.pdf

9 Simon Michaelides, executive board, commercial director, UKTV, interview 13 May 2015

10 Yelin, H, Wise, J, Phillips, C, Willis, M, Boston, E, Chandler, L, Hales, L, Jordon, J, Goldman, S and Ali, S, Institute of Practitioners in Advertising, Gold, IPA Effectiveness Awards 2008

11 Drucker, P, quoted in Whitney, D and Trosten-Bloom, A (2010) *The Power of Appreciative Inquiry: A practical guide to positive change*, Berrett-Koehler Publishers, San Francisco

12 Yelin, H, Wise, J, Phillips, C, Willis, M, Boston, E, Chandler, L, Hales, L, Jordon, J, Goldman, S and Ali, S, Institute of Practitioners in Advertising, Gold, IPA Effectiveness Awards 2008

13 Yelin, H, Wise, J, Phillips, C,Willis, M, Boston, E,Chandler, L, Hales, L, Jordon, J, Goldman, S and Ali, S, Institute of Practitioners in Advertising, Gold, IPA Effectiveness Awards 2008

14 Urban Dictionary (2015) [accessed 6 July 2015] [Online] http://www.urbandictionary.com/

15 Aaker, D and Joachimsthaler, E (2000) The brand relationship spectrum: the key to the brand architecture challenge, *California Management Review*, 42 (4), pp 8–23

16 Steve North, general manager, entertainment, UKTV, interview 27 June 2015

17 Steve North, general manager, entertainment, UKTV, interview 27 June 2015

18 Steve North, general manager, entertainment, UKTV, interview 27 June 2015

19 Yelin, H, Wise, J, Phillips, C, Willis, M, Boston, E, Chandler, L, Hales, L, Jordon, J, Goldman, S and Ali, S, Institute of Practitioners in Advertising, Gold, IPA Effectiveness Awards 2008

20 Yelin, H, Wise, J, Phillips, C, Willis, M, Boston, E, Chandler, L, Hales, L, Jordon, J, Goldman, S and Ali, S, Institute of Practitioners in Advertising, Gold, IPA Effectiveness Awards 2008

21 http://www.redbeecreative.tv/work/dave-channel-rebrand?service=brand-identity

22 Yelin, H, Wise, J, Phillips, C, Willis, M, Boston, E, Chandler, L, Hales, L, Jordon, J, Goldman, S and Ali, S, Institute of Practitioners in Advertising, Gold, IPA Effectiveness Awards 2008

23 UKTV (2015) Dave: More than Just a Name, Marketing Society Excellence Awards, June

24 Simon Michaelides, executive board, commercial director, UKTV, interview 13 May 2015

25 http://www.redbeecreative.tv/work/dave-channel-refresh?service=brand-identity

26 Simon Michaelides, executive board, commercial director, UKTV, interview 13 May 2015

27 UKTV (2015) Dave: More than Just a Name, Marketing Society Excellence Awards, June

28 Winfrey, L (1991) [accessed 27 July 2015] Courtroom Network Banks On Real-life Drama, *Pittsburgh Press*, 7 July [Online] https://news.google.com/newspapers?id=u-khAAAAIBAJ&sjid=7GMEAAAAIBAJ&pg=6980,1261106&hl=en

29 Turner Entertainment Network (2007) [accessed 27 July 2015] Television Network Brand Name – truTV, Press Release [Online] http://www.igorinternational.com/clients/truTV-naming-TV-network-rebranding.php

30 Learmonth, M (2011) [accessed 27 July 2015] Why 500 Channels Means 19 Shows About Pawnshops, Advertising Age, 8 August [Online] http://adage.com/article/media/500-channels-means-19-shows-pawnshops/229153/

31 Buckman, A (2011) [accessed 27 July 2015] TruTV Is King Of The Road With Four Tow-Truck Shows [blog], Xfinity, 21 August [Online] http://my.xfinity.com/blogs/tv/2011/08/21/trutv-is-king-of-the-road-with-four-tow-truck-shows/

32 Learmonth, M (2011) [accessed 27 July 2015] Why 500 Channels Means 19 Shows About Pawnshops, Advertising Age, 8 August [Online] http://adage.com/article/media/500-channels-means-19-shows-pawnshops/229153/

33 Puja Vohra, executive vice president, marketing and digital, truTV, interview 8 July 2015

34 Puja Vohra, executive vice president, marketing and digital, truTV, interview 8 July 2015

35 O'Connell, M (2014) [accessed 27 July 2015] TruTV Looks To Complete Makeover With Tweaked Logo, Four New Series Orders, *The Hollywood Reporter*, 10 July [Online] http://www.hollywoodreporter.com/live-feed/trutv-looks-complete-makeover-tweaked-717513

36 Puja Vohra, executive vice president, marketing and digital, truTV, interview 8 July 2015

37 Michael Vamosy, chief creative officer, Stun Creative, interview 10 June 2015

38 Puja Vohra, executive vice president, marketing and digital, truTV, interview 8 July 2015

39 Daniel Dörnemann, executive creative director, loyalkaspar, interview 11 June 2015

40 Puja Vohra, executive vice president, marketing and digital, truTV, interview 8 July 2015

41 Puja Vohra, executive vice president, marketing and digital, truTV, interview 8 July 2015

42 NBCUniversal (2012) Universal Channel Rebrand Pitch Brief, August

43 NBCUniversal (2012) Universal Channel Rebrand Pitch Brief, August

44 Lee Raftery, executive vice president, marketing and communications, NBCUniversal International, interview 8 May 2015

45 Lee Raftery, executive vice president, marketing and communications, NBCUniversal International, interview 8 May 2015

46 Marco Giusti, senior vice president, creative, NBCUniversal International, interview 8 May 2015

47 Swaim, M (2008) [accessed 8 July 2015] Cracked.com, Every Episode of *House* Ever, 22 November [Online] http://www.cracked.com/blog/write-your-own-house-episode/

48 Giusti, M (2014), NBCUniversal Case Study presentation, PromaxBDA Europe, Conference, March

49 http://www.redbeecreative.tv/work/universal-channel-global-brand-identity

50 NBCUniversal International, 12 months on % change versus 4 weeks prior to refresh

51 Lee Raftery, executive vice president, marketing and communications, NBCUniversal International, interview 8 May 2015

CHAPTER FOUR

THE 800lb GORILLAS
Building a big broadcast brand

*What we're talking about here, okay, is major brand surgery.
This is, like, beyond botox, it's kind of open heart, rip it out, start over,
okay? As of now it's, like, a dinosaur, okay, but where we're going with
this, okay, what we do is we make it into, like, a rhinosaur... like a
dinosaur that... so now it doesn't even exist yet, but that totally should
exist. Here's the thing with that. As an idea, as a concept, it's way cool.*

SIOBHAN SHARPE, *W1A – REBRANDING THE BBC*[1]

– THE BIG THREE –

We are not 100 per cent sure why the term '800lb gorilla' has become so inextricably linked with big, dominant TV organizations, in the UK at least, but it was Greg Dyke, the BBC's former director-general, who used the phrase most memorably. Inspired no doubt by the old joke (*Where does an 800lb gorilla sit? Anywhere it wants to!*), he stated when interviewed by Nils Pratley for the *Guardian* back in 2003:

> There are two 800lb gorillas around in this market. We [the BBC] are one and Sky are one... I think you need a third 800lb gorilla. You used to have it with ITV but ITV has been squeezed in the marketplace. I believe we should be looking at the advertiser-funded marketplace and working out how you get a third 800lb gorilla, because that's what you need.[2]

Given Greg Dyke's roots in commercial broadcasting, he will no doubt have been pleased to see the resurgence of ITV in recent years. A big part in ITV's revival as a commercial TV powerhouse in the UK (and, when it comes to production, beyond) has been its brand and the way its marketing team has built and nurtured it. ITV's 2014 Annual Report makes this clear:

> ITV's competitive advantage is underpinned by three strategic assets: high quality content, our strong brand and our talented, creative people.[3]

In CEO Jeremy Darroch's statement in the Sky Annual Report 2014, he mirrors this when he talks about 'the strength of our brand' and Sky's growing ability to extend it into new segments of the entertainment market.[4] While, unsurprisingly, we couldn't trace any overt mentions of brands in the BBC's latest Annual Report, in our experience over many years working with the corporation the importance of the BBC brand in relation to its public service remit and viewer goodwill is never far from the top of the marketing agenda.

So, how are these broadcaster brands built and nurtured? How is it possible for them to have clear, well-defined identities when they have to embrace such a wide range of channels, services and sub-brands? What is the role of their flagship channels? And how, in the case of the dominant commercial networks, are their masterbrands developed and supported in a way that delivers competitive advantage? In this chapter we stay in the UK and look at these questions in relation to the BBC, ITV and Sky – branded houses all – with a brief detour to Australia and its public service broadcaster, the ABC.

– IN THE FRAME –

In Chapter 3 we introduced Magnus Willis and his 'flag channels' and 'frame channels' concept. He uses the term 'frame channel' to describe those TV channels in the UK that you will find on the first page or two of the programme guide. Take the Sky 'all channels' guide, for example. It is still generally the case that people start to navigate on the first page, where what Magnus terms the 'old school terrestrial brands' are exactly where you would expect to find them:

> 101: BBC One
> 102: BBC Two
> 103: ITV
> 104: Channel 4
> 105: Channel 5
> 106: Sky 1

Magnus describes how the 'frame' concept works like this in the context of channels:

> It borrows from the world of terrestrial TV where in essence everyone was a generalist and what united the channel was not something at its centre... but something that encapsulated and framed everything... framing lots of interesting stuff that people sort of had a sense of. There is a sense of BBC One-ness... The world knows what BBC One is like even though it

covers a whole load of genres, from news to fact-ents to sport, everyone has a sense of BBC One, and even though probably BBC Two has never quite been as clear, still people have got a sense of what BBC Two is about, likewise ITV, and likewise Channel 4, so you have those brands that are sort of understood even though if you came to defining what the core proposition of them was you'd probably run aground.[5]

What Magnus refers to as 'BBC One-ness' is disproportionately important in shaping the British public's overall perceptions of the BBC and its value to the nation. BBC One remains the most watched TV channel in the UK, with nearly two-thirds of adults switching on at least once a week.[6] In the words of legendary TV designer Martin Lambie-Nairn, who led major rebrand projects for the channel in 1991 and again in both 1997 and 2002:

> BBC One is the corporation's most recognized face, and consequently the praise or blame that attaches itself to the BBC usually gets directed that way first.[7]

These words were written nearly 20 years ago but they remain true today.

– CLOCKS AND GLOBES –

Although the relationship that viewers have with the BBC, and BBC One in particular, has been formed over many years and shaped by multiple experiences, there is no doubt that a major influence on people's perceptions has been the channel's brand identity. A number of websites run by enthusiasts (including TV Ark) have painstakingly catalogued the on-screen identities of all the UK's major TV channels, going back as far as the BBC Television Service's first tuning signals in 1937. A notable example was 'the corporation's first on-screen logo', the so-called Bat's Wings, created in 1953 by Abram Games (who had previously designed the iconic logo for the 1951 Festival of Britain).[8] However, for over 50 years the prevailing visual manifestation between the programmes on BBC TV and, as it was called after the launch of BBC Two in 1964, BBC One, was a ticking clock and/or a single rotating globe. The graphic design of the globes and clocks evolved over the years, but they became such a permanent and familiar fixture on the UK's TV screens that it is no surprise that BBC Television's former head of graphic design, John Aston, described the BBC One identity as 'where angels feared to tread' and a subject that 'everyone had an opinion about'.[9]

During a period of 11 years, the formidable partnership of the design agency Lambie-Nairn and the BBC's highly respected director of broadcasting and presentation, Pam Masters (full disclosure: our former boss), transformed the visual identity of BBC One in three stages. In 1991 a more contemporary and sophisticated globe was introduced. Then, in 1997, the globe became a distinctive orange hot air balloon, gliding serenely above landscapes across the length and breadth of the UK to represent the way in which BBC One brought the world to every corner of the nation. For the first time, instead of just one visual symbol of the channel there were multiple (in fact, over 50) idents, each with its own soundtrack. Five years later, in a drive led by new controller Lorraine Heggessey to bring more energy and modernity to BBC One, the long tradition with the globe was broken with the introduction of a completely new set of idents based on rhythm and movement: dancers and acrobats, clad in red, performing ballet, capoeira, salsa and even the Maori haka in outdoor locations across Britain.

There is no doubt that this radical (and, amongst some critics, controversial) change in identity did a lot to shift perceptions of the channel, along with its new red logo and on-screen presentation. However, by autumn 2005 the BBC One controller (Peter Fincham, until recently ITV's director of television) and marketing team decided that another change in identity was needed. With the advent of the digital TV age, there was a need for BBC One to assert its unique strengths as: 'The place... that will unite big audiences and give them a sense of common experience around a wide range of quality programmes.'[10]

The stated target audience was, quite simply, 'everyone'. New channel idents topped the list of key deliverables for a competitive pitch that we were invited to take part in alongside, from memory, eight of the best design agencies in town.

– CIRCLE TIME –

Looking back at our original pitch, it is remarkable that even then, over 10 years ago, we quoted a number of academics and journalists predicting the transformational impact of 'narrowcasting' and personalization made possible by new digital technology, which would sound the death knell for the collective experience in broadcasting. Just as we differ now, we didn't share that view then. We believed strongly that, as media increasingly proliferated and fragmented, there would be an even greater need for people to have somewhere to go for shared viewing moments.

Peter Fincham agreed. In a TV industry conference speech in April 2006 he said the following, quoting a surprisingly low percentage of UK homes (3 per cent) that had more than one television playing at a time:

> What we aim to do (for BBC One), across a huge range of genres, is find those programmes that have a broad, mainstream appeal. We like big audiences, and we like family audiences. It's a commonly held view that family viewing is dying out... It's actually something of a misconception. We like watching television together.[11]

For a competitive creative pitch with such high stakes attached, the brief we set ourselves was extremely simple. We had to find a distinctive and entertaining way to capture BBC One's unique ability to bring the nation together in mainstream TV viewing, particularly in its channel idents. In the early stages we got very excited about a concept based on the Korean Mass Games (no, really), which we dubbed Together as One. It would be the world's first mass participation identity and a potent symbol of a nation united by its most watched TV channel.

However, Fincham and the BBC One marketing team challenged us to push for something more extraordinary: people doing amazing things together. They also asked us to think of a symbol of togetherness for the idents, not just content-related images and the channel's logo. The solution was pretty obvious. The most universally recognized icon of togetherness is a circle: a wedding ring, the Olympic rings, yin and yang... the list goes on. From that starting point we realized that a circle is also the way we have traditionally shared stories. We found a rich selection of images to illustrate that fact, from tribal campfires to nursery-school circle time to the girls in *Sex and the City*. To complete the circle (no pun intended) of logic, we realized that, dating right back to its first-ever tuning signals, through its various clocks and globes, via Abram Games's Bat's Wings (and with just a brief detour to dancers in red), the visual identity of BBC One had always been in the form of a circle. The world's best brands respect their design heritage. BBC One's symbol of the collective viewing of shared stories, particularly bearing in mind the O in its name, could only be a circle.

The idea was always about extraordinary things happening when people or objects come together. To celebrate togetherness as a force for good, forming a circle was not enough, it had to create something never seen before. From this tough self-imposed brief came the building of the moon, impossible football practices and, later, fairy circles and penguins in ice rinks.

We're not sure where the first executional idea came from. Maybe subliminal memories of David Attenborough documentaries? The initial ident concept sketched on a layout pad was a circle of hippos swimming in a perfectly synchronized circle. We didn't even know at first whether hippos could swim. We soon established that they don't, unless you count walking fast under water and bouncing off the bottom, but we thought that would make the ident more charming.

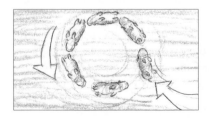

An early sketch for the BBC One hippos ident concept
Source: Reproduced by permission of the BBC

Other ideas flowed quickly: motorcycle stunt men riding a circular wall of death; extreme kite flyers forming a circle of giant red kites; a ring of footballers kicking balls to each other at high speed. Presenting the first batch of concepts to Peter Fincham and his team was one of the most joyful meetings of our careers. There was no debate, just an instant and unanimous recognition that the idea was a perfect fit for BBC One.[12]

The go-ahead to production came almost immediately and from that point our thoughts turned to how the media would react. We were well prepared by the BBC's press team. They knew that, rightly or wrongly, the launch of a new BBC One identity would attract coverage and comment from every single national newspaper in the UK, mostly on their front pages. Predictably, the *Daily Mail* led the assault, with a typically alarmist headline:

> BBC blows £1.2m on 80 seconds of hippos, kites and surf scenes[13]

Ahead of the press launch we had all been reminded of the key message that the previous set of idents had been aired 43,000 times over a four-and-a-half-year period (on average, over 30 times a day), a fact that some of the outlets were happy to quote.[14] Set in that context, the cost of production seems extremely modest. (More to the point, many of the idents we first created back in 2006–07 are still running on BBC One today, over nine years on from the launch.) Within a couple of days of the launch, Peter Fincham and his team were delighted to see that viewers were already posting spoofs on YouTube:

> My favourite, which you might have seen, was based on the shower scene from *Psycho*, in which as the blood – conveniently coloured red to reinforce BBC One branding – soaks down the circular plughole, the new BBC One graphic circles emerge. That's one we might use, maybe just before *Songs of Praise*.[15]

Since then we have created a diverse range of seasonal and topical versions, embracing events such as the football World Cup and programme brands such as *EastEnders* and *Doctor Who*, working with collaborators including Aardman (for a *Wallace & Gromit* Christmas special) and the BBC's Natural History Unit. More recently, with the aim of generating more warmth and variety in a cost-effective way, we have developed a series of simple illustrated idents in which the O in One has been rendered as, for example, an Alka-Seltzer tablet on New Year's Day, a red nose for Comic Relief and the zero in number 10 (Downing Street) for the general election. The idea here is that BBC One is waking up on the same day as its viewers and therefore still uniting the nation in shared experiences.[16] As the BBC's latest Annual Report states (citing programmes such as *The Great British Bake Off*, coverage of the World Cup and the night when Lucy Beale's killer was revealed on *EastEnders*):

BBC One... can still bring audiences of all ages and backgrounds together for must-see programmes.[17]

The BBC One idents are probably the most universally viewed pieces of TV content in the UK. They precede the widest possible variety of programming, from *Casualty* to *Strictly Come Dancing*, from *BBC News* to major sporting events such as the 2012 London Olympics. Virtually everyone in the UK sees them and recognizes them. Over the years they have also proved the only effective means of explaining to people outside the TV industry what exactly we do for a living. When asked the question, eyes glaze over if we talk about innovative on-screen presentation or complex transmedia marketing campaigns, but we get an instant reaction when we say 'we created the swimming hippos on BBC One', much like the artist Tracey Emin commented in the early days:

> Have you seen the BBC hippos? Every time I watch them... I'm lulled into a whole sense of enchantment. It's probably one of my favourite, most comforting things of the year. And what's strange is when I mention it to other people, their faces light up with glee.[18]

BBC One's swimming hippos displaying perfect unity
Source: Reproduced by permission of the BBC

– SHOUTING TO THE BLUE SUMMER SKY –

Before we explore the ways in which ITV built the brand identity of its flagship channel, we want to take a quick trip down under to look at how the BBC's public service equivalent in Australia, the Australian Broadcasting Corporation (ABC), has expressed its own part in the life of the nation compared with the BBC's approach. Back in 1997 the ABC had commissioned a new set of idents from an ad agency, Batey Kazoo, which became an iconic fixture on Australian television. The beautifully simple idea was to film real Australians, reflecting the country's diverse and multicultural make-up, tracing the ABC's distinctive logo – officially a 'lissajous curve' (part of the wave form of an oscilloscope, apparently) but known affectionately as 'the worm' – accompanied by a three-note mnemonic. When planning a rebrand of the ABC in 2014, marketing head Diana Costantini sought inspiration in those late-1990s idents, more than 90 of which ran over a three-year period:

> They were brilliant and everyone remembers them and still refers to them to this day. Having Australians endorse a brand, by drawing the logo in the air, had never been done before and was the perfect solution for being inclusive and giving ownership of the public broadcaster back to all Australians. The idents were simple, elegant and genuine. In our recent rebrand, we wanted to capture the essence of that work but add a new twist.[19]

Diana and her team were tackling challenges familiar to us with general entertainment channels and public service broadcaster brands: the need 'to be all things to as many people as possible' and 'to lighten up' and 'inject some exuberance to tackle the negative perceptions around stuffiness'. The answer was a revival of the idea of real-life Aussies featuring in personalized idents: micro-stories of life in regional communities, resolving with captions like 'It's Dave's ABC' or 'It's Taylah & Shontaye's ABC' blending into the hashtag #ourABC next to colourful versions of the 'worm' logo, with contemporary renditions of the three-note mnemonic.

Real life in Australia's regional communities reflected in ABC's idents
Source: *Reproduced by permission of Australian Broadcasting Corporation*

Talking about how much harder idents will need to work for TV channels in a world of increased viewer choice, Diana shared this opinion:

> Gone are the days of lingering, beautifully crafted, stand-alone spots, unfortunately. As we continue to find ways to keep our brand linked to our key content, we'll see more of a marriage between brand and content. The result will be fewer traditional idents and an increase in channel brand/image spots and shorter/stickier breaks.[20]

For the ABC that 'stickiness' was achieved with a wide variety of idents (16 in total so far) featuring, in Diana's own words, 'Australians telling their stories – warts 'n' all'.[21] The best of the individual idents were then compiled into a longer brand film set to a universally loved anthem by the Australian band Hunters and Collectors, 'Throw Your Arms Around Me' (sample lyrics: 'Whatever world you come from, Whatever tongue you speak, We may speak a thousand languages, But you will make me call your name, And I'll shout it to the blue summer sky'[22]).

The respected journalist Paul Daley was one of the many viewers who appreciated what the ABC was trying to achieve. Describing the film as a 'stirring visual interlude between programmes' that reflects Australia's diverse ethnic and indigenous make-up, he went on to say:

> If, like me, you love this new ABC station ID, then you'll probably pause, as I do every time I see it now, to contemplate whether it captures the true heart of Australia. It is certainly a reminder of what I want Australia to be.[23]

(Having now described how both the BBC and the ABC have used idents as such an integral part of their on-screen brands, the subject of idents deserves a discussion of its own, which we pick up again in Chapter 6.)

– 'YOU'RE GOING TO REAP JUST WHAT YOU SOW' –

Public service broadcasters have varying ways of expressing the fact that they belong to the people of the nation they serve. The ABC relies on the Australian government for most of its income, but the BBC is funded by a unique method underpinned by a royal charter reviewed every 10 years or so: a TV licence fee paid by everyone in the UK who watches or records TV programmes. Every charter review period fosters a high-profile national debate about the public purposes of the BBC and how they should be paid for. At times like these the management of the BBC is faced with the question of whether to allow the output and brand identities of the TV channels and other services to speak for themselves, or to run some form of overt communication about the overall value of the BBC to justify the licence fee.

Probably the most celebrated example of the BBC doing the latter was the 'Perfect Day' promotional film of 1997. We can both remember our spines tingling when we first saw the full four-minute version: a visually spellbinding montage of some of the most famous musical artistes of the day performing, in sequence, what was then a relatively obscure Lou Reed track. Featuring lines delivered by singers and musicians from David Bowie and Bono to the BBC Symphony Orchestra via Tammy Wynette and Lou Reed himself, along with many other Britpop, rock, R&B and reggae artistes less well known now than they were at the time, the song was released as a charity single for BBC Children In Need and reached number one in the UK music charts. (Several commentators pointed out the irony that the appeal of the song led us to pay for a single that was originally designed to celebrate something we had already paid for.) It is often overlooked that 'Perfect Day' was not primarily an ad for the diversity of music on the BBC, although it did that job extraordinarily well. The whole point was to talk about the value delivered by the BBC thanks to its method of funding:

> Whatever your musical taste it is catered for by BBC Radio and Television. This is only possible thanks to the unique way the BBC is paid for by you. You make it what it is.[24]

A similar message sat at the end of an earlier campaign, from 1986, featuring the comedian John Cleese ranting in a pub in a pastiche of his legendary 'What have the Romans ever done for us?' scene from Monty Python's *Life of Brian*, with 'the Romans' being replaced by 'the BBC'. An array of recognizable BBC stars and presenters answer his question with an exuberance that proved, again, that the licence fee value-for-money story can be told in memorable and entertaining ways. Writing in the *Independent on Sunday*, Tim de Lisle said this of 'Perfect Day':

> It left you with a warm feeling, and the hope that you might bump into it again... Arty but uplifting, subtle yet populist, this was the public information film for people who don't like public information films.[25]

Justin Bairamian, now director of BBC Creative, is in a unique position to comment on this subject since he was part of the team at Leagas Delaney, the advertising agency that created 'Perfect Day':

> I have always personally had a passion for the BBC having an expression of what it's about. I have always felt the BBC is better when it does that... The BBC should be talking about itself. Brands that are confident do that.[26]

We agree. However, the management of the BBC has not always shared this view. Contrasting the regimes of John Birt (director-general at the time of 'Perfect Day') and Mark Thompson (who held the role from 2004–12), Justin suggests a clear reason why:

> The guy at the top has to believe in it. It comes down to that... Mark Thompson... did not believe in this stuff... He just fundamentally disagreed

with the BBC saying anything about itself... David Abraham at Channel 4 now believes in it, fundamentally, and you can see it... Unless you've got someone at the top creating the space for it and believing in its importance, it doesn't happen.[27]

In 2015, under the leadership of Tony Hall as director-general and faced with another period of intense public and media scrutiny in the run-up to another charter review, the BBC returned to overt communication of an overall brand message. Ad agency RKCR/Y&R created a campaign (known within the BBC as the 'For' campaign) that did not directly address the licence fee or carry a value-for-money message, but lovingly assembled memorable BBC moments from a diverse range of programmes and services. A gentle Yorkshire-accented voiceover was provided by popular actress Jodie Whittaker:

For waking us up
And getting us going
For making us laugh
And making us cry
For expanding our minds
And broadening our horizons
For standing us on the shoulders of giants
And taking us to new worlds
For all our hopes
And our dreams
For not just watching
But living too
For all the days of our lives
And all the moments we share
For all of us.[28]

The 'For' campaign saw scenes as universally loved as Andy Murray winning Wimbledon, news footage of the newborn Princess Charlotte and the victory moment of *Strictly Come Dancing* jostling with images of BBC mobile apps and the *Radio 1 Breakfast Show*. It proved that there is indeed still a place for what the ABC's Diana Costantini would call 'lingering, beautifully crafted, stand-alone spots', for the BBC at least.

Describing the difficulty during the 2015 charter review period of talking overtly about the licence fee (because the heartland audience might see it as cheapening the BBC brand while non-approvers might be antagonized), Jane Lingham, who is responsible for the BBC's overall brand strategy, explains what the campaign intended to achieve:

The best way to remind people that we [the BBC] are good value for money, is to remind them what they get from us, and that's where the 'For' campaign came from. It's a campaign that's designed to remind people... about all the range and breadth of what the BBC does and the role it plays in the daily lives of people across the UK. The BBC is a thread that pulls together daily life for millions of people, and demonstrating that is a good way of reminding people that the BBC is good value for money. The universality of the BBC licence fee is also fundamentally important to what we offer (everyone pays so everyone wins) so we also wanted to draw attention to that. That's why we used the endline 'For All Of Us'.[29]

– A BRAND IN POOR HEALTH –

Perhaps ironically for the UK's biggest public service broadcaster, over the last 20 years or so there have been many examples of excellent marketing and brand building from the BBC. Until 2011, the same cannot be said of the major commercial network, ITV. Part of the reason for that has been the fragmented nature of the organization, divided as it was by the mid-1990s into 16 regional franchises, some with long-standing brand identities familiar to their local audiences.

One of our collaborators at the University of Nottingham, Cathy Johnson, writes about this extensively in her excellent book *Branding Television* (the most thorough academic study of this subject that we're aware of). Cathy underlines the fact that introducing a consistent overall ITV brand identity was not a straightforward process, so it is no surprise that Rufus Radcliffe, arriving as group marketing and research director in 2011 after 10 years building his reputation as a bold and innovative marketer at Channel 4, immediately realized that ITV had a brand issue:

I looked at our visual identity over the years and there was very little equity in it at all... there was nothing in our existing identity that was resonating.[30]

However, for Rufus the problem ran much deeper than just the look and feel of the brand:

I was told that we didn't really have a statement of purpose. What is the point of ITV? How do you define your business over and above that of making money?... That was one of the things I was keen to do when I arrived at ITV ... to define the organizing principle around our brand and what we do.[31]

The ITV marketing team was quick to identify the impact of a weak brand on the network's commercial performance:

Despite ITV broadcasting some of the biggest and most loved shows, our audiences felt little for the ITV brand. Whilst 90 per cent of us watched

ITV every month, a staggering one-third of viewers thought that 'ITV didn't have anything for them'. These low expectations were a real problem. No matter how good the programming was, performance was always going to be stifled if we didn't address the issue with the brand.[32]

Two years into an ambitious five-year plan set out by CEO Adam Crozier in 2010 to transform ITV's business there were encouraging signs of improvement, but a year-long research study carried out in 2012 demonstrated clearly that ITV's 'brand health' correlated closely with its share of viewing. In general, viewers had poor expectations of ITV. The brand had become a barrier to watching. Clare Phillips, ITV's head of brand planning, sums up the issue like this:

> If viewers have poor expectations of your channel brand, it makes it harder to get them to watch your new show. Given that new programmes are launched every week, it's critical that people view your channel brand positively. The question is: how do you make viewers like and value your channel brand?[33]

– A RALLYING CRY –

A far-reaching decision was made to revitalize the entire ITV brand: not just via a fresh coat of paint for the channel identities or an advertising campaign but by identifying the 'organizing principle' that Rufus Radcliffe referred to, carrying it through to every nook and cranny of ITV and expressing it in a completely new identity for the ITV brand across all its channels and services, globally. A big ambition like that needed a big statement of purpose. More audience research confirmed an acknowledgement amongst viewers that, at its best, 'ITV tells stories we all care about, that we all want to share and talk about.'[34] ITV's overall position was defined as: The Heart of Popular Culture.

Rufus describes it like this:

> It's not an overly complicated set of words but it feels to us like when we're absolutely in the sweet spot of what we do we're at the heart of popular culture, we're shaping conversations, we're mirroring conversations, we're absolutely at the beating heart of the culture of modern Britain... it can swing from powerful current affairs, Jimmy Savile's exposure, (the) leaders debate, brilliant news reporting right through to extraordinary drama or family entertainment for all the family.[35]

Unlike, say, The Home of Witty Banter, The Heart of Popular Culture didn't appear as an advertising endline or channel tagline. It was more of a rallying cry to everyone within the ITV organization to feel a greater sense of pride in their cultural contribution to the UK and the appeal of ITV's content to mainstream British viewers on a huge scale, with the most popular programmes of the day including *Downton Abbey*, *Britain's Got Talent*,

The X Factor, Coronation Street and *Emmerdale*. In Rufus Radcliffe's words: 'It wasn't even a network rebrand, it was an entire business rebrand.'[36]

Although this project was much, much more than just the launch of a new visual identity for ITV, as part of the process ITV decided to transform the way the brand was presented across all its channels, services and buildings... and to launch the new identity on a single day across its entire global operation. To stand any chance of achieving this bold ambition, Rufus realized that the creative development process had to be an inclusive one, involving as many people as possible across ITV in workshops and roadshows, talking about the new statement of purpose, sharing creative work in progress and giving people a sense of ownership. He also decided that the core task of creating the new visual identity needed to be an iterative one, so rather than the more traditional approach of asking a number of creative agencies to pitch for the project he built what he describes as 'a team of Galacticos' led by Matt Rudd, a talented graphic designer Rufus had worked with successfully at Channel 4:

> We got the very best people with different skill sets together to form a team. We hired a space at [post production house] Envy in Soho for three months and we populated it with brilliant people. We would go in every week to catch up and chew the fat and see what was going on. We had a combination of brilliant external talent and... great ITV talent and gave them a lot of creative freedom to go away and think really bravely about it. We gave them quite a lot of protection as well.[37]

One of the key outputs of this 'pop-up studio' was a new logo for ITV, taking its place at the centre of a more coherent brand architecture (in the classic branded house tradition) in which the '1' in ITV's main channel, ITV1, was dropped in favour of renaming it, simply, ITV. (Incidentally, the ABC in Australia did exactly the same thing with ABC1 as part of its 2014 rebrand.) The new ITV logo was genuinely innovative. Based on a 'colour picking' function, it took on a chameleon-like ability to change its colours to blend with the tones of the different programme content it was designed to sit on: bright and colourful for populist entertainment shows (think *Ant and Dec*), or more muted for serious documentaries or current affairs. The new logo system was a really clever way to address the familiar challenge of creating a brand identity flexible enough to work effectively across a diverse, multi-genre channel. Recognizing the need to maintain a high level of variety, the main ITV channel moved from running six idents to over 100, all intended to capture the 'magic to be found in the everyday... real people going about their daily lives'.[38] The first batch featured such diverse scenes as inflating a hot air balloon, washing a dog in a sink and fire eating: not everyone's definition of 'everyday', perhaps, but eminently watchable. New visual identities were also created for ITV2, ITV3, ITV4 and CITV.

'*Magic in the everyday*': ITV *idents with their chameleon-like logo*
Source: *Reproduced by permission of ITV plc*

ITV's marketing team was keen for the organization's transformation to be marked with a real 'moment' and it came on 14 January 2013. Writing to all ITV employees across 18 locations, from London to Stockholm and Sydney, CEO Adam Crozier put it like this:

> Today is a landmark day in the history of ITV as our rebrand goes live. We are rebranding all five of our channels in the UK, six ITV Studios production offices around the world, ITV Studios Global Entertainment plus our online and on-demand products including ITV Player. Our new identity will also stretch across our buildings, our stationery, our communications and everything else ITV.[39]

The audacity of this undertaking drew admiration from across the UK TV industry, not least from the BBC's Justin Bairamian: 'The identity was a masterstroke I think. It was extraordinary, and the fact that they did it overnight, it was transformative.'[40]

Although ITV didn't create a 'Heart of Popular Culture' brand campaign along the lines of the BBC's 'Perfect Day' or 'For' campaign, or the ABC's anthemic #OurABC, brand advertising did play a significant part in ITV's revitalization. To address the brand health issue ITV's marketing team found that advertising for a whole genre of programming was more effective than simply promoting individual titles, with drama being the genre that could shift quality perceptions the most. A house of drama campaign was developed, including a beautifully produced film in which the camera tracks through a large house as if from the audience's point of view, passing recognizable stars of ITV dramas past and present: lead characters from *Downton*

Abbey, *Doc Martin* and *Mr Selfridge* mashed up seamlessly with 'gone but not forgotten' stars of classic ITV dramas such as *Inspector Morse* and *Prime Suspect*, resolving with the endline: 'Where Drama Lives'.

Doc Martin (Martin Clunes) and Mr Selfridge (Jeremy Piven) play cards in ITV's 'house of drama'   Source: *Reproduced by permission of ITV plc*

So, how did ITV's brand revitalization work? The ITV marketing team produced a highly impressive case study that, like our Dave case with UKTV six years earlier (see Chapter 3), was recognized in the UK's advertising effectiveness awards. ITV demonstrated a string of 'before and after' effects, including the fact that the rebrand led to significant improvements in ITV's brand health, with increases amongst all adults in positive statements like 'quality', 'something for me' and 'warm-hearted'. ITV's main channel grew 3.4 per cent in 2013: the only UK terrestrial TV channel to increase its share that year and the first time in over 20 years that the ITV main channel had grown. The drama campaign played a key role, delivering a short-term return on investment of 14 per cent. In total, nearly £30 million in additional advertising revenue was attributed to the brand revitalization over the first 18 months, and ITV's share price rose 74 per cent over a year, outperforming the FTSE 100 by six times.[41] Effects like these (interrogated with the help of econometric analysis) demonstrated the important role played by ITV's talented marketing team in restoring true 800lb gorilla status to the company's financial performance. (In the interest of balance, at the time of writing, despite a strong overall financial performance, ITV had just reported a drop in viewing figures. Competition in the mainstream TV market continues to be tough and unrelenting, but the ITV brand is arguably stronger than it has ever been at a national level to confront these challenges.)

– GOOD ENOUGH IS NOT ENOUGH –

One of the most notable elements of the ITV rebrand was the way its defined brand purpose – 'The Heart of Popular Culture' – was brought to life across the whole organization. The third member of UK broadcasting's big three, Sky, has also articulated a brand expression intended not just as a line on corporate communications (although in Sky's case it does perform that role) but as a mantra for everyone in the company to live by. It could be argued that the challenge for Sky in finding a brand property to unite the whole organization was even greater than that faced by ITV because for many years it tended to be seen as a satellite television provider with a primarily transactional relationship with its customers, with perceptions dominated by its Sky Sports and Sky Movies channels, rather than a fully rounded entertainment company. Robert Tansey, Sky's brand director, content products, describes how the task was approached:

> Because we are both a content provider and a retailer, having something that was singularly focused on one area was always going to be difficult, so it had to be something that was much more about the spirit of the company. Through a series of stakeholder interviews what became clear was that right from its inception Sky had always been an organization that had not settled for the status quo, that was always a little bit restless, always wanting to try and improve everything it did, stemming in part from a recognition that because we are a pay service and there are very good free offerings in the UK we have to make a very compelling offer to customers for why they should choose to put their hands in their pockets to pay for either our content or services.[42]

Working closely with the creative agency group Engine, the Sky marketing team developed a very simple expression of this restlessness, this constant drive to improve: Believe In Better.

In recent years Sky has used this line consistently as a sign-off across a wide range of its communications, including campaigns for both content and services. It works particularly well in advertising that neatly links some of Sky's technology-delivered services with major entertainment franchises such as *The Walking Dead* and *Game of Thrones*, for example when delivered by Joanna Lumley and more recently Idris Elba as part of TV advertising campaigns for Sky Box Sets. However, as evidence of the fact that Believe In Better is not just an advertising tagline, Tansey emphasizes the extent to which it has infiltrated daily life at Sky:

> As we develop marketing campaigns and new product development it's an ethos that underpins all of that... We will constantly evaluate work by 'is it demonstrating either why we have made something better or why

what we have is better than the alternatives that are out there?' It is often mentioned in meetings. If people don't think something is quite up to scratch they say, 'Come on guys, we believe in better, let's make sure we can improve this, it's not quite good enough.'[43]

Believe In Better has become a philosophy that is truly embedded in the Sky culture and an important factor in helping the organization on its journey from a satellite TV provider to a fully rounded entertainment company.

– THE BIG BRAND BUILDERS –

Whether via universally recognized idents, overarching brand campaigns or expressions of purpose that act as rallying cries throughout the whole organization, marketing has played and continues to play a critical role in building the UK's largest and most successful TV brands. BBC One unites the nation in shared viewing experiences and, in turn, plays a big role in the British public's perception of the value for money delivered by the BBC in total. ITV sits at the heart of popular culture. Sky believes in doing everything bigger and better. These are the 800lb gorillas in the diverse menagerie of British TV, surrounded by smaller, aggressive competitors such as Dave, Universal Channel and the Channel 4 portfolio. Competing with the gorillas means doing things differently, being creative and taking risks. In the next chapter we look at how to build a TV brand with personality and attitude.

NEXT
★ 'Typical Channel 4'.
★ A new kind of pop artist.
★ The flamboyant artist and the passionate guide.
★ A street fighter of a network.
★ A fearless storyteller and a fearless marketer.
★ A 'yeoman application'.

LATER
★ Elizabethan viral marketing.
★ 800-TBS-FUNNY.
★ Mary Berry's extraordinary goal celebration.

NOTES

1 BBC (2015) [accessed 4 August 2015] Rebranding The BBC – W1A: series two, BBC Two [online] https://www.youtube.com/watch?v=YCQJEAcYSCw

2 Pratley, N (2003) [accessed 4 August 2015] Dyke Bangs Drum For British Broadcasting, *Guardian*, 11 June [Online] http://www.theguardian.com/media/2003/jun/11/broadcasting.bbc1

3 ITV plc (2014) [accessed 4 August 2015] ITV Annual Report And Accounts 2014
   [online] http://www.itvplc.com/investors/announcements/annual-report-and-
   accounts-2014

4 Darroch, J (2014) [accessed 4 August 2015] Chief Executive's Statement
   [online] https://corporate.sky.com/investors/annual-report-2014/
   strategic-report/ceo-statement

5 Magnus Willis, founding partner and joint chairman, Sparkler, interview,
   27 May 2015

6 BBC (2015) [accessed 4 August 2015] BBC Annual Report And Accounts
   2014/15 [online] http://downloads.bbc.co.uk/annualreport/pdf/2014-15/
   bbc-annualreport-201415.pdf

7 Lambie-Nairn, M (1997) *Brand Identity for Television: With knobs on*,
   Phaidon Press, London

8 TV Ark (nd) [accessed 4 August 2015] BBC One: November 1936–April 1964
   [online] http://www.tv-ark.org.uk/mivana/mediaplayer.php?id=bf0443529db0d
   6d0cf4f3d9f22bbdb0c&media=bbc_batwings_ident_t1383&type=mp4

9 Lambie-Nairn, M (1997) *Brand Identity for Television: With knobs on*,
   Phaidon Press, London

10 BBC (2005) Brief for a New BBC One Identity, provided directly to the authors
   (Autumn)

11 Fincham, P (2006) [accessed 4 August 2015] After The BBC Charter:
   What Future For Pluralism In Public Service Broadcasting? 26 April [Online]
   http://www.bbc.co.uk/pressoffice/speeches/stories/fincham_voice.shtml

12 http://www.redbeecreative.tv/work/bbc-one-channel-rebrand?service=brand-
   identity

13 Daily Mail (2006) [accessed 4 August 2015] BBC Blows £1.2m On 80 Seconds
   Of Hippos, Kites And Surf Scenes, *Daily Mail*, 26 September [Online]
   http://www.dailymail.co.uk/news/article-407046/BBC-blows-1-2m-80-seconds-
   hippos-kites-surf-scenes.html

14 Sweney, M (2006) [accessed 4 August 2015] BBC One Unveils New Channel
   Indents, *Guardian*, 26 September [Online] http://www.theguardian.com/media/
   2006/sep/26/broadcasting.bbc2

15 Fincham, P (2006) [accessed 4 August 2015] BBC One – Risk, Creativity,
   Challenges And Audiences, 16 October [Online] http://www.bbc.co.uk/
   pressoffice/speeches/stories/fincham_rts.shtml

16 http://www.redbeecreative.tv/work/bbc-one-channel-refresh

17 BBC (2015) [accessed 4 August 2015] BBC Annual Report And Accounts
   2014/15 [Online] http://downloads.bbc.co.uk/annualreport/pdf/2014-15/
   bbc-annualreport-201415.pdf

18 Emin, T (2006) [accessed 4 August 2015] Tracey Emin: My life In A Column
   Independent, 22 December [Online] http://www.independent.co.uk/voices/
   columnists/tracey-emin/tracey-emin-my-life-in-a-column-429604.html

19 Diana Costantini, head of ABC Creative, interview 8 June 2015

20 Diana Costantini, head of ABC Creative, interview 8 June 2015

21 Diana Costantini, head of ABC Creative, interview 8 June 2015

22 Hunters and Collectors (2013 – updated release; original release 1984)
   'Throw Your Arms Around Me', Mushroom Records, November

23 Daley, P (2014) [accessed 4 August 2015] Can The ABC's Rebrand Get The Nation Singing The Same Song? *Guardian*, 24 July [Online] www.theguardian.com/commentisfree/2014/jul/24/can-the-abcs-rebrand-get-the-nation-singing-the-same-song

24 BBC (1997) [accessed 4 August 2015] 'Perfect Day' – BBC Promotion [online] https://www.youtube.com/watch?v=WJpQJWpVJds

25 de Lisle, T (1997) [accessed 4 August 2015] Oh, It's Such A Perfect Song, *Independent*, 9 November [Online] http://www.independent.co.uk/arts-entertainment/oh-its-such-a-perfect-song-1293130.html

26 Justin Bairamian, director of BBC Creative, interview 22 July 2015

27 Justin Bairamian, director of BBC Creative, interview 22 July 2015

28 BBC (2015) [accessed 2 November 2015] The BBC: For All of Us [Online] http://www.bbc.co.uk/corporate2/insidethebbc/whatwedo/bbc-for-all-of-us

29 Jane Lingham, director, BBC Brand, interview 29 July 2015

30 Rufus Radcliffe, group marketing and research director, ITV, interview 14 April 2015

31 Rufus Radcliffe, group marketing and research director, ITV, interview 14 April 2015

32 Phillips, C, Radcliffe, R and Bateman, E (2014) ITV Brand Revitalisation: Winning back the hearts of the nation: Institute of Practitioners in Advertising, Silver, IPA Effectiveness Awards

33 Clare Phillips, head of brand planning, ITV, interview 24 April 2015

34 Phillips, C, Radcliffe, R and Bateman, E (2014) ITV Brand Revitalisation: Winning back the hearts of the nation: Institute of Practitioners in Advertising, Silver, IPA Effectiveness Awards

35 Rufus Radcliffe, group marketing and research director, ITV, interview 14 April 2015

36 Rufus Radcliffe, group marketing and research director, ITV, interview 14 April 2015

37 Rufus Radcliffe, group marketing and research director, ITV, interview 14 April 2015

38 ITV (2013) [accessed 2 November 2015] A Taster Of Some Of The New ITV Idents [online] https://www.youtube.com/watch?v=PDuBEO9Mt3A

39 Phillips, C, Radcliffe, R and Bateman, E (2014) ITV Brand Revitalisation: Winning back the hearts of the nation: Institute of Practitioners in Advertising, Silver, IPA Effectiveness Awards

40 Justin Bairamian, director of BBC Creative, interview 22 July 2015

41 Phillips, C, Radcliffe, R and Bateman, E (2014) ITV Brand Revitalisation: Winning back the hearts of the nation: Institute of Practitioners in Advertising, Silver, IPA Effectiveness Awards

42 Robert Tansey, brand director, content products, Sky, interview 26 June 2015

43 Robert Tansey, brand director, content products, Sky, interview 26 June 2015

CHAPTER FIVE

THE RISK TAKERS
Building a TV channel brand with attitude

Dr Roger Spain (Dr House won't hire him because of a tattoo): 'Wow! I thought you'd be the last person to have a problem with nonconformity.'

Dr Gregory House: 'Nonconformity – right. I can't remember the last time I saw a twentysomething kid with a tattoo of an Asian letter on his wrist. You are one wicked freethinker! You want to be a rebel? Stop being cool... and get a haircut like the Asian kids that don't leave the library for twenty-hour stretches. They're the ones who don't care what you think.'

HOUSE[1]

– A REVOLUTION –

Any book attempting to celebrate the world's best TV brand builders needs to reserve a special place for the UK's Channel 4. Since its launch in 1982 the Channel 4 brand has been built in line with its unique public service remit by bold marketers and creative people. The current management team led by CEO David Abraham, who spent the early part of his career at some of the UK's most creative advertising agencies, has maintained Channel 4's reputation for innovation and risk taking across its portfolio. But Channel 4 doesn't have a monopoly on courageous marketing, as we will see when we look at FX Networks in the United States and, briefly, CANAL+ in France.

Although the first programme on Channel 4 was the decidedly mainstream gameshow *Countdown*, what led into it was a short piece of content that, from its earliest seconds of broadcasting, set the tone for the channel's revolutionary approach to creativity. Its launch idents changed the way that TV marketers thought about on-screen brand symbols. Having already touched on idents in relation to channels like BBC One, ITV, Dave and ABC, we look at the topic in more detail in Chapter 6, so we will hold off talking more about the impact of Channel 4's on-screen identity until then. This, along with a succession of highly creative campaigns for individual programmes (examples of which we illustrate in later chapters), has built a characterful brand personality, but in recent years the management team has felt the need to go further to communicate its values and achievements in relation to its remit. Charged by the UK Parliament to be creatively experimental and to appeal to a culturally diverse society and younger audiences, it is notable that in its 2013 Annual Report Channel 4 talked extensively about its marketing:

> With our public service remit to be 'innovative and distinctive', Channel 4 must remain at the cutting edge of TV and online marketing. And with our status as a commercially funded not-for-profit broadcaster we must do so with enough style and success to cut through an ever-more crowded media landscape and be noticed.[2]

The most interesting case study cited by Channel 4 at the time was its 'Born Risky' campaign. Having set out on a journey to discover whether it would be possible to capture the essence of the Channel 4 brand (particularly for younger audiences who didn't have 20–30 years of past experience of the channel), marketing and communications chief Dan Brooke explains how research to track perceptions of Channel 4 in relation to its remit identified a fertile territory:

> The value where we not only scored highly but where the gap between us and competitors was highest was about a channel that takes creative risks. And when you go and talk to viewers, people in lots of different ways say 'Oh, yes, Channel 4, that's the risqué one,' 'Channel 4, that's the one where they always try something a bit different,' so there's an experimentation element to that too. Born Risky then came out of thinking about younger viewers and a subtle way of saying, 'We've always been like this.'[3]

In October 2013 Channel 4 launched a (not so subtle) 60-second film packed with challenging and provocative clips from some of its hardest-hitting programmes: edgy dramas, investigative journalism, documentaries on people with extreme disabilities and dark comedies. Introduced by Channel 4 News anchor Jon Snow, as if warning viewers of distressing news footage, the programme clips were interspersed with captions that summed up (sometimes ironically) perceptions and dimensions of the brand:

★ TYPICAL CHANNEL 4
★ NOT SAFE FOR POLITICIANS
★ WTF?
★ MAY CHALLENGE PREJUDICES
★ NOT EVERYONE'S CUP OF TEA

As a central visual motif for the film, Channel 4 revived the red triangle device that had been used briefly back in 1986 to warn viewers about the potentially offensive content of X-rated art movies running in late-night slots. A voiceover at the end summed up Channel 4's remit in uncompromising terms:

> Channel 4 was set up to take creative risks and put its profits back into programmes. We were born to experiment, born to challenge, born risky.[4]

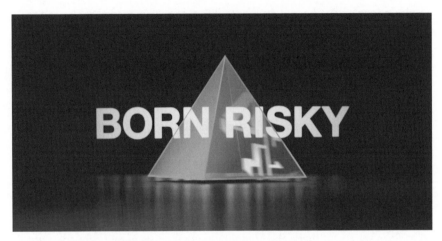

The red warning triangle revived in Channel 4's first 'Born Risky' campaign
Source: © Channel 4 Television

Channel 4 CEO David Abraham sums up what the campaign was intended to capture:

> There are two types of risk. There's a risky programme that is so challenging that viewers find it difficult to tune in to or there's the surprising, delightful, unexpected product of a risk-taking creative approach, which I'd like to think is where we score and where we succeed... The product of the risk-taking editorial approach is to do things that should delight the viewer, but of course it also means that sometimes we are very challenging. Programmes like *Utopia* or many of the things that are on *Channel 4 News* or *Dispatches* are not designed to be 'easy listening' as it were. We're not trying to appeal to all of the people all of the time. We are here to complement... other channel choices and appeal to everyone some of the time, when they are in the right mood for something more challenging, and that's why I think the Born Risky campaign encapsulates part of what we're here to do.[5]

Early research carried out by Channel 4 reassured the team that the campaign was hitting the mark: the channel's reputation for taking risks increased from 47 per cent to 69 per cent and, significantly, the belief that 'having a broadcaster that takes risks is important' rose from 50 per cent to 72 per cent.[6] Clare Phillips, who was head of audience research and insight at Channel 4 at the time the campaign was developed, explains the way this worked in much the same way as we described the application of heuristics in Chapter 2:

> It was all about having a shortcut... People need to have an idea about a brand in order to make up their minds about it. People had a vague idea about what Channel 4 was all about, but we managed to crystallize it for them. At its best Channel 4 is about taking risks, challenging the establishment and the status quo. And it's been like that since the very beginning of the channel. We expressed this as Born Risky. When viewers saw this expression it made sense to them and they could easily find the evidence amongst the shows to back it up.[7]

Over the two years that followed the 'Born Risky' launch, the campaign was further developed in a number of typically diverse executions. In February 2014, armed with the broadcasting rights to the Sochi Winter Paralympic Games, the Channel 4 marketing team and Jay Hunt, chief creative officer, decided to draw attention to Russia's anti-gay laws. In the words of James Walker, head of marketing, Channel 4 wanted to:

> Make a statement that... the homophobia that exists in that country is not acceptable but do it in a way that feels like laughing in the face of it and is joyous.[8]

The result was a temporary re-version of the channel logo in the rainbow colours of the lesbian, gay, bisexual and transgender (LGBT) pride flag and an audacious film based on a camp cabaret performance of a song with a message to competitors in Sochi: 'good luck gays on Gay Mountain'. The final frames showed the red triangle transformed into a rainbow snow pyramid with the endline Born Risky.[9]

A few months later, Musharaf Ashgar, the acutely stammering hero of the popular reality series *Educating Yorkshire*, presented another compilation of dramatic programme clips with a moving manifesto for Channel 4's remit.[10] Then, as viewers settled down to watch the 2014 final of ITV's *The X Factor*, in one of the commercial breaks they were confronted by a music video of a very different genre. The 'new kind of pop artist' was Viktoria Modesta, and the twist was that the singer and model had a prosthetic lower leg. The full-length (six-minute) video ended with a stunning sequence of the singer portrayed like a menacing life-size puppet against a bright red backdrop, her left leg a lethal-looking metal cone, with captions preceding the red triangle and Born Risky pay-off line: 'Some of us were born to be different. Some of us were born to take risks.'[11]

'Some of us were born to be different': Viktoria Modesta in Channel 4's Prototype music video   Source: © Channel 4 Television

Joint heads of Channel 4's in-house 'agency', 4Creative, Chris Bovill and John Allison, were quoted as saying:

> Pop stars these days are painfully dull and manufactured. Modesta is the perfect partner for Born Risky and Channel 4 as she embodies our governmental remit of championing alternative voices and establishing new talent.[12]

– A BODY WITH ARMS –

We asked the Channel 4 team whether all this brand-building communication is intended to cover the entire portfolio of channels and services, or just the main TV channel. As we saw in Chapter 3, Channel 4 has developed its portfolio as a set of endorsed brands, each with its own identity yet all feeding off the Channel 4 masterbrand: in particular, E4, with its youth focus and vibrant personality embodied in shows such as *Made in Chelsea* and *The Inbetweeners*, and More4, with its schedule of lifestyle programmes, documentaries and US dramas. Dan Brooke is very clear on this:

> In terms of the brand I don't really distinguish between them. They all have a set of shared values. Some of them have a focus on a subset of the values but there are none really that are outliers... Because Channel 4 is the biggest and the most diverse brand and the one that commands the most viewer attention, all the values sit within Channel 4, and then E4 has a subset of those, More4 has a subset of those, which are particular primarily to the audience subset that they aim at and also the genre of programming that they focus on more.[13]

There are strong parallels here between Channel 4 and another of the world's most respected and fiercely individual TV brands: CANAL+ in

France. Launched two years after Channel 4 as the fourth television channel in its home country, CANAL+ has a similarly proud tradition for supporting original creative voices and production. In Chapter 3 we illustrated how the CANAL+ portfolio is a classic example of a uniform branded house, but the values of the brand are far from conventional. Positioned as 'the flamboyant artist and the passionate guide', CANAL+ shares with Channel 4 the values of courage, risk taking and independence. Olivier Schaack of CANAL+ eloquently describes the relationship between the masterbrand and the many sub-brands in its portfolio:

> It's really like a single channel that just has a few arms. It's like a being with several arms and legs, they all belong to the same person and that's CANAL+... an independent mind, a free mind – that's the body. And then the channels are the arms.[14]

Olivier stresses the extent to which the CANAL+ masterbrand has to work across multiple platforms and services and this is a point also made strongly by Channel 4's James Walker:

> Now it's about what does your brand look like on an EPG on Virgin or Sky, what does your brand look like when it's available on YouView, on PlayStation? There are so many different places that it's accessible, so creating a sense of a whole or a motherbrand is really important.[15]

So the Channel 4 masterbrand stands for bold experimentation, challenge and alternative voices. And the essence of this brand positioning sits at the heart of all the sub-brands in the Channel 4 portfolio. Dan Brooke wonders if this is truly unique:

> Are there any other brands that zero in on the fact that they're risk taking?[16]

Well, our team could nominate campaigns created for BBC Three, a channel aimed primarily at a 16 to 30-something audience, bearing the line Never Afraid To Try New Stuff. One film in particular sticks in our memory, in which comedians including Johnny Vegas, Matt Berry and Ralf Little attempt daring activities, including parkour and motorcycle stunt riding.[17] BBC Three's imminent move to an online-only channel, which we will come back to in Chapter 16, is certainly a bold step for the BBC. And if we cross the Atlantic again we can see that there is at least one network that shares Channel 4's appetite for risk: FX Networks.

– DIPPING A TOE –

While Channel 4 was launched in a blaze of publicity in the UK, with first-night highlights including the controversial soap opera *Brookside*, FX had more humble beginnings. In June 1994 it was introduced (with a lower-case 'f' and standing for 'Fox extended') as a new cable network from 20th Century Fox. Based initially in an 'apartment' in Manhattan's Flatiron district, its schedule included an unpromising mix of pet shows, live talk shows and repeats of classic old series such as *Batman* and *Wonder Woman*. Since those early days it has rewritten the rules of what a basic cable channel can achieve, taken on HBO as a respected commissioner of successful adult programming (complex, edgy and groundbreaking dramas and comedies) and established the credibility, since 2013, to bear the positioning line: Fearless.

This is no marketing bolt-on without substance. Just as Channel 4 armed itself with extensive research before its 'Born Risky' campaign, the marketers at FX are at pains to emphasize how carefully they approached the development of any audience-facing brand positioning statement or tagline.

FX was initially set on its path to distinction with the breakout success in 2002 of gritty police drama *The Shield*. Gaining then-record audience numbers for basic cable, and following this with unexpected awards recognition at the Emmys and Golden Globes, *The Shield* proved several years before the likes of AMC, TNT and USA Network that distinctive original scripted programming was not the exclusive preserve of subscription-only brands such as HBO (and, later, Netflix). FX followed that success with further original series launches: sophisticated dramas including *Nip/Tuck* and *Rescue Me*, and quirky comedies such as *It's Always Sunny in Philadelphia*. Since 2004, with the arrival of current CEO John Landgraf, FX has successfully grown into what the *Los Angeles Times* TV critic Mary McNamara describes as 'a tough little street-fighter of a network'.[18] It wasn't until three years after Landgraf joined, though, that the FX marketing team felt the channel was ready for a 'line'. According to John Varvi, EVP, on-air promotions:

> By 2007, audience research showed a consistent perception among FX viewers, backed by critics, that FX was delivering a distinctive viewing experience by way of its original series. Now we had a portfolio of original programming that warranted the development of a brand position.[19]

That brand position was defined as: There Is No Box.

FX Networks's top marketer Stephanie Gibbons explains the rationale behind it, subverting the 'buzzword bingo' phrase 'thinking outside the box':

> Our proposition was... we're not going to acknowledge that there is a box, so forget about going outside of it. We're not going to exist in a comparative world that asks, 'What are our competitors doing, how do we realign our strategy?' It was about saying we have a particular path: we seek the great, we seek the fresh, we seek the new, we seek the unusual.[20]

John Varvi goes on to explain how it was introduced (in early 2008):

> While we 'launched' with a series of brand spots, the There Is No Box positioning was used primarily as a visual tag on end boards. We did not market it as a 'campaign' in the customary fashion or with the fanfare one would normally see from a national television network. We were, after almost six years (since *The Shield*), putting our toe into the branding waters.[21]

Given the respect for the quality of the FX team's work amongst the global TV marketing community (as we mention in our Introduction, multiple Marketing Team of the Year award winners), it is notable that their take on network brand positioning is far from the technocratic approach found in some TV organizations with less distinctive cultures. You might even call it surprisingly hesitant. In John Varvi's words:

> It was a number of years before we even contemplated doing this, starting with There Is No Box, because we knew we couldn't arbitrarily decide that 'this will be our brand position, let's convince the world'. It was really about the feedback that we received – whether it was through ratings, research or anecdotally – that convinced us that the audience we were serving, primarily a psychographic audience, was getting what we believed we were sending out. It wasn't until we felt there was an alignment between what we thought we were doing and what the audience was feeding back to us that we started to discuss the notion of publicly representing a brand perspective.[22]

– BRAIN, HEART AND GUT –

There is no doubt that, by the end of the 2000s, FX had carved out a distinctive territory in the US TV landscape. Further original scripted programmes, including *Justified* (a law-enforcement drama based on an Elmore Leonard story) and *Sons of Anarchy* (the adventures of an outlaw motorcycle club), along with edgy comedy *Louie*, further established the network's reputation for bold creative bets. As we described with USA Network in Chapter 2, great things can happen when a channel's positioning is in complete harmony with its programme strategy, and this can serve as a valuable framework for determining what will and will not work. This point is illustrated by a piece in the *Hollywood Reporter* entitled 'When TV Brands Go Off Brand', examining the case of buddy-cop drama *Terriers* when it looked like being axed after just one season of disappointing viewing figures on FX (it was). From the creator of *Ocean's Eleven*, with strong characters and clever writing, *Terriers* had been critically acclaimed and had built a loyal core of fans. However, big ratings did not follow and the *Hollywood*

Reporter offered a clear reason: the real issue was that *Terriers* simply did not fit the FX brand:

> Series on FX have balls... They are aggro, not Zen... In *Terriers*, no amount of clever riffing can mask that it's about as edgy as *Murder, She Wrote*... The show has always felt out of place... (and) that certainly speaks to the power of a brand. It's less of an indictment of *Terriers* and more affirmation that FX has almost always been on point.[23]

While continuing to keep the brand 'on point', by 2012 the FX marketing team began to feel that There Is No Box was not the strongest possible encapsulation of the essence of the network. With the continued success of shows such as *Sons of Anarchy* and the emergence of hard-hitting anthology series *American Horror Story*, FX was forging a more emotional connection with its viewers. In that context, There Is No Box was seen as somewhat cerebral and esoteric. The opportunity was to create a positioning line that was more visceral: one that, in the words of Stephanie Gibbons, 'felt more from the brain, the heart and the gut all at once'. However, she goes on to emphasize her team's caution in doing this:

> We abhor the notion of packaged, one-word identities, we actively resisted it for as long as we could until there were certain scenarios where it was essential to have some sort of shorthand. Still for us it's cumbersome, we didn't like having it because our programming and our relationship with our consumers is complex and we want to exist in places that defy a one word description.[24]

It would be easy when writing a book about TV marketing to attempt to present a neat and fail-safe formula for expressing a channel positioning: a 'cookbook' approach – follow these simple steps and ta-dah! But it isn't as simple as that. As we have discussed in the previous chapters, a TV channel is made up of diverse and dynamic content. Amongst all the marketers we talked to, no one stressed more than FX the importance of the organic relationship that viewers have with individual shows and the complex cumulative impact of a number of strong individual programme brands on an overall network brand. As a result, the FX marketing team was very reluctant to reduce all this, as if in a crucible, to one phrase or one word. However, focus groups confirmed that if they were going to settle on one word, a perfect word to go with would be Fearless. The concept was first proposed by New York agency Leroy & Clarkson, working in collaboration with strategic consultant Lee Hunt (who had been so instrumental in the development of the 'characters' positioning for USA Network), following a brand workshop with the FX management team. FX's research concluded that, at best, Fearless represented a 'trifecta', applying to characters, series and the whole network:

Respondents commented on how certain FX series characters are fearless... Many respondents associated the campaign with FX's series (*Louie, Justified* and *Sons of Anarchy*)... Some respondents perceive it as promoting the entire network.[25]

Lee Hunt underlines the fact that Fearless is a heartfelt positioning, driven from the top of the network:

They're an outlier brand and they purposely break the rules, they do things differently, and the creative they do is often surprising or shocking or unexpected. And they really do live up to that idea of fearless storytelling. And that actually all comes from John (Landgraf). And so often the brand really emanates from a person who leads with vision. John obviously is a fearless storyteller and that has become a part of everything they do. Stephanie (Gibbons) is a fearless marketer too.[26]

For that fearless marketer, though, the introduction of the new one-word tagline had a very practical rationale. Stephanie Gibbons describes Fearless as a 'yeoman application' with an important role to play.

Promotional endpages for 'Fearless' FX Networks shows The Strain *and* Justified
Source: *Reproduced by permission of FX Networks, LLC*

Despite the team's reluctance to sum up the complex relationship between FX viewers and programmes in a single word, Fearless acts successfully as shorthand to sum up what the audience is thinking about FX and therefore why they should try a new show, or one they have not yet watched. Again, this is heuristics at work. This becomes all the more important in an on-demand world, as John Varvi emphasizes:

It's a necessity now. There are platforms everywhere that would love nothing more than to absorb our content and turn it into their own. I remember not that many years ago when the notion that brands didn't matter was being championed but today they matter more than ever.[27]

– A FEARLESS NETWORK –

Importantly, Fearless works as a brand statement across the full FX suite of four outlets: the well-established FX channel; FXX (a comedy-driven channel with a younger target audience); FXM (predominantly a movie channel); and FXNOW (FX Networks's video on-demand service). John explains how the brand works across the whole portfolio:

> They are all one and the same, serving overlapping audiences, and what they have in common is their desire for unique and provocatively entertaining dramas and comedies. The only thing that differentiates them – the linear channels anyway – is our skew demographically... and for our content to exist across those four channels and on other platforms that are somewhat out of our control, it's really important for the world... to understand that the origin of the programmes comes from the 'Fearless' suite of FX Networks.[28]

There are strong parallels here with Channel 4 in the UK: a heroic flagship channel that embodies the distinctive values and personality of the brand, with a small number of demographically targeted sister channels endorsed by that masterbrand together with an on-demand platform that pulls together content from the whole portfolio.

FX's Fearless philosophy has helped the network to close the gap on HBO as the leading source of high-quality TV in the United States. Speaking at the Television Critics Association in January 2015 John Landgraf presented data compiled from end-of-year lists from critics of the best TV across the previous year. HBO shows got 250 mentions across 115 lists but FX was close behind with 213, well ahead of AMC (74) and Netflix (67). Landgraf asserted that:

> The race for the best in TV is really only a competition between two channels... The rest of the pack is way behind.[29]

The power of Fearless is well summed up by Michael Vamosy, chief creative officer of agency Stun Creative, who spent five years in the FX Networks in-house creative team:

> FX has always been creatively different... They really take risks... They didn't run out there with a statement like 'FX. Fearless' before they could own it... They were smart because they proved that they were fearless and then they claimed that they were fearless. They did a good job of not overpromising their brand.[30]

– THE RISK TAKERS –

Channel 4, CANAL+ and FX Networks have a lot in common. Their brand personalities are not based on empty words or superficial marketing concepts but encapsulations of their authentic cultures, beliefs and actions in the form of the challenging programmes they commission. They have earned the right to call themselves 'fearless', 'the flamboyant artist' or 'born risky'. They are channels with attitude – and bold marketing has played a big part in their success.

NEXT

★ Neon signs, hay bales and pylons.

★ Taking an alpaca for a walk.

★ Fluffy 2's birthday party.

★ How MTV killed 'boring'.

★ Setting the blocks free.

★ The origin of the 'kryptonite'.

LATER

★ John Actor plays Monkfish.

★ Katy Perry's 'left shark'.

★ Inside the Truth Terrorist's lair.

NOTES

1 *House*, 'Kids' (2004) season one, episode 19, Fox, 24 May

2 Channel 4 (2013) Television Corporation Report and Financial Statements

3 Dan Brooke, chief marketing and communications officer, Channel 4, interview 26 June 2015

4 Channel 4 (2013) [accessed 9 September 2015] Born Risky, *Channel 4* [Online video] https://www.youtube.com/watch?v=8j5QHoVn5Vk

5 David Abraham, CEO, Channel 4, interview 26 June 2015

6 Channel 4 (2013) Television Corporation Report and Financial Statements

7 Clare Phillips, head of brand planning, ITV, interview 24 April 2015

8 James Walker, head of marketing, Channel 4 Television, interview 25 June 2015

9 Channel 4 (2014) [accessed 9 September 2015] Gay Mountain, *Channel 4* [online] https://www.youtube.com/watch?v=-6RID82Ru-k

10 Channel 4 (2014) [accessed 9 September 2015] Born Risky, *Channel 4* [online] www.youtube.com/watch?v=H-jwTptI8Sg

11 Channel 4 (2014) [accessed 9 September 2015] Prototype, *Channel 4* [Online] https://www.youtube.com/watch?v=jA8inmHhx8c

12 West, G (2014) [accessed 9 September 2015] Channel 4 To Challenge The Ideals Of Pop Music Introducing Alternative Pop Star During X Factor Final Ad Break, The Drum, 12 December [Online] http://www.thedrum.com/news/2014/12/12/channel-4-challenge-ideals-pop-music-introducing-alternative-pop-star-during-x

13 Dan Brooke, chief marketing and communications officer, Channel 4, interview 26 June 2015

14 Olivier Schaack, director of creative services, CANAL+, interview 11 June 2015

15 James Walker, head of marketing, Channel 4 Television, interview 25 June 2015

16 Dan Brooke, chief marketing and communications officer, Channel 4, interview 26 June 2015

17 BBC (2008) [accessed 9 September 2015] 'Never Afraid To Try New Stuff', BBC Three Trail [Online] www.youtube.com/watch?v=e9G5s3M4MwA

18 Milliken, M (2014) Swimming Away From 'Sea of Sameness', US Network FX tests TV waters [Online] http://www.reuters.com/article/us-television-emmys-fx-idUSKBN0GK1C420140821

19 John Varvi, executive vice president, On-Air Promotions, FX Networks, (FX, FXX, FXM, FXNOW) interview 6 August 2015

20 Stephanie Gibbons, president of marketing, digital media marketing and on-air promotions, FX Networks, interview 26 June 2015

21 John Varvi, executive vice president, on-air promotions, FX Networks, (FX, FXX, FXM, FXNOW) interview 6 August 2015

22 John Varvi, executive vice president, on-air promotions, FX Networks, (FX, FXX, FXM, FXNOW) interview 26 June 2015

23 Goodman, T (2010) [accessed 9 September 2015] When TV Brands Go Off Brand, *Hollywood Reporter*, 23 November [Online] http://www.hollywoodreporter.com/news/tv-brands-brand-47791

24 Stephanie Gibbons, president of marketing, digital media marketing and on-air promotions, FX Networks, interview 26 June 2015

25 FX Tagline Research Insights & Conclusions (2013) Internal Document, FX Research, February

26 Lee Hunt, managing partner, Lee Hunt LLC, interview 24 March 2015

27 John Varvi, executive vice president, on-air promotions, FX Networks, (FX, FXX, FXM, FXNOW) interview 26 June 2015

28 John Varvi, executive vice president, on-air promotions, FX Networks, (FX, FXX, FXM, FXNOW) interview 26 June 2015

29 Littleton, C (2015) [accessed 9 September 2015] John Landgraf: HBO, FX Lap The Field In 'Race For TV's Best', *Variety*, 18 January [Online] http://variety.com/2015/tv/news/fx-tca-louie-the-comedians-to-premiere-april-9-pamela-adlon-pilot-ordered-1201408314/

30 Michael Vamosy, chief creative officer, Stun Creative, interview 10 June 2015

CHAPTER SIX

IDENTS
Giving a channel a personality

When the package is this pretty, no one ever cares what's inside.

JOEY TRIBBIANI, *FRIENDS*[1]

– PUZZLES AND BLOCKS –

The 1982 Channel 4 launch identity was universally hailed as a significant creative breakthrough. In the words of Jeremy Myerson, most recently Helen Hamlyn Chair of Design at the Royal College of Art:

> Channel 4 marked the first expression of a properly branded television channel. It needed to differentiate itself from its competitors and fight for viewers. It did so without having to resort to the staple fare of the television identity... a standard logo designed for the cover of an annual report given a gratuitous twist or wobble on screen.[2]

In this chapter we reflect further on the general subject of idents, the influence of Channel 4 and why idents are infinitely more popular amongst TV marketers in Europe in building a channel's personality than they are in the United States.

The first Channel 4 idents seem a little quaint now, 33 years on from their launch, but at the time they were startlingly original. They were created by Martin Lambie-Nairn, several years before he would have a chance to reinvent the BBC's on-screen presentation, with the loyal support of his client Pam Masters (who had been lured from the BBC by Channel 4 CEO Jeremy Isaacs to help launch the channel before returning 'home' to the BBC seven years later). Lambie-Nairn realized during the early stages of a three-way pitch for the project that an innovative approach was needed to create something very different from the convention at the time for a single on-screen symbol:

> From the start, we knew that the Channel 4 identity was not going to play by the rules... We believed... if Channel 4 wanted to be fresh and surprising,

it had to have a family of idents, each a variation on a basic theme, helping to establish a unique personality for the station.[3]

A key fact about Channel 4 had a defining influence on the creative development process: rather than produce its own programmes, it would commission its output from a wide range of different sources and put them together in a coherent channel. Lambie-Nairn thought about wooden puzzles that fit together in much the same way and developed an idea in which a number of multicoloured component parts of a figure 4 could be assembled, via computer animation, to create the new channel's on-screen logo.

One of Lambie-Nairn's original 1982 'puzzle' idents for Channel 4
Source: © Channel 4 Television

The 'puzzle' idents were finally replaced in the 1990s with relatively unmemorable concepts based on circles and horizontal scrolling bars, but in 2004 Channel 4 won the renewed admiration of the industry with a radical reinvention of the original 1982 idea. Under the brilliant leadership of creative director Brett Foraker the 4 logo was again broken down into its nine constituent blocks but this time ingeniously camouflaged in (initially) 12 different forms in exterior locations (for example, neon signs outside an American diner, hay bales on a stubbled field and electricity pylons). Rather than the blocks moving, as they did in 1982, this time the camera moved, revealing the blocks coming together fleetingly in the form of the classic 4 at the midpoint of the scene. They were beautiful and spellbinding.

These idents remained an iconic fixture of British television until late 2015, when Channel 4 took another radical change of direction in its on-screen presentation. We will come back to this later, but first let's consider the role of channel idents, which is a subject of much debate, particularly with US TV marketers.

– PACKAGING WITH A PURPOSE –

The liking for idents is a European and Asian phenomenon. In the United States, the preference has long been to minimize the risk of losing viewers

Pylons and neon signs: two of Channel 4's long-running idents launched in 2004
Source: © *Channel 4 Television*

to a rival network during a commercial break by moving from one show to another as swiftly as possible (perhaps via the kind of talent spot we described in Chapter 2 with USA Network). This has brought about techniques such as hot switching, where the end of one programme leads directly into the next, which can result in a commercial break appearing uncomfortably soon after the opening title sequence of a show. The financial pressure to retain audiences, and the homogeneous nature of a typical US network's programming, has led to interstitial content with an emphasis on individual programme brands and their stars. This is instead of anything that expresses a message about the network brand except, as we have seen, taglines on promos with overarching propositions (Characters Welcome,

Way More Fun, Fearless...). Cathy Johnson of the University of Nottingham says:

> In the UK context, channel branding is seen as particularly useful for uniting the range of programming provided in the public service broadcaster's mixed programme schedule, whereas in the United States the far less pronounced variety of programming found on the networks is seen as undermining the usefulness of channel branding.[4]

So, how do idents work and why do so many broadcasters outside the United States still commission them regularly and run them in virtually every junction between programmes?

Idents are an example of the interstitial content that US academic Jonathan Gray would call 'paratexts': acting as 'airlocks' to texts that 'establish frames and filters through which we look at, listen to, and interpret (those) texts' (in this case, the programmes themselves).[5]

There's that word 'frames' again. At their most basic level, idents form part of the flow of a channel's content and help viewers to orient themselves. James Walker, Channel 4's head of marketing, puts it like this:

> They are incredibly important... In the linear television world they create the beautiful packaging that goes around the content and they create a sense of place, but in a more on-demand world they are also a stamp.[6]

Idents for a TV channel are a particularly unique creative challenge. They cannot rely on dialogue or music, as they are often dipped under a continuity announcer talking. They can have a narrative structure but, in the case of dynamic channels such as BBC One and Channel 4, have to have an ending known as a 'living hold', which needs to last up to 30 seconds, so you never really know when the 'story' is going to end. Beyond this, broadcasters and content owners are recognizing the growing importance of reinforcing ownership of their programme assets in online media. Short, recognizable pre-roll idents or stings can be effective at doing this.

Channel idents also have to be flexible. They need to be engaging, and capable of having topics as diverse as genocide documentaries and Saturday night gameshows introduced over them. Because they often need to act as a gear shift in a junction between just those sorts of varied genres, having a batch of idents with varying moods and tones, from upbeat to contemplative, is important. For BBC One there is always at least one ident that is neutral enough to carry news of sombre national importance. For the 2002 'dance' idents this was particularly challenging, and a balletic ident filmed at Minack Theatre in Cornwall was chosen in advance. Sadly, the very weekend that the idents went live the Queen Mother passed away, and so for days nothing but a group of funereal ballerinas was screened. To some observers the entire identity never really recovered from this unfortunate start.

In the hands of the best TV brand builders, idents have now moved a long way from their origins as simple numeric signifiers and animated logos to become brand messages with meaning. Our own team has played its part in this evolution, from people (or hippos) coming together for BBC One (see Chapter 4) to kittens and hamsters in unexpected settings for The Home of Witty Banter (see Chapter 3). We have filled programme junctions with fun facts about elephants and mosquitos for Russia's first national children's channel (reputedly launched at the request of President Putin as an antidote to a growing diet of US kids' channels),[7] we have mashed up videos and photos for Ireland's youth-focused channel RTÉ2[8] and captured DreamWorks's best-loved characters for the first time in a TV channel identity.[9] When executed well, idents can act as succinct brand statements to sum up those two positioning questions that we looked at in Chapter 3: who is the channel for and what does it offer them? During the development of the 100% Characters rebrand for Universal Channel there were many discussions with NBCUniversal's US stakeholders about whether idents were needed. The London-based marketing team believed strongly that they were:

> Outside of the constraints of promoting specific content (idents were/ are) an expression of the channel. They are a way to make it easier for our viewers to just 'get it'. The Universal Channel idents are not just there to communicate the brand logo, they are there to communicate the Characters' positioning. They are a key part of driving home the brand positioning.[10]

Like all the other elements of the Universal Channel identity, the idents had to communicate consistently and effectively in over 100 countries, without the benefit of access to US-based talent to call into a studio at short notice. We therefore created a series of visual metaphors to dramatize the fact that Universal was the home of '100% Characters'. For example, a line of dog walkers on a beach promenade ends with a girl nonchalantly strolling with a large white alpaca on a leash, and a drive-in movie is enjoyed by a chilled-out couple eating popcorn in the back of a trailer equipped with its own hot tub. Idents like these, and others featuring a lobster-eating cop in a lunchtime diner and a junior doctor doing a ward round on a Segway, did not just establish Universal Channel's positioning but also helped to create a new personality for the network.

Philip Almond, the BBC's director of marketing and audiences, has a very clear view of the role of idents:

> They give a channel a personality... It comes from the pace of an evening and how you create an evening. You need a gap between programmes. If there were no trailers, no idents, it would be an incredibly jolting experience, so you need that space, but also you're in people's living rooms

Taking an alpaca for a walk: one of the '100% Characters' from Universal Channel's idents Source: *Reproduced by permission of NBCUniversal International*

and you're there by permission. Idents give a personality and an identity to the channel and it's particularly important on diverse channels like BBC One and BBC Two that you need some kind of glue, otherwise at times it could seem a very random experience.[11]

This point is reinforced by the academic Cathy Johnson:

Over the 1990s the principal role of the junctions in UK terrestrial television shifted from providing clarity and order to the flow of broadcasting, to constructing branded identities that conveyed a personality for the channel over and above its individual programmes.[12]

– THE 2s –

Apart from Channel 4, the UK channel whose personality has been enhanced most famously over many years is BBC Two. It was Martin Lambie-Nairn, again, who was the driving force behind a complete rebrand back in 1991, which was when viewers were first introduced to the stubby, sharp-edged '2' logo that, over the years, has become such an iconic feature of British television. The channel controller at the time, Alan Yentob, was quoted as saying that the previous logo (a stylized upper-case 'TWO') 'made no impact... was singularly unmemorable and told you nothing about the personality of the channel'.[13] BBC Two was regarded as 'snobbish', 'middle class' and 'highbrow': attributes that were an increasingly poor fit with

Yentob's more varied and vibrant programme strategy.[14] Martin Lambie-Nairn describes the creative development process:

> As we developed creative themes... we felt that the brand values BBC Two had to convey – witty, innovative, surprising – could not be communicated effectively by a single ident. I imagined... a whole family of idents that could be developed in a variety of ways to reflect the different programming moods of the channel.[15]

Appearing first in sophisticated form, for example a steel-grey '2' being splashed with turquoise paint, covered in billowing silk or flickering in the form of a neon sign, successive generations of 2s became more playful, zipping around like a remote-controlled car or bounding across the screen like a fluffy toy puppy. In the hands of the BBC's own talented graphic design team, many of whom later became colleagues in our agency, BBC Two's animated idents won creative award after creative award, including a coveted D&AD Black Pencil, as the 2s took on many other forms, including a venus fly trap, a helium balloon and a group of tiny baby 'swans'.[16]

Two 2s: classic BBC Two idents   *Source: Reproduced by permission of BBC*

When asked to pitch for another BBC Two rebrand in 2006, following the popularity of our work for BBC One, we felt strongly that the animated 2 character should be retained and, if anything, given more freedom. We wanted to take it out into the real world, unconstrained by a table-top film studio, to develop its personality. The then controller and head of marketing disagreed. There was a feeling that the animated 2 had run its course, and a new identity was commissioned from a leading ad agency based on the idea of the channel logo serving as a 2-shaped 'window on the world' through which various scenes could be viewed from BBC Two's perspective. In our view this was a mistake. Brand properties like the animated 2 are incredibly rare in television and we felt this was a classic case of a client team getting bored with something long before viewers ever would, with the personality of the channel losing out as a result. Happily, though, our team has recently had opportunities to maintain the playfulness and fun of the iconic 2 on a number of topical occasions: a 2-shaped butterfly and caterpillar for the wildlife programme *Springwatch* and a 'tennis ball' for BBC Two's coverage of Wimbledon, to quote recent examples.[17]

The 2 becomes a caterpillar and butterfly for BBC Two's Springwatch
Source: *Reproduced by permission of BBC*

The 50th anniversary of the channel in 2014 gave us the idea of throwing a birthday party for all the most memorable 2s of the past, which resulted in everyone's favourite – the puppyish white fluffy 2 – burying its 'nose' greedily in a birthday cake supposedly donated by *The Great British Bake Off*'s Mary Berry[18] and, maybe a little worse for wear, squeaking along karaoke-style to 'I Will Survive'. As if inspired by the message of that song, several of the original idents have been running again on the channel recently and they look as fresh today as they did when first launched. In the words of the BBC's brand director, Jane Lingham:

> It is testament to those idents that they still can work and they can be updated. They are simple enough and straightforward enough that you can just keep going with them. They're very flexible. People are fond of them.[19]

This is no mere assertion. Jane refers to qualitative research carried out recently by the BBC in which she doubted whether viewers would be able to talk about the personality of individual channels, but it was not a problem:

> It always amazes me how much of a point of view people have about channel idents and how much they can recall... People have such a clear sense of what the channels stand for and they would talk about all the idents really easily.[20]

A 50th birthday party for the BBC 2s   Source: *Reproduced by permission of BBC*

– KILLING 'BORING' –

Our former colleague Clare Phillips, now head of brand planning at ITV and with recent experience also at Channel 4, has a balanced view of the role of idents on a TV channel:

> Idents are important. But we place an overimportance on them. The junctions as a whole are what we should be concerned with.[21]

According to Clare, one of the key ways to maintain viewer engagement throughout the junctions is through variety and keeping the idents fresh. We saw in Chapter 4 how ITV in the UK and the ABC in Australia have both shown a recent preference for a large selection of different idents to choose from, and a brand that has recently applied this philosophy in a highly innovative way on a global scale is MTV.

In fact, a book about TV brand building would be incomplete without a mention of the pioneering influence of MTV. At the time of its launch in 1981, according to one of the founders, Tom Freston:

> Television had never really had brands before – people watched programmes rather than channels. But our format was borrowed from radio, with videos playing the role of records. We had to create a sense of cohesion so that the audience would identify with the channel and stay with it.[22]

One of the most iconic moments in television history was MTV's first broadcast, featuring doctored footage from the Apollo 11 moon landing with Neil Armstrong planting a multicoloured graffiti-style MTV flag as a lead-in to the symbolic words of the Buggles song 'Video Killed the Radio Star'.[23] From those opening seconds MTV established a new television language, with a seamless flow of music videos interspersed with logos, idents and promos. Over many years, diverse and creative idents helped to establish for MTV a distinctive personality as the definitive music channel for young audiences.

However, like all channels, MTV has been continually evolving in the face of intensifying competition. While still being positioned as 'the world's premier youth entertainment brand',[24] today's programming mix, with its emphasis on popular reality shows such as *Jersey* (and, for the Brits, *Geordie*) *Shore*, *Teen Mom* and *Ex On The Beach*, led to a recent realization by the global marketing team that a new approach to on-screen identity was called for. Kerry Taylor, who has lead responsibility for the MTV brand internationally, explains:

> We are now seeing that 83 per cent of our audience have got smartphones around the world, over 80 per cent of them are on social media, so our audience is completely living in that space... We started changing our content strategy so now there's the linear show and then... an equal amount of content that lives in a social media space... but we've got this very broadcast aesthetic and the audience are living in a place where the

aesthetic is completely different... We know that they want TV in a linear immersive experience when they come there but the whole look and the way that they want to collaborate with the brand has changed.[25]

In response, and guided by a huge research project with a sample of 15,000 18–34-year-olds, the MTV team arrived at a radical new approach to interstitial content, devised to work equally well across over 160 countries and in 32 languages. At the press launch (appropriately at the 2015 Cannes Lions festival of creativity), this was summed up neatly as a move from the iconic call to action in the 1980s when the original channel was trying to establish itself as a must-have on US cable TV packages, 'I Want My MTV', to today's 'I Am My MTV'. Not a tagline, but a way of thinking about MTV's philosophy of co-creation with artists and its audience. The creative expression was described by Adam Sherwin, writing in the *Independent*, as 'a riot of garish, clashing colours, emojis and GIFs, incorporating social media videos'.[26]

At the heart of this fresh approach to brand identity was a reinvention of MTV's idents as 'bumps': 5- to 15-second pieces of interstitial content. Working with self-styled 'storytellers and technologists' at B-Reel in New York, with the manifesto 'Make Stuff. Get It On Air. Take Control of MTV', a web-based platform was built.[27] This connected to a global content management system to enable young people to submit their own videos from Instagram and Vine, with the potential to be run on air within two hours of submission.[28]

Companion initiatives included MTV Canvas, which gave fans a 'digital sticker book' of assets with which to create their own idents, and MTV Art Breaks, which allowed MTV to build on its legacy of introducing the work of new artists (for example, in the early days, Keith Haring and Jean-Michel Basquiat) in the form of experimental video content.

A big practical advantage of this approach to idents, according to Kerry Taylor, was the way it liberated its in-house creatives around the world. Rather than 'just pumping out stuff from the centre', creatives across all MTV's markets were given a 'digital toolbox':

They've got 300 backgrounds, 300 what we're calling 'invaders'... (and we say) these are all the elements that you can use on air as you see fit, or add to them, so by handing that out you suddenly move away from 'I can't believe they gave me that and they don't understand my market' to saying 'Our philosophy is to kill boring, just be creative, do things differently.' It's about letting the audience participate, but you've got complete freedom to do that in a way that you feel works best for your market, so wherever you go around the world MTV will look similar, but it just won't look the same.[29]

As MTV first did back in the 1980s, it is once again leading the way in creating new approaches to building a channel brand personality that is match-fit for today's changing patterns of TV viewing.

MTV Bump and MTV Canvas: tools to enable viewers to 'take control' of MTV's interstitial content   Source: *Reproduced by permission of Viacom International Media Networks*

– SETTING THE BLOCKS FREE –

Conscious of innovation like MTV's happening in other parts of the television landscape, the marketing team at Channel 4 and their in-house 'agency', 4Creative, had been toying for some time with the idea of refreshing their main channel's identity. They felt there was no urgent need to tackle the challenge: viewers had not grown tired of the classic 'perspective' idents that had been running for over 10 years. However, in line with their bold moves to communicate Channel 4's remit with campaigns emphasizing its stance as a risk taker and a champion of alternative voices (as we saw in Chapter 5), the team felt there was an opportunity for the on-screen identity to work harder. More than simply telling viewers what channel they were watching, could it give them more of a sense of what Channel 4 stands for?

For 4Creative's joint heads, Chris Bovill and John Allison, replacing a much-loved and award-winning identity was a daunting task that they eventually decided they should tackle before viewers told them they had to, as John sums up:

> It was procrastination on a huge scale. It's like being a student – you do the dishes, you do anything to not do your homework, until we realized 'We're going to have to do this now.'[30]

In approaching the brief, 4Creative set out to create a concept with the potential to be much bigger than a set of idents with a large number 4 centre-stage, however imaginatively that could be done. The goal was to capture Channel 4's diverse qualities: 'irreverent, innovative, alternative and challenging'.[31] A further objective was to develop a creative theme that would work hard across every element of the channel's on-screen presentation: not just idents but, for example, promo end boards, menus and 'opticals' (short interstitial blips of content).

Chris and John explained to us that the breakthrough came when they realized that, after over 30 years, Lambie-Nairn's famous blocks could be set free. They no longer had to be bound by the constraint of coming together to form the 4 logo. They could be liberated in a way that could symbolize Channel 4's diversity. This was a eureka moment that unlocked the whole identity. Chris describes how this gave them a highly flexible concept that could be developed over time:

> We had to do something that could evolve like the channel, because the channel is a shapeshifting and pretty schizophrenic thing, from *Countdown* to *Muslim Drag Queens*, so it had to be something that could shift and play.[32]

The solution for the on-screen presentation system, developed in collaboration with Grant Gilbert and his agency DBLG, was for the blocks to be assembled and reassembled in a wide variety of dynamic and playful combinations: different colours, different numbers, different configurations to carry information to help viewers navigate. They could be yellow for *The Simpsons*, green for *Cucumber* or a clean white stack for a 'coming next' menu. Chris Bovill explains further:

> We have set the blocks free and we can send them off in loads of different ways. They can be programme specific, we can play with 3 blocks, 9 blocks, 100 blocks. We can make them out of things – chalk for *Educating*, blood trails for *Fargo* – so there are layers to where this thing can go. We're not locked in. The 4 doesn't have to be a 4, it can just be these really distinctive blocks that only Channel 4 owns.[33]

Much like we saw with ITV in Chapter 4, the new Channel 4 identity was the work of a 'dream team', led by 4Creative and at various stages drawing on the talents of not only DBLG but also the globally renowned designer

Setting the blocks free: new on-screen presentation for Channel 4 launched in 2015
Source: © Channel 4 Television

Neville Brody and director Jonathan Glazer. Brody was commissioned to create two new typefaces, which were also based on Lambie-Nairn's original nine blocks and christened Horseferry and Chadwick (the two London streets on which Channel 4's HQ is located). Alice Tonge, creative director at 4Creative, described Horseferry, the new headline font, to *Creative Review*:

> You can find all the little blocks. They're all buried within it... It's got loads of character – it's occasionally spiky, sometimes smooth, sometimes goes against the grain, doesn't always follow type rules. Full of personality, and something that only Channel 4 could own.[34]

This chapter set out to discuss the importance of idents in giving a channel a personality, but we have seen recently, with MTV and Channel 4 for example, that this is no longer a job for idents alone. All elements of a channel's interstitial content can work together to create a distinctive identity.

– THE ORIGIN STORY –

However, the team at Channel 4 realized that idents still had a vitally important role to play in holding the programme junctions together. Having relieved the blocks of their duty to form a large number 4, 4Creative saw an opportunity to develop a much richer back story. Chris Bovill talks about how the first batch of new idents were developed to explore the origins of the blocks:

> Because we are going to be doing so many things with them, we needed to set them up as being special and precious, giving them these unique properties because they're not just kids' building blocks. These things have a currency, like kryptonite, so let's give them an origin story, so you discover them.[35]

Four somewhat unsettling short narrative films directed by Jonathan Glazer offer glimpses of the blocks in elemental form. We discover their 'kryptonite', for example, glowing like crystals under a spectacular water-fall, adorning a shaman's ritual costume or being gathered from a hillside of rubble by a swarm of sinister figures in white protective clothing. An atmospheric score by Mica Levi, who worked with Glazer on the arthouse sci-fi movie *Under the Skin*, adds to a haunting, mesmerizing feel that is different from anything seen before in a TV channel identity.

With these first four new idents the Channel 4 team have followed the 'rules' we described earlier in this chapter, but in a sense broken them too. There is no dialogue, they are not reliant on music (although the sound design is striking), they are open ended and flexible. They are there to form a bed for a continuity voice, which is the basic function for any TV ident. At the same time, there is a sense that there is more to discover. We feel we are at the beginning of an intriguing story, with more to unfold over the coming months and years. Yet again Channel 4 has elevated the craft of the humble ident to absorbing and thought-provoking TV content in its own right.

The origin of the blocks – two of Channel 4's 2015 idents   *Source: © Channel 4 Television*

— AN ENDURING ROLE —

From the rich tradition of Channel 4, evolving from its original 1982 coloured blocks via neon signs and hay bales to its latest shamanic dance and eerie waterfall, to the iconic playfulness of the BBC '2s' and MTV's latest innovations in viewer participation, we can see that outside the United States there is still a significant role for idents in forming the personality of a TV channel. In fact, some of the most groundbreaking creativity in the TV marketing world over the past 30 years or so has come from these short pieces of content, with their practical requirements for flexibility and diversity. But the best TV marketers do not settle for traditional and predictable ident formats. As Viacom's Kerry Taylor concludes:

> You need them. They have a really important part to play. It's just that what constitutes an ident, or what an ident should be, is now much more of a question.[36]

NEXT
★ The ratings totem pole.

★ Breaking the fourth wall.

★ The subconscious themes.

★ The three-act structure.

★ Launching second seasons.

★ 'Who's been hit?'

LATER
★ The world's cheapest billboards.

★ 'Lillian Thomson'.

★ 'Binge Responsibly'.

NOTES

1 *Friends*, 'The One Where Chandler Doesn't Like Dogs' (2000) season seven, episode eight, NBC, 23 November

2 Myerson, J, quoted in Lambie-Nairn, M (1997) *Brand Identity for Television: With knobs on*, Phaidon Press, London

3 Lambie-Nairn, M (1997) *Brand Identity for Television: With knobs on*, Phaidon Press, London

4 Johnson, C (2011) *Branding Television*, Routledge, Abingdon. (It is interesting to note that in late 2015 US network TBS introduced a new set of short idents created by agency 99 Tigers, whose creative director David Seeley was quoted as saying that logo IDs as an art form had 'fallen by the wayside' and had started to make a comeback; see http://brief.promaxbda.org/content/99-tigers-ushers-in-tbs-logo-with-memorable-idents. It will be interesting to see if this becomes a new trend in the United States.)

5 Gray, J (2010) *Show Sold Separately: Promos, spoilers and other media paratexts*, NYU Press, New York

6 James Walker, head of marketing, Channel 4 Television, interview 25 June 2015

7 https://www.youtube.com/watch?v=_0SODuGYCqo

8 http://www.redbeecreative.tv/work/rte-channel-rebrand?service=brand-identity

9 http://www.redbeecreative.tv/work/dreamworks-tv-launch

10 Marco Giusti, senior vice president, creative, NBCUniversal International, interview 8 May 2015

11 Philip Almond, director of marketing and audiences, BBC, interview 14 September 2015

12 Johnson, C (2011) *Branding Television*, Routledge, Abingdon

13 Williams, S (2004) [accessed 3 November 2015] Ten Into Two, *Off The Telly*, April [Online] http://www.offthetelly.co.uk/oldott/www.offthetelly.co.uk/indexcb13.html?page_id=1772

14 Williams, S (2004) [accessed 3 November 2015] Ten Into Two, *Off The Telly*, April [Online] http://www.offthetelly.co.uk/oldott/www.offthetelly.co.uk/indexcb13.html?page_id=1772

15 Lambie-Nairn, M (1997) *Brand Identity for Television: With knobs on*, Phaidon Press, London

16 BBC Two (2015) [accessed 3 November 2015] BBC Two Idents And Continuity [Online] http://www2.tv-ark.org.uk/bbctwo/index.html

17 BBC (2015) [accessed 3 November 2015] Butterfly – Springwatch – BBC Two Ident [Online, Red Bee video] https://www.youtube.com/watch?v=5gCu51WatZE; also see: BBC (2015) [accessed 3 November 2015] Caterpillar – Springwatch – BBC Two Ident [Online] https://www.youtube.com/watch?v=VYtlpRqC0Jg; also see: Red Bee (2015) [accessed 3 November 2015] BB2 Wimbledon Ident [Online] https://www.youtube.com/watch?v=Pa-VSiOXcEo

18 https://www.youtube.com/watch?v=CgK7JWk-O3o&list=PLDsg58IUh5wS4yz QiKYVTUY1K3X4fw3xS&index=3 Also see: https://www.youtube.com/watch?v= q-_hIY6yYJI&list=PLDsg58IUh5wS4yzQiKYVTUY1K3X4fw3xS&index=4

19 Jane Lingham, director, BBC Brand, interview 29 July 2015

20 Jane Lingham, director, BBC Brand, interview 29 July 2015

21 Clare Phillips, head of brand planning, ITV, interview 24 April 2015

22 Tungate, M (2004) [accessed 9 September 2015] The Making Of MTV, *Media Week*, 17 August [Online] http://www.mediaweek.co.uk/article/516339/making-mtv#Spb9dKED3ijFiWd7.99

23 Elias Arts, LLC (2012) [accessed 9 September 2015] MTV ID 'Moon Landing' [Online] https://www.youtube.com/watch?v=HmBp6RwOUbg

24 MTV (2015) [accessed 9 September 2015] *MTV UK and Ireland Press Centre* [Online] http://www.vimn.com/press/mtv/corporate-information/mtv

25 Kerry Taylor, senior vice president, youth and music, Viacom International Media Networks, interview 2 July 2015

26 Sherwin, A (2015) [accessed 9 September 2015] The Media Column: MTV Rebrand Aims To Put The Channel Back In The Driving Seat Of The Cultural Revolution, *Independent*, 28 June [Online] http://www.independent.co.uk/news/media/the-media-column-mtv-rebrand-aims-to-put-the-channel-back-in-the-driving-seat-of-the-cultural-revolution-10351288.html

27 B-Reel (2015) [accessed 9 September 2015] Featured Work [Online] https://www.b-reel.com/projects/mtv-bump

28 B-Reel (2015) [accessed 9 September 2015] MTV Bump [Online] https://www.b-reel.com/projects/mtv-bump

29 Kerry Taylor, senior vice president, youth & music, Viacom International Media Networks, interview 2 July 2015

30 John Allison, joint head, 4Creative, interview 5 October 2015

31 Channel 4 (2015) [accessed 3 November 2015] Channel 4 Refreshes Iconic Main Channel Brand, Press Release [Online] http://www.channel4.com/info/press/news/channel-4-refreshes-iconic-main-channel-brand

32 Chris Bovill, joint head, 4Creative, interview 5 October 2015

33 Chris Bovill, joint head, 4Creative, interview 5 October 2015

34 Williams, E (2015) [accessed 3 November 2015] Channel 4 Rebrands, With Help From Jonathan Glazer And Neville Brody, *Creative Review* [Online] https://www.creativereview.co.uk/cr-blog/2015/september/channel-4-rebrands-with-help-from-jonathan-glazer-and-neville-brody/

35 Chris Bovill, joint head, 4Creative, interview 5 October 2015

36 Kerry Taylor, senior vice president, youth & music, Viacom International Media Networks, interview 2 June 2015

PART THREE

BUILDING AND PROMOTING TV PROGRAMME BRANDS

CHAPTER SEVEN

MARKETING DRAMA
Glimpsing the future, unravelling the helix and speed dating

Starting to watch a television show that might run for years isn't a decision to take lightly. I'm wrestling with a big commitment issue here.

SHELDON COOPER, *THE BIG BANG THEORY*[1]

– WHY IT MATTERS SO MUCH –

Dramas form the structural pillars and joists that all general entertainment channels are built on. Alongside top sporting rights, they are the battering rams that new entrants to the broadcast market utilize to achieve scale of viewing and critical acceptance. Dramas can define a brand – as they have done so successfully with USA Network or AMC – and they are the ratings totem pole that networks such as ITV rise and fall around.

It is no wonder, then, that drama sees the highest levels of marketing investment, and the greatest innovations in off-screen campaigns. For example, Sky's premium drama channel Sky Atlantic was reported by *Private Eye* to have spent £7.5 million on promoting the series *Fortitude* to a settled consolidated weekly audience of 1.5 million viewers.[2]

From ABC in the United States floating thousands of messages in bottles for the launch of *Lost*, and branding a million dry cleaning bags with *Desperate Housewives* ads – 'Everyone has a little dirty laundry' – to Channel 4's pop-up shop for 'Persona Synthetics' launching *Humans*, and ITV's fake newspaper-stall headlines for *Broadchurch*, the most successful dramas have nearly always been preceded by the most creative marketing.

Chapter 14 on storyworlds develops a number of these case studies in which fiction is woven into the real world. Often these are extensions of a campaign though, amplifying the sense of event for launches and rewarding existing fans of established shows. The battle for eyeballs with drama, as indeed with most genres, is won and lost with the quality of the TV spots, and the strength of the key art. Drilling down to find the essence of a new show that has the expectations of a whole network riding on it is the greatest challenge of the responsible marketing teams. No one in the world currently does that better than FX Networks in the United States. Stephanie Gibbons, the inspirational marketer at the helm, explains their approach:

> How we approach dramas is to say we're going to do the trailers, we're going to show the work as it exists in its completed form, but we also want to take the drama apart strand by strand. We want to unravel the helix, we want to think about it the way we would think about literature – in the most basic of classes, by asking, where does the foreshadowing exist, what are the subtexts behind the protagonists, what is their Achilles heel, what drives them, what doesn't, what are the themes that the creators thought about before they put anything to paper? That's how we market dramas.[3]

Writers from Hollywood and the theatre have been attracted to the 'small screen' because global television is embracing more sophisticated thematic and mature dramas, and moving away from formulaic plots and hospital ward fare.[4] The richness of the texts following this shift means that Stephanie's approach becomes ever more important.

Yet equally, as the growing creative muscle of television attracts A-list names, so the oldest form of dramatic promotion – star power – needs examining too.

– SPEED DATING –

Since the posting of playbills for the productions of the Lord Chamberlain's Men theatre company at the Rose or the Globe theatres in London – an Elizabethan form of viral marketing – the simplest promotion of drama has adopted a fairly familiar guise. Priority is given to named talent, both in front of camera/proscenium arch, or indeed behind it as writers. Richard Burbage was an excellent box-office draw for the Lord Chamberlain's Men, William Shakespeare a headline act.

For a 10-year period, Britain's largest commercial broadcaster ITV would put bankable stars Robson Green or Stephen Tompkinson into any drama and the viewers would flock to it. A promotional and commissioning trope brilliantly skewered in *The Fast Show* comedy's Monkfish sketches: 'Coming soon to BBC One, John Actor plays tough, uncompromising detective/vet/doctor/Scottish detective, etc... Monkfish'.[5]

For marketers it was easy and unchallenging and, in many instances, it is entirely the right thing to do. But there is a subtler blend of reasons that can and should be used to capture an audience for a drama. A blend based on emotional engagement with the characters, universal underlying themes and a sense of impending jeopardy in the situation. Let's explore these individually.

– EMOTIONAL ENGAGEMENT –

Perhaps more than any other form of television, watching the first episode of a drama is a moment of potentially heavy commitment. A decision that could lead to 24 hours of your precious time being spent with a programme and a channel. It's like entering into a long-term relationship, in comparison with a 53-minute dalliance with a one-off documentary or dipping in to gawp at a 'structured reality' half-hour. Good dramas retain an audience because they form an emotional relationship with characters – an empathy that lasts beyond the closing credits. As such it is important that you use the time within your trailer as a speed date for your characters. If you read any guide to speed dating you will find advice that is useful in drama promotion:

> Make an effort! Be yourself. Be engaged – 55 per cent of communication is body language.

Of these, the third phrase is particularly apt in this context: *Be engaged*. It is unusual in the process of making a drama to be unduly focused on the audience beyond the moment of commission. Indeed the audience can often be construed as peers and critics. In the bad old days of the early 1990s, veteran drama producer Verity Lambert phoned to complain to one of us about the time slot that her drama trailer (on the nation's most mainstream channel) was getting – saying indignantly: '7 pm on a Friday... but that's when everyone is leaving town for the weekend'.

– DOWN THE LENS –

One way of addressing this issue head-on in trailers is by capturing the leading characters talking directly to camera. There is then a direct acknowledgement of the presence of another party in the whole endeavour – the viewer.

Indeed there is an interesting lesson for all brands here, in the power of direct one-to-one communication. In the interruptive model of advertising there was a sense that the direct communication of a 'brand spokesperson' to camera smacked of regional sofa stores dropping prices. However, in an online environment, where people are used to the one-on-one communication relationship formed by social networking, it is a comfortable and trusted means of communicating – drawing more on the presenting styles of television than the artifice of the TV commercial.

So within the wider lesson of giving the audience a reason why they should commit to spending time with you, specially shot trailers in which the cast breaks the invisible fourth wall and looks directly down the lens have that power of human engagement.

A great example was the relaunch of the BBC's global smash hit brand *Doctor Who*. In 2005 that success was in no way guaranteed, however. The show about a time-travelling alien space hero had launched in 1963, but had been off the screen for many years. Lorraine Heggessey, the BBC One channel controller, and Jane Tranter, head of drama, had hatched a plan to reinvigorate the Saturday teatime slot with a family drama. It now seems an obvious fit, but at the time, years before the successes of *Primeval*, *Merlin*, *Atlantis* and *Robin Hood*, it was a major gamble. They had in showrunner Russell T Davies, however, the perfect blend of science fiction fan and master storyteller.

How could we launch a rebooted and suited *Doctor Who* onto the national consciousness though?

Our early pitch to Davies, Julie Gardner (who had been charged with development for BBC Wales) and Jane Tranter was that we needed something that was going to make a dramatic connection with the viewers. We drew inspiration and pitched the idea as being the modern-day equivalent of Shackleton's famous expedition-recruitment press advertisement:

Men wanted for hazardous journey. Low wages, bitter cold, long hours of complete darkness. Safe return doubtful. Honour and recognition in event of success.[6]

This became a direct invitation, from Christopher Eccleston as the Doctor, to join the voyage of discovery.

Filming Eccleston to camera also enabled us to do something you will rarely see outside *House of Cards*, or *Sex and the City* – a character talking directly down the lens. This in itself makes the resulting trailer leap out in the junction. It also enabled us to hold back as much as possible from the 'science fiction and fantasy' visually and to land the Doctor – fresh as he was emerging from the time wars – as an adventurer... an Indiana Jones figure who wanted you as his companion along for the ride. The minute we saw his exhortation on the studio monitors... 'Do you want to come with me... because if you do I should warn you...' we felt sure we had a marketing hit on our hands.[7]

A challenge for the regenerated show was that, in the 18 years since it had last been regularly on TV screens, the expectation level that audiences had of visual effects (spoilt by a diet of billion-pound computer game and blockbuster movie budgets) were now a galaxy apart from what a teatime show could deliver. Away from the narrative of the show, where you are swept along by story and character, a trailer can sometimes expose rather than celebrate CGI work. So we decided early on that glimpsing, rather than 'celebrating', the monsters, the planets, the worlds, was the way to go. Less is more. In many ways that became a mantra to the cutting of *Doctor Who* trailers for many series to come. Matt Scarff, Richard Senior (who would go on to direct episodes of *Doctor Who*) and Jason Thomson all became adept at cinematic flashes to black, teases and beats, rather than extended scenes in the promotions.

Inevitably there was a creative tension, a deliberation with our counterparts in the BBC's marketing team over the brief... and a compromise. How could the Doctor ask you – the viewer – to be his companion when he already had one? Billie Piper's presence was also felt to be vital to the reboot in terms of widening the demographic appeal. So a slightly uncomfortable end shot was agreed that doesn't sit naturally in the cut (see: **https://www. youtube.com/watch?v=1hQyujVvRcY**).[8]

The body language itself is also reflective of the mood on the set, where we now know that a new Doctor was already being cast. David Tennant was on his way.[9]

In any event, the trailer launched across the BBC channels with radio versions airing from the *Today* programme to Radio 1. And it worked. Over 10 million viewers accepted the leather-coated Eccleston's invitation and the programme had set off on its journey to global powerhouse. Throughout this chapter we will return to *Doctor Who* as an object lesson in brand building and audience retention within the fiction genre.

Remaining with 'breaking the fourth wall' for a moment though, US dramas have for years employed this technique of marketing campaigns having direct viewer relationships. *Desperate Housewives* paraded, flirted, flaunted and seduced its way through series launch after series launch. Take season two for ABC, memorably soundtracked with the song 'Juicy' by alt-rock band Better than Ezra, as the cast brought to life a moment from their own title sequence – Eve plucking an apple from the tree – in a series of lascivious vignettes, while singing the word 'Juicy' directly down the lens.[10]

Or our launch campaign in the UK for season two of *Mistresses* for BBC One, where four equally glamorous leads struggle to escape a vast web of ensnaring red ribbons, glancing all the time at the viewers, as if to make them complicit in their dance. Building with great pacing to an apposite literary quote from Sir Walter Scott's *Marmion*.[11] The encapsulation indeed of the single-minded promise:

Oh, what a tangled web we weave,
When first we practise to deceive![12]

Similarly when launching the second series of *Luther*, a BBC police series almost defined by Idris Elba's portrayal of the titular character, we deliberately ended the trailer in which Luther trashes his office in mesmeric slow motion with a moment in which he recovers his poise, almost delicately replaces his phone receiver and looks straight down the lens. It was a 'stop whatever you are doing' moment.[13]

Working with drama producers on a marketing campaign, this can be the moment of creative tension. They are used to crafting the introductions to the cast – slow reveals of character and motive – whereas in the trailer we are having to grab attention and offer a shorthand and, of necessity, heightened portrayal of a character's motives, desires and flaws.

Chris Spencer, who ran the on-air promotions team for HBO for 25 years and is responsible for a vast array of their award-winning campaigns, remarks that the style that became a trademark in their specially shot promotions had its origins in creative challenge:

> The whole style of HBO's epic original programming shoot campaigns was born out of something that would normally be considered a negative in the creative process. Carolyn Strauss, then head of HBO Original Programming, did not want the on-air department writing dialogue for the actors to recite in promos, and she couldn't spare the show writers to draft lines because they had a show to write. What emerged from this was HBO's iconic approach to show promotion – beautiful portraiture of the talent in sometimes surreal environments (a desert, a supermarket, a void), without voices at all or with snippets of show dialogue underneath. The net result was something that felt more like a dream of the show than the show itself, and with all the clarity of hindsight it became our look and we acted like it was what we had always intended. The important lesson for me was that 'no' is not always the death of creative, that sometimes 'no' gives you structure you can use to your advantage.[14]

– UNIVERSAL THEMES –

For FX's Stephanie Gibbons, establishing underlying, often subconscious, thematic tones is the essential first step to creating the network's individual and highly awarded marketing:

> To a certain extent dramas are about the human experience, hopefully in its broadest terms, its narrative and storytelling. So often in our marketing we go to the subconscious themes, not necessarily what the show is but the primordial seed from which the show emerged. For *American Horror Story* we marketed the first season before the pilot script was completed. We sat down and had a conversation with Ryan Murphy and he told me the kinds of things he was thinking from a thematic standpoint. We had no script or even any certainty of who was going to be cast. It was truly a matter of working at a thematic level, and we do that to this day with *American Horror Story* and all our dramas. What were the subliminal themes that went into the script? What was in the writer's mind before his fingers touched the keyboard?[15]

Stephanie expands on this, citing the second season of *American Horror Story* (*Asylum*) as an example. Amongst many stand-out pieces of key art, the one that was used most prolifically across print and social media was that of a 'crying nun', her pale white face streaked with black tears:

> What are the themes of *Asylum*? You had a protagonist who was an alcoholic and prostitute, and when she killed a child while driving drunk, she realized she had to get away and get herself together. She turned to the Catholic Church for sanctuary and structure. She essentially took the

Dark subconscious themes: key art for American Horror Story: Asylum

Source: Reproduced by permission of FX Networks, LLC

covenant and decided, 'This is who I am.' One of the themes that may not even have reached 90 per cent of the people who watched was the notion of institutional corruption, and what happens when one has aligned oneself so fully to an ideology and belief system. In this case Jessica Lange was the protagonist who discovered corruption at the most hyperbolic levels and in a fashion that only creator Ryan Murphy could have conceived.[16]

For any programme in any genre, viewers do not want or need a list of reasons to watch, they just need one very good one. As Robert McKee, Hollywood's foremost guru in plot craft, would undoubtedly tell you, in the end with drama it ultimately comes down to the story:

> And so storytelling is, by far, the greatest way to hook and hold. The best people have that talent, or they learn that craft and they know how to beguile people and move them and excite them with their visions and persuade them.[17]

– GLIMPSING THE FUTURE –

Why does every movie trailer tell you the story? Why does the 'In a world where...' voice-over man always begin by telling you just how bad things have got?

To give the audience the moment of crisis, to set out the hero's quest. It is a common complaint for people coming out of movie trailers to say 'But they showed me everything that was going to happen... why bother watching now?' Indeed the directors of two major Hollywood blockbusters (*Terminator Genisys*, and *Jurassic World*) have taken their own marketing teams to task for just that issue in the summer of 2015.[18]

But the best trailers are capable of giving you that glimpse of the future – the probability of a murder, the likelihood of an affair or the possibility of whip-smart exchanges. That glimpse is also knowledge that even the protagonists at the start of the adventure don't have. Look at these glimpses from two launch trailers:

> 'What you call love, was invented by guys like me... to sell nylons.'
>
> Don Draper, *Mad Men*[19]

or

> 'Mr Mayor, fellow members of the City Council. In less than two hours liquor will be declared illegal by decree of the distinguished gentlemen of our nation's Congress. (Toasts) To those beautiful, ignorant bastards.'
>
> Nucky Thompson, episode one, *Boardwalk Empire*[20]

When Steve Buscemi appeared, a whole year before HBO officially screened *Boardwalk Empire*, in a dazzling 120-second launch trailer, those were the words that Martin Scorsese, the executive producer, used to hook us in – Robert McKee's 'moment of crisis', around which the whole series hangs. When we approach any long-running drama, it is these underlying questions that keep an audience engaged. 'What is the island?' (*Lost*). 'Will Nucky Thompson be brought to his knees?' (*Boardwalk Empire*). 'Will Don Draper ever be unmasked?' (*Mad Men*). 'Will Gregory House ever cure his own demons?' (*House*).

A 'glimpse of the future' is a useful phrase because of that powerful word – glimpse. It is another reminder to be single minded and reductive with how the drama is pitched. Even the most emotionally complex and narratively unconventional drama can, in the hands of a good creative, become a brilliantly simple promise. Take *Mad Men* and the launch of the seventh and final series on AMC. Soundtracked by Alice Russell's 'Breakdown', the specially shot promo featured all of the main characters on the move. Filmed in an airport – travelling, restlessness, the search for something, moving on. Don steps off a plane; Betty waits for a taxi; Roger flirts in a departure lounge. Resolved in one simple caption: 'It's all up in the air' – a promise that the final season would free itself more than before from the confines of the Madison Avenue office to set the characters on one last quest. The quest that, from Don to Peggy, Roger to Betty, we have followed for all the previous years. The search for happiness or, if not happiness, at the very least contentment (see: **https://www.youtube.com/watch?v=jkl2vWAwAOI**).[21]

Unsurprisingly for a Matthew Weiner show, the trailer is meticulous in establishing within that glimpse of the future a sense of time, of place, of mood. Bloggers quickly spotted cultural references (again, something that a single-minded specially shot trailer can achieve far more than any clip-based spot). For example, there was a very heavy nod to Hitchcock's seminal movie *North by Northwest* – shown around the time of the series launch at MoMI, in a film season curated by Weiner himself and titled Required Viewing: *Mad Men*'s Movie Influences.

Linda Schupack, AMC's EVP of marketing, explains that Matthew Weiner's choice of key art for the final series was similarly created to highlight the theme of moving on:[22]

> In the case of this last season, 7B, where that image is of Don driving in a car – is he driving away, is he driving to a place? We had conversations with Matt (Weiner) about what the arc of the narrative was going to be and we kicked around a couple of different concepts, finally landing on the image of Don driving – in our minds it was leaving a city but with *Mad Men* we always want to suggest... we want never to absolutely literally represent something, and we knew there was going to be a spiritual theme in a sense, that Don was going to be searching for non-material things.[23]

Glimpses of the future can even at first glance be infuriatingly opaque, as with Channel 4's launch of *Lost* in the UK. Directed by David LaChapelle, the cast impeccably styled in tattered evening wear waltz in a haunting slow-motion danse macabre around the burning remains of Oceanic Flight 815 to Portishead's track 'Numb'... 'I'm ever so lost, I can't find my way'... while the whispered voice-over intones: 'All of us have a secret.'[24]

As the Lostpedia notes, foreshadowing is everywhere – Locke and Walt conducting, Kate swapping partners from Jack to Sawyer to Jack again – and, perhaps as an overall glimpse of the future, 'infuriatingly opaque' was the best encapsulation possible. What both these spots for *Mad Men* and *Lost* achieved was extraordinary standout in the clutter of a TV channel's breaks and junctions. You couldn't fail to notice them, they demanded your attention. It is perhaps surprising, then, how infrequently dramas look to a specially filmed and constructed trailer to achieve this, traditionally leaning more heavily on a grammar that has its roots in decades of movie trailers.

– THE THREE-ACT STRUCTURE –

A typical beginner's guide to movie-trailer making will talk about the need to mimic the scriptwriter's own structural cornerstone – the three-act structure:

Act One. Setting the stage: introducing your characters and their world.

Act Two. Presenting the dilemma: complicating the world and highlighting the obstacles that the characters experience.

Act Three. Intensification of the challenge. Ratcheting up the obstacles and the obstructions facing your heroes on their journey.

Beyond the need to set the stage in any Act One, there is the dual requirement to begin in as impactful a way as possible. Legendary drama producer Mal Young, then the showrunner for BBC continuing dramas *EastEnders*, *Casualty* and *Holby City*, allegedly and only semi-jokingly instructed his writers and producers to start every drama with 'a f*ck or a fight'. In any form of trailer making, the first five seconds are as important as the first five minutes of the programme. Is the first set-up, the first line of dialogue, the first revelation of crisis to come as compelling as it can be?

Clearly the two- to three-minute duration of cinema trailers give a very different canvas to paint on than the smash and grab of the 30- or 40-second TV spot often accorded to drama launches. For those theatrical spots the three acts can unfold in a more systematic way. Furthermore, as with any set of rules or principles, many of the outstanding artists will deliberately subvert or avoid following them. As a shorthand to deconstructing the vast majority of drama trailers, however, it serves a useful purpose. Even those that at first glance seem looser in form can be usefully explained using the technique.

The launch of *True Detective* on HBO manages to condense the wooziness and multilayered heat of the series into its 100 seconds, while actually having a traditional structure:[25]

> Act One. Introduce the characters. The opening shot. Detectives Cohle and Hart in their sedan. 'Do you wonder ever if you're a bad man?', 'The world needs bad men, we keep the other bad men from the door.' Their voice-overs set up the classic odd-couple partnership 'steady and smart'. The world they inhabit painted in lingering landscape shots of swampy Louisiana. 'This is a world where nothing is solved.'
>
> Act Two. Present the dilemma: 'Do you ever see something like this?', 'No Sir.' A remarkable crime, a challenge to even the most experienced. Totemic rituals and symbols flash past us. 'Like a lot of dreams it had a monster at the end of it.'
>
> Act Three. Intensification of the challenge. At 1 minute 15 seconds, exactly two-thirds of the way through the trailer, we see a breakdown to black, the track stops, and everything accelerates. The violence becomes visceral, the sex more explicit, the landscapes burn. 'Just what is it you found?', 'Something deep and dark.'

With established series it is possible to skip Act One (our audience has a pre-existing relationship with the characters and world) and hurl yourselves boldly into the dilemma and the intensification. Science fiction hit series *Torchwood* illustrates this with the trailer for mini-series *Children of the Earth*. We know as an audience that *Torchwood* is an agency that exists to protect us from alien threats. So the role of our promo is merely to make this particular threat unmissable.[26]

To a haunting version of the children's nursery rhyme 'Twinkle, Twinkle...', it adopts a reverse countdown structure, establishing a threat in stark graphics. 'On the fifth day the Earth will be at war, on the fourth day our government will conspire, on the third day the sky will burn, on the second day our defences will fall, on the first day it will start... when our children stop.' Here the third-act intensification is honed to a single chilling moment: children screaming.

The trick when working within any expected set of guide rails is to avoid predictability. The legendary film-trailer maker Mark Woollen, in an interview with *Wired* magazine when asked if he rejects the traditional three-act structure, replies cautiously that it is only true to a degree, because in the first act you are usually establishing a character and a situation:

> And depending on the film you're often setting up a conflict or obstacle – Act Two. But it's all about the pace and style in which it's handled.

The worst feeling is when you get to the end of Act Two and feel like, 'Here we are rounding the corner and then this is going to happen!' That's kind of miserable.[27]

– MUSIC AND RHYTHM –

Above all else drama trailers, like movie trailers, are about rhythm. Examining the same *True Detective* promo as above, the music of Hans Zimmer's 'Wheat' and the layered slow mix edits that echo the title sequence all contribute to the suffocating swampy rhythm. As Stephen Garrett writes in *Filmmaker* magazine:

> A trailer, cut well, will have a flowing motion to it, a sense that everything plays off everything else, and will propel the viewer through the experience of the film. Trailers build up excitement and anticipation, and a keen sense of rhythm heightens those sensations.[28]

Perhaps the finest example of music setting mood lies in the series three launch of Channel 4's teenage drama *Skins*. The trailer itself charts a single wild night in a pub, from chaotic arrival of the Skins gang, through descent into orgiastic riot, and police-bothering departure. Filmed with bravura cinematography, a rich palette of flares, pill popping and shagging in toilets, watched over by disapproving and crucially older locals, the trailer dares viewers to throw themselves in with the mob. Anyone in the target market wants to be there. Anyone older wishes they could still be there. And all of this is catapulted into a hedonistic whirl by the track 'Halfway Home' from the 2008 album *Science* by US band TV on the Radio. Has ever an opening line more conjured up the spirit of a show: 'The lazy way they turned your head into a rest stop for the dead'?

In an interview with the *Observer*, director Neil Gorringe noted how the footage worked against both massively downtempo and massively uptempo tracks – the staples of most trailer makers. He said he had spent the past month 'constantly listening to music, reading thousands of blogs and putting every track I can think of into Last.fm (the custom internet radio station that creates endless playlist chains), then following the spiralling chains.[29]

The track worked particularly well as it is almost formed of two parts itself, a drunken and distorted opening, gradually succumbing to a relentless patter of toms and angular guitars that accelerate as the party descends into various levels of hell. As Gorringe describes, it's 'more of a music video than a drama trail...'

– FINDING A VOICE –

One of the biggest challenges for creatives working on drama is how to keep a sense of an overarching channel brand, when the dominant tone is clearly being established by the narrative, mood and rhythm of the story itself. This challenge is exacerbated by stylistic tropes of editing that mean all channels' drama trailers can blur into one morass, where interchangeable casts all turn their heads to folksy ballads by female singer-songwriters. The best way to swim against this tide is to seek originality of creative execution.

Stephanie Gibbons of FX Networks again points the way:

> The notion of a portfolio is critical for us. We haven't focused a great deal on brand advertising. We're strong believers in the idea that branding really is the sum of our parts and that speaking in those terms runs a little bit counter to our culture. We have always marketed from a theatrical perspective, which is to say that each individual programme has a brand that's developed against it, that's packaged from the ground up uniquely and originally.[30]

As ever, then, it is vital to seek originality of creative execution, if not through specially shot material or graphic styling, then through script.

Drama trailers driven by a voice-over script are increasingly rare, as they are mistakenly seen as relying on a dated technique, but this means that when done well they truly leap off the screen. Two examples of this craft stand out over the years.

First, the launch of *The Virgin Queen*, a 2005 BBC historical drama mini-series focusing on the personal life of Elizabeth 1, and in particular her relationship with Robert Dudley, Earl of Leicester. Even though the drama looked at her relationships with deliberate ambiguity, Ann Marie Duff was instructed by the director, Coky Giedroyc, to play the part true to her lifelong virginity. This led to the idea for our trailer, a love letter written from the queen to her one true passion – her country. Written by creative Joe Lee and movingly performed by Duff to a perfectly paced soundtrack of Bloc Party's 'So Here We Are':

> Where men faltered you stood firm / where they brought darkness / you were the light / when they mocked / and doubted me / you always believed. / Like me they grow old / But your beauty endures / Only you my true love / Have never let me down / To my England, with love.[31]

Second, and by complete contrast, Showtime's launch of comedy drama *House of Lies* featured a highly entertaining monologue from lead character Marty Kaan (Don Cheadle), mirroring a device from within the show itself where Kaan regularly breaks the fourth wall to address the audience while the remainder of the cast are oblivious:

> 310 million people in the US alone, that amounts to billions of decisions every day, what jeans to wear, what bank to trust, what coffee to order, what phone to buy. Like it or not, we have a hand in all of them. While you sleep, while you work, while you play, we keep America

running like clockwork. We're the secret handshake, the wizards of Oz, the hand up your skirt when no one's looking. We keep big business in business by telling them what they need, when they need it. Truth? We're just stealing their watch to tell them the time. And they're paying us millions for the favour.

Big fish. Big pond. Big cojones.[32]

The visuals inevitably counterpoint much of what Kaan is saying as the rest of the cast display anything but the ruthless professionalism he hints at. Altogether it is a hugely infectious piece that intentionally recalls *Glengarry Glen Ross* and *The Wolf of Wall Street*.

– DIVIDE AND CONQUER –

A question often posed by marketers (who are used to neatness and single-mindedness as a measure of judging a creative approach) is this:

Is it possible to make very different creative solutions to talk to totally different audiences, without profoundly mis-selling to at least one of them?

Surely a show has an editorial integrity that demands that you can only position it in one way?

Wrong.

Two shows, separated by 16 years and with profoundly different ambitions, make interesting case studies of how one programme can be marketed very differently to discrete audiences without overpromising or misleading how the series is positioned. The first is Fox's breakout hit *Empire*, which in 2015 was launched with what was described by Joe Earley, Fox TV Group's chief operating officer, as 'a very broad campaign with niche overlays'. The second is the BBC's 1999 drama serial *Warriors*, written by Peter Kosminsky, about the United Nations peacekeeping force in Bosnia.

Empire, which could be described as a black family saga, in the mould of *Dallas* and *Dynasty*, is one of the network's biggest-ever breakout hits. There were many contributing factors to its success as a marketing campaign, many of them borrowing on learnings that we will outline in Chapter 14. The timescale of the promotion alone, the scale of the media buys, and sponsorship – from major PPV boxing bouts to Black Friday promotions – shopping bags, checkout screens at Target and Walmart, *Empire*-themed Adidas shoes and jewellery.

Another clear point of success was the release strategy, as outlined by *Deadline* magazine, where every new episode was immediately released and then kept available on FOX NOW and VOD platforms to allow new audiences to come in at any point up to episode five. Of particular interest to this chapter, though, is how they targeted different audiences with different trailers. For soap fans, the show played up the family dynamic and conflict; for music fans the roles of music producer Timbaland and guest stars such as Mary J Blige were the focus; for younger fans the soundtracks were heavily hip-hop influenced; for the viewers of *Scandal*, fun lighter cuts were prepared.

Joe Earley also explained to *Adweek* how they segmented and targeted. 'This was a show for everyone, but we knew we were going to have to sell the show to targeted audiences,' Earley said. And, importantly, they needed to do so without using the term 'soap opera':

> It's a big, broad soap, but you don't sell a soap as a soap, though that's what we know that it is.[33]

Instead, for mainstream scripted fiction fans, they focused on the family drama and the music empire aspect, and then created bespoke work for everyone from African-American communities to fashionistas to LGBT communities (one of the main characters is a gay singer). 'There's even a little *Sex and the City* in *Empire*,' Earley added. The crafted promos extended to one that centred around Taraji P Henson's breakout character, Cookie, which they felt would appeal to *Real Housewives* fans.[34]

In 1999, BBC One promoted Peter Kosminsky's drama *Warriors* to three very carefully segmented audiences, using all of the BBC's breadth of reach to be as targeted and discrete as possible. Set in Vitez in Bosnia during the Lašva Valley ethnic cleansing, *Warriors* tells the story of the UNPROFOR force, torn between their peacekeeping mandate and the urge to intervene to stop the atrocities being committed against the civilian population. It was immensely powerful and brilliantly written, but as a drama for BBC One it was a 'difficult sell'. In the end the three 'cuts' that were produced all shone a light on profoundly different aspects of the story.

For a broadly female 'ITV drama' viewership, the trailer focused on the relationships between the soldiers, their local female interpreters and their wives back home. The drama powerfully showed the psychological damage inflicted on the soldiers and the impact that it had on characters such as Emma, played by Jodhi May, and three of the finest male leads of their generation – Matthew Macfadyen, Ioan Gruffudd and Damian Lewis. For that demograph it was positioned as a film about unique pressures on human interactions. For a more male audience, characterized as action fans, the trailer played up the war story, the action and tension produced within the tight confines of the Warrior armoured car of the show's ironic title. Finally, and importantly for the BBC, a third trailer was cut with a primary audience of 'opinion formers'. The drama did more than any current affairs programme of the time to give understanding and context to an immensely complicated conflict, and the final promotional trailer focused exclusively on the moral and political dimensions at its heart.

As we move into a world of streamed series, internet-connected televisions and sophisticated customer relationship marketing, will this degree of tailoring messages more tightly to individuals grow exponentially? Indeed, is the future of all content marketing a more programmatic one? A 'brand share' article in *Adweek*, titled 'What entertainment marketeers stand to gain from programmatic advertising' certainly believes it is an essential new tool:

> Programmatic creative is a valuable strategy... A consumer's entertainment choices are based on personal preference. Some watch sci-fi because they're drawn to futuristic stories; others watch documentaries because they like the depth and realistic angle. Our interests and tastes compel us to seek out additional content that fits these designated parameters, and programmatic creatives can deliver ads based on the same.[35]

You can read more on personalization in Chapter 16 and in the bonus online chapter entitled 'TV Channel Design in a Multiscreen World', available for download at: **www.koganpage.com/TheTVBrandBuilders**

– WILL IT WORK ON A PENCIL CASE? –

What turns a programme into a brand... into a culturally resonant force of nature with global reach, and enduring appeal? Clearly if there was an easy answer then the TV schedules would be packed with them. But there are some key factors, and one is this. If you look across the shows that fit that criterion, from *The Walking Dead* to *Top Gear*, they have all embraced the power of marketing from the first frame of the show to the last note of the credits. Marketing is not, and never will be, just about the trailers, the posters, the bought media. It begins with a title sequence, a theme tune, a logo. In the case of the current *Doctor Who* logo, it began with a superb bit of design thinking from two creatives, neither from a design background – Tony Pipes and Matt Rhodes. Like all good bits of creative thinking it was preceded by great planning and a tight brief. The job in 2009 for series five was to try to persuade a core boy audience to reappraise the show alongside the exponential growth in superhero movie franchises. We decided that a defining note of those shows – *Superman*, *Batman* – was that they had a logo you could draw on your pencil case. And so the letters 'D' and 'W' were sketched into the iconic TARDIS shape. A shape that now sits on books, top trumps cards, T-shirts and toys, from Dorking to Delhi.

It is hard to think of a successful drama brand in recent years that hasn't benefited from strong design work. As mentioned earlier, the use of double exposures in Elastic Studios's titles for *True Detective* did much to establish the overall tone of the show.[36] *Mad Men*'s 'Falling Man' and the way it resolves into its iconic silhouette image did more than anything to define a tone and style for the show.[37] Producer Cara McKenney told the specialist blog on

An early sketch of the Doctor Who *logo*
Source: Reproduced by permission of BBC

title design 'Art of the Title' that the idea itself came fully formed from creator Matthew Weiner:

> Matthew had a distinct point of view and came to us with a compelling brief: a man walks into an office building, enters his office, places his suitcase down and jumps out of the window.[38]

Two brands that have benefited from exceptional care and thought in the logo itself are the periodic table-referencing *Breaking Bad* and Fox's *24*. George Montgomery and Siren Creative created the iconic clock device and logo for *24* after showrunner Joel Surnow was looking for an analogue edge to a version of the '24' he had been using in his own early rough cuts of the pilot. Conceptually the sense of counting down, echoing the timer on a bomb in reverse, develops an urgent sense of anticipation at the outset. The unique real-time nature of the drama is established from the off. The strength of the brand can be seen in its pure unchanged state lasting for nine series, including spin-offs.[39]

Beyond logos, the best programme brands have creative assets that enable their host channel to embrace them in a wide variety of ways. As we will see in Chapter 10, ABC's 'House' campaign saw all of their programme talent living together – beautifully blending *Lost* and *Desperate Housewives*, for example.[40] *Doctor Who* has been integrated into BBC channel identities in myriad ways. Christmas trees decorated with mini TARDII and sonic screwdrivers dematerialized in 2015, a BBC '2' transformed into Davros's minion in the mid 1990s, David Tennant rode a TARDIS pulled by reindeer in another Christmas identity in 2009, and most surprisingly a Dalek rolled through Stansted Airport clutching a bag of duty free in a Christmas tie-in with comedy sketch show *Come Fly with Me*.[41]

Crucially and fortuitously one of the strengths of the BBC Wales drama team was that they understood that part of the enduring appeal of the *Doctor Who* brand was its ability not to take itself too seriously.

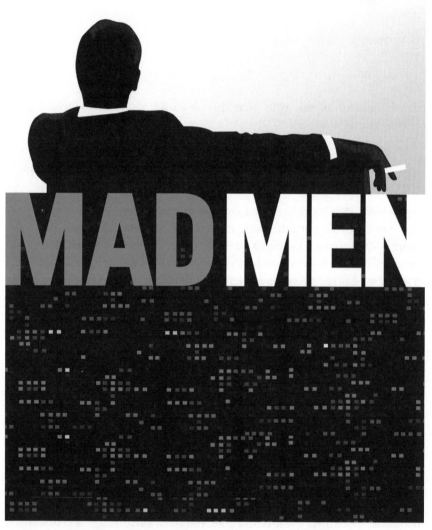

The iconic Mad Men *silhouette: season one key art*
Source: *Still taken from* Mad Men *provided through the courtesy of Lionsgate*

– RETURNING IN THE FALL –

Writing in *Broadcast* magazine in a customarily insightful piece about channel ratings, Stephen Price wrote the following:

> *Luther*'s return to BBC One was by no means a shoo-in, as series one began well but slipped dramatically. This second series defied this gravitational logic; Tuesday's opener was as strong as last May's launch episode of 5.6 million/25 per cent.[42]

As a seasoned student of drama ratings, and their typical erosion over time, Price appeared genuinely baffled that this change in the natural order could occur. To an observer of marketing, however, it was not a surprise. As discussed above, our second series trailer of *Luther* succeeded in capturing the nation's attention, bringing Idris Elba's powerful on-screen persona to prominence. Moreover it had significant marketing investment behind the creative idea. But compared with the costs of the series as a whole, and the risk of it continuing on a gradual ratings decline, the investment was miniscule, and the return on investment in those viewing figures palpable.

Experience suggests that launching the second series of dramas actually requires more promotional investment in creativity and airtime than the first. To begin with you don't have the initial press flurry around talent, the 'shock of the new' in feature pieces and PR, and second, an 'accepted wisdom' will have been established in the viewers' heads around the first series – was it a slow burn, a flash in the pan, a 'hard watch', or a 'mustn't miss'? In fact most of the people exposed to those opinions will not have actually seen the show for themselves, and so with a second series there is a chance to break those fragilely held opinions if the marketing campaign has sufficient standout.

Chris Spencer, responsible for launching second series for myriad HBO titles, explains that the network's deliberate strategy was to allow first seasons to 'find an audience' and settle in, before they committed marketing dollars behind specially shot trailers. From the tease shot on the darkened studio sets of *The Newsroom*,[43] to the theatrically staged tableaux of the *True Blood* shoot,[44] Chris and his team were given licence to tease and creatively explore in 'sophomore' runs far more than debut series. With *The Sopranos* season two in 2000, this sudden injection of marketing interest provided an interesting test of the showrunner's vision:

> The pressure was on – the *New York Times* had called the show 'the greatest work of American popular culture in the last 25 years' and we wanted to relaunch the show in style and with scope. We produced an enormous promo shoot over several days with the entire cast. Everything went beautifully; even Jim Gandolfini, not a big fan of promo chores, pitched in to make it a success. The edit process was fluid, the spots cut

almost effortlessly to land 'Family Redefined'.[45] I was supremely confident when I strode into David Chase's office with the finished results, feeling that I was about to receive a well-deserved pat on the head.

The silence that greeted it was uncomfortably long. I mean, LONG long. Then David said, 'What the hell is this? This is not my show.' True. But no amount of explaining could convince him that the show and the marketing for the show could be separate things.

I thought I would never try for another promo shoot again with *The Sopranos*, but when it came to the final episodes I had an idea that I couldn't let go of: Tony Soprano, alone in the Meadowlands of New Jersey, contemplating the end. A perfect metaphor, a man alone in a bleak landscape, one long tracking crane shot. We cut a cacophonous swell of show dialogue underneath the image.[46] I thought it was a solid piece, but remembering my last experience with David, it was a much more humble man who crept into his office (some seven years after that first encounter).

There was a shorter silence after this one finished.

'Better,' he said.[47]

Liz Dolan, CMO at Fox International Channels, acknowledges that for second and third seasons the balance of promotional focus might shift somewhat towards supporting a channel's overall positioning, referencing the bold work done for the launch of hit series *Wayward Pines*:

I think in the first season, the show has to be forward, you really have to make people interested in what's unique about it. With *Wayward Pines*, you see the Fox channel branding integrated, but the marketing, the on-air and everything else was designed to support the show brand, to create the idea that it was a provocative, unusual *Twin Peaks*-type mystery. After season one, when presumably the show identity is established, the channel brand needs to become the primary message, because you want to keep people on your channel. You want to make those two things inextricably linked, the show brand and the channel brand. In our case, we want them to know that the show lives on Fox and they should keep watching it here. Our challenge is that by the time season four launches, Netflix will have seasons one, two and three.[48]

Key art for Fox's mystery thriller Wayward Pines *Source: Reproduced by permission of Fox.*
WAYWARD PINES © *2014 Bluebush Productions, LLC. All Rights Reserved.*

For returning series the degree of standout needed can be harder to achieve using programme material given preconceptions and familiarity of the story-world: not impossible, but harder. What the *Luther* campaign, ABC's *Desperate Housewives* Juicy trailer and many other examples, from *Being Human* and *Ashes to Ashes* in the UK to *Boardwalk Empire* and *Big Love* in the United States, all managed to do was to present a second or third or fourth series as unmissable, event television. HBO's award-winning 2012 trailer for season three of *Boardwalk Empire* shows Nucky Thompson surrounded by the ghosts of his past, crowding in on him, generating a tangible sense of a show building to a climax.[49]

Furthermore, as John Varvi of FX Networks notes, if you keep in step with your audience you can increasingly use more subtle and sophisticated signifiers within your marketing:

> So in the first two or three seasons of *Sons of Anarchy*, we spell out the title, but then we're able to just use 'Sons' and then we're able to say 'S.O.A.' and then we're able to just show a skull from The Reaper, and the audience not only gets it but they appreciate that we understand the show in the same context that they do.[50]

Subtle shorthand for an established show: Sons of Anarchy *final season key art*
Source: Reproduced by permission of FX Networks, LLC

Stephen Price's suggested gravitational logic would have resulted in Luther series two launching with 1.5 million fewer viewers than it actually achieved and, for a public service channel or commercial broadcaster, 1.5 million extra viewers is certainly worth investing in.

It all comes back to story. In John Yorke's definitive book on screenwriting, *Into the Woods*, he quotes Aaron Sorkin: 'The real rules are the rules of drama, the rules that Aristotle talks about.'[51]

Ultimately every drama discussed in this chapter shares one truth. They all have a narrative urge that begs you to turn the page, to stay tuned in, to discover what happens next. Or in the box-set era, to watch just one more. The role of a trailer is to crystallize that need into a compelling 30 seconds. Two final examples. For the launch of *House of Saddam*, a BBC drama around the last days of the dictator's family in Baghdad, the creative director Mina Patel felt the need to move the audience's preconceptions away from the geopolitical lens through which Iraq was inevitably seen – to make it instead a story about family and power. To achieve this the creative team took a single photographic still of the cast and, through clever post-production, showed Saddam's family slowly and disconcertingly melting.[52]

The particular skill is when an audience knows how a story will end, convincing them to watch for the manner of the telling.

In contrast, drama marketing at its purest: at the end of season one of Sorkin's *The West Wing*, President Bartlett and his team leave a town hall meeting, to be met by a hail of bullets from hidden gunmen. As staffers are flung to the ground, we simply hear the radio of a Secret Service agent asking: 'Who's been hit, who's been hit?' The quintessential cliffhanger. The page-turn moment to end all page-turn moments. So when NBC trailed season two, the only reminder needed was that an answer was imminent: 'America has been asking one question all summer. Who's been hit?'[53]

NEXT

★ 'What type of comedy is it?'

★ Picking 30 seconds that work.

★ The circus of the earth.

★ 'Precision Engineered Comedy'.

★ Snuffleupaguses.

★ The best exit line.

LATER

★ 'Never Stop Asking'.

★ Beardy men fixing cars.

★ Teresa Giudice's pancakes.

NOTES

1 *The Big Bang Theory*, 'The Commitment Determination' (2015) season eight, episode 24, Warner Bros. Television, 7 May

2 *Private Eye* (2015) **1393**

3 Stephanie Gibbons, president of marketing, digital media marketing and on-air promotions, FX Networks, interview 26 June 2015

4 Willens, M (2015) [accessed 10 August 2015] Why So Many Writers Now Move Between TV And Theatre, *The Atlantic*, 3 January [Online] http://www.theatlantic.com/entertainment/archive/2015/01/why-so-many-tv-writers-turn-to-theater-and-vice-versa/384133/

5 Daily Motion [accessed 2 March 2016] The Fast Show – Monkfish [Online] http://www.dailymotion.com/video/x2tmarq

6 Watkins, J (2013) *The 100 Greatest Advertisements 1852–1958: Who wrote them and what they did*, Dover Publications, New York

7 BBC One (2006) [accessed 10 August 2015] Doctor Who Series 1 Boxset Easter Egg Trailer [Online] https://www.youtube.com/watch?v=hQINlUB3Kww

8 BBC One (2007) [accessed 10 August 2015] Doctor Who – Series 1 Trailer 2005 [Online] https://www.youtube.com/watch?v=1hQyujVvRcY

9 Martyn (2011) [accessed 10 August 2015] Eccleston Explains Why He Left Doctor Who, *Bad Wilf*, 20 July [Online] http://badwilf.com/eccleston-explains-why-he-left-doctor-who/

10 ABC (2006) [accessed 10 August 2015] Desperate Housewives – Juicy Promo Season 2 [Online] https://www.youtube.com/watch?v=XBRkgnbtb8E

11 Red Bee [accessed 2 March 2016] BBC One Mistresses [Online] https://www.youtube.com/watch?v=CJFqplnO5Ag&index=78&list=PLDsg58IUh5wSL0PL9GLVpuYRGnrTHCvfk

12 Scott, W (1887) *The Poetical Works of Sir Walter Scott*, Wildside Press LLC, Holicong PA, p 138

13 BBC (2011) [accessed 3 November 2015] Luther – New Series 2011 Trailer – BBC One [Online] https://www.youtube.com/watch?v=am0Ujh_0GO4

14 Chris Spencer, former senior vice president, HBO Promotions, interview 26 October 2015

15 Stephanie Gibbons, president of marketing, digital media marketing and on-air promotions, FX Networks, interview 26 June 2015

16 Stephanie Gibbons, president of marketing, digital media marketing and on-air promotions, FX Networks, interview 26 June 2015

17 McKee, R (2010) [accessed 3 November 2015] Big Think Interview with Robert McKee [Online] http://bigthink.com/videos/big-think-interview-with-robert-mckee

18 Pulver, A (2015) [accessed 10 August 2015] Jurassic World Director Criticised For Revealing Too Much Of Film, *Guardian*, 7 July 7 [Online] http://www.theguardian.com/film/2015/jul/07/jurassic-world-director-colin-trevorrow-criticises-trailer-showing-too-much

19 *Mad Men*, 'Smoke Gets In Your Eyes' (2007) season one, episode one, AMC, July 19 [Online] https://www.youtube.com/watch?v=LfuMhXcLa-Q

20 HBO (2010) [accessed 10 August 2015] Boardwalk Empire: Trailer #1 (HBO) [Online] https://www.youtube.com/watch?v=e6z71l6HQwQ

21 AMC (2014) [accessed 10 August 2015] Mad Men Season 7 Trailer [Online] https://www.youtube.com/watch?v=jkl2vWAwA0I

22 Movieweb [accessed 2 March 2016] Final Mad Men Poster Released [Online] http://movieweb.com/mad-men-season-7-poster-final-episodes/

23 Linda Schupack, executive vice president of marketing, AMC, interview 11 June 2015

24 Channel 4 (2009) [accessed 10 August 2015] Lost David La Chapelle, Trailer (Full) [Online] https://www.youtube.com/watch?v=bQSSyRbVqos

25 HBO (2013) [accessed 10 August 2015] True Detective: Official Trailer (HBO) [Online] www.youtube.com/watch?v=fVQUcaO4AvE

26 BBC One (2009) [accessed 10 August 2015] Torchwood: Children Of Earth Trailer – BBC One [Online] https://www.youtube.com/watch?v=qtYmtQfzueM

27 Kehe, J and Palmer, K M (2013) [accessed 10 August 2015] Secrets Of A Trailer Guru: How This Guy Gets You To The Movies, *Wired*, 18 June [Online] http://www.wired.com/2013/06/online-trailers-mark-woollen/

28 Garrett, S (2012) [accessed 10 August 2015] The Art Of First Impressions: How To Cut A Movie Trailer, *Filmmaker Magazine*, 13 January [Online] http://filmmakermagazine.com/37093-first-impressions/#.VcjeI_lVhBc

29 Davis, J (2009) [accessed 10 August 2015] Get With The Programme, *Guardian*, 15 February [Online] http://www.theguardian.com/music/2009/feb/15/television-music-skins; see also https://www.youtube.com/watch?v=Ho69_sCkwyI

30 Stephanie Gibbons, president of marketing, digital media marketing and on-air promotions, FX Networks, interview 26 June 2015

31 Red Bee [accessed 2 March 2016] The Virgin Queen Trailer [Online] https://www.youtube.com/watch?v=cEGCzTMmoGU

32 Showtime (2013) [accessed 10 August 2015] House Of Lies: Season 1 Trailer [Online] https://www.youtube.com/watch?v=pNLlHYJnj8I

33 Lynch, J (2015) [accessed 10 August 2015] How Fox's Marketing Fanned The Flames Of Empire, One Of The Biggest New Shows In Years, *Adweek*, 29 January [Online] http://www.adweek.com/news/television/how-foxs-marketing-fanned-flames-empire-one-biggest-new-shows-years-162612

34 Lynch, J (2015) [accessed 10 August 2015] How Fox's Marketing Fanned The Flames Of Empire, One Of The Biggest New Shows In Years, *Adweek*, 29 January [Online] http://www.adweek.com/news/television/how-foxs-marketing-fanned-flames-empire-one-biggest-new-shows-years-162612

35 Celtra (2015) [accessed 10 August 2015] Why Entertainment Marketers Should Be Flocking to Programmatic, *Adweek*, 14 April [Online] http://www.adweek.com/brandshare/what-entertainment-marketers-stand-gain-programmatic-164020

36 Clair, P (2014) [accessed 3 November 2015] HBO's True Detective – Main Title Sequence [Online] https://vimeo.com/84017154

37 Woods, C (2009) [accessed 3 November 2015] Mad Men Title Sequence [Online vide] https://vimeo.com/6380514

38 McKenney, C; Fuller, S and Gardner, M (2011) Mad Men, *Art of the Title*, 19 September [Online] http://www.artofthetitle.com/title/mad-men/

39 Seacad Media (2014) [accessed 3 November 2015] 24 Opening Sequence + Previously on 24 [Online] https://www.youtube.com/watch?v=yKJQ8jJ4dI0

40 Rue005 (2009) [accessed 3 November 2015] ABC House – Teri Hatcher [Desperate Housewives] & Matthew Fox [Lost] [Online] https://www.youtube.com/watch?v=LgsjhxFKhBM

41 Red Bee [accessed 2 March 2016] BBC One Christmas Ident – Come Fly With Me And Dalek [Online] https://www.youtube.com/watch?v=t9T1iRfPsP4

42 Price, S (2011) [accessed 10 August 2015] Sun Fails To Shine On ITV, *Broadcast Now*, 23 June [Online] http://www.broadcastnow.co.uk/sun-fails-to-shine-on-itv/5029050.article

43 HBO (2013) [accessed 3 November 2015] The Newsroom: Season 2 – Tease (HBO) [Online] https://www.youtube.com/watch?v=5EP7aBZ2DuI

44 Sick (2009) [accessed 3 November 2015] True Blood Season 2 Trailer [Online] https://www.youtube.com/watch?v=RsAhDweVTBk

45 Sopranos Addict (2014) [accessed 3 November 2015] The Sopranos Season 2 Trailer [Online] https://www.youtube.com/watch?v=NNZG9vYU950

46 INFLUX Magazine (2013) [accessed 3 November 2015] The Sopranos Final Season 6 Official Trailer With James Gandolfini [Online] https://www.youtube.com/watch?v=ch-X-9J73aQ

47 Chris Spencer, former senior vice president, HBO Promotions, interview 26 October 2015

48 Liz Dolan, chief marketing officer, Fox International Channels, interview 11 June 2015

49 HBO (2012) [accessed 10 August 2015] Promotion, Marketing And Design Award Winner – Dramatic Program Spot [Online] https://www.youtube.com/watch?v=c-ksXpic0JA

50 John Varvi, executive vice president, on-air promotions, FX Networks (FX, FXX, FXM, FXNOW), interview 26 June 2015

51 Yorke, J (2013) *Into the Woods: How stories work and why we tell them*, Penguin Books, London

52 Red Bee Media (2009) [accessed 3 November 2015] BBC House of Saddam [Online] http://uk.adforum.com/award-organization/6650374/showcase/2009/ad/34446801

53 MTVCops (2012) [accessed 3 November 2015] 2000 NBC Promos: West Wing Season Premiere, Titans, Yasmine Bleeth, Victoria Principal [Online] https://www.youtube.com/watch?v=SrNSwiaWp9I

CHAPTER EIGHT

TIMING AND OTHER SECRETS

A guide to promoting TV comedy

Tim: *Well, for starters, I think we could really 'up' the comedy.*

Beverly: *Oh my gosh, if you could get it up that would be wonderful!*

EPISODES[1]

– THE HARDEST PART –

Legendary comedy writer Laurence Marks tells the story in an interview with the *Telegraph* newspaper that, on their first morning together as professional comedy writers, his partner Maurice Gran said: 'It's half past nine. I suppose we'd better go upstairs and make 15 million people laugh.'[2]

If you ask any writer who has attempted both disciplines – to make someone cry or to make them laugh – from Peter Shaffer to Aaron Sorkin, they will all tell you that it is infinitely easier to make someone cry.

The same is true of the difference between editing a trailer for a drama and a comedy. In fact we would go so far as to say that comedy is without doubt the most difficult programme genre to promote.

It is for this reason that it is often advisable to try to avoid complexity of messaging. Marketers who are keen to establish 'what type of comedy' a programme is, or 'how it reflects and touches on important national concerns', should be told politely and firmly that the trailer has one simple and single-minded mission, which in 30 seconds will be hard enough: make people laugh.

In a similar context, Yan Elliott, creative director of Fabula, writer of many of the hilarious Orange Wednesday Gold Spot ads, told *Campaign* magazine:

We have been involved in many conversations with brands concerning 'What sort of funny are we?' This always makes me laugh. I tend to picture Eric Morecambe or Seth MacFarlane sitting in a room procrastinating over what style of funny they want to be: 'Am I belly-laugh funny, or more of a warm, knowing wit?'[3]

Steve North, the general manager of UK channel Dave, agrees that the simpler the solution when trailing comedy, the better:

> People are often reticent about committing to a new piece of comedy... I might be offended, I might not find it funny... so they don't give it a go, they often wait to be reassured by other people. If you then layer marketing on top that doesn't really highlight what the show is giving you, you just make it even harder for an audience to come into it. I'm always a fan of a clip-based promo that just says look, here's a funny joke from the show, here's a little moment that shows you the kind of humour and scenarios to expect. But it's hard because it's so subjective.[4]

Walter Levitt, chief marketing officer of Comedy Central in the United States, has the same approach:

> One of the things we often talk about here is trying not to step on the comedy of the content, in other words not trying to out-comedy the comedy in the marketing... Often the best way to showcase a piece of comedic content is to put it out there and show it to people and use the content as the marketing... As an industry we like to try to reinvent the wheel and do our own thing but sometimes the magic formula we have found is simply to show the funniest moments... and let the comedy play out.[5]

In short, no one will watch a comedy for rational reasons, for curiosity or for broadening the mind. They will watch it if the marketing has made them laugh. Period. So why is it so hard?

– CRIMES AGAINST COMEDY –

Jennifer Saunders developed an almost pathological dislike of the teams responsible for trailing her programmes, from *French and Saunders* through *Absolutely Fabulous* to *Jam and Jerusalem*. None of those involved really knew what they had done to provoke her ire, which got so bad it was a subject she regularly brought up in interviews and, we seem to recall, she even name-checked the marketing department in a derogatory fashion in one of her shows. What caused this degree of animosity is lost in the mists of time, but we strongly suspect it would be on account of an early creative team committing one of two sins. Revealing a key gag 'before its time', or ruining a gag by meddling with the timing.

Let's examine why both of these crimes occur.

The fact that many programme makers are reluctant to let their best material be 'thrown away' in a trailer is on the face of it baffling. As fans who knew every word of every Monty Python sketch off by heart, it is safe for us to assert that the best laughs stand repeated viewing. Yet many programme makers think an audience should only see their show exactly as they constructed it, with the reveals occurring in the exact context they were created in. Jennifer Saunders falling down the stairs in *Ab Fab* is always funny, even as a stand-alone 10-second clip (see: **https://www.youtube.com/watch?v=OhFt7HsseNg**),[6] but when carefully built up to within the dramatic arc of the whole episode then clearly it hits higher notes.

So why is comedy so difficult a genre to promote? A primary cause is the very nature of shorter time lengths and durations and what they do to the natural rhythm of comedy. What makes a joke funny is as much about the time the scene takes to play out, or the elaborate set-up over multiple scenes, as it is about the actual punchline itself. Promo makers who don't understand this will hack feedlines from payoffs, jokes from set-ups and wonder why an executive producer is furious with them, when all they have done is clearly include the line that appears to get all the laughs.

Some comedies are written with a more machine-gun-like joke delivery, or have a high preponderance of visual jokes, pratfalls and one-liners. Take *Friends* or *Seinfeld* in the United States for instance, or *Miranda* and *The Inbetweeners* in the UK. Others built over time on catchphrases and the nature of repetition, like *The Fast Show* or *Father Ted*, also make much easier edits.

All of these shows are gifts to the creatives and channels from E4 to Comedy Central in the UK, TBS to TV Land in the United States, have long exploited their repeatability both in the schedule and in the numerous ways that the same material can be cut up and remixed to give a channel's particular take on them.

So how should creatives handle shows where the comedy is more paced and more reliant on character – say *Peep Show*, *Louie*, *The Office* (on either side of the Atlantic), *Rev.* and *Parks and Recreation*? One firm recommendation is to pick a scene and let it play in its entirety. Even the slightest inclination to trim the pacing will rightly incur the wrath of the production team. Pick 30 seconds that work, and as long as it's funny that is enough. Similarly, marketing briefs that ask you to name-check or face-check multiple cast members will have to be firmly managed. With comedy there is no deader hand than a montage of gurning faces and head turns from characters.

– THIS TIME NEXT YEAR WE'LL BE MILLIONAIRES –

So, for all these reasons, it might be best to think on select occasions about constructing a specially shot conceptual trailer for comedy. Creatives working on promoting such a range of comedies inevitably become mimics and magpies, able to turn their writing style to copy that of the talent they are promoting. Frequently, all this will achieve is to give the programme team a draft for them to improve on, but in some rare and celebrated instances it will be deemed perfect. See the section on *The Simpsons* later in this chapter for one such case study.

When writer John Sullivan first brought back *Only Fools and Horses*, the UK's most successful sitcom of all time, after a five-year break from the screens, he was very reluctant to release any of the material. This was partly due to the reasons outlined above, but also because the plot very quickly revealed that the Trotter family – whom we last saw in 1996 becoming millionaires – had lost all their wealth. Moreover, in the intervening years the archive episodes of the show were being regularly featured in repeats both on the BBC and its co-owned digital channel UK Gold, and thus the need to stress the newness of the material was paramount. So, how could we make a splash, remind the viewers of the point in the plot and not show any footage?

We decided that a single visual would do the job. The trailer opened on the Trotters' most famous prop – their iconic three-wheeler yellow van – and slowly pulled out to reveal... more and more and more of the van, which we had actually turned into an extraordinary stretch three-wheeler limo, parked in front of the casino in Monte Carlo. In a single 20 seconds the premise of the show was landed, with a memorable visual gag, which in its originality promised a new series.

Walter Levitt of Comedy Central talks about two further situations in which it can make sense for marketers to create original promotional content: when launching a new show and, conversely, when the audience has a strong affinity with a well-established comedy. On the first of those points he says:

> When we have a brand new comedic voice that we're trying to introduce, often we need to shoot something custom... When it's someone brand new who you have never heard of, just showing them already in context in their piece of content, in their show, is sometimes a step ahead of the consumer and so sometimes we need to start from the beginning, start from 'Here's who this person is and here's why they're funny.'[7]

The Trotters' stretch three-wheeler promoting a returning series of Only Fools and Horses   *Source: Reproduced by permission of BBC*

To illustrate the potential role of shooting a conceptual trailer for an established series, Walter talks about a campaign produced by Comedy Central for the fifth season of its sitcom *Workaholics*. Safe in the knowledge that fans knew and loved the characters (college roommates evolving towards adulthood), the Comedy Central marketing team wanted to create something 'fun and celebratory and, most importantly, memorable',[8] so they shot a pastiche of an action-movie trailer:

> We shot for three days in the desert with the three stars in every typical action movie trailer set-up, from a shoot-out to fight scenes, and we cut together this trailer that had nothing to do with what was actually in the show but that was clearly highly comedic and clearly said to the fans 'We understand that you love these guys, you love these characters, you love the show,' and the punchline of the trailer was 'This season on *Workaholics* none of this happens.'[9]

Comedy Central's action movie trailer for season five of Workaholics

Sometimes necessity can be the mother of invention. Channel 4's in-house creative team, 4Creative, found themselves faced with limited access to their star performer, Alan Carr, and no access to his guests. They therefore imagined that Alan had been chatty all his life, rabbiting away about anything and everything as a very young child, and as a result the line 'Born to Chat' emerged. The result, with incredibly sophisticated post-production hidden behind a low-fi Super 8 look and feel, saw a baby Alan proving hilariously garrulous.[10]

A 'baby Alan Carr' in Channel 4's 'Born to Chat' promo   Source: © Channel 4 Television

Even the notoriously controlling, detail-minded Louis CK has encouraged original material in his marketing campaigns. FX launched season four with a promo on its Facebook page: 'Louie. Everybody's doing it.' The black-and-white video features fans in various spots around New York City, singing the theme song... or attempting to sing the theme tune might be more accurate.[11]

From a different end of the comedy spectrum, Noel Fielding and Julian Barratt from cult show *The Mighty Boosh* launched their third series for BBC Three via cinema commercials in which their on-screen selves squabbled over the very direction of the trailer, climaxing in a phalanx of glitter-ball-headed guitarists accompanying Noel Fielding in a glam rock riot.[12]

– DECONSTRUCT AND RECONSTRUCT –

All of the above challenges (and more) probably weighed heavily on the marketing and creative team at FX Networks in the United States, when they were told that their channel FXX had bought the syndication rights to the longest running, and undoubtedly most consistently funny, US sitcom ever: *The Simpsons*. Moreover, a show that had already had its fair share of original marketing around the world, with Sky One's remake of the title sequence as a live action film directed by Chris Palmer standing out as just one highlight.[13]

As Stephanie Gibbons, who leads the FX Networks marketing team, told us:

> With *The Simpsons*, we had the advantage of working with a property that was already branded so strongly that it completely unburdened us from having to deal with that lens on the work. We knew going in that this brand had countless marketers and creatives who had worked on it over a 24-year period. We were really daunted by all the amazing work that had been done against it, and it was clearly a brand that was part of society, both reflected and mirrored. So our goal was, first and foremost, to have fun. It's *The Simpsons*. We weren't marketing a prison, we were working on a comedy, something that is joyful and ironic and has multiple generations of people who have either grown up with it or are being exposed to it for the first time.[14]

The platform for an exceptional campaign was well laid with the tactical scheduling decision to play every single episode of the series back to back, leading swiftly to the campaign line: Every. Simpsons. Ever.

First meetings with creators Matt Groening and Jim Brooks, whilst initially terrifying, gave the FX team huge licence with a one-word brief from Brooks that the work had to be 'revolutionary'. Allied to FX's positioning of 'Fearless' (see Chapter 5), this demanded really bold work, and the campaign did not disappoint. Based on the premise that the show was so culturally resonant that it could be reduced down to a colour, an ear, a string of pearls, and still be instantly recognizable, the theme of deconstructing and reconstructing those base elements led to joyful off- and on-air imagery, from the Simpsons reimagined in the style of Picasso to the FXX logo itself, which, as Steve Viola, FX's SVP of broadcast design, told *Promax Daily Brief*, 'literally merged the deconstructed Simpsons brand with FXX branding'.[15]

From that brief, FX threw open the doors to a multitude of collaborators. As Stephanie Gibbons reasons:

> It couldn't have one piece of key art, it had to have 20, it had to have a million different iterations because it was like the circus of the earth... We had so much to celebrate, so many sub-franchises, so many characters, so many tools, so essentially it was a sawed-off shotgun of joy.[16]

The approach avoided traditional 'matching luggage' marketing and let myriad TV, web, social and outdoor ideas fly. John Varvi of FX explains:

With a lot of the graphic designers who grew up with the show, when they asked 'What are the parameters?' we were able to say, 'Well, there are none.' We couldn't stop them from sending us stuff.[17]

The hero trailer was again based on those early conversations between the FX marketing team, Groening and Brooks. When the creators were told that the channel was going to run all 552 episodes consecutively, Groening exclaimed that people's heads were going to explode. The creative team took that apocalyptic scenario one stage further, with a dystopian vision of what the world would look like after the marathon screening. In a phrase: 'We're all gonna die.'

An apocalyptic vision of the outcome of FXX running 'Every. Simpsons. Ever'
Source: Reproduced by permission of FX Networks, LLC

Perhaps uniquely for a campaign of this size, The FX marketing team created a vast amount of these assets in advance of the campaign being signed off by Groening and Brooks. Working like an agency themselves, they gambled and spent 16 weeks preparing the work for the pitch of their lives. John Varvi says:

When we met and presented, basically we just opened up our veins and said 'We hope you like the blood you're getting,' because in the back of our minds we were thinking, 'If you don't like what we're giving you, we don't know where we're going to go next.' It was everything we had.[18]

– OFFICIALLY VERY FUNNY –

It is of course possible to define your channel's approach to comedy with a campaign that focuses on your own brand's specific credentials. TBS in the

United States decided to zig away from the dramatic direction taken by most of its general entertainment competitors with a brand campaign under the simplest of slogans: Very Funny.

Possibly inspired by stablemate TNT's successful staking out of the drama category, and a precursor to the repositioning of truTV that we explored in Chapter 3, Turner's Steven R Koonin told the *New York Times*: 'In cable, unless you stand for something, you're doomed... TBS will be for young adults who want television to make them laugh.'[19]

The move, in June 2004, saw the channel sacrificing some of its slate of bankable dramas such as *Little House on the Prairie* in favour of sitcom reruns, such as *Friends*, and theatrical release comedy films. To flag the new focus TBS launched a high-profile and award-winning campaign – 800-TBS-FUNNY – in which the channel claimed the highest ground possible of being the national arbiter of what was funny. Written by the ad agency Publicis New York, with an estimated production and media spend of $50 million, the campaign was set in a TBS call centre that the nation would call to clarify whether they could laugh at a particular colleague, or situation. According to a case study from the online publisher Warc:

> The campaign won awards, and critics in such publications as *Adweek* and Advertising Age's *Creativity* described the television spots as 'inspired', 'verbally adroit', 'outrageously funny' and 'one of the best TV promo campaigns in the history of the genre'.[20]

In the United States, where the rights to re-air successful series are almost as fiercely fought over as the best original series ideas, the arrival of a famous show to your channel can be brand defining in itself. But the best marketing will still allow you to talk about what you stand for.

When *Modern Family* moved to USA Network for syndication and windowing earlier series, the channel went out of its way at its advertising 'Upfronts' presentation to showcase the news. They specially filmed the cast in brilliantly funny remakes of many famous scenes from the show, as if they had been made under the more permissive censorship guidelines that govern cable channels. Or, perhaps, what the cast imagined those cable channels would permit. A truly 'not safe for work' version indeed. To give you one example, Phil Dunphy shows his kids into the newly acquired RV, and when his wife Claire says, 'I know where this is going,' Phil retorts, 'You, me, two hookers and a bag of smack.'[21]

BBC Two has twice earmarked airtime and production budgets to establish its credentials as the UK's leading generator of original comedy. The first campaign under the tagline Pedigree Comedy (drawing on its unparalleled heritage from the 1960s onwards) paired the channel's leading talent, including Catherine Tate, David Mitchell and Stephen Fry, with a fluffy and mischievous number '2' (a precursor to the '2' character we revived for the channel's 50th anniversary, as we discussed in Chapter 6). Filmed with complex puppetry, the channel was brave enough to allow its brand icon to frantically mount comedian Rob Brydon's leg in a series of sexual thrusts while Brydon wearily told someone on the end of the phone that it was 'hard to say when he'd be done'.[22]

Three years later, under pressure from BBC Three (as a generator of edgy young comedy), and from E4, Comedy Central and Dave (increasingly owning US sitcoms and talent from the stand-up circuit respectively), BBC Two carved out another distinctive position, under creative director James de Zoete: Precision Engineered Comedy. Comedy that was written and performed with true craftsmanship. Brilliantly playing against this line, Peter Capaldi, star of savagely satirical political comedy *The Thick of It*, talked eloquently about how he saw himself as a Shakespearean wordsmith, before launching into an entirely bleeped out Malcolm Tucker tirade of filth.[23] Satirist Charlie Brooker even took part, putting aside his long-held suspicion of all things promotional. Indeed it was the second time he actively played against type. Memorably, in 2007, he promoted his *Screenwipe* series (in which a running bête noire of Brooker's was continuity announcers who talk over the credits of programmes) by wandering in front of BBC Four's idents, dismantling the very ident itself while arguing with the continuity announcer: 'See? You don't like it when it's done to you.'[24]

Finally, Dave itself has developed perhaps the most consistent and distinctive tone of voice within the comedy genre in the UK. Sardonic, wordy, dry and witty, every trailer script, continuity announcement or menu slide is written with the brand in mind first, the show second. The overall success

Charlie Brooker invading BBC Four's idents to promote his TV review show Screenwipe   *Source: Reproduced by permission of BBC*

of the Dave brand was discussed in Chapter 3, but within our team the secret to much of Dave's success was a combination of the use of virtual 'table writing' techniques borrowed from the United States, where the strongest gag had to survive intense competition, and spontaneity and improvisation on the day. Regular collaborators such as comedian Jake Yapp also helped shape the tone of continuity and trailers alike.

– THE SECRET... –

As with feature films, the best editors are not noticed. The best cuts are invisible, or so clever that it is only an expert eye who will spot the subtle genius that lies behind where a splice is one frame right or left.

Perhaps one of the finest examples of the kind was for a double bill of programmes on UKTV's channel Gold: *The Catherine Tate Show* and *The Vicar of Dibley*. Gold is a cable and satellite home to a lot of the BBC's finest comedies and, increasingly, new commissions. Often the challenge when promoting Gold, however, is to bring a freshness to old material and encourage reappraisal of comedies that you may have either missed or loved the first time around.

Our creative who worked on the campaign, Richard Senior, brilliantly cut together a conversation between Tate's teenage nightmare character Lauren: 'Miss. Are you the Vicar of Dibley?' and Dawn French playing the eponymous vicar. Flipping some shots so that the head angles were perfect for the conversation, and cutting so beautifully to the music, as Lauren reaches her ultimately cutting comment 'Do you like Cliff Richard, Miss?' the song 'Devil Woman' bursts into life.[25] This is a trailer that somehow gave space to both of its component parts to be funny, but also created a piece of genuine original hilarity on top. The cuts, the beats, the pauses, the looks, the speed, the timing. In the end, as the old joke has it, the secret to great comedy is always...

...the timing.

– IF YOU WORK IN MARKETING, KILL YOURSELF –

We discuss in Chapter 9 how there is an inherent tension between the editorial need for explanation and balance versus marketing's needs to be reductive. Similarly there can be a tension within comedy for shows that seek to prick the bubble of hype, gloss or 'marketing speak', and which then need those same tactics to promote them. Many a creative has the words of someone they revered as a near god – comedian Bill Hicks – ringing in their ears:

By the way if anyone here is in advertising or marketing... kill yourself. It's just a little thought; I'm just trying to plant seeds. Maybe one day they'll take root – I don't know. You try, you do what you can.[26]

The solution inevitably has to be found by genuinely attempting to promote the programme, whilst remaining true to its central, single-minded premise. In other words, satirizing the very act of advertising can sometimes lead to the campaign itself.

The Chaser's War on Everything was a hugely popular and wildly controversial satirical show produced by the ABC in Australia. A regular thorn in the side of the Australian government, and frequently courting controversy and indeed even being arrested for some of their stunts and sketches, the *Chaser* team had a brilliantly imaginative approach to marketing: notably in 2007 when they announced that they had 'demanded' launch posters for their series in their contract from the ABC, but claimed that the network was honouring it by buying the cheapest billboard sites in the world.

Publicity shots began to emerge of poster sites promoting 'The Chaser', as it was known, in Iraq, Estonia, Iceland and India. In Iceland the site bought was in front of the least popular tourist attraction, a very drab glacier, and in India the sign was hand-painted in Bollywood tradition, by a firm that

One of 'the world's cheapest billboards' promoting ABC's The Chaser's War on Everything *in Valsad, India*

Source: Reproduced by permission of Australian Broadcasting Corporation

assured an 80 per cent 'likeness to the subjects'. Shooting down those who were quick to shout 'Photoshop', Reuters sent out a reporter to assert the validity of the programme's promotional effort in Baghdad, and Diyar Outdoor in Iraq supplied an invoice charging the ABC a grand $US150 for each billboard.

All told, a superb case story of satirizing artists' promotional demands, the financial straits of a national broadcaster and even the way in which many international countries' cultures were covered in Western media, all while gaining masses of column inches in the newspapers and huge volumes of online hits (on the website you could even watch webcam coverage of some of the live sites). Interestingly the whole campaign was created in a very traditional manner by an advertising agency – The Glue Society.[27]

In the UK, a country with a rich satirical tradition on television, the same dilemma frequently appears. BBC Two's *W1A*, a series that ruthlessly skewers the inner workings of the BBC, has at its heart a monstrous parody of marketing in the form of Jessica Hynes's brilliant creation Siobhan Sharpe, supremo of agency Perfect Curve. 'Siobhan Sharpe' filmed several trailers for the second series with us, spending at one point five minutes discussing the branding of the broadcaster she is airing on:

> Future forward you free yourselves of visual clutter totally, like logos, schmogos, instead you become one of the first brands in the world, like, that's *in the world*, to have an audio logo and we're halfway there already with 'Beeb'... but where we're heading is like 'Beeep'... it's way cool... 'BeeeeP'... in branding terms you've got like blind loyalty from the get go, which is like 'slap me a dunk'.[28]

(For another sample see the epigraph to Chapter 4.)

– TAKING THE MARKETING ON THE ROAD –

An interesting new marketing approach has been tried a couple of times recently with comedy shows in the United States: taking the stars of the show out to live comedy venues. Showtime, recognizing the skills of the cast of its crossover comedy drama hit *House of Lies*, booked them into LA's Upright Citizens Brigade Theatre for long-form improvisation theatre shows. Taking it one step further and with a wholly unknown programme was the launch of NBC's *Undateable*. Bill Lawrence, a comedy showrunner with impressive credentials, explained to the Grantland website how the idea of a live comedy tour was born partly out of desperation to get noticed. They knew it would be hard for NBC to launch the show straight after the Olympics where it was airing:

It's tricky for networks nowadays – they can't just air promos and hope people see them. The landscape is too vast. Luckily, our cast is composed of stand-up comedians... so we decided to use them in a grass-roots effort... We will go on a national comedy tour... take *Undateable* to the people, and we shall win them over.[29]

It's easy to picture the meeting where this felt like a good idea. But, as Lawrence goes on to explain, the metrics of TV viewership are not quite that simple, and nudging the ratings dial requires more than a few live dates. Indeed those TV spots that he was so concerned about being ineffective might still be the best hope that the show has:

Here's the utter stupidity behind a 'grass-roots' promotional tour. The Nielsen ratings decide your show's fate. Roughly 30,000 homes represent what the entire country is watching. I've never once met a Nielsen family. They are like Snuffleupaguses to me. I don't believe they are real. This tour will not 'reach' one of them.[30]

– GO OUT ON A LAUGH –

As other chapters have also reinforced, great marketing is ultimately about reduction and impact. So what better note to end on than probably the finest, cleverest reduction of a comedy show. And also the best exit line. Channel 4 brilliantly promoted the last-ever episode of *Friends* with a poster campaign featuring the distinctive logo for the show, against a funereal black backdrop, with the seven letters reworked into the simplest of anagrams. ENDS. FRI.[31]

A perfect send-off: Channel 4's press and poster campaign for the final episode of Friends
Source: © Channel 4 Television

NEXT

- ★ Finding an angle.
- ★ The thirst to be first.
- ★ Chasing tornadoes.
- ★ Monstering.
- ★ The democratization of news.
- ★ The NewsWall.

LATER

- ★ A megaphone, a rose and big red balls.
- ★ Beware of things made in October.
- ★ The floating Gallifreyan fob watch.

NOTES

1 *Episodes* (2015) [accessed 5 August 2015] season four, episode five, Showtime, 8 February

2 Marks, L (2011) [accessed 5 August 2015] Tragedy Is Easy – It's Comedy That's Hard, *Telegraph*, 22 January [Online] http://www.telegraph.co.uk/culture/8276048/Tragedy-is-easy-its-comedy-thats-hard.html

3 Connell, R and Woodward, C (2012) [accessed 5 August 2015] Kings Of Comedy, *Campaign Magazine*, 18 October [Online] http://www.campaignlive.co.uk/article/1155310/kings-comedy

4 Steve North, general manager, entertainment, UKTV, interview 26 June 2015

5 Walter Levitt, executive vice president, chief marketing officer, Comedy Central, interview 25 August 2015

6 Absolutely Fabulous (2006) [accessed 5 August 2015] Ab Fab Stairs [Online] https://www.youtube.com/watch?v=OhFt7HsseNg

7 Walter Levitt, executive vice president, chief marketing officer, Comedy Central, interview 25 August 2015

8 Comedy Central (2014) [accessed 6 November 2015] The Return Of Workaholics [Online] https://www.youtube.com/watch?v=9wbGDM8QtPM

9 Walter Levitt, executive vice president, chief marketing officer, Comedy Central, interview 25 August 2015

10 Channel 4 (2010) [accessed 5 August 2015] Alan Carr Chatty Man [Online] https://www.youtube.com/watch?v=DMXLKKLqaEI

11 Louie CK (2015) [accessed 6 November 2015] Louie. Everybody's Doing It [Online] http://thelaughbutton.com/news/people-on-the-street-sing-louies-theme-song-for-season-4/

12 JKNEifer3 (2010) [accessed 6 November 2015] The Mighty Boosh 3 Trailer [Online] https://www.youtube.com/watch?v=L58D_twUmVo

13 Sky One (2014) [accessed 5 August 2015] The Simpsons Go Real Life [Online] Available: http://www.dailymotion.com/video/x198rvj_the-simpsons-go-real-life-sky-one-ad_shortfilms

14 Stephanie Gibbons, president of marketing, digital media marketing and on-air promotions, FX Networks, interview 26 June 2015

15 Viola, S, quoted in Sanders, J (2015) [accessed 5 August 2015] The Rise And... Rise Of 'Every. Simpsons. Ever'. Promaxbda, 6 November [Online] http://brief.promaxbda.org/content/the-rise-and-rise-of-every.-simpsons.-ever

16 Stephanie Gibbons, president of marketing, digital media marketing and on-air promotions, FX Networks, interview 26 June 2015

17 John Varvi, executive vice president, on-air promotions, FX Networks (FX, FXX, FXM, FXNOW), interview, 26 June 2015

18 John Varvi, executive vice president, on-air promotions, FX Networks (FX, FXX, FXM, FXNOW), interview, 26 June 2015

19 Koonin, S, quoted in Elliott, S (2004) [accessed 5 August 2015] The Media Business: Advertising – TBS Puts Serious Money Into Promoting Itself As A Place For Laughs, *New York Times*, 22 April [Online] http://www.nytimes.com/2004/04/22/business/media-business-advertising-tbs-puts-serious-money-into-promoting-itself-place.html

20 Bailey, R (2007) Turner Broadcasting System, Inc.: TBS Very Funny Campaign, *Encyclopaedia of Major Marketing Campaigns*, vol 2, pp 1659–65

21 USA Network (2013) [accessed 5 August 2015] Modern Family R-Rated For Cable [Online] https://www.youtube.com/watch?v=uFwyMGhYtcA

22 https://www.youtube.com/watch?v=nzul0Xye_lM&list=PLDsg58IUh5wSL0PL 9GLVpuYRGnrTHCvfk&index=90

23 https://www.youtube.com/watch?v=WW6lsgXLW9o

24 http://www.dandad.org/awards/professional/2008/tv-cinema-graphics/16355/charlie-brookers-screen-wipe/

25 UKTV Gold (2012) [accessed 5 August 2015] Vicar Of Dibley And Catherine Tate UKTV Gold [Online] https://vimeo.com/38422142

26 Hicks, B (1993) [accessed 5 August 2015] Revelations [Transcript] http://genius.com/Bill-hicks-on-advertisers-and-marketing-annotated

27 MacLeod, D (2007) [accessed 5 August 2015] Chasers War On Billboards. The Inspiration Room, 4 June [Online] http://theinspirationroom.com/daily/2007/chasers-war-on-billboards/

28 Red Bee (2015) [accessed 5 August 2015] Siobhan Sharpe – W1A Exclusive Online Extra [Online] https://www.youtube.com/watch?v=uUzdGaepo0M

29 Lawrence, B (2014) [accessed 5 August 2015] The 'Undateable' Comedy Tour: How To Launch (Or Not Launch) A TV Show In 2014, *Grantland*, 28 May [Online] http://grantland.com/hollywood-prospectus/the-undateable-comedy-tour-how-to-launch-or-not-launch-a-tv-show-in-2014/

30 Lawrence, B (2014) [accessed 5 August 2015] The 'Undateable' Comedy Tour: How To Launch (Or Not Launch) A TV Show In 2014, *Grantland*, 28 May [Online] http://grantland.com/hollywood-prospectus/the-undateable-comedy-tour-how-to-launch-or-not-launch-a-tv-show-in-2014/

31 Channel 4 (nd) [accessed 5 August 2015] Friends Farewell Artwork [Online] http://files1.coloribus.com/files/adsarchive/part_603/6036105/file/friends-tv-programme-ends-fri-small-90502.jpg

CHAPTER NINE

SELLING THE NEWS

The Day Today: *slamming the wasps from the pure apple of truth.*

CHRIS MORRIS, *THE DAY TODAY*[1]

– EDITORIAL BALANCE VERSUS MARKETING REDUCTIVENESS –

There is an inherent contradiction lurking at the heart of promoting most news and current affairs output. The contradiction lies between the broadcaster's stated aim (and often statutory regulated mission) for impartiality and the natural creative instincts in marketing to simplify, to use hyperbole, to 'find an angle'. Unless you are working for a news outlet with a blatant agenda – Fox News springs to mind as a poster boy – then the tension between the need to explain and contextualize, and the need to provoke interest, runs like a constant seam between editorial teams and marketers.

And yet. And yet. Perhaps out of any of the programme formats and genre types, news and current affairs need communication to punch harder and shout louder to gain attention than virtually any other. Viewing figures for news and serious current affairs have been in sharper decline for the last two decades than any other genre.[2] The growth of 24-hour news has cannibalized newscasts, inevitably, and can account for some of the decline, but the total ratings for shows such as *60 Minutes* in the United States, or *Dispatches* or *Panorama* in the UK, have all seen marked drops as well.[3]

Of course it is perfectly possible to make standout advertising campaigns that take neutrality or impartiality as the very bedrock of a brand, most memorably in the case of two UK newspapers: the *Independent*'s 'It is. Are you?' 1986 launch campaign,[4] or BMP's triumph of storytelling for the *Guardian*: 'An event seen from one point of view...'[5]

In most regulated European markets, however, neutrality is not a brand distinction. Nor is the ability to explain (possibly challenging several marketing campaigns that have done just that). Any journalist would say that their role is to explain. *Deutsche Welle*, the *Washington Post* and *Al Jazeera* would all make that claim with equal merit.

If you are going to stake a claim for balance and impartiality then it is wise to do so with credible support. BBC World's 'Never Stop Asking' campaign beautifully edited together a string of politicians being stumped by tough questions from BBC journalists. Never has hesitation been used so effectively as a creative device. A giant microphone thrusting up through the floor of Hauptbahnhof station in Berlin was just one experiential metaphor of our 'Never Stop Asking' campaign.[6]

A giant microphone in Berlin's Hauptbahnhof dramatizes the fact that, with BBC World, 'you can't bury a powerful question'   Source: *Reproduced by permission of Red Bee*

– CHOPPERS, DOPPLERS AND BOOTS ON THE GROUND –

So how do you approach finding an angle? For years US broadcasters have looked to technology for something more tangible to make a claim about, whether it is the quality of the cameras mounted on the 'news chopper' or the 'Doppler predictor' for their weather services.

Understanding why these 'technical firsts' have not been a feature of UK broadcasting is interesting. They certainly have been happy to make their cross-platform and digital engagement stories a focus of campaigns, but never the means of actually capturing the news itself. Perhaps this is down to 'The Day Today' effect, which so brilliantly skewered the tropes of 24-hour news and its overreliance on graphical gimmickry in the early years – 'the currency cat', for example – that it may have had a profound effect on how the media felt it could credibly talk about itself.[7]

International broadcasters have also engaged in an arms race of statistics about the number of 'boots they have on the ground'. Whether they have a numerical advantage in correspondents, foreign bureaus, or countries they report from, if it stands up as a claim, it has been promoted. The fact that the majority of these promotions look exactly the same – journalists talking earnestly to camera intercut with shots of satellite dishes, streams of data and so on – is another thing entirely.

CNN has used its credibility in the market for 'boots on the ground' as a basis for its 2015 brand positioning campaign, 'Go There'. 'With an unmatched global footprint, CNN has the capabilities to go where no one else can.'[8] Where the campaign exceeds mere statistical flummery is in the use of the line to signify the brand's willingness to confront subjects they claim no one else does. At first glance, in an era of Vice News fundamentally unlocking many formerly taboo areas in journalism, the claim could feel exposed, but vindication lies in the print ads where truly unlikely CNN storytellers such as Morgan Spurlock are highlighted as 'going there to tell the inside story'.[9]

– THE FIGHT TO BE FIRST –

A further point of advantage is always sought out in 'who is first'. The gag told by rivals about Sky News's claim has always been: 'Never wrong for long'. But the fact that it is used as a defensive joke by their rivals shows the degree to which the channel's relentless focus, for years, on the 'first' message has cut through. In news promotion, as with any form of advertising, persistence – even persistence built on the flimsiest credibility – will have an effect. The fictionalized race for first pictures from even the most mundane local events in Dan Gilroy's 2014 film *Nightcrawler* is a high-octane but extremely credible portrayal of the pressure that surrounds news executives.

But the debate around Sky News's 'First for Breaking News' line extended beyond mere joking, when a 2009 report by Cardiff University, 'The Thirst to be First', called into question the veracity of the claim.

The university's report examined the output of three rolling news channels, including ITV News and BBC News. The central question surrounded the percentage of what was claimed as 'breaking news' actually being wholly predictable or routine events. Some even diaried in advance. The Cardiff report asserted that for Sky News it was an astonishing 79.4 per cent, compared with ITV's 32.1 per cent and the BBC's 12.5 per cent. The report concluded:

> The growth in breaking news is a perfect example of a victory of style over substance. Breaking news is there because it has a certain *feel,* rather than because of the significance of its content.[10]

A furious Sky rebuttal claimed that the report was BBC funded and only took a brief snapshot of the channel, which was not representative. Peter Horrocks, then the head of BBC News 24, claimed that the findings revealed the 'First for Breaking News' line to be: 'Nothing more than a marketing trick'.[11] The whole affair was a skirmish in the increasingly fractious battle between the rolling news channels, but it is interesting that the dismissive words of Horrocks use the word 'marketing' as a pejorative. Of course it was a marketing trick. Highly effective, single-minded and relentlessly pursued marketing.

In one remark, though, the tension mentioned at the beginning of this chapter between editorial probity and advertising reductiveness is laid bare. Robert Tansey, Sky's brand director, content products, believes that even today it is 'still motivating internally as well as being motivating to the consumer':

> If you talk to the journalists at Sky News they're still very proud of the fact that they're more fleet of foot, more nimble, better at getting to the stories more quickly than any other news organization.[12]

Wind forward to 2014 and Peter Horrocks, by then in a global role responsible for the BBC's international rolling news channel, is quoted in an official press release trumpeting a new study that showed:

> We are just as fast as our competitors and are number one for breaking news from around the world. The BBC's breaking news is authentic news – rather than the non-existent or minor developments in stories that other broadcasters label 'breaking news'.[13]

A long-running claim and source of pride for Sky News
Source: Reproduced by permission of Sky News

So it seems that the claims and counter-claims around being first are here to stay as a vital 'marketing trick' for all news providers.

Before the 2015 'Go There' rebrand, CNN themselves had used 'be the first to know' since 2001, trademarking it internationally, and fiercely contesting the launch of the BBC Arabic channel's marketing material, which it complained used an Arabic translation of the same line. As we explore later in the chapter, perhaps it is the explosion of new social streams such as Twitter and Instagram that have made it increasingly difficult for any broadcaster to own 'first to air' any more.

– MOVING A MOUNTAIN –

The desire to stake ownership to being 'first' is understandable because, as shown above, it is deemed more important for news providers than other brands to be able to prove a claim empirically. Compare it with another former CNN slogan: 'The most trusted name in news'. This is a claim that might stand up in certain parts of the United States but would almost certainly fall under a withering crossfire from the BBC World Service in other parts of the globe, to mention just one rival.

A 2001 BBC brand campaign featured the most remarkable spokesperson – the Dalai Lama – singing the BBC World Service signature tune, and remarking how vital it had been as a source of trusted information in his youth. (The filming of this campaign at the Dalai Lama's home in Tibet provided one of the more surreal moments in broadcast promotion. Attempting to find a suitable framing shot for the Dalai while filming on the terrace outside his home, the director Steve Kelynack discussed with his director of photography that they could move a mountain that was protruding over the Dalai's shoulder in post-production. In a general sense of wonderment the Dalai remarked that even the almighty was not capable of moving such a mountain.)

In American broadcasting the empirical claim is rebranded a POP – 'proof of performance'. *Business Alabama Monthly* explains, in an article headlined 'Chasing Tornadoes and Snatching Up Market Share', that there is a predictability to how local stations will cover a weather event. Imagining a scenario in which a swathe of thunderstorms are threatening the Tennessee Valley, the coverage plays out much as you would expect with weather crews mobilized for reporting from the scene, and providing context and analysis back in the studio. The strength and intimacy of live television are in the living room with you as the storm approaches and passes:

> But the next day, the same weather images are back – clipped and tidied into a commercial, with musical backbeat and colourful, spiralling graphics. 'Exclusive!' the narrator touts. 'WE brought it to you FIRST. And we

covered it BEST.' The pitch extends into technological ballyhoo – storm trackers and Doppler radars. Then the kicker – lives saved, a community sheltered from the storm.[14]

The article concludes that even as news broadcasters are covering an event, they are in effect letting you know how well they are covering it. What technology they brought to that coverage, and just how quickly they managed to turn it around.

The inherent problem facing news marketers without these 'POP' moments is the very unpredictability of the content, particularly for rolling news channels. Sky News in the UK believes, as do many similar news channels, that there are two solutions. The first is to pick the few big events where you can predictably get ahead of the curve and throw everything at those set pieces. They call it 'monstering'. The general election in the UK is one such set piece, with the predictability of occurring only once every five years. Robert Tansey believes that even within that 'monstering' you can be targeted and thematic:

> In and around the 2015 election it was about how you engage with young people, how do you get the 18-24 year olds to vote and how do you use your different channels to do it?[15]

The second approach is to wrap a theme around a particular week – traditionally in an expected thinner 'hard news' week:

> Editorially they are looking for ways of leading the agenda, but doing it in such a way that you know marketing can then help you to support it. If then there's a massive national disaster, you have to put your plans on hold for a week because the disaster is going to dominate the airwaves. But if it's just another week in October Sky News will decide what we're going to be focusing on. So, we'll get the right guests on, we're leading the agenda, we're doing an open letter, and then marketing's challenge is how you promotionally package that up.[16]

– ANCHORMAN –

Another way to find an angle for news broadcasters, and again one perfected by US networks from Walter Cronkite to Ron Burgundy, is the cult of personality. While whole networks have rested much of their advertising on the broad shoulders of legendary reporters such as Christiane Amanpour and Peter Jennings, and while larger-than-life characters such as Richard Quest have become transfer prizes as much for their name recognition as their contact lists, it is something that the European broadcasters tend to shy away from.

There is perhaps a fear among journalists that self-promotion can damage their credibility. Often they are cross-examining the very smoke-screen that other public figures are putting up in their own PR. In 20 years of working with the BBC, the occasions when we have focused on the individual strengths of Jeremy Paxman, John Humphrys and Stephanie Flanders, etc, can be counted on one hand.

Foreign correspondents tend to be different. They are happy to talk about their experiences for the network's good and this then becomes one of the most repeated and successful tropes in the news channel repertoire – the extended montage of flak-jacketed figures, counting down to camera, recounting tales of 'first into Basra' experiences. 'This is Kate Adie from Baghdad', 'Gavin Esler from Washington'.

– CLOSER TO THE PEOPLE –

Perhaps surprisingly, few news channels use the end users as spokespeople for their brands. Surprisingly because, as with newsprint, fierce loyalties can be created, particularly with local stations across the North American continent.

In an article for TV Newscheck, David Johnson, the VP of creative for Toronto-based local news service CP24, talks about his award-winning campaign from 2013 in which they posed the question online: 'Why do you watch CP24?' and were so overwhelmed with the naturalness of how viewers expressed their affinity that they then captured in understated documentary style that emotional connection. As one viewer says: 'It's a part of Toronto. Wherever you go, it's always on – barber shops, gyms, bars, laundromats. It's not appointment viewing; it's like a companion.'[17]

Al Jazeera has increasingly pitched its brand as being closer to the streets and to the voices of real people (perhaps surprisingly for a channel owned by a royal family). 'Hear the Human Story' is the largest marketing campaign it has run since the channel's launch, based on its stated belief that humanity should always be reflected in its reporting. It features stories from the Philippines, Spain, Rwanda and a wonderful story of a school that is run under a motorway bridge in India. Arguably reflecting humanity is a given entry point for any news channel but, as stated at the outset of this chapter, finding genuine differentiators within the market is exceptionally hard, and a marketer's job might rely more on shining a bright and consistent light on a category generic.

– MAKING PEOPLE CARE –

For decades, news broadcasters have built up databases that give them strong rating indicators of the respective topics they cover. If you wonder why certain news stories always lead the US bulletins, it is based on hard advertising dollars.

So, the biggest question facing the promoters of news and current affairs is not 'Why should people care about how my brand of news is reporting this story?' but rather 'Why should the audience care about this story at all?'

Channel 4's *Dispatches* has consistently excelled in its promotion, and put huge production budgets behind trailing programmes that have little hope of big audiences, with the primary intention of talking to a small opinion-forming audience. 'China's Stolen Children' was one such case in point. The 48-sheet poster of the Great Wall of China plastered with missing-children posters was a powerful and resonant image.

The approach is often deliberately provocative, none more so perhaps than the advertising promoting Sri Lanka's Killing Fields, with a sea crimson with blood set against a traditional palm-tree-and-blue-sky background. Dan Brooke, Channel 4's chief marketing and communications officer, highlights the degree of reach that such advertising can have: 'People in Sri Lanka started using it on placards, protestors in Sri Lanka were using it.'[18]

This leads us to *Panorama*, and Rwanda as a case study. In 1994 the genocidal massacres in Rwanda had been reported for a couple of weeks within the UK but were buried in paragraphs within the broadsheets' international sections, or late in bulletins.[19]

Fergal Keane had returned to the *Panorama* cutting rooms with his producer Tom Giles and quite astonishingly harrowing footage of rivers choking with bodies.

Here is a quote from the programme transcript:

> You do not just see death here, you feel it and smell it. It is as if all the good and life in the atmosphere have been sucked out and replaced with the stench of evil. There are two thoughts then, that of the mortal terror, which must have been in the minds of the people who knew they were going to be killed, and the hatred and savagery in the hearts of those who were going to kill them.[20]

Keane sat in an edit suite and showed image after image that, for reasons of taste, were unlikely even to make the cut of the final programme. He was visibly shaking, both with what he had seen and with anger at the total lack of interest in the story being shown within the UK. Foreign affairs also always saw a ratings slump for *Panorama*, compared with other topics covered by the programme, and it was particularly hard to get any sort of audience for stories from Africa. Ceri Evans, the BBC creative director then responsible for news promotion, asked the question that was so often to be the unlocking of a string of award-winning *Panorama* trailers: 'What do you want the viewers to think, Fergal?' Keane paused and replied: 'Just the scale of it, Ceri, we have to tell them the scale of it.'

So we wondered how to make an audience consider the magnitude of the events, when we couldn't show any of the imagery that demonstrated it. As is so often the way, creative strictures led to the most interesting solution. We tracked down the sort of typical footage of British high streets that is usually used to accompany reports on retail forecasts. The only shot from Rwanda itself was the end shot, a six-year-old refugee boy playing with a wooden jigsaw map of the African continent, chiming with the penultimate line of the script, read with measured understatement by Stephen Kemble:

> If the killing in Rwanda happened here, and the entire population of Bristol was hacked to death...
> And the people of Leicester were mutilated with knives and axes...
> While the children of Glasgow had their homes burned to the ground...
> You'd want to know more wouldn't you?
> Bad luck for the people of Rwanda that they don't live a little closer to home.
> *Panorama* reports from a forgotten land. Monday 9.30. BBC One.[21]

The trailer was pulled from the airwaves on the Sunday night by an overprotective presentation editor after the duty log received a handful of complaints that the trailer was upsetting. To which an irate Ceri Evans bawled down the phone: 'Genocide is f*cking upsetting.'

Everyday life in Britain contrasted with massacres in Rwanda: trailer for the BBC's Panorama   *Source: Reproduced by permission of BBC*

– RE-CREATING THE NEWS –

Integrity is vital to any news broadcaster, which leads us to examine another ethical question that regularly faces news marketers. Is it ever ethical to re-create a news event in order to capture it for marketing purposes? As a general policy most broadcasters would say a definitive 'no'. There was a storm of controversy in 2001 when the BBC produced a trailer for its news coverage, with a complicated post-production technique that involved a seamless camera move through a multitude of different news events to communicate the arrival of BBC News as an online brand. Clearly it would have been impossible to use that technique without creating fictional news stories. But the backlash, inevitably led by the *Daily Mail*, was fierce. Tory culture spokesman Peter Ainsworth said:

> I think it's an appalling amount to spend staging a bogus news item that is fake and so lacks integrity. The BBC could have used archive footage. We don't pay the licence fee to have people fly to South Africa to make fantasy films.[22]

It is understandable that staging car bombs is deemed to be crossing the line in a modern editorial context for a public service broadcaster. But, as ever, there are shades of grey. Is it acceptable to film a weather trailer with a weather presenter where you use a rain machine? That seems more justifiable. So what if we filmed a trailer with a weather presenter in a boat while they talked about the impact of flooding? Again that seems okay. But what if the boat is not on a river, it's filmed on a stage-set road that we had flooded to represent the impact of floods more visually? Is that re-creating a news event? The nuances are subtle but fraught, particularly if they take place in the febrile atmosphere of press scrutiny.

– THE BIGGEST STORIES SELL THEMSELVES –

Some stories by their scale and exclusivity transcend the traditional need to find 'USPs' to magnify. In 1995, four people stood in the control room of VCA1 (Versioning and Captioning Area) of BBC Television Centre, watching Stephen Kemble, a voice-over artist, finalizing a trailer for what would be the highest-rated current affairs show in the history of British television, with 22.78 million viewers tuning in.[23]

Those four people, Tony Hall (director of BBC News), Steve Hewlett (editor of *Panorama*), Mike Robinson (programme producer) and Alan Yentob (controller, BBC One) were the only people, alongside the cameraman Tony Poole and the creative for the trailer, who had seen any of the footage on the screen. The angled head, the downcast eyes, the quiet answers that would become one of the most defining pieces of news footage ever:

'Yes I loved him, yes I adored him. I'd like to be a queen of people's hearts, in people's hearts...'

Diana, Princess of Wales, talking to Martin Bashir, 1995

If you get the right story, the marketing takes care of itself.

Of course where the challenge lies in these one-off current-events specials is that they do not build up any momentum for future episodes. Dan Brooke at Channel 4 cites it as a wider problem within broadcast news:

> For Channel 4 News those things might just be a 10-minute story in one programme and, on the whole, unlike newspapers, who when they get subjects that they really care about return to them, television's a bit more 'Okay, we've done that, what's next?'[24]

– FUTURE CHALLENGES –

Looking to the future, the challenge to news broadcasters is coming from a mixture of new digital-only providers – Vice News, Huffington Post and Yahoo News – and traditional print providers moving into video. The hiring of the BBC's ex-director-general, Mark Thompson, as CEO of the New York Times Group in 2012 was a totemic example of the convergence of provision. Looking to the former category, Vice is a poster boy for what we could categorize as the democratization of news reporting. A report by Ofcom, the British broadcasting regulator, in July 2015, highlighted that the switch to online viewing as a primary source of news was especially prevalent with younger viewers:

> The trend towards online news consumption is even more pronounced for young people, with three-fifths accessing news online, nearly half (45 per cent) considering the internet their most important source of news about the UK, and 50 per cent citing the internet as their most important source for news about the world. Vice Media provide a range of news content in a style that is more appealing than traditional TV news to many young people.[25]

Rafael Sandor, the head of TV marketing and creative for Vice Media, can see a clear explanation for the appeal of Vice to millennials:

> What's particularly fascinating for me as a viewer of Vice – an online viewer – is when I saw it from outside I saw this very honest brand, very honest people going round the world doing these things because they care about them, and when I got inside Vice I got exactly the same thing. The people are just for that. And that's a problem of this democratization of media – it's more a problem of ethos than at any time before, because ultimately big corporations can talk like democratic media, but they're not, they're a big corporation.[26]

The array of new challenges includes 'click bait' headlines on social feeds, investigations into areas that traditional editorial sensitivity has not covered in Ofcom-regulated waters and, of course, simply the reach through viral sharing.

The response has been a mixture of 'me-too' behaviour such as bite-sized packages for shorter attention spans, embracing the latest social tools such as Periscope and Meerkat, and broadening the range of editorial topics covered. The *Daily Mail* and ESPN are just two news sources using Snapchat 'Discover'. Brevity certainly seems to be re-emerging as a new demand, driven by technology such as Apple's watch. As Emily Bell wrote in the *Guardian* in April 2015:

> The *New York Times* illustrates its own offering by a series of text alerts – all that will fit on the watch face and remain legible. It is not the whole story, but during a run around the block it is enough. As screen space shrinks consumers will make more selective choices about what their 'bare essentials' are in communications.[27]

It has led to soul searching amongst the editorial and marketing communities of news. *Washington Post* journalist Barry Ritholtz wrote about how he discovered the tragic bombing of the Boston marathon:

> Monday afternoon at 2:56 pm, three hours after the fastest runner of the Boston Marathon crossed the finish line, my Twitter feed lit up. Someone in the office yelled: 'Explosions at the Boston Marathon, may be terrorism.' Within seconds, there were first-hand reports, photos and even video circulating. Not on CNN or Reuters or the Associated Press. On Twitter.[28]

In response to this threat, and returning to the earlier theme of the chapter and Sky News's 'First for Breaking News' brand line, Robert Tansey admits:

> We certainly questioned it a few years ago when we were probably behind the curve of stuff like Twitter. How can you credibly say you are first for breaking news when the public are breaking news before you possibly can? As we have now done much more than other news providers to digitize the offering and be present on those platforms it retains its credibility and its motivating factor.[29]

A few services are beginning to be more experimental with their marketing. The BBC's *Newsnight*, under the editorship of Ian Katz, hired from the *Guardian*, has been particularly bold using existing YouTube talent, animators and musicians to broaden the brand perception. Radio 1's *Newsbeat* is launching a video service as part of the move online of the BBC's youth TV channel BBC Three.

CNNMoney created a digital war room to track the most popular stories both on its own site and across the web. The data allows CNN's producers to create stories around the moment's hottest topics and helps them to A/B test headlines (ie compare two alternative versions to see which performs better). The BBC are using Instagram to get shorter stories out to otherwise hard-to-reach audiences.[30]

Perhaps headlines are in fact the acceptable form of marketing, where reduction is allowed in an editorial context. Possibly drifting closer to the sort of nightmare predicted by satirists from Chris Morris to Charlie Brooker comes 4NewsWall: a Tumblr-hosted website built up from the day's headlines, targeted squarely at a 16- to 24-year-old demographic, and utilizing bold text over animated GIFs (graphics interchange formats). Interestingly this last example was not born out of traditional editorial development but from the marketing community at Channel 4. Dan Brooke explains:

> The NewsWall came from News saying that we need to think about this in a different way so let's go to a different set of people than we normally go to, so rather than going to online news specialists they essentially said let's go to some young people in 4Creative – and they got something completely different as a result.[31]

What both of the above examples can undeniably achieve is a speed of communication. Though as Ed Murrow, the legendary US broadcast journalist and inspiration for the George Clooney film *Good Night, and Good Luck* wisely said when receiving the Family of Man award in 1964: 'The speed of communications is wondrous to behold. It is also true that speed can multiply the distribution of information that we know to be untrue'.[32]

So a plethora of voices remains, and finding genuine distinctiveness stays key. Ultimately the originality and exclusivity of the story, and the quality and

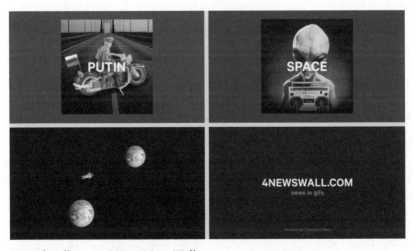

News headlines as GIFs: 4NewsWall   Source: © Channel 4 Television

timeliness of the storytelling, will always win in a news and current affairs environment and these must remain the focus of any brand marketing within the genre.

NEXT	**LATER**
★ The Orwellian eye.	★ Making science sexy.
★ Three waves of PR.	★ 'America Start Your Engines'.
★ A singing baby and a singing raven.	★ *The Choir*'s singing tweets.
★ A robotic Cheryl.	
★ James Corden on a crane.	
★ *The X Factor* mash-up.	

NOTES

1 *The Day Today* (1991) season one, episode one, BBC Two Talkback Productions, 19 January

2 Pew Research Center (2014) [accessed 7 July 2015] Network TV: Evening News Share Over Time By Channel [Online] http://www.journalism.org/media-indicators/evening-network-news-share-over-time/

3 Pew Research Center (2014) [accessed 7 July 2015] State Of The News Media 2014 [Online] http://www.journalism.org/packages/state-of-the-news-media-2014/

4 How To Get Ahead in Advertising (2015) [accessed 7 July 2015] *Independent* [Online] http://www.independent.co.uk/news/media/advertising/how-to-get-ahead-in-advertising-2069073.html?action=gallery&ino=4

5 https://www.youtube.com/watch?v=_SsccRkLLzU

6 Sweney, M (2008) [accessed 7 July 2015] BBC World News Unveils Global Promos *Guardian*, 17 November [Online] http://www.theguardian.com/media/2008/nov/17/bbc-world-news-promo

7 Gsedinburgh (2007) [accessed 5 November 2015] The Day Today – Chris Morris – BBC 'Finance' [Online] https://www.youtube.com/watch?v=D0uE1qi2A68

8 CNN (2014) [accessed 7 July 2015] CNN Worldwide Launches Brand Campaign: 'CNN. GO There' [Online] http://cnnpressroom.blogs.cnn.com/2014/04/10/cnn-worldwide-launches-brand-campaign-cnn-go-there/

9 Troika (2015) [accessed 7 July 2015] CNN Go There [Online] http://www.troika.tv/cnn-go-there/

10 Lewis, J and Cushion, S (2009) The thirst to be first, *Journalism Practice*, 3 (3), pp 304–18

11 Brand Republic (2005) [accessed 7 July 2015] Sky News Record For Breaking News Just A 'Marketing Trick' [Online] http://www.brandrepublic.com/article/530002/sky-news-record-breaking-news-just-marketing-trick

12 Robert Tansey, brand director, content products, Sky, interview 26 June 2015

13 BBC (2014) [accessed 7 July 2015] BBC World News Best For Global Breaking News [Online] http://www.bbc.co.uk/mediacentre/worldnews/2014/bbc-best-for-global-breaking-news

14 Business Alabama Monthly (1996) [accessed 7 July 2015] Chasing Tornadoes and Snatching Up Market Share [Online] http://www.31alumni.com/newswars.htm

15 Robert Tansey, brand director, content products, Sky, interview 26 June 2015

16 Robert Tansey, brand director, content products, Sky, interview 26 June 2015

17 Greeley, P (2013) [accessed 7 July 2015] PromaxaBDA: Making A Great News Promo, TV News Check, 2 June [Online] http://www.tvnewscheck.com/article/67943/promaxbda-making-a-great-news-promo

18 Dan Brooke, chief marketing and communications officer, Channel 4, interview 26 June 2015

19 Giles, T (1994) [accessed 7 July 2015] Media Failure Over Rwanda's Genocide, *BBC News* [Online] http://news.bbc.co.uk/1/hi/programmes/panorama/3599423.stm

20 Keane, F and Giles, T (2004) *Killers*, BBC One, 4 April

21 MoonHunter69 (2015) [accessed 5 November 2015] Panorama Rwanda Trailer 1997 BBC One [Online] https://www.youtube.com/watch?v=2LXNRhBIeWQ

22 Ainsworth, P, quoted in Conlon, T (2012) [accessed 7 July 2015] BBC Spends £100,000 On 60-Second Trailer, *Daily Mail*, 27 July [Online] http://www.dailymail.co.uk/news/article-27712/BBC-spends-100-000-60-second-trailer.html

23 Douglas, T (2012) [accessed 7 July 2015] Tracking 30 years Of TV's Most Watched Programmes, *BBC News*, January [Online] http://www.bbc.co.uk/news/entertainment-arts-16671101

24 Dan Brooke, chief marketing and communications officer, Channel 4, interview 26 June 2015

25 Glennie, A (2015) [accessed 7 July 2015] Only Half Of Young People's Viewing Is Traditional Scheduled TV, *Guardian*, 2 July [Online] http://www.theguardian.com/media/2015/jul/02/young-people-live-tv-bbc-iplayer-youtube-netflix

26 Rafael Sandor, head of TV marketing and creative, Vice Media, interview, 11 June 2015

27 Bell, E (2015) [accessed 7 July 2015] Apple Watch Highlights Need For Shorter News As Screen Sizes Shrink, *Guardian*, 26 April [Online] http://www.theguardian.com/media/media-blog/2015/apr/26/apple-watch-shrinking-news-apps

28 Ritholtz, B (2013) [accessed 8 July 2015] How Twitter Is Becoming Your First Source Of Investment News, *Washington Post*, 20 April [Online] http://www.washingtonpost.com/business/how-twitter-is-becoming-your-first-source-of-investment-news/2013/04/19/19211044-a7b3-11e2-a8e2-5b98cb59187f_story.html

29 Robert Tansey, brand director, content products, Sky, interview 26 June 2015

30 Taube, A (2015) [accessed 8 July 2015] The Importance Of CNN In The Age Of Snapchat, *Native Advertising*, 10 April [Online] http://nativeadvertising. com/cnn-brings-its-video-know-how-to-the-web/

31 Dan Brooke, chief marketing and communications officer, Channel 4, interview, 26 June 2015

32 Kendrick, A (1969) *Prime Time: The life of Edward R Murrow*, Little Brown, Boston

CHAPTER TEN

PROMOTING ENTERTAINMENT SHOWS
Scrubbing the shiny floors

> *Statler:*   *This show is awful.*
> *Waldorf:*   *Terrible.*
> *Statler:*   *Disgusting.*
> *Waldorf:*   *See you next week?*
> *Statler:*   *Of course.*
>
> THE MUPPET SHOW[1]

– PRESSURE IN THE SPOTLIGHT –

In Chapter 1 we recounted a story of an entertainment show launch that took 37 scripts to be written and presented to multiple executive producers, commissioners, agents, artists and channel controllers – all of which were rejected by one or another... until finally, with the airdate looming, we ended up successfully making the very first script we had presented.

This was not an isolated occurrence, or indeed an extreme one. When it comes to entertainment marketing, more than any other genre, there seems to be extraordinary pressure on all concerned. Tony Pipes, executive creative director of ITV Creative, offers the most likely theory for why this is:

> It's a weird balance of power because those shows are so valuable, creatively and commercially – finding that format is such a hard thing to crack at every level that, no matter what brief you write to, if a senior stakeholder with commercial interest in the show's success says 'I don't think that's right' then you are back to square one. It's like a house of cards.[2]

The stakes are indeed incredibly high, and incredibly lucrative if a format is a success, but the sheer difficulty of creating the next winning entrant to

Saturday night TV is shown by the age of the 'big beasts' of ITV today. *Britain's Got Talent* is approaching 10 years, *The X Factor* is in its twelfth year, and *I'm a Celebrity... Get Me Out of Here!* is in its fourteenth year. Meanwhile, over on the BBC, *Strictly Come Dancing*, the mothership format for *Dancing with the Stars*, is 12 years old. In the United States, *Survivor* is 16 years old and entering series 32. *Big Brother*, the daddy of them all, launched in the Netherlands in 1997.

So when they work, they really work. They provide a live 'must see' moment to any network, and typically a younger-skewing audience in large numbers.

A list of shows that all the contributors to this book launched in the hopes of becoming the next big thing in entertainment would fill another volume. *Pets Win Prizes* was one of our personal fondest efforts. So is it possible to point to any magic bullets, any secret elixir that has contributed to the success of those that made it?

– LASTING BRANDS –

One of the common factors in all of the shows that have stood the test of time, and in most cases have become successful formats internationally, is a strong design identity.

The *Big Brother* 'eye' is a standout example of a clear and memorable brand icon. Artist Daniel Eatock, when initially approached, did not feel that the show needed a logo, but fortunately Peter Bazalgette, then head of Endemol who had developed the show, had a bigger vision for the programme.

Bazalgette suggested eyes, and Eatock blended this with his early thoughts of TV flickers, to create something that Eatock describes as echoing 'the main ethos of the show' and reflecting 'the Orwellian sense of concealment, typified by the surveillance cameras distributed around the house'.[3] Eatock went on to devise the eye for multiple series, though the title sequences and graphic packages were produced by a range of agencies, including our own. Of course, a format's branding is so much more than just a logo. The music, the lighting and the set design are all key elements of an overall design brand aesthetic. For *Who Wants to Be a Millionaire?* the swooping downward lighting changes are almost as recognizable as the formatted verbal tics of the host: 'Is that your final answer?' Noticeably when the UK's *Big Brother* moved at the end of its 11-year run on Channel 4, and the format rights were picked up by Channel 5, nearly all the elements that had made the show a success were retained. The title music composed by DJ Paul Oakenfold as part of music production duo 'Elementfour' transferred, as did the eye logo and even the voice-over narrator Marcus Bentley (who had originally been a continuity announcer on Channel 4 itself).

Indeed there is an interesting paradox in the degree to which a host broadcaster invests in the marketing and development of a property that is ultimately as transferable as an entertainment format. Every Channel 4 poster that turned the *Big Brother* eye into a national emblem was in some part playing a long-term marketing function for Channel 5. Even Channel 4's typically understated farewell to the show played with the logo as the centrepiece of a poster campaign that read: R.I.P.

Channel 4's farewell to Big Brother   *Source: © Channel 4 Television*

What is harder to transfer of course is presenter talent, who often will have contracts with the channel rather than the production company. This was most noticeable in the fallout following the departure of the presenting team from the BBC's blockbuster show *Top Gear*. While the faces of the three presenters were unarguably the biggest draw to the show, it was noticeable that the brand icon that was used globally was a wholly anonymous member of the presenter team – The Stig, whose white-helmeted presence is a highly marketed symbol. There are 'Stigs' as part of the team in the United States, Russia, Korea, France and Australia... and their uniform appearance is a merchandise designer's dream.

Of course memorable brand icons can be found at any stage in any format, but it is unquestionable that to succeed as an entertainment show, you need some simple visual mnemonics. In 2009 ABC in the United States ran a highly successful campaign in which the stars of all of their big shows lived together in one house: 'Your Favourite Shows Live Here'. In one launch spot, all the entertainment shows are marked by their big visual cues. *Total Wipeout*'s big red balls, *The Bachelor*'s single rose, *Extreme Makeover*'s megaphone, *Dancing with the Stars*'s score paddles[4] – all easily globally translatable and transferable iconography. Other memorable logos and brand assets, from *Pop Idol* to *Who Wants to Be a Millionaire?*, from

The X Factor to *The Voice*, all point to the need for greater up-front investment with marketing expertise than many production companies are used to.

– THE GREAT SURVIVOR –

In the United States, *Survivor* would be grouped under the 'reality' banner – it was the success of the show in 2000 for CBS that really gave networks renewed enthusiasm for non-scripted formats. Unsurprisingly, given the thrust of this chapter, it was a show that was born with marketing at its heart. Anne O'Grady, senior VP of marketing for CBS at the time, is quoted in *The Business of Entertainment* as saying: 'We were more involved with *Survivor* than any other show launched on the network. It was a marketing project from the beginning.'[5]

Everything from the mantra of the show – 'Outwit, Outplay, Outlast' – to the branding and, crucially, the introduction of product placement and product logo placement into the promotions, points to this close collaboration between creator Mark Burnett and the marketing team.

Product placement is critical to the business-case success of *Survivor* – now entering its thirty-second season. In that first season it is estimated that about 1 million dollars in advertising was linked to product integration. Burnett realized that the rewards for the contestants winning tasks could justifiably be 'luxury items' such as Mountain Dew, Bud Light and even Dr Scholl soles, without the intrusion being too jarring for viewers.

– CREATING AN EVENT –

In researching this book, there has been a tendency to focus on the parts of the entertainment marketing mix that sit within the more traditional advertising and design portfolio, but for marketing entertainment and reality shows the majority of the heavy lifting is taken on by their close relation, variously described by TV networks as PR, Publicity or Communications.

The symbiotic relationship between media outlets and entertainment shows came to its peak with the joint ownership of Express Newspapers and Channel 5 (when the UK tabloid the *Daily Star* pretty much ran no front-page news that wasn't related to the contestants in *Big Brother* for the whole of its three-month run), but that was an extreme example of what has become a very common and mutually beneficial relationship. For any entertainment show there are broadly three waves of PR activity. There are the pre-launch reveals of contestants and format points. Then, during the bulk of the production, the weekly placing of stories related to contestants that maintain the subplots and intrigues that prevent viewership drifting. Finally, the hype is brought to fever pitch during and after a 'final', with winner profiles and back stories. The PR machine borrows from its work with multiple other industries during this cycle. In the pre-launch phase, snippets are released with the careful timing plans usually seen in the music industry. *Strictly Come Dancing* in the UK has moved from announcing all of its contestants in a single big show to a bi-weekly leak of individual names to carefully choreographed media outlets, culminating in what is close to a film premiere red carpet launch. Philip Almond, the BBC's director of marketing and audiences, acknowledges that this is a more important phase perhaps than even than the trailers themselves:

> You start to get to this view of marketing and the arc of a programme through first window, discussion programmes around it, second window... marketing across the entire life cycle of the show rather than just a trail to say 'This is what's on tomorrow.' There's a real sense in which *Strictly* builds up as an event and then is released. And then of course there is the marketing spin-off of the tour... so you start to think of content marketing in a very different, broader way than just the ATV promotion of the TV show. And that's what I mean about branding in the future. There will be some programmes that are brands, and *Strictly* would be one of them for us, where how you manage that across the piece across all those touch points is important – from show ticket releases, to studio tours, to live events as part of the experience.[6]

The other key phrase used by Philip is the acknowledgement of secondary programmes, the 'discussion programmes'. They have become an important component of the ongoing hype around entertainment shows, and from the first known example – *Big Brother's Little Brother* – they have grown to be a critical part of any show's success. Now in the UK *Strictly Come Dancing* has *It Takes Two*; *The Great British Bake Off* has *An Extra Slice*; *The Apprentice* has *You're Fired*. This is not just lazy broadcasters exploiting every shred of airtime out of their hits; it is an acknowledgement of the impact, in particular, that social media has had on entertainment shows – the need to analyse and discuss immediately after an episode. To Philip Almond these spin-off shows have one clear purpose:

> You could argue that the entire *It Takes Two* every night, half an hour on BBC Two, is marketing, like *The Xtra Factor*. It's further collateral – is it marketing, is it programme content in its own right? It wouldn't get commissioned in its own right, but it's keeping the conversation going and keeping the sense of event.[7]

– THE PHONE LINES ARE OPEN NOW –

As we see in other chapters on factual and children's marketing in particular, one of the keys to success for linear television lies in ever-more involving ways of audience participation. The entertainment show revival in the UK can be traced firmly back to the introduction of phone voting, as audiences suddenly found themselves thrust into the heart of the TV narrative in a way that fiction and documentary never could, with broadcasters discovering an unexpected income stream in premium-rate phone lines to boot. Peter Fincham, until recently director of television at ITV, was involved in the creation of *The X Factor* when his production company Talkback co-produced the first series with Simon Cowell's Syco Entertainment, and he then inherited the second series of *Strictly Come Dancing* as controller of BBC One. In an interview with the *Guardian* celebrating *The X Factor*'s 10 years he acknowledged the role that those shows' interactivity plays:

> After a period when Saturday night TV was being described as 'moribund', these formats brought back the idea of everyone sitting down together on a Saturday night. And the shows turned out to be a clever way of bringing together various elements, including interactivity and competition. From the beginning, these series weren't a short snack: they were long and involving entertainment.[8]

Constant reappraisal of formats to find new ways of involving the audience also creates a virtuous circle as it provides marketers with something new to talk about. As *Survivor* entered its thirty-first series in its sixteenth year, it took the unprecedented step of allowing its fans to choose all the contestants from a pool of previous failed 'Survivors'. The show's host for all 31 seasons, Jeff Probst, told the *New York Times*:

> When I told some producer friends what we were doing, almost every one of them said, 'You mean pick one contestant?' I said, 'No, the entire group.' They said, 'You're trusting an entire season to the fans?' The answer's yes, because our fans get it. They're a part of our longevity.[9]

The dynamic generated by this one decision shows the strength of content and marketing being truly entwined. In addition to advertising the plot twist to fans and encouraging their participation, viewers had a reason to go to YouTube to watch contestants' profiles, to watch analysis by the host on all the potential cast, to come back for thank you videos, and generally to interact for three months with a show before anyone even sets foot on the shores of Cambodia.[10]

Dancing with the Stars, for the launch of season 18, also placed a big new format twist in the hands of the viewers: the ability to switch partners between the dancing couples throughout the season. You can see in the launch work created by agency Troika for ABC how that simple idea super-charges the creative approach:

> Monday 17 March, nothing can come between *Dancing*'s hot new cast and their partners... except you.[11]

As Tony Pipes, responsible for drawing an audience to all those ITV shows, plaintively remarks:

> The difficulty with returning series is that you basically have the same proposition every year. So the hardest bit is finding something unique about it every year, when it's a format that is known and loved.[12]

What *Survivor* and *Dancing with the Stars* clearly understand is which format points to twist to give refreshed unique selling points, without undermining the integrity of what brought an audience to the show in the first place. Justin Bairamian, director of BBC Creative, goes further in stressing that marketing should have a role in helping to guide these format changes, as the people responsible for audience relationship management:

> The role of marketing is as much about helping editorial teams to keep the format fresh as it is about this year's trail. Where we get it wrong is we often get put in 'What is this year's trail?' guise and marketing at best should be involved in how the editorial is shaped and how it lands with the audience.[13]

– HOSTS OR FORMAT? YOU DECIDE –

The mention of Jeff Probst above leads into another conundrum for marketing entertainment shows: working out whether the draw for an audience lies more in the presenting talent that the audience will know and have an affinity with, or in the format itself, which will likely create future stars of its unknown cast. In 2015 ITV chose to go heavily in one direction, as Tony Pipes explains:

> We had a real focus on 18- to 35-year-olds, as attracting that new heartland audience is always a priority. It is something that Simon Cowell understands really well and it was his idea to be confident with the brand, have fun and sort of tackle the critics head on. If we were not taking ourselves too seriously, then how could they? It was a real gear shift, but suited the new judges' personalities and the younger audience.[14]

The resulting trailer is a high-concept, hugely entertaining and glossily produced introduction to *The X Factor* 'Factory', with a robotic cloned Cheryl Fernandez-Versini and Simon Cowell masterminding the production line.[15] Similarly the BBC's trailers for *The Voice* have focused squarely on the

Inside The X Factor's *glamorous factory*   Source: Reproduced by permission of ITV plc

'mentors'. (The word 'judges' is banned in an attempt to market the show as a positive, feel-good alternative to *The X Factor.*) Successive trailers created by our team led by CD Andy Booth have showcased those mentors at the point they first hear an extraordinary voice. From the maternity ward of a hospital with a baby singing 'What a Feeling' (tagline 'A Star will be Born'),[16] to a late-night bar where a raven gives an impromptu performance of Ram Jam's 'Black Betty' with all four mentors joining in (subtly underlining their vocal abilities again as another point of difference with their rival ITV show).[17]

There is a sense that in these big shows what is important is who the general public want to share their Saturday night sofa with. The judges/mentors in *Dancing with the Stars, Strictly, The X Factor* or *Bake Off* are not just watchable characters in the narrative, they are watchers *of* the narrative alongside you at home. They see the performances as you see them, comment as you comment. The role of marketing should be less about elevating their status than letting their genuine personalities shine through. Hence a robotic Cheryl is a hugely likeable Cheryl, as she clearly sees the funny side of the press criticism.

Our trailer for *The Great British Bake Off* during the 2014 football World Cup, which saw Mary Berry, the venerable judge of all things cake, flick-flacking her way across the summer lawns while screaming 'yessss' in an extraordinary goal celebration, can be seen in this light.[18] So can Sir Alan Sugar, host of *The Apprentice*, accidentally gunning down passers-by with his 'You're fired' finger point in another promo. Even the 'bad cops' in entertainment shows need to be lovable.[19]

Ant and Dec are two presenters on whose shoulders ITV's commercial success weighs heavily. They host three of the four juggernaut entertainment shows that the network's schedule is built around. *I'm a Celebrity... Get Me Out of Here!* (IACGMOOH), *Britain's Got Talent*, and *Saturday Night*

Takeaway. The trailers for IACGMOOH in particular always show the boys in variety show-style sketches.[20]

As Tony Pipes explains, they are happy to work with the marketing team in devising where the focus of the promotional effort should fall:

> It depends on the property – they have a big vested interest in *Takeaway* because it's their production company and their idea. So that is very much about selling the show and the format. How do we let people know it's live, for instance? It's a really difficult brief because it's such a varied show and hard to explain... so they are always really involved in that. With *I'm a Celebrity* they are happier to do more comedy, sketch-type ideas and be more 'personalities' really rather than worry about the format themselves. They are really good to work with, they understand advertising and marketing. They're clever and they have a lot of respect for what we do.[21]

Ant and Dec as castaways to promote series 15 of I'm A Celebrity... Get Me Out of Here! *Source: Reproduced by permission of ITV plc*

The launch of James Corden into the world of the late-night talk shows in the United States is instructive here too – how adopting 'low status' is often important in establishing new likeable characters. When talking about his work on agency DDB's legendary VW advertising in the 1960s, art director Helmut Krone said, 'a little admission gains a great acceptance'.[22] The launch campaign made much of Corden's relative anonymity in the market. He was hoisted up on a crane to stand next to a giant billboard overlooking the CBS lot in LA: '*The Late Late Show* with this guy' was scrawled in handwritten paint with an arrow pointing to Corden.[23]

The agency Stun also produced trailers in which Corden went out into local shopping centres to ask people: 'What do you think of the new host James Corden?' As *Variety* magazine reported, the clever self-deprecation of the new host being unrecognizable to the passers-by played out brilliantly:

One woman says she doesn't like the man, so he pushes her on her reasons: 'Is it because he cut his long hair? Is it because he's so thin?' 'Yes, he looks like he's wasting away,' she replies. Suddenly suspicious, she asks, 'He's not behind me, is he?' With a wink to the camera, Corden says, 'No, we would never do that to you.'[24]

Indeed it wasn't the first time that Corden had proved himself happy to be the fall guy in a marketing campaign. Sky One in the UK created a launch trailer for their sports panel show *A League of Their Own*, which cast Corden in a mock heroic parody of a Nike commercial starring Fernando Torres. Written by Rafaela Perera and directed by Ben Winston (a long-time Corden collaborator and now executive producer of his CBS show), the trailer featured super slow-motion footage of Corden, whose lack of sporting prowess leads to disastrous and incendiary consequences.[25] The print and poster campaign continued the theme of pricking the pomposity of Adidas and Nike's portentous statements of ambition, with headlines such as:

Impossible is Impossible

Float like a butterfly. Drink lots of tea

My game is unstoppable. Until the ad break

Of course the success of Corden in cracking the US market is less to do with the traditional launch marketing campaign than with his instinctive understanding of social media and the new digital media environment. For Corden every show becomes a sequence of short-form marketing material the minute it is aired, ready to be instantly shared, recut, reposted and replayed. As executive producer Rob Crabbe told the *Hollywood Reporter*:

We could never count on ratings to start because James is an unknown quantity. But what we could go for is relevance – by being part of the conversation and getting videos put up and having people, hopefully favourably, mentioning things said on the show on a blog post and linking to the YouTube video. That's been incredibly helpful in getting James out there.[26]

So, 'Carpool Karaoke with Stevie Wonder' is a trailer.[27] 'Dodgeball with One Direction' is a promo.[28] All content is marketing. At the time of writing the YouTube channel exceeded 2.5 million subscribers and Carpool Karaoke with Justin Bieber and Adele had both attracted over 50 million views.

The love-in between Google's video platform and *The Late Late Show* culminated in August 2015, when an entire episode was given over to celebrating the talent and diversity of the 'stars of YouTube'. Billed as a celebration of 10 years of YouTube and filmed entirely in the reception area of the brand's 'space' in LA, it was also a clever marketing ploy to reach out to the demographic group who would not be allowed to stay up to *The Late Late Show*'s witching-hours start time. Some 2,000 plus applied to be the lucky audience of 100, and they were all there expressly to see the YouTube stars: from the Epic Rap Battle team to the Slow Mo Guys. *Late Late Show* executive Ben Winston acknowledged to the *Hollywood Reporter*:

> We'd be lying if we said we weren't reaching out to a certain extent to that new crowd to say, 'This show is for you, and late night is for you.'[29]

The new mutually beneficial relationship between online video-sharing sites such as YouTube and entertainment shows is a growing area of focus for marketers across the world. The Ylvis brothers, stars of TV Norge in Norway's talk show *I kveld med Ylvis* (Tonight with Ylvis), discovered global fame with a song written in part as a promotion for the show. 'The Fox – What does the Fox Say?' became the most watched video globally in 2013. Their collaboration with renowned hit-makers Stargate was meant to be a terrible parody of manufactured pop, but instead became an international phenomenon. As one of the brothers admitted to the *New York Times* following their appearance on the Jimmy Fallon show: 'From a comedian's perspective, it would be much more fun if we misused their (Stargate's) talents,' Bard said. 'We go make that song, we come back to our talk show and we say, "Sorry, guys."'[30]

– SOCIABLE. SHAREABLE –

Entertainment marketing relies on social currency, and establishing the right tone of voice in Twitter feeds, Instagram posts and Vine headlines needs as much care and attention as the crafting of billboard campaigns. Tony Pipes explains the growing role that social media is playing in ITV's campaigns for *The X Factor*, particularly as they target a declining younger demographic:

> This year [2015] rather than buy off-air we have done a lot of social support for *The X Factor* trying to reach that younger audience. Lots of social films in particular. We did lots of snippets and interviews with the talent themselves. When we shot the main trailer we had two studios – one dedicated to social. So the talent went in there and were reminiscing about their favourite *X Factor* acts and moments. They did 'who could hold a note for the longest' for example, lots of fun things, and because all of the judges did it we had a lot of material and a really good roll-out plan, including seeding and paid social for weeks before the first episode.[31]

This understanding of the impact of YouTube also influenced the marketing of the 10th anniversary season of *The X Factor*. ITV Creative worked with world renowned DJ Robin Skouteris to create a remarkable mash-up of the countless stars produced by the show, from Leona Lewis and Little Mix to Amelia Lily and Joe McElderry, not to mention One Direction. The idea perfectly suited the YouTube environment and swiftly racked up hundreds of thousands of views. As Tony says:

> It was perfect... and the weird thing is, we said that's what you should go with for the whole campaign, and all the commissioners were saying 'No, you need something specially shot.' There's always the default to the big conceptual spot, yet this got more traction than anything else and it cost about £3,000.[32]

There was also the added benefit of a PR storm around the artists who were not included in the mash-up, with headline-generating 'fury' from Matt Cardle.[33] Remember, with entertainment shows, PR always trumps traditional bought advertising.

– TAKING THE SHOW ON THE ROAD –

Interaction with entertainment formats extends beyond the marketing campaign, though, and into product extensions. For decades, brand merchandise and licensing deals have seen everything from board games to computer games and pub quiz machines flourish on the back of big shiny floor shows. From Nintendo Wii versions of The Amazing Race, to Deal Or No Deal and The Voice on the app store.

In 2010 Channel 4 took interactivity to new levels with an online game mechanic for new quiz format *The Million Pound Drop*. The game mirrored the show in allowing players to gamble 'a million pounds' on the answers to questions being asked live on linear television. Host Davina McCall could then refer live to how well or badly online players were getting on. The creative director of developers Monterosa, Tom McDonnell, explained why playing along live added so much to the experience:

> Integrating real-time participation with a format is challenging but we've worked closely with Endemol and Channel 4 to integrate the two creatively. The pay-off is a greater sense of event, and being able to engage fans of the show more.[34]

The further advantage for all game extensions is clearly a marketing one. Taking the brands into viewers' homes builds both loyalty and visibility.

But if you cannot take your entertainment brand into their homes, the next best thing is to take it to a town nearby.

We saw in Philip Almond's earlier quote the increased importance that the BBC places on the live tour element of growing a super brand like *Strictly Come Dancing*. For the BBC it is less about the financial returns of an arena tour than it is about being able to bring a physical manifestation of one of their bigger hits out on the road to get closer to tens of thousands of licence fee payers. *Dancing with the Stars* has similarly ambitious live tours every year, taking in 40 US cities through the summer months. Live tours have the added advantage of keeping marketing visibility high for a brand when it is off air.

CBS had a whole marketing team dedicated to what they called the 'outernet', physically taking shows into surprising places – including once sponsoring a family motor home to tour across the United States with the whole RV wrapped in *Amazing Race* signage.[35]

– PUTTING ON THE PARTY FROCK –

There are drama channels, comedy channels, documentary channels, children's channels, news channels and reality TV channels. There are no entertainment channels (a possible exception might be Challenge in the UK, which is predominantly an archive of gameshows). It is interesting to consider why this might be the case. Entertainment shows are high-octane, 100 mile an hour shows that require intensive audience concentration and/or participation. Perhaps a diet exclusively of these shows is unlikely to sustain an entire evening's viewing, let alone a 24/7 schedule.

The result is that most entertainment shows sit on channels with a broad range of programming, whose brands and junctions need to embrace a wide variety of tones. Often this presents a problem when designing a brand identity for broad genre channels. The ability to slip into the party shoes and glittery frock needed to match the right tone of voice of Saturday night entertainment needs careful consideration when creating the design elements for such a channel. For channels like CBS, BBC One and ITV the gear change between programmes can be pronounced. For BBC One we create a raft of idents with the express intention of introducing this content. The neon of Blackpool illuminations and *Strictly* glitterballs are both corralled into service. But it is very easy for such pronounced shifts in tone to feel clumsy.

In 2010, BBC One was trying to protect its Saturday night viewing figures against the behemoth of ITV's *Britain's Got Talent*. An identity and brand campaign was devised based around the iconic circular structure of the BBC's studio complex Television Centre. The work itself was based on the genuine experience for those lucky enough to work there: you would see aliens filming *Doctor Who* queuing in the canteen behind *Strictly Come Dancing* dancers, while chat and music host Graham Norton conversed with football presenter Gary Lineker – all in the building for their respective shows.

A bright, 2D animation style turned this thought into a colourful 'House of Fun' to create idents, menus and in-programme pointers (IPPs). Tellingly the IPP, which is rarely used in the UK, goes by the less salubrious name

'Violator' in the United States. It is where a small graphic pops up a few minutes before the end of a programme to alert viewers to what is coming next.

During a deeply emotional speech from Matt Smith's Doctor Who, at the climax of the episode 'City of Angels', animated entertainment host Graham Norton popped up and danced around at the bottom of the screen. (He was promoting the hunt for a new musical star in *Over the Rainbow* – to give full context.) It was a painful lesson in how not to upset the devoted *Doctor Who* audience, and some 6,000 rang the BBC Duty Office to complain about this jarring insertion of Saturday night jazz hands.[36] Thankfully, Twitter had yet to become a global phenomenon.

Shiny floor shows, at their best, work as cardiac paddles on a channel, pumping unpredictable, audience-involving, fast-paced, water-cooler moments into the heart of a schedule. The best marketing for them mirrors these qualities. Like ITV's *The X Factor* 10th anniversary trail, or Ylvis's 'What Does the Fox Say?', they are social at heart, high energy, and aware that their primary purpose is also to entertain.

NEXT

★ The biggest thing on television in 200 million years.

★ President Obama's preview screening.

★ Reinventing *The Beverly Hillbillies*.

★ Save Snuffy.

★ Propelling Sigur Ros to fame.

★ Running with Sean.

LATER

★ 'It's about who you want to lose.'

★ Sir Jonathan Ive's *Blue Peter* badge.

★ The household campfire.

NOTES

1 *The Muppet Show*, 'Don Knotts' (1977) season two, episode 201, CBS/ITC, 18 November

2 Tony Pipes, executive creative director, ITV Creative, interview 16 September 2015

3 Eatock, D (nd) [accessed 28 October 2015] Big Brother 2: Logo And Graphic Identity Commissioned By Channel 4, *Daniel Eatock Artist Page*, http://eatock.com/project/big-brother-2/2/

4 Evafanaticcom (2009) [accessed 28 October 2015] ABC House Campaign Promo #2 [Online] https://www.youtube.com/watch?v=GsjP21ByUMQ

5 O'Grady, A, quoted in Sickels, R (ed) (2008) *The Business of Entertainment*, Greenwood Press, Westport, CT

6 Philip Almond, director of marketing and audiences, BBC, interview 14 September 2015

7 Philip Almond, director of marketing and audiences, BBC, interview 14 September 2015

8 Lawson, M (2014) [accessed 28 October 2015] Ten Years Of The X Factor: The Show-Off Show With A Talent For Survival, *Guardian*, 29 August [Online] http://www.theguardian.com/tv-and-radio/2014/aug/29/the-x-factor-television

9 Probst, J, quoted in Koblin, J (2015) [accessed 28 October 2015] 'Survivor' Defies Gravity To Hang On As CBS Ratings Stalwart, *New York Times*, 30 September [Online] http://www.nytimes.com/2015/10/01/business/media/survivor-defies-gravity-to-hang-on-as-cbs-ratings-stalwart.html?_r=2

10 CBS (multiple dates) [accessed 28 October 2015] 'SurvivorOnCBS Video Collection' [Online] https://www.youtube.com/user/SurvivorOnCBS/videos

11 Troika (2014) [accessed 28 October 2015] ABC Dancing With The Stars Season 18 Launch [Online] http://www.troika.tv/abc-dancing-with-the-stars/

12 Tony Pipes, executive creative director, ITV Creative, interview 16 September 2015

13 Justin Bairamian, director of BBC Creative, interview 22 July 2015

14 Tony Pipes, executive creative director, ITV Creative, interview 16 September 2015

15 ITV (2015) [accessed 5 November 2015] X Factor – Brand New Trailer – ITV [Online] https://www.youtube.com/watch?v=23pOX0-apB4

16 https://www.youtube.com/watch?v=K7A71XjNe_M&list=PLDsg58IUh5wSL0PL9GLVpuYRGnrTHCvfk&index=22

17 http://www.redbeecreative.tv/work/bbc-one-the-voice-series-4-launch?service=entertainment-marketing

18 https://www.youtube.com/watch?v=y_TTLYdxKTg&feature=youtu.be

19 https://www.youtube.com/watch?v=SIG_-2JAU_g&feature=youtu.be

20 ITV (2015) [accessed 5 November 2015] I'm A Celebrity: Get Me Out Of Here! Brand New 2015 Trailer, ITV [Online] https://www.youtube.com/watch?v=zi50W2J-Dko and ITV (2015) [accessed 5 November 2015] I'm A Celebrity: Get Me Out Of Here! Brand New 2015 Trailer, ITV [Online] https://www.youtube.com/watch?v=WBHmi4mQSxI

21 Tony Pipes, executive creative director, ITV Creative, interview 16 September 2015

22 Krone, H, quoted in Muir, C (2015) [accessed 28 October 2015] Volkswagen Crisis: Brand That Invented Modern Advertising Is Dented, *The Conversation*, 25 September [Online] http://theconversation.com/volkswagen-crisis-brand-that-invented-modern-advertising-is-dented-48186

23 Bronner, S (2015) [accessed 28 October 2015] With James Corden, The Era Of Late-Night Feuds May Finally Be Over, *Huffington Post*, 10 March [Online] http://www.huffingtonpost.com.au/2015/03/09/james-corden-late-late-show_n_6820514.html?ir=Australia

24 Birnbaum, D (2015) [accessed 28 October 2015] James Corden On Taking Over 'The Late Late Show' And Winning Over America, *Variety*, 3 March [Online] http://variety.com/2015/tv/news/james-corden-late-late-show-new-host-interview-1201444685/

25 Rich Thrift (2010) [accessed 28 October 2015] A League Of Their Own [Online] https://vimeo.com/10351674

26 Crabbe, R, quoted in Jarvey, N (2015) [accessed 28 October 2015] Tyler Oakley, Jenna Marbles And A Host Of Online Stars Stop By The Aug 21 Episode Shot On Location At YouTube Space LA, *Hollywood Reporter*, 21 August [Online] http://www.hollywoodreporter.com/news/how-james-corden-built-a-816701

27 The Late Late Show with James Corden (2015) [accessed 28 October 2015] Stevie Wonder Carpool Karaoke [Online] https://www.youtube.com/watch?v=qqrvm2XDvpQ

28 The Late Late Show with James Corden (2015) [accessed 28 October 2015] Dodgeball with One Direction [Online] https://www.youtube.com/watch?v=QYMGgESFd7E

29 Winston, B, quoted in Jarvey, N (2015) [accessed 28 October 2015] Tyler Oakley, Jenna Marbles And A Host Of Online Stars Stop By The Aug 21 Episode Shot On Location At YouTube Space LA, *Hollywood Reporter*, 21 August [Online] http://www.hollywoodreporter.com/news/how-james-corden-built-a-816701

30 Itzkoff, D (2013) [accessed 28 October 2015] The Fox Says, 'I Can Make You Famous', *New York Times*, 11 October [Online] http://www.nytimes.com/2013/10/12/arts/music/ylviss-unlikely-hit-started-as-a-joke.html?_r=1

31 Tony Pipes, executive creative director, ITV Creative, interview 16 September 2015

32 Tony Pipes, executive creative director, ITV Creative, interview 16 September 2015

33 Doran, S (2013) [accessed 28 October 2015] WATCH: The Ultimate X Factor Mash-up [Online] http://entertainment.ie/tv/news/WATCH-The-Ultimate-X-Factor-Mash-Up-Minus-Matt-Cardle-and-co/203307.htm

34 Laughlin, A (2010) [accessed 28 October 2015] CP4 Boosts Online For 'Million Pound Drop', *Digital Spy*, 20 May [Online] http://www.digitalspy.co.uk/tech/news/a220898/c4-boosts-online-for-million-pound-drop.html#ixzz3p8GuGTj0

35 Blackmon, J (2006) [accessed 28 October 2015] CBS Outernet Campaign Includes Survivor Terry Deitz, *Reality TV Magazine*, 17 July [Online] http://realitytvmagazine.sheknows.com/2006/07/17/cbs-outernet-campaign-includes-survivor-terry-deitz/

36 Lusher, T (2010) [accessed 28 October 2015] BBC Apologises To Doctor Who Fans After Thousands Of Complaints Over Programme Trailer, *Guardian*, 26 April [Online] http://www.theguardian.com/tv-and-radio/tvandradioblog/2010/apr/26/bbc-apologises-doctor-who-trailer

CHAPTER ELEVEN

DOCUMENTARIES AND REALITY

Stories and storytellers

Homer: Lisa, honey, I bought you something. A DVD!
Lisa: Not interested.
Homer: It's a documentary... by the BBC... in cooperation with CANAL+.
Lisa: (gasps) Gimme, gimme, gimme!

THE SIMPSONS[1]

– WHY WE WATCH WHAT WE WATCH –

Ultimately there are two reasons to watch a documentary. You are interested in the story, or you are interested in the storyteller. That, in a sentence, would encapsulate every creative decision made in every factual campaign over the last 50 years.

So, a pretty short chapter then?

Fortunately what lies beneath this simple mantra is a world of more complex and nuanced marketing approaches, but at its most basic every creative brief will attempt to highlight one or other of these approaches. In the reductive pressure cooker of a 30-second trailer it is virtually impossible to land both pillars equally. Louis Theroux's *LA Stories* inevitably becomes a trailer about Louis Theroux, whereas *Extreme Fishing with Robson Green*, despite the headline billing, is a programme about big fish, watched by people interested in big fish.

The history of factual television has seen the balance of commissioning shift between the two pillars. From the cult of personality, where no travelogue was complete without a comedian discovering themselves, to rafts of identikit programmes looking at previously unremarked topics or communities of interest, from storage lockers to repo truckers (see Chapter 3 in relation to truTV).

The attraction of these new non-scripted programmes lies of course in their relatively low budgets. Away from the global filming and hefty CGI of landmark documentaries, which we will return to later, observational documentaries and factual entertainment can be low cost, highly formatted and capable of filling hours of prime time at a fraction of the cost of drama, comedy or sports rights. They don't rely on big name talent with their retinue of agents, and they don't involve heavy upfront investment in writing teams and showrunners. In short, if you can find the right pawnbrokers, deep sea fishermen, driving instructors or vets, then it is a licence to print advertising revenue.

But today we are seeing the balance returning to what we could call 'serious factual'. Robin Garnett, VP of creative for Discovery UK, speaks with fierce pride of Discovery Channel's new brand mantra 'Make Your World Bigger', and how it has come to define commissioning and marketing alike:

> We had our eyes opened when, after many years of year-on-year growth, last year ratings started to drop off. Our affiliates have always wanted us to champion our blue-chip factual reputation, and for the first time we started to get viewers saying the same thing as well. 'You keep giving us all these American copy-cat turbo programmes and they aren't even as good as the original ones.' We had just launched this idea of 'Make Your World Bigger', and the content we had simply didn't live up to it – beardy men fixing cars in a garage in Texas makes your world smaller than ever – so we had a big think about who we are. What are we for, what do we believe? If we're saying we 'Make Your World Bigger' we have to mean it, we have to live it – through our content, our mix of programmes and our behaviour.[2]

A mantra for Discovery Channel: 'Make Your World Bigger'
Source: Reproduced by permission of Discovery Networks

Equally Liz Dolan, responsible for National Geographic channel's marketing worldwide, makes a similar point:

> The content has to be more premium. We have a premium brand, but we have not always had premium content. That has been the challenge for that channel for a long time. When people describe the National

Geographic brand, they describe something that is in their imagination but not on their screen. I'd rather have that than the reverse when they think we have awesome programmes but are some crappy brand. But your number one marketing tool is your content so our number one marketing goal is to improve our content.[3]

Certainly an analysis of key art for *Ax Men* on History Channel,[4] versus *American Loggers* on Discovery,[5] suggests that there was a period when brands had all but given up any attempt to mark out meaningful and distinctive territories. Writing in 2010, TV marketing guru Lee Hunt noted in his Annual Best Practices presentation:

For 15 years Discovery Channel stuck 'Explore Your World' onto every promo, ad and ID. And while the channel always scores through the roof in brand awareness, the line had almost zero recall. At the end of the day it's all about how you create emotional resonance with a tag.[6]

So, as factual channels begin to return to premium content documentaries, it becomes more important than ever to produce a return on that upfront investment with strong and distinctive marketing campaigns.

PROGRAMMES
– VISIBLE FROM –
SPACE

A phrase you will often hear echoing around the vaulted halls of television festivals is that of 'landmark factual' – commissioners seeking landmark factual programmes, SVPs and controllers announcing landmark factual deals. There is a revealing semantic tic at play here. What do they mean by 'landmark'? Visible from a distance, an assumption of immense stature. When we have sat in channel controller forward-planning meetings where programmes are given the 'green-light tick', and then go on to spend four years in the making, it gives one an understanding of the scale and impact meant by the term 'landmark'.

Perhaps the defining example of the genre, and still one of the biggest rating series in the world, ever, was the BBC/Discovery co-production *Walking with Dinosaurs* – a landmark factual project so big it was probably visible from space. (It certainly found a place in the *Guinness Book of World Records* for being the most expensive documentary by minute of footage.)[7]

The most important consideration when launching a programme of this size and originality is to make it feel like an unmissable event. So we launched it – with a similarly understated claim:

Get ready for the biggest thing on television in 200 million years.

Teaser trailers ran weeks ahead of launch giving tantalizing snatches of producer Tim Haines's extraordinary creations. Often, when taking a viewer to new worlds and new wonders, the trick in marketing is to hold back, preventing the spectacle becoming too familiar in the period before launch. Showing a glimpse of ankle, but no more. Many of the marketing techniques discussed in other chapters also came into play, from outdoor posters to channel idents, in which the then BBC One icon, a globe-shaped balloon, drifted over a lumbering stegosaurus.[8]

It launched in the UK to breathtaking viewing figures, an audience of 18.9 million.[9] This pattern was matched worldwide, with *Walking with Dinosaurs* becoming the most watched programme ever on Discovery Channel in the United States and garnering 400 million viewers in total across the globe.[10]

The series also marked a new departure in sales and marketing for factual, as BBC Worldwide, the public service broadcaster's commercial arm, began to build 'global brands'. Beyond the traditional brand extensions of books and DVDs, *Walking with Dinosaurs* was reimagined as an arena tour,[11] and in 2014, a theatrical release film provided another reboot of the franchise.

In 2015, another series worthy of the landmark tag was launched globally by Fox and National Geographic channel: *Cosmos: A Spacetime Odyssey*.

A sequel to Carl Sagan's definitive 1980 series on PBS, it was championed and executive produced by Seth MacFarlane (of *Family Guy* fame) and Sagan's widow and original co-author Ann Druyan, and presented by the charismatic Neil deGrasse Tyson.

The 16-year gap between *Walking with Dinosaurs* and *Cosmos* reveals an interesting change in marketing tactics for broadcasters. The growth of the web has fundamentally changed global release patterns. In 1999 it didn't matter hugely when each geographical territory showed the series. By 2014 the impacts of illegal file downloading, social sharing of imagery and the digital marketing footprint meant that the release windows needed to be closer and closer. Fox decided to make this a deliberate feature of their launch with a simultaneous same 'day and date' airing of episode one in every country across the world. Liz Dolan of Fox explains:

It was super-ambitious for us, but we made the decision in the rest of the world to do it differently from the US. In the US, *Cosmos* was shared by Fox and Nat Geo so it premiered on Fox on Sunday nights, which was gutsy for Fox, and essentially was repeated on

Nat Geo on Monday nights. In the rest of the world, we needed to marry it to our one big science brand Nat Geo, but it had all of these entertainment values, all of this drama, all of the amazing visual storytelling. So we premiered it across our entire portfolio – all the Fox channels, all of our Nat Geo channels, we even put it on Fox Sports.[12]

Liz goes on to say that part of the reason for the cross-scheduling onto their entertainment channel portfolio was a bid to broaden the reach from those predisposed to watch factual:

It's a show about science, the vastness of the universe and the creation of the world. People just seeing that on their EPG might not think it's the most compelling choice at the end of a hard day. We believed we could hook people if they could see even a little of it... so we got people to surprise sample it. The original *Cosmos* was such a cultural institution but someone had to step into Carl Sagan's shoes. They made an amazing choice with Neil deGrasse Tyson. Neil has the ability to make science so popular... he's on the *The Daily Show* all the time... he's got this huge Twitter following, and he makes science sexy.[13]

The launch trailer followed a similar pattern to that of *Walking with Dinosaurs*, using the language of unmissable film launches – 'The greatest cosmic story science has ever told'[14] – but then unusually went on to list all seven channels that would carry the programme, perhaps with the subtext that it was so large it couldn't merely be held on one channel alone.

The digital campaign included online advertising and extensive social media to engage the 37 million National Geographic fans, fabulous 3D GIFs, and an off-air campaign built around the key art of a human eye immersed in a galaxy.

Tyson and Druyan travelled to four continents to host question and answer sessions and preview screenings – and then came the biggest stunt of them all.

On the opening night the series was introduced by a special guest – President Barack Obama. Having hosted a preview screening at the White House as part of its first Film Festival, the president appeared before the premiere inviting a generation to explore new frontiers, 'Open your eyes and open your imagination' because 'the next great discovery could be yours' (possibly an unfortunate turn of phrase to name-check a great rival factual brand there).[15] Like *Dinosaurs* before, the marketing campaign paid off, as Liz describes:

It turned out to be the highest-rating series in the history of National Geographic Channel (partly because of the opening multichannel stunt). For me, *Cosmos* was the best example of what is possible for us because we took everything we know how to do – original entertainment, compelling

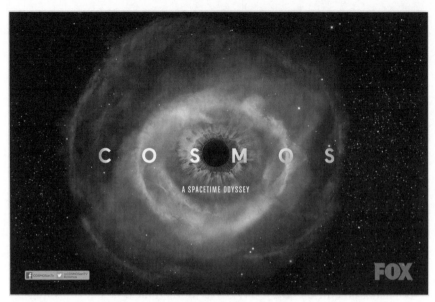

Cosmos, '*a show about science, the vastness of the universe and the creation of the world*' *Source: Copyright © 2014 Cosmos Studios, Inc. TRADEMARK ® COSMOS: A SPACETIME ODYSSEY by Druyan Sagan Associates, Inc. All rights reserved. This material cannot be further circulated without written permission of Cosmos Studios, Inc. and Druyan Sagan Associates, Inc.*

factual content, big event buzz, talent promotion, global reach, everything – and we bet it all on one big ambitious show.[16]

– CREATING FACTUAL STARS –

To return to this chapter's opening remarks, if we look at those programmes that are watched not for the subject but for the storytellers, we can subdivide them in three distinct ways: specialist experts bringing their enthusiasm and passion to a subject with the hope that it will spread infectiously to the watching public, the 'naive' presenter who serves as the eyes of the audience entering a new world for the first time and, finally, the subjects of an observational format themselves.

Let's look first at the specialist. Animal Planet built much of its ratings success on the back of Steve Irwin, 'The Crocodile Hunter', a man whose enthusiasm was so infectious that any attempt to contain him within the confines of a marketing message seemed foolhardy. David Attenborough on the natural world, Brian Cox on space, Michael Moore on gun control... the key to marketing is to capture that presenter spark and trap it successfully in the reductive time of a trailer. One of the finest examples is Discovery Channel UK's launch of *Bear Grylls – Born Survivor* in 2011 – an edit that strips the series back to its very visceral movement and grunts of endeavour, as Grylls leaps from mountain rock to jungle branch in a non-stop race.[17]

A brand ad for BBC Two, adroitly creative directed by James de Zoete and Andy Booth, took every factual star on the channel and edited footage of them all walking away from camera. It was highly original in execution – who shows just the backs of their biggest stars? – but wonderfully captured their constant questioning. What is around the next corner? Or, as the voice-over put it: how far is too far?

The second area is the star as the discoverer of new worlds of knowledge. Michael Palin became the original adventurer on behalf of the sofa bound. Indeed his impact on the places he visited for the travelogues – *Around the World in 80 Days, Pole to Pole, Full Circle* – created the 'Palin Effect', which saw large increases in visitors to the visited destinations. The BBC invested heavily not just in the production but in the marketing of the shows, allocating off-air poster sites to promote his Himalayan travels, for example. There was commercial sense behind this as the add-on sales of DVDs, books and other merchandise turned the explorer into a lucrative global brand. The format of 'celebrity adventurer' is now as well travelled as Palin's suitcase itself, with some of the latest incarnations being seen on Showtime in the United States, where *Years of Living Dangerously* saw stars including Harrison Ford, Don Cheadle and Jessica Alba explore climate change. As the *New York Times* reviewed, the strength of these shows can lie in the naivety of the presenter asking simple questions. Yet in their trailer, Showtime cleverly elevated the show, both by branding it an 'event series' as opposed to just a series, and increasing the celebrities' status by captioning them as 'correspondents'.[18] As the review summarized, there is no loss of journalistic credibility:

> The truth is, Mr Ford and Mr Cheadle are just as good as any seasoned television correspondent at the news magazine drill: parachute in, digest a lot of material gathered by producers and researchers, ask reasonably intelligent questions, make small talk, look concerned. On the basis of the first episode, they're probably better.[19]

The third area of focus on storytellers is the emerging 'reality stars' of observational documentaries. The great advantage for people marketing these series, as they run over multiple seasons, is that they become dramas, with storylines that twist and turn with all the themes of human interaction found in fiction. Robin Garnett explains the change over the years in how Discovery have marketed *Deadliest Catch*, as characters and personalities emerge:

> Deadliest Catch could be a one-off documentary about crab fishermen in the Bering Sea and you'd watch and think 'Yeah, I didn't know that existed' and say 'That's interesting,' but that show has lasted for 10, 12 series and it's still rating well. People come back and it's clearly for something more than knowledge.

When we began marketing it was 'the most dangerous job in the world', and you're going to want to watch how they do it and how they survive. But now we market it more like a soap like *EastEnders* or *Coronation Street* – what are the storylines that people want to follow, who are the characters people love or love to hate? Because that is why people are coming back to it – it's absolutely the formula of soap operas, but in a form, location and tone that is acceptable to men.[20]

An interesting example of how a single show can be positioned differently on two networks lies in a revealing picture of school life, *American High*, a series sold on Fox as 'reality' TV, and then rerun on PBS and marketed as a 'documentary' series. As Susan Murray writes in her book *Reality TV: Remaking television culture*: 'Executives at both networks believed they could alter the reception context of *American High* to suit their particular needs.'[21]

One of the channels that pioneered the heavily formatted observational documentary genre in America was A&E. Michael Vamosy of Stun Creative was tasked with launching their massive hit series *Duck Dynasty*, and he talks about how the key was to establish the family as characters with depth, in much the same way we have discussed in Chapter 7 on drama:

We kind of reinvented the Beverly Hillbillies. There they are standing in front of a gorgeous mansion but they happen to be in their hip waders and tuxedos. The tuxedos are gorgeous, the women look beautiful in their dresses, but the guys have these hints of their personality coming through the formal wear: a camouflage lapel, a camo bow tie. It was just that hint of sophistication, to position that show as 'Yes, they're rich, but they're not what you were expecting.' And we helped set that up and start the conversation with the viewers and A&E did a great job of taking it and running with it and turning that show into a huge success.[22]

– CHILD LABOUR –

In the UK, a major development within observational documentaries arrived with 'fixed-rig' camera shows. This filming technique allowed us into the places and professions of people in a way that conventional documentary crews could never capture. One of the most successful in the genre has been the *Educating* series on Channel 4. The characters of teachers and pupils alike from the featured schools across the UK have become genuine stars in their own right, without any of the fakery and flummery of 'scripted reality' shows like *T.O.W.I.E* or *Jersey Shore*: Essex Deputy Head Mr Drew, and Musharaf, the student who was brilliantly and movingly coached to overcome a profound stutter (and later turned up in Channel 4's 'Born Risky' campaign, which we described in Chapter 5). Channel 4 shepherded the conversation around the social channels using the #educatingessex hashtag, which generated around 100,000 tweets during the first series alone.

When tasked with marketing the second series set in Yorkshire, Channel 4's in-house 'agency' 4Creative, realizing that the children were the stars of the show, came up with the idea to make the marketing campaign part of the schoolchildren's educational life. They handed over the brief to the children, who threw themselves into the project, producing over 100 drawings and paintings to illustrate the off-air campaign, many of them perfectly on Channel 4's mischievous tone of voice.

Light relief on the school timetable: creating the advertising for Educating Yorkshire
Source: © Channel 4 Television

– WHAT TYPE OF STORYTELLER ARE YOU? –

The inherent breadth of topics, styles, moods and subgenres that lie underneath the factual banner makes attempts to pinpoint a broadcaster's overarching brand promise within documentaries particularly challenging. Both of the UK's biggest broadcasters have struggled. In ITV's case, Tony Pipes, executive creative director, admits that trying to unify such a diverse portfolio under a single thought is fraught:

> There is a real shift between what we show before 9 pm and what we run after 9. After 9 pm you get Trevor McDonald on *Inside Death Row* and these serious heavyweight documentaries, and before 9 pm it's lighter, more Griff Rhys Jones walking the hills of Scotland. Our factual team have always struggled to define ITV in that genre with one line.[23]

In 2008 the factual marketing team at the BBC signed off on an ambitious and powerful piece of brand communication, creating a clear lighthouse identity for what makes a BBC story. The creative team of Oliver Harnett and John-Paul McKeown used the words of Jack Kerouac from his acclaimed novel *On the Road*, and striking vignettes from acclaimed photographer and director Stuart Douglas:

> I shambled after as I've been doing all my life after people who interest me, because the only people for me are the mad ones, the ones who are mad to live, mad to talk, mad to be saved, desirous of everything at the same time, the ones who never yawn or say a commonplace thing, but burn, burn, burn like fabulous yellow roman candles exploding like spiders across the stars and in the middle you see the blue centrelight pop and everybody goes 'Awww!'[24]

The trailer concludes with the single promise: 'Meet the most interesting people in the world. BBC Documentaries'.[25]

The trailer ran into much debate about whether it accurately caught the breadth of tones of voice within the 'documentary genre'. That same yin and yang, push and pull, that ITV equally wrestled with. To our minds, it was warm, powerful and engaging, as all the best documentaries should be. Clearly defining the voice of a single 'storyteller', as a brand campaign seeks to do, is a challenge, but some brands have been successful in identifying a unique position. A&E in the United States marketed all of their content under the tagline: Real Life. Drama. A clever play on their switch from the genres of their original name to the pillars of their new schedule.

For UKTV History (now renamed Yesterday) our team developed a brand campaign using the line 'Why we are who we are'. For channels that specialize in historical factual, there is a perceived need to show the contemporary relevance of their content, and this was one of the more successful executions of that strategy. Each promotional film put the spotlight on a historical episode that had shaped our world today, using mixed-media animation and a wide variety of tones. In one spot we see the creation of the 'unlucky third match' during the trenches of the Somme, in another the birth of the Channel Tunnel.

Perhaps the most awarded of factual channel campaigns came with the launch of BBC Four in 2002. Creative directors Anton Ezer and Ben Friend positioned the brand squarely as an oasis of intelligent programming, defining the channel against all other television almost as clearly as 'It's Not TV. It's HBO' did: BBC Four. Everybody Needs a Place to Think.

Beautiful and powerful films showed where great artists, athletes and writers had found inspiration. Mary Shelley creating Frankenstein in the Villa Diodati on the shores of Lake Geneva, Jesse Owens preparing for the

1936 Olympics in a clapboard church in Cleveland, Ohio, and Ian McEwan walking the ploughed fields of his beloved Chilterns.[26] Posters showed Philip Glass in Central Park, Sam Taylor-Wood (now Taylor-Johnson) in Regent's Park and Dennis Hopper in Venice, California.[27]

Artist Sam Taylor-Wood in her 'place to think': BBC Four's launch campaign
Source: Reproduced by permission of BBC

What the campaign did so brilliantly was to create a lasting and clear position for the channel. It is not a broad consumption entertainment brand. It is a public service brand filling a vital role of exploring places that no other channel will. It has successfully maintained that positioning while broadening and lightening its tone of voice with award-winning 'season' campaigns such as *American Culture*[28] and the *Medieval Mind Season*.[29]

– SEASONS AND STUNTS –

Seasons have proven a strong marketing tactic for factual channels, providing a single unifying headline thought to often disparate pockets of content. The scheduling reality of factual TV is that there are a lot of one-off or three-part documentaries and it is important for 'umbrella' messages to give viewers a reason to keep coming back to the channel. The growth of long-running character-driven series such as *Deadliest Catch* has to some extent replaced the need for seasons, as the format itself drives return viewing through more conventional plot devices. Discovery Channel, however, has been home to the most globally recognized and consistently scheduled season in TV history.

– SHARK WEEK –

At the PromaxBDA conference in 2015, the Discovery US marketing team celebrated three years' worth of marketing campaigns around the enduring franchise Shark Week. The 'Save Snuffy' campaign from 2013 remains one of the most talked about launch trailers. The spoof news clip in which the rescued Snuffy the seal is cruelly snatched from the jaws of safety by a great white shark is a true viral phenomenon, which the marketing team capitalized on brilliantly by airing fan-reaction videos, generating vast amounts of Save Snuffy merchandise and garnering coverage across myriad traditional news sites.[30]

Can Snuffy be saved? Marketing campaign for Discovery Channel's Shark Week
Source: Reproduced by permission of Discovery Networks

What it didn't give them, however, was a single image to unify the campaign under, a gap that they sought to rectify with the following year's 'King of Summer' campaign in which Rob Lowe jet skis towards camera on the back of a pair of sharks, tossing chump steak to them as he races. The King of Summer campaign also demonstrated the ability for marketing teams to commercially exploit seasons, with the launch of an entire beach festival in Hermosa complete with headline acts such as Jimmy Buffett.

As ever, one of the greatest accolades any brand can achieve is that of being blatantly copied by competitors. A fact hilariously owned up to in the 'Sharkfest' commercial created by the Nat Geo Wild channel to promote their own take on fin-related programming, scheduled to run at exactly the same time as Discovery's:

> We want you to confuse the two, and you will, and we don't care because it gets ratings... sharks cannot sign an exclusive contract with a network... we're pretty certain on that.[31]

Channel 4 have also used the season strategy successfully to corral diverse one-off programmes: *Mating Season* being a standout example. They also used humour and grandiose overstatement to powerful effect in promoting their 2014 'Live from Space' season. Director Neil Gorringe harnessed Hawkwind's epic track 'Silver Machine', as an astronaut straddled a lunar rocket blasting into space.[32] A truly filmic spectacle for a documentary launch.

Channel 4 campaigns for themed documentary seasons
Source: *Mating Season – Noma Bar illustration/design for Channel 4. Live From Space* © *Channel 4 Television*

− TREAT IT LIKE A THRILLER −

Where factual channels fall behind general entertainment channels and sports networks is in the challenge of creating 'must watch live' moments. Linear television viewing has proved remarkably resilient, supported by the twin pillars of live entertainment events and their phone vote interactions, and fiction reveals that warrant immediate social commentary and water-cooler discussions. Can documentaries ever build up the escape velocity to enter either of those brackets? Not for want of trying. From *T-Rex Autopsy Live* to *Eaten Alive*, factual channels have tried to create big single 'must watch' moments. Marketing these events draws heavily on theatrical release marketing. Bold key art, countdowns and viewer competitions abound. An early mentor advised us to 'treat every documentary like a thriller', and this advice can certainly be seen in the work for *T-Rex Autopsy* or *Skywire Live*.

Interestingly, though, the more the format appears to be pumped up to 'unmissable' status in its promise, the less watchable it can seem – the classic advertising tension between stimulus and response. Perhaps a better model lies in theatrical release trailers themselves. One of the biggest shifts in movie-going in recent years has been the growth in popularity of the documentary genre, and trailers for *Man on Wire*,[33] *Virunga*,[34] *Searching for Sugarman*,[35] and more, are great examples of creating a sense of event for a single simple story.

– SCORING THE THRILLER –

Using all the ingredients outlined in theatrical release film trailers brings us to music. One of the most impactful and successful matches of music to story in TV promotional history resulted in a record-breaking factual campaign. The BBC's *Planet Earth*. Editor Thomas Ioannou had the idea of using the epic song 'Hoppipolla' by Icelandic band Sigur Ros. Opening with a simple piano fugue as the sun peeped around the edge of the world from space, the ethereal soprano vocals chimed with the sense of wonder evoked from the undersea photography, and then the soaring strings crescendoed over some of the most spectacular visuals ever captured by the BBC's Natural History Unit (and the first to be filmed in HD).[36] It was a particularly bold choice as the series already had an original score by award-winning composer George Fenton, and serves to highlight, as we see so often in this book, that what is appropriate for a 60-minute programme may well not be right for a 60-second trailer.

Many of the UK public service broadcasters have a 'blanket music agreement' with the major music companies, which for an annual fee gives permission for all tracks from those labels to be used on trailers with an 'appointment to view' message. So while Sigur Ros would not have been paid directly, Jonsi from the band has acknowledged that the use of the song had a transformative effect on their career in the UK and beyond.[37] From another perspective the band and label benefited from a promo video shot over five years and costing $25 million.

– FUTURE FOCUS –

Inevitably when looking to the future of factual marketing, it is important to embrace new digital possibilities. Perhaps with 'knowledge-based' programming the key is not about creating more expansive storyworlds, in the way we will discuss in Chapter 14 for drama or comedy. Certainly anyone wanting 'more information' or greater depth on any subject will find it online. As Robin Garnett, Discovery UK's vice president of creative, puts it:

> With the emergence of the internet, the idea of coming to factual TV for just knowledge is redundant. If you want to know something, you know what you want to know, and you can find it in a click. You are off on your own knowledge journey.[38]

That change itself has forced a marked reappraisal of what the role of digital platforms is for brands such as Discovery. Robin refers to a move from a purely TV-based knowledge brand, to a broader experience brand, where:

> We are in the centre of the fabric of your life – an app on a phone that gives me tips to 'Make My World Bigger', we are interested in anything that enables you to expand your world with the Discovery brand, not purely relying on TV content, it's an idea that lives beyond ATV. Because we don't know where it's going to go. Is Discovery the trusted brand that you would go to for actual experiences, adventure parks, events, etc? It should be a strong enough brand that if you took the TV content away it would still be a thing that meant something.[39]

Robin illustrates this with the example of Sean Conway, a most unlikely sporting hero, who dresses like Forrest Gump, and had an epiphany in his thirties that led to him attempting a 'length of Britain' triathlon. The first year cycling Land's End to John O'Groats, the next year swimming it, and in 2015 running it. Discovery took this journey as being a fantastic metaphor for 'Make Your World Bigger' and used their social and digital channels to create a very new factual experience. While the programme itself was pro-moted as a final destination, the whole marketing plan geared up to support his run; the campaign idea: '#RunwithSean'. As Robin explains:

> You could turn up physically to certain points along the route and run a mile with Sean, or bring him some cake, or a beer. He's quite an unconventional sportsman – for him he wasn't trying to do it in the quickest time, he was trying to make it the richest experience, so you could tweet him and say 'I'll meet you here, why don't you come this way,' or 'Go past there because there's an amazing view,' and he'd go off the beaten track a bit. So he's a living embodiment of 'Make Your World Bigger'. A lot of marketing

went into promoting your ability to experience this thing with him; there was a programme at the end and we did promote it and it did very well, but it was a whole shift in the marketing from promoting content to promoting experience.[40]

So creating immersive experiences is one direction for digital outreach of factual, and perhaps the other lies in the means of delivery itself. A&E Networks' History channel recently launched 'Asterisk', a website resembling BuzzFeed in editorial style, which according to Evan Silverman, senior VP of digital media at A&E, represents a new way of TV adding an entertainment filter to knowledge quests:

Most people are not searching for history on a daily basis. But they enjoy getting history in their lives in a fun and entertaining way... Asterisk is looking at life and culture through a historical filter.[41]

In other words, despite the seemingly overwhelming advance of information online, factual channels still have a place, reaching out to invite people to discover 'why we are who we are'.

NEXT
★ Think and feel like a fan.
★ It's not the despair. It's the hope.
★ Aspiring to *Ski Sunday*.
★ Man versus cheetah.
★ 'Meet the Superhumans'.
★ 'The Game Never Ends'.

LATER
★ Re-creating Doc McStuffins's clinic.
★ Sherlock's 'fatal' fall.
★ The 'Battle for the Handle'.

NOTES

1 *The Simpsons*, 'Marge Gamer' (2007) season 18, episode 17, Fox, 22 April
2 Robin Garnett, vice president of creative, Discovery UK, interview 29 September 2015
3 Liz Dolan, chief marketing officer, Fox International Channels, interview 11 June 2015
4 History Channel (2015) [accessed 5 November 2015] AxMen Promotional Artwork [Online] http://editorial.sidereel.com/Images/Promos/ax_men_poster.jpg
5 Discovery Channel (2015) [accessed 5 November 2015] American Loggers Season 1 Artwork [Online] http://www.sanity.com.au/media/Images/fullimage/275482/TSA_2192966_2015-17-4--00-56-35.jpg
6 Hunt, L (2010) [accessed 12 October 2015] Lee Hunt's New Best Practices 2010: PromaxBDA Conference [Online] http://www.leehunt.com/articles/

LeeHunt_BestPractices2010_video.pdf?bcsi_scan_7f6001589688e1d7=Pw74Y
3Ds4zoytGatjj67AHc97Ls1AAAA7XIA8A==&bcsi_scan_filename=LeeHunt_
BestPractices2010_video.pdf

7 Guinness World Records (1999) [accessed 12 October 2015] Most
Expensive Television Documentary Series by Minute [Online] http://www.
guinnessworldrecords.com/world-records/most-expensive-television-
documentary-series-per-minute/

8 TV Ark (2015) [accessed 12 October 2015] BBC One – Walking With
Dinosaurs Ident From 1999 [Online] http://www.tv-ark.org.uk/mivana/
mediaplayer.php?id=1603f3da67c7b12a78726a6fb0f5aec5&media=
bbc1balloondinosaurs1999&type=mp4

9 Broadcasting Audience Research Board (nd) [accessed 12 October 2015] TV
Since 1981 [Online] http://www.barb.co.uk/resources/tv-facts/tv-since-1981/
1999/top10

10 h2g2 (2015) [accessed 12 October 2015] 'Walking With Dinosaurs' – The
Television Phenomenon, 12 January [Online] http://h2g2.com/edited_entry/
A87827629

11 Global features and BBC Worldwide (2015) [accessed 12 October 2015] Walking
With Dinosaurs: The Arena Spectacular [Online] http://www.dinosaurlive.com/
creative/bruce-mactaggart/

12 Liz Dolan, chief marketing officer, Fox International Channels, interview
11 June 2015

13 Liz Dolan, chief marketing officer, Fox International Channels, interview
11 June 2015

14 National Geographic Singapore (2014) [accessed 12 October 2015] Cosmos:
A Spacetime Odyssey – Promo 3 [Online] https://www.youtube.com/
watch?v=XKO_BZ_PiCM

15 National Geographic (2014) [accessed 12 October 2015] President Obama's
COSMOS Introduction [Online] https://www.youtube.com/watch?v=
qcdYYISYh0I

16 Liz Dolan, chief marketing officer, Fox International Channels, interview
11 June 2015

17 Payne, C (2011) [accessed 12 October 2015] Bear Grylls Cinema Ad [Online]
https://vimeo.com/28503251

18 Years of Living Dangerously (2014) [accessed 12 October 2015] Years Of
Living Dangerously Trailer [Online] https://vimeo.com/78162825

19 Hale, M (2014) [accessed 12 October 2015] A Climate Of Complexity:
'Years Of Living Dangerously,' Celebrity-Filled Documentary, *New York Times*,
11 April [Online] http://www.nytimes.com/2014/04/12/arts/television/
years-of-living-dangerously-celebrity-filled-documentary.html?_r=2

20 Robin Garnett, vice president of creative, Discovery UK, interview 29 October
2015

21 Murray, S (2008) *Reality TV: Remaking television culture 2e*, New York
University Press, New York

22 Michael Vamosy, chief creative officer, Stun, interview 10 June 2015

23 Tony Pipes, executive creative director, ITV Creative, interview 16 September
2015

24 Kerouac, J (2000) *On the Road*, Penguin Modern Classics, London

25 Douglas, S (nd) [accessed 12 October 2015] Nice Shirt Films [Online] http://niceshirtfilms.com/director/stuart-douglas/

26 Friend, B (nd) [accessed 12 October 2015] BBC Four: Shelley [Online] http://www.friendicus.com/projects/bbc_four/bbc_four.php?m=1&p=1

27 Friend, B (nd) [accessed 12 October 2015] BBC Four: Everybody Needs A Place To Think [Online] http://www.friendicus.com/projects/bbc_four/bbc_four_print.php?m=3&p=4

28 BBC (2011) [accessed 12 October 2015] The All American Season Trail – BBC Four [Online] https://www.youtube.com/watch?v=QXjGbEST3b4

29 https://www.youtube.com/watch?v=Enxqm85WFxI

30 Swift, A (2013) 'Shark Week' Kills Snuffy The Seal, Humans Overreact – Watch, *Hollywood Life*, 27 June [Online] http://hollywoodlife.com/2013/06/27/shark-week-snuffy-the-seal-commercial-video/

31 Baker, A (2015) [accessed 13 October 2015] Sharkfest 'Rant' [Online] https://vimeo.com/131421624

32 Channel 4 (nd) [accessed 12 October 2015] Live From Space Season Trailer [Online] http://www.channel4.com/programmes/live-from-space/videos/all/live-from-space-season-trailer

33 Magnolia Pictures and Magnet Releasing (2008) [accessed 12 October 2015] Man On Wire Trailer [Online] https://www.youtube.com/watch?v=EIawNRm9NWM

34 Netflix (2014) [accessed 12 October 2015] Virunga – Main Trailer – Netflix [Online] https://www.youtube.com/watch?v=Wu-vjWd7Tb8

35 Top Documentaries (2012) [accessed 12 October 2015] Searching For Sugar Man Trailer [Online] https://www.youtube.com/watch?v=8hEojBYmR-o

36 CrashUser (2013) [accessed 5 November 2015] Planet Earth BBC Trailer HD [Online] http://www.disclose.tv/action/viewvideo/137676/Planet_Earth_BBC_Trailer_HD/

37 Bychawski, A (2006) [accessed 12 October 2015] Sigur Ros Re-Release Single Due To Public Demand, *NME News*, 6 April [Online] http://www.nme.com/news/sigur-ros/22716

38 Robin Garnett, vice president of creative, Discovery UK, interview 29 October 2015

39 Robin Garnett, vice president of creative, Discovery UK, interview 29 October 2015

40 Robin Garnett, vice president of creative, Discovery UK, interview 29 October 2015

41 Spangler, T (2015) [accessed 12 October 2015] A+E Launches Asterisk Internet-Media Brand With New Spins On History (Exclusive), *Variety*, 13 April [Online] http://variety.com/2015/digital/news/ae-launches-asterisk-internet-media-brand-with-new-spins-on-history-exclusive-1201470981/

CHAPTER TWELVE

FASTER, HIGHER, STRONGER, LONGER

The hyperbolic world of TV sports promotion

Thousands and thousands of hours of football, each more climactic than the last! Constant, dizzying, twenty-four-hour, year-long, endless football! Every kick of it massively mattering to someone, presumably. Watch it all, all here, all the time, forever, it will never stop, the football is officially going on forever! It will never be finally decided who has won the football! There is still everything to play for, and forever to play it in! So that's the football! Coming up! Watch it! Watch the football! Watch it! Watch it! It's gonna move... Watch the football! It's football!

DAVID MITCHELL, *THAT MITCHELL AND WEBB LOOK*[1]

– MORE IMPORTANT THAN LIFE AND DEATH –

Unlike previous chapters where marketing teams are attempting to introduce brand new programmes to a prospective audience, waving furiously for attention, with sports marketing they are frequently pushing at an open door. Your broadcaster has bought the rights to a competition or tournament, and there is a horde of devoted fans of participating teams just waiting for it to be shown. So where are the challenges promoting sport? First, because of the viewer's very predisposition. The consumers' relationship with a sports brand is more complex and passionate than most other consumer brands. They have lifelong loves and hates. Second, because the tournament or club will have a heritage and perception that are frequently outside your control as broadcaster; and third, for the simple reason that there is a vast amount of really, really good advertising done in this sector and therefore the quest for originality is alarmingly daunting.

Perhaps more so than any other genre, we feel there is a need for the majority of sports marketing to be devised by people with a passion for sport. This is partly because it avoids embarrassing moments of ignorance when dealing with the sports department's producers. (We still cringe at the memory of a marketer proclaiming on a written brief that the key selling point of the BBC's next cricket coverage of the England v Australia Ashes test matches was the addition in the commentary box of one 'Lillian Thomson'. For non-cricket-loving readers, Dennis Lillee and Jeff Thomson were the greatest fast bowlers ever produced by Australia.) However, the key reason for needing to be passionate about what you are promoting is that in order to talk to sports fans you have to think and feel like a sports fan. You have to understand what is being said on the terraces, thought on the bleachers or shouted from the stands. You have to feel the black humour and tribal loyalties, the fickle adorations and eternal vendettas. You have to know that 'it's not the despair, it's the hope' that gets to supporters. You have to know that history matters, that superstitious conditioning leads them to believe they can influence a game, and that occasionally, just occasionally, it is acceptable to appreciate greatness from a rival team player.[2] To think and feel like a sports fan, you have to know what music to play, what colours to paint with, what technology to employ, what words to choose.

Aaron Taylor, former SVP of marketing at ESPN, explains how the entire network's positioning pivots around this insight, derived from the early days of ad agency Wieden+Kennedy's work on the brand:

> At the time, back in the early 1990s, Jerry Cronin drafted what we refer to as the manifesto – the internal monologue of a sports fan talking about how special it feels to be a sports fan – and the headline on the manifesto is: 'ESPN isn't a large network. It's a huge sports fan.' So being that embodiment of the fan ourselves leads us to act in a certain way when we are communicating with fellow fans. From this manifesto there came some basic fundamentals: we talk with fans not at them, we try to relate to them on their own level, we take them inside with unparalleled access to provide the best coverage in the business, we help them become better sports fans, we capture their passion for sports and serve it up in our voice. We have fun. We take sports seriously, but we don't take ourselves too seriously. Those are some of the fundamentals that guided how we operate when we speak fan to fan in marketing communications.[3]

From the knowledge and understanding of sports fans come the key factors that we will outline for successful sports promotion. Insight. Humour. Partisanship. Music choices. Technology.

ESPN isn't a large network.
IT'S A huge sports fan. **ESPN**

Headline from ESPN's brand manifesto   Source: Reproduced by permission of ESPN, Inc

– UNDERSTANDING A SPORTS FAN –

In what was a landmark shift in sports promotion, Sky Sports launched a new season of Premiership football promotion in 1996 with an anthemic speech voiced by Sean Bean that claimed exactly this territory. We understand you.

> It's ecstasy, anguish, joy and despair
> It's part of our history
> Part of our country
> And it will be part of our future
> It's theatre, art, war and love
> It should be predictable... but never is
> It's a feeling that can't be explained but we spend our lives explaining it
> It's our religion
> We do not apologize for it
> We do not deny it
> They're our team, our family, our life.
>   Football
> We know how you feel about it
> 'Cos we feel the same[4]

The trailer was written by Barry Skolnick (still a key creative director within Sky), who ironically told the *Racing Post* in 2001 that it was inspired by being dumped by his girlfriend and his belief that 'the only thing I could rely on was Leeds United' (ironically, one would suggest, given Leeds's spectacular fall through the leagues that began at exactly that point in time).[5]

It could have been hyperbolic and ludicrous, but somehow the music, the choice of Bean as spokesman and the inherent credibility of the broadcaster kept it on just the right side. That could not be said of some of the match trailers and monthly packages that would follow over the years of Sky Sports dominance, which came to be so brilliantly skewered by British comedians Mitchell and Webb in the sketch featuring in this chapter's opening epigraph: 'football, football, football'. In it, David Mitchell strides around a

*'We know how you feel about it': Sean Bean's rousing speech for
Sky Sports' football coverage*   Source: Reproduced by permission of Sky Sports

football pitch ranting about the 'clash of the South Coast titans' and 'the battle of the North West between Shrewsbury and Macclesfield in a match that has already been described as "on this Sunday"'.[6]

The reason that hyperbolic excitement feels so comically inappropriate is, of course, because that is not how even the most hard-core fans feel about their teams. There is nothing as changeable or unpredictable as a sports fan's mood – just talk to Leeds United supporters – and as a broadcaster you have got to be agile enough to track their temperamental changes. Remember you can wake up feeling confident and enthusiastic about your team's chances and by lunchtime, having read two pundits' verdicts and heard the injury news, you might be cataclysmically depressed, and an upbeat promo script might sound totally hollow and out of touch.

An analysis of the BBC and ITV's promotion of major tournaments involving the England football team would show a graphic decline in nationalistic fervour, as the side consistently underperformed, to be replaced by executions that focused on the range of international talent taking part, and indeed the allure of the host country. NBC cannot possibly promote the Tour de France in the same way after the decade-long unveiling of drug cheats. Indeed their 2015 trailer explores the brutality of the course with the stark and double-sided question: 'Who will survive?'[7]

– KNOWING THE TRIBES –

Understanding the tribalism of sports fans is essential, the deep-seated rivalries that surpass all understanding. Brands have long exploited their awareness of this for commercial credibility, though few have executed it as well as ESPN with their wonderful study of twin Mancunians on the red and blue sides of the city, as they speak in identical soundbites of the innate stupidity of their brother in fandom: 'If I'd been born a red/blue I'd have been a right muppet, a miserable git...'[8]

Aaron Taylor, formerly of ESPN, explains the rationale behind it:

> They are the same fan, the same person. They can't get past their loyalties even though at the very heart of it they are the same person. It was a concept that rang true to us in the States – the rivalries that everyone talks about, whether it's University of Michigan versus Ohio State, Red Sox and Yankees. Choosing the rivalry and shooting it overseas just gave it a more interesting perspective on a universal truth about fandom.[9]

Brothers in fandom on two sides of the city of Manchester in ESPN's 'Born Into It' campaign   Source: Reproduced by permission of ESPN, Inc

Indeed, in the English Premier League the fierceness of the inter-fan rivalry adds to its commercial value, as Olivier Schaack, the man tasked with promoting it for CANAL+ in France, remarks:

> The Premier League is one of the sports competitions that's the easiest to promote using passion, because there are so many cameras and the crowd is so close to the field that on every Premier League game you have pictures of fans, the coaches, and there is this passion and excitement all the time. With the French league I tried it, and for the FIFA World Cups you have different cultures of fans and you get something interesting, but with the Premier League you sometimes feel that the crowd is shouting so loudly that the camera moves. It's big.[10]

The 6 Nations, the rugby tournament that pits all four British home nations alongside Italy and France, is also built on a rivalry that has long been the promotional focus of the public service broadcaster. In 2011 a trailer was produced with exceptional insight. Filmed all over the country by director Chris Balmond, a succession of puzzling vignettes sees fans palpably from

Scotland, Wales, Ireland, France and Italy all passionately cheering the name England. The reveal comes after 40 seconds of identical 'Englands', when a caption reads: 'The 6 Nations. It's not about who you want to win. Its about who you want to lose.'[11] The trailer ends with a group of England fans puzzling in a pub to answer the same question with myriad different responses: 'France... Scotland... Wales?'

It was a promo born of a basic truth – all the other teams have one simple and single enemy. This is a truth that a fan of any hue would acknowledge, and rugby is always played and supported with a knowing sense of warm humour. Yet the ad proved hugely difficult for us to sell up through the stakeholders. We were successful, only at the last minute for the good officers of the English RFU to object to the BBC head of sport. The trailer was pulled and replaced with tame vox pops from the same shoot. Two years later, when the trailer leaked online, it became a massive viral hit and, as anticipated, was loved and shared by fans of all hues – including the English. After all, it was an entirely English team that had made it. Self-deprecation, insight, the humour of the terraces... in short, a world away from how a governing body might see their sport.

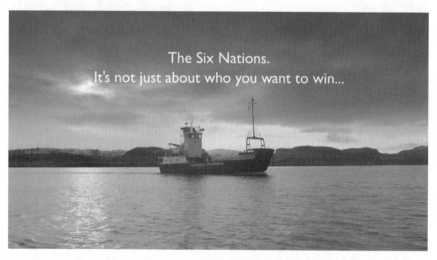

'It's about who you want to lose': the 'banned' 6 Nations rugby trailer
Source: Reproduced by permission of BBC

– SEEING THE FUNNY SIDE –

Humour is an essential part of what makes a sports fan, along with blinkered judgement and elephantine memories. Broadcasters that can appeal to the darkly comic nature of caring so much about the outcome of where a little ball goes can instantly demonstrate 'We know how you feel about it because we feel the same.' We will see how ESPN built their entire brand around a light self-deprecatory tone later, but their great rivals Fox Sports have also long been comic masters. This time it is comedy born out of understanding fans' obsessiveness. Their campaign idea that 'all other sports would be better if they were hockey' from the late 1990s cleverly underscored which rights they had sole ownership of and flattered the NHL fans and franchises alike. Particularly joyful is the 'Bowling Would Be Better if It Were Hockey' promo in which Christie Allison ends up with a very difficult spare – spoilers avoided for those wishing to enjoy online (see **https://www.youtube.com/watch?v=xt1ynyKP5NU**).[12]

Taking a similar deadpan tone, their Cannes Lion Gold-winning and Emmy-nominated 'Beware of Things Made in October' for Major League Baseball shows the disastrous consequences on the manufacturing industry of the dedicated screen time that any baseball fan will put in during the playoffs.[13] (The inspired editing of the 'Nail Gun' spot was down to Hank Corwin who went on to edit *JFK* and *Natural Born Killers*.)

From Australia their sister channel, Fox Sports, picked up on a very human truth about the innate competitiveness inherent in any cricket fan – from television watcher to playing in the back garden with their very small children. Seeing a dad charging in to bowl from five houses away may have little to do with the Australia versus South Africa one-day internationals briefly captured in the final five seconds of the trailer, but says everything about their passion and understanding of cricket devotees. Their endline 'The Game Never Ends' is an even better encapsulation of that state of heightened fandom.[14]

CANAL+ and their agency BTEC Paris highlighted the technical quality of their football coverage, not with a dull list of historic competencies but with the brilliant idea of showing how their camera operators get closer to the action by literally inserting them into the action in hilarious mimicry of the players they are tracking.[15]

Celebrating camera crew in a CANAL+ football promo
Source: Reproduced by permission of CANAL+

Surprisingly Sky, such a dominant force in the UK, rarely use humour in their marketing. Robert Tansey, brand director, believes that in part it dates back to their initial need to establish serious credentials:

> When we came into the market and launched, the necessity was to show that we were incredibly professional and our standards were high. It plays out even in how our people on screen look: they always wear shirts and ties and that's driven by, if we're getting people to pay for it, we've got to be incredibly professional. Then, humour in marketing doesn't match necessarily with what's on screen. That's possibly one of the reasons why we have found it a harder place to go to than lots of other broadcasters.[16]

Of course humour, as Chapter 8 on comedy explores in greater detail, is the hardest art to master. When done badly, the brand is more likely to suffer adversely in a way that a clip-based trailer, however dull, will probably avoid. Setanta Sports and Des Lynam spring to mind as a foot-in-mouth example.[17] This is not to recommend the clip-based promo as a better solution, however. Indeed it is vital to challenge the normal conservatism of the sports departments, who traditionally are the hardest client body. Not least because they find it difficult to understand that there might be an audience that doesn't share their own fixed predisposition to watch. As Olivier Schaack from CANAL+ comments:

> When you do it the way sport production people do it you only talk to the sport fans and so you could never increase your audience.[18]

Aaron Taylor, formerly of ESPN, agrees with the view that you first need to gain credibility as a brand for your journalism, coverage and overall sense of authority before using humour:

> We have an overall brand promise that ESPN is 'sports with authority and personality'. Sports is what we do. Authority is how we do it. And, our personality is what sets us apart. The credibility that we are the best in delivering live events coverage and the best in sports journalism gives us the ability to leverage humour as a device of relatability.[19]

– NOT GIVING IT 110 PER CENT –

Beyond the clip-based compilation of sporting action, sports promotion is equally prone to some of the most excessive use of clichéd imagery in broadcast trailer making. A few to avoid at all costs include:

★ Comparing the upcoming sporting fixture to a battle and/or general war imagery (this includes any reference to gladiators, Vikings, Greek gods, etc).

★ Man versus animal comparisons (especially cheetahs, lions and so on).

★ Showing viewers getting closer to the action, by sticking a couple on a sofa next to the pitch/track/golf course.

★ And, of course, the following bits of music: Carl Orff's 'Carmina Burana', David Bowie's 'Heroes', Coldplay's 'Fix You' and Guns N' Roses' 'Welcome to the Jungle' – as four that are representative of uninspired thought processes.

– IN TUNE WITH THE NATION –

In the words of the BBC's director of marketing and audiences, Philip Almond:

> If you are uniting people you need an anthem. That's why we stand up before football matches and sing them. If you get it right for the nation you probably get it right for the BBC brand.[20]

Music is vital as a tone setter in sport. The BBC for many years have viewed the trailer and the title sequence of their major tournaments as being the place to define the style and mood of their coverage through the choice of a track. The quintessential example was the choice of 'Nessun Dorma' for the Italia 90 football World Cup, a choice of such emotive power and crescendoing passion that it felt almost prescient of a tournament that would end with England's talisman Paul Gascoigne in floods of tears. It made ITV's choice of theme tune – Rod Argent and Peter Van Hooke's 'Tutti Al Mondo' – sound lacklustre and limp, and indelibly started a period of perceived superiority of coverage from the BBC. Olympic trailers have equally become a moment where music matters and, unlike the World Cup, creative agencies have turned to original compositions from two of the UK's great contemporary rock band composers. Firstly for the Beijing Olympics, the twin creative talents of Damon Albarn (from Blur and Gorillaz) and animator Jamie Hewlett combined on a spot of evocative and ambitious storytelling. The two-minute sequence was inspired by the Chinese folk tale 'Journey to the West' about an 'epic quest for enlightenment'. It featured three characters: Monkey, Sandy and Pigsy, journeying to the Olympic 'Bird's Nest' stadium and being called on to use a variety of Olympic skills such as javelin and hammer throwing, diving and running while defeating foes.[21]

For the 'home' Olympics, London 2012, the BBC turned to the band Elbow to compose the music. Our team made a fly-on-the-wall documentary charting the creation of the music for the trailer, and Guy Garvey described the pressure of walking in the footsteps of previous musical giants, admitting that he aspired to the heights of Ski Sunday.[22]

He also spoke to the BBC website about the project, saying:

It's a real challenge because it's designed to fit important images nationally and people's endeavours, people have trained their whole lives for that moment.

For our music to be sound tracking it, there was a big feeling of responsibility but also we're just dead proud to be doing it. And strange as well with none of us really being athletic.[23]

Markus Schmidt, founder of Munich-based agency United Senses, shares our passion for sport and has a long track record for distinctive design and promotional work in the sports sector. He goes as far as to say that:

In sport, music is much more important than in any other field of marketing and promotion because it really, really sets the emotion and sets the tone. It entirely decides what the emotional outcome of a piece will be.[24]

– ANIMATION TO AVOID ELIMINATION –

The creative agency RKCR/Y&R chose animation to accompany the Elbow composition – entitled 'First Steps' – for the BBC's London 2012 campaign. Abstracting the competitors into animated avatars avoids three of the many challenges of sports promotions. First, the difficulty of access to the biggest sports stars who are locked into sportswear endorsements and/or protective team managers. Second, athletes injuring themselves and withdrawing – after you have spent months making a trailer or sequence featuring them. Despite that, Nike, in creating an animated commercial featuring all of their star football players for the 2010 World Cup, still suffered with a 'curse' that virtually all of their featured players were knocked out or sent home early from the tournament.[25] Third, sometimes it is just about rights restrictions themselves.

Better, then, to create generic sportsmen and women to represent the competitors as the BBC did – running, swimming and jumping across the whole country within a giant 'Stadium UK'.[26] As the BBC's Philip Almond explains:

The skill is doing it in a way that shines a light on the content, while giving the values of the BBC. That concept, both in the way it was executed in the animation and also with the underlying theme of bringing the different parts of the UK together, did that beautifully.[27]

The UK as a giant 'stadium': the BBC's London 2012 campaign
Source: Reproduced by permission of BBC

– A SUCCESSFUL CAMPAIGN –

One of the greatest failings in broadcast promotion and marketing versus the wider world of brand advertising is the lack of consistency and magpie-like chasing of the next shiny thing. As we discussed in Chapter 1, broadcasters rarely think enough about long-term brand-building properties. It is essential when transforming your media brand that you have a core long-term property that is true, ownable and flexible enough to work for you for a number of years. Why this lack of campaign planning exists in television marketing is puzzling, but all roads lead to the short-term overnight fixations of the channel controllers that tend to influence all behaviour.

It is even more baffling when, in our opinion, the greatest set of promotions in the history of television have all been born from one deeply single-minded campaign. After 20 years and well over 400 spots, ESPN's 'This is SportsCenter' proves that, as with football management, perseverance is often the key. As *Adweek* magazine acknowledged in 2012, the most remarkable thing about 'This is SportsCenter' is 'perhaps how little it has changed'. The basic principle is a *This is Spinal Tap*-type spoof observational documentary series set in the channel's Connecticut headquarters, where sports stars work in mostly menial roles alongside the channel's genuine presenters and backroom staff. The concept came fully formed in the first presentation from agency Wieden+Kennedy, and was superbly structured to allow for constant refreshment and endless topicality. Combined with a pitch-perfect ear for comedy and an almost 100 per cent success rate in recruiting talent (until now only Michael Jordan seems to have escaped the net), the campaign flourishes to this day. Furthermore, its speed and flexibility to respond allow scope to deal with the mood swings of those irrational and emotional fans:

> While Nike and every other sports marketer portrayed athletes as superhuman, ESPN presented them as absurdly yet relatably human – enduring life's endless small humiliations. By bringing them down to size, in a way sports fans loved, ESPN built a larger-than-life campaign that athletes now practically beg to be involved in. After 17 years, it shows no sign of slowing.[28]

Everybody has their favourites from this campaign. Ours is a lovely throwaway turn from Maria Sharapova, but it is hard to top Arnold Palmer mixing his namesake drink or hockey player Alexander Ovechkin's Russian Spy role. (Another strength of the campaign is its refusal to explain any jokes. If you're in on them, that's part of the reward; if you're on the outside – tough – watch more sport.)[29]

Late, great ESPN anchor Stuart Scott about to surprise Maria Sharapova with the old snakes-in-a-tube trick in a classic 'This Is SportsCenter' spot
Source: *Reproduced by permission of ESPN, Inc*

Aaron Taylor, who in his words 'stewarded' the campaign for 14 years, agrees with the view that its reactiveness is key:

> I love spots where we demonstrate that we are nimble, topical and of the moment. Right after the Super Bowl last year when the social world was all abuzz about the 'left shark' in Katy Perry's half-time performance... I got a script at 5 pm on a Thursday afternoon from Wieden+Kennedy... and that night we had negotiated with Katy Perry's people to secure the costumes. We shot on Monday and were on air on Tuesday or Wednesday, so we were part of the dialogue that was still happening and we looked really smart for being that topical... We did the same thing with the Brett Favre spot when he was contemplating coming back to the NFL – 'One if Retired, Two if Unretired' with the UMass Minuteman (like 'One if by land, two if by sea')... The timeliness of it, I love being that smart and nimble when there is something going on in the world of sports we want to comment on.[30]

So many subsequent campaigns around the world owe a debt to 'This Is SportsCenter'. Take Reebok's 2009 NFL Fantasy Football campaign 'Pick Me'[31] or even the first year of our own longest-running campaign for the BBC, the FA Cup.

For this the creative team of Anton Ezer and Ben Friend devised a positioning based on its unique unpredictability (it is the only football tournament where an amateur local team could legitimately end up playing against a Champions League giant) and summarized that with the endline: Great Drama from the BBC. With one strong single ownable premise there was a platform for infinite variety. In the first year we took a couple of England footballers, Joe Cole and Teddy Sheringham, well out of their comfort zones by demonstrating that just because the FA Cup was great drama, they wouldn't necessarily be good at any other form and placed them into the BBC's most successful soap operas.

Then, the next year, we demonstrated drama by showing the fear that the footballers had at being drawn against lower league opposition and created a bogeyman figure to come and frighten them with the balls from the draw mechanism – generating more superb acting from the likes of Gianfranco Zola, Jamie Redknapp and Ashley Cole.[32] Then, in year three, we showed that because the FA Cup was great drama in and of itself, it didn't need any other form of hype – and got the king of hype himself, Don King, to prove it in a wonderful part-scripted, part-improvised rant to two English gentlemen from the Football Association.[33]

– THE BIG ONES –

The level of spending on sports rights is a graph that closely resembles the vertical take-off of a Harrier jump jet. Global rights are predicted by

Deloitte to hit £17 billion in 2015, marking the second year of double-digit increases.[34]

So why is sport so important for broadcasters? Clearly there is not space in this book to track the success of the world's largest sports broadcasters in both starting a market and then dominating it in the way that Sky in Europe, SuperSport in sub-Saharan Africa and Star in Asia have, to give three examples. But beyond the channels that depend on sport for their basic livelihoods, the arms race extends to all of the major multi-genre networks.

For the BBC, CBS, ITV, NBC and so on, the importance of sports is partly driven by changes in viewing behaviour. As on-demand channels increase audience fragmentation, live events are one thing that still bring large viewing figures, and nothing draws advertising dollars like a sense of event and a high volume of watching eyeballs. You can either try to create a live event – hence the vast investment in talent shows and entertainment formats (see Chapter 10) – or you can buy in the more guaranteed appeal of gloriously unpredictable and passionately followed sport.

Clearly the bigger the innate support base of any sport, the larger the marketing investment, and there is no bigger supporter group than that brought by those behemoths – the World Cup and the Olympic Games. The BBC even has a term within its marketing lexicon, 'main eventers', to describe the armchair fans who will only come in for events on the scale of the Olympics.

For NBC the 2014 Winter Olympics in Sochi generated $946.8 million in advertising spending, while the 2012 Summer Olympics in London brought in US$1.3 billion, according to Kantar Media.[35] No surprise then that in 2014, with the added muscle of its Comcast owners, NBCUniversal signed a deal to carry the Olympics through 2032.[36] In short, for the rights holders on either side of the Atlantic, every four years is their own 100 metres final.

NBC begin branding their channel via on-screen bugs as the Olympic broadcaster for some 12–18 months ahead of the actual event. The Rio Olympics campaign began on 1 August 2015 as John Miller, the EVP of marketing, told the *Wall Street Journal*: 'To a large degree, it's the official kickoff of our campaign... It won't be a continual, year-long effort, but we take a year out to say, "This is where it all begins."'[37]

Where US broadcasters always seem to have an edge over virtually any other channel globally is their ability to lock their star 'front of camera' talent into contracts that guarantee their participation in marketing campaigns, and they use them to seamlessly weave in cross-promotion from their other entertainment properties.

A favourite campaign saw the stars of NBC's hit sitcom *The Office* suggest their own improvements to the Olympics. Dwight reels off his plans for a 'centathlon' because decathlons are for wimps: 'Animal mimicry, wall climbing, hide the hamster.'[38]

But the importance of the biggest events can also be in their brand-defining role, as Channel 4 in the UK proved with their coverage of the 2012 Paralympics. Our former planning director, John McDonald, noted in a blog at the time:

> The 'Superhumans' campaign very clearly reinforces the parent brand. By firstly championing alternative voices and fresh perspectives and secondly challenging people to see the world differently.[39]

Many column inches and a deserved shower of awards have already greeted Channel 4's launch trailer for the event: a film in some ways notable for its unremarkableness. It is quite conventionally, though beautifully, directed by Tom Tagholm. There is a familiarity from scores of trailers past of shots of athletes going about their training and competitive regimen. As Scott Harris wrote in the *Telegraph*, it feels after a few seconds that we very much have the measure of it:

> The hip-hop track 'Harder Than You Think', by Public Enemy, is an apt but unsurprising accompaniment to images of these inspiring athletes. We think we have already inferred what the trailer exists to tell us: Paralympians are serious athletes who have overcome serious challenges and deserve to be taken seriously. We shouldn't overlook disabled sport. It's harder than we think. And so on.[40]

And then... everything changes, in the course of one remarkable breakdown in the music track... A bomb explodes. A soldier we assume to be in Iraq or Afghanistan is thrown skywards. A car crashes. A pregnant mother is given disturbing news. Scott continues:

> The images are arresting and shock us out of the safety of our assumptions, about the trailer and about the athletes in it. Suddenly, we see those athletes

Channel 4 inviting us to 'Meet the Superhumans'   Source: © *Channel 4 Television*

as they are: not something less than normal athletes, but something more. The words 'Meet the Superhumans' appear onscreen. It's clever, succinct filmmaking.[41]

Dan Brooke, chief marketing and communications officer at Channel 4, notes the power that the campaign had in reshaping perceptions, beyond the narrow confines of sport:

It said something much bigger about people with disabilities and I think said something about Britain and our progressiveness as a country. What was great about it was it was a rare thing, a complete overlap of the values of the Paralympics and the values of Channel 4, occurring at a time when the world's biggest event outside of war was occurring in Britain.[42]

It is an example of brand marketing at its purest, as James Walker, Channel 4's head of marketing, confirms:

Clearly the positive payback to our brand in terms of people seeing Channel 4 doing something that it should do, that's part of its intrinsic values, delivering its remit. It was a perfect circle in that respect, so the success of it would never entirely be measured on the number of people who watched the event. But clearly, the more people you could get to spend hours of their time engaging in Paralympic sport, the more positively they would feel about Paralympic sport and disability, and change attitudes, and the more positively they would feel about Channel 4 as well.[43]

– SHARED MEMORIES –

The capacity to invoke collective memories is a powerful tool for any brand, but when you have been as central to those memories as a host broadcaster usually is, then it can become a vital marketing tool – from defining lines of commentary to camera angles that become etched onto national consciousness. Framed well, it will guarantee hairs rising on the backs of necks across a nation. Done badly and it is more as if someone has trampled on your wedding dress. As we said in Chapter 1, it can be about knowing when to get out of the way of the content.

Regional broadcaster BBC Wales championed this technique some decades before Sky, with reactive trailers that were made in the hours following 6 Nations rugby matches (rugby is Wales's national sport and is followed with something approaching religious fervour). Under the leadership of Ceri Evans and John Morgan, the promo team would perfectly capture the mood of the nation with a well-chosen song, and expertly edited highlights within minutes of the game finishing, and this would air in junctions as a pure brand campaign. At times it would drive the agenda of the whole country's press, such as the moment in a trailer for an upcoming England versus Wales match in 1993, where a dominant England were expected to roll over the

Welsh team. The promo team picked on one England player's fallibility under the high ball and, to a slow heart beat, showed Jonathan Webb repeatedly dropping the ball, interspersed with the single word 'Beatable'. The trailer roused the country and Wales won a dramatic encounter 10–9.[44]

Olivier Schaack of CANAL+ is a firm believer in what he terms 'goosebump marketing':

> In 2010 to promote the World Cup we asked Zidane, and the former coach Jacquet, to tell us a World Cup story, but not as a player, as a viewer, so normally when they were kids, and they all had a story and this created a lot of emotion. So the culture, the history, the legends = number one.[45]

– PUTTING THE TALENT UPFRONT –

Clearly access to a soccer legend such as Zinedine Zidane could be in and of itself a massive advantage for any broadcaster in giving immediate credibility. But in this media-wise postmodern age, most armchair pundits will see an array of 'ambassadors' such as those signed up by new entrant to the market BT Sport and be aware that footballers will do pretty much anything if the cheque is big enough. So, if you are to benefit from access to talent, either as pundits or indeed as paid endorsers, you still need to give them a role in your campaign that is rewarding to the viewer. ESPN's 'This Is SportsCenter' and the 'Great Drama from the BBC' FA Cup campaign are great examples from earlier in this chapter. Sky, increasingly confident in the quality of the analysis from their pundit teams, have also begun to rely on those same faces for their marketing drives, as Robert Tansey confirms:

> The quality of your talent and your analysis and their association with your brand has become more important for us, so if you look back over the last couple of years we've done a lot more with Gary Neville, Jamie Redknapp, Jamie Carragher in football – and we have done more and more with the cricket and the rugby talent as well.[46]

A technique not employed enough by broadcasters is to highlight the calibre of their commentary teams. The voices that accompany our memories of sporting glory are powerful and resonant. In 2003, we created a striking campaign promoting the radio football commentary team for the BBC. Noticing the similarity in improvised verbal dexterity between the commentary team and rap battles, as captured in Eminem's film *8 Mile*, director Ron Scalpello captured two top commentators in an epic underground club head-to-head 'commentary battle' to a thumping 'Lose Yourself' soundtrack.[47] Selected as one of *Campaign* magazine's top five ads of the year, it highlighted that talent behind the microphone could be an untapped promotional opportunity for sports broadcasters.

– A P McCOY CLINGS ON –

As we discussed in Chapter 9 (on news), it is also possible for broadcasters to seek to promote their coverage based on a technological advancement. This is fantastic and powerful if you are first to market with a genuinely new bit of kit. It can make you look like your brand is forward thinking, agile, brave and innovative. You can reflect well on the sport you are promoting and on the parent channel. Crucially, though, it needs to be of real audience benefit.

If you are the sixth broadcaster to go to air promoting your HD channel by showing droplets of water flying off a football shot on a Phantom camera at 1,000 frames a second, the very best you get for your money spent is abject indifference and, worse, you could look like you have no original thought.

To show the level of detailed insight BBC Sport bring with the analysis of their pundits, we produced with agency Circus a campaign for the BBC using pioneering time-slice photography. Freezing moments of sporting endeavour from such greats as jockey A P McCoy, Irish rugby hooker Keith Wood and the leading goal scorer in the Premiership, Andy Cole, to the accompaniment of uniquely untold facts about them. In the early days of time slice a bank of 100 rigged 35 millimetre cameras and a bank of lights were erected around a Grand National-sized jump that McCoy was due to guide a borrowed horse over (borrowed because most owners would not go near such a foolhardy enterprise). In a torrential rain storm, A P charged towards the fence, but the horse, bucking furiously at the bank of lights, only served to kick over the stand holding the cameras. A P calmly said, 'We have one more shot at this if we go right away,' so the entire crew held up the cameras for what probably remains the only hand-held time-slice sequence in history. He jumped perfectly... as ever.[48]

– BUMPING AND GRINDING –

Sometimes a piece of work emerges that harnesses everything we have demonstrated as key to sports marketing in this chapter – humour, insight, great music, buy-in from talent, partisanship and technical prowess.

In 2015 NBC realized that they had an opportunity with their broadcast of the Super Bowl to recharge another sporting franchise that they were rights holders to: NASCAR. With a nation embracing its artisan heart, from coffee shops to bearded hipsters, they also felt it was a perfect moment for a genuine blue-collar sport to reclaim its place at the nation's heart. So they turned to the perfect spokesperson for that heartland: the star of their own sitcom *Parks and Recreation*, Nick Offerman. In a two-minute spot entitled 'America Start Your Engines', Offerman sings a campaign song that urges

Americans to get some NASCAR in their life. Prescribing a gut check for the entire nation, he intones:

> If the founding fathers saw us huddled in our little cocoons, texting each other smiley faces, they'd hang their powdered wigs in shame... When our idea of danger is eating gluten, there's trouble afoot.[49]

The level of expenditure in making the film in which Offerman stars as multiple characters in his own music video – driver, team owner, fan, mechanic, etc – would have been dwarfed by the amount of money NBC would have given up in potential earnings for the Super Bowl spot – some $4.5 million according to *Adweek*.[50] This proves that in 2015, matching the growing investment in rights, sport also remains the most heavily marketed programming in the television world.

– 'THE GAME NEVER ENDS' –

Maybe as lifelong sports fans we would be expected to say this, but in this chapter we have talked about some of our all-time favourite TV marketing campaigns. Sport is such a rich and fertile territory for creativity. With a nod towards the final chapter of the book, however much the TV industry is disrupted in the future by technological, entrepreneurial and consumer-driven changes, as comedian David Mitchell might well have said in this chapter's opening epigraph: 'the marketing of televised sport is officially going on forever'. Markus Schmidt of creative agency United Senses sums it up beautifully:

> Sport is just a great field of entertainment. It has so many things that other disciplines have to script – big drama, big emotion, heroes, disasters, it has everything... it's just life, it's just happening... and it's probably the one thing that will save linear television as we know it, because everything else is available everywhere else, but sport, you have to see it live. The last big programme will probably be a football game, I guess.[51]

NEXT	LATER
★ Inside *The Umbrellas*.	★ The Lost Experience.
★ Select your 'Horrible Hero'.	★ canadiansexacts.org.
★ Cartoon Network's mash-ups.	★ *Mad Men*'s 'quilt of fan experience'.
★ Introducing the green slime.	
★ Star Wars's 'Generation Dad'.	
★ Phillip and Gordon or Andi and Edd?	

NOTES

1 Mitchell, D (2008) [accessed 5 November 2015] Mitchell & Webb – Football, Football, Football [Online] https://www.youtube.com/watch?v=VF_uOgyBK1c

2 Whitbourne, S (2011) [accessed 7 September 2015] The Psychology Of Sports Fans: Are You A Fair Weather Fan? 30 December [Online] https://www.psychologytoday.com/blog/fulfillment-any-age/201112/the-psychology-sports-fans

3 Aaron Taylor, former senior vice president of marketing at ESPN, interview, 23 September 2015

4 Sky Sports (2009) [accessed 7 September 2015] Watch Sean Bean In 1997 Sky Sports football Ad [Online] http://www.theguardian.com/media/video/2009/feb/05/sky-sports-sean-bean

5 McGovern, D (1997) [accessed 7 September 2015] An Advert That Has To Be Bean To Be Believed [Online] http://www.compleatseanbean.com/skyad.html

6 BBC (2008) Watch The Football! – That Mitchell And Webb Look BBC 2 [Online] https://www.youtube.com/watch?v=MusyO7J2inM

7 NBC Sports (2015) [accessed 7 September 2015] 2015 Tour De France: Who Will Survive? [Online] https://www.youtube.com/watch?v=AoZqdxbJ01w

8 https://www.youtube.com/watch?v=0ms_b_NH3P4

9 Aaron Taylor, former senior vice president of marketing at ESPN, interview, 23 September 2015

10 Olivier Schaack, director of creative services, CANAL+, interview, 11 June 2015

11 Marcopepito (2014) [accessed 7 September 2015] [HUMOR] Six Nations 2012 Clip Trailer Banned On BBC Sport [Online] https://www.youtube.com/watch?v=UmkbJlYx1v8

12 Appie (2014) [accessed 7 September 2015] 'Bowling Would Be Better If It Were Hockey', Fox Sports NHL Commercial [Online] https://www.youtube.com/watch?v=xt1ynyKP5NU

13 King, E (2015) [accessed 7 September 2015] FOX SPORTS 'Nail Gun' / 'Leafblower' [Online] http://ericking.tv/2002/09/02/fox-sports-nail-gun/

14 MrCodlaa (2007) [accessed 7 September 2015] Fox Sports: Serious Cricket [Online] https://www.youtube.com/watch?v=GMvgIASnGAs

15 BETC Paris (2014) [accessed 7 September 2015] CANAL+ Football – Cameramen [Online] https://www.youtube.com/watch?v=aUDbLqgyUHc

16 Robert Tansey, brand director, content products, Sky, interview 26 June 2015

17 Hewelt, J (2007) [accessed 5 November 2015] Setanta Sports TV Advertising [Online] https://www.youtube.com/watch?v=VjCJPGXtMVo

18 Olivier Schaack, director of creative services, CANAL+, interview 11 June 2015

19 Aaron Taylor, former senior vice president of marketing at ESPN, interview, 23 September 2015

20 Philip Almond, director of marketing and audiences, BBC, interview 14 September 2015

21 BBC Sport (2008) [accessed 7 September 2015] BBC Sport's Olympics Monkey [Online] http://news.bbc.co.uk/sport1/hi/olympics/monkey/7521287.stm

22 https://www.youtube.com/watch?v=QYp8KLwD4bQ&list=PLDsg58IUh5wTr DqRtJzFrCGZzcjgvVZI7&index=78

23 Garvey, G (2011) [accessed 5 November 2015] London 2012: Elbow Compose BBC's Olympic Theme [online] http://www.bbc.co.uk/news/mobile/uk-15856028

24 Markus Schmidt, founder, United Senses, interview 1 September 2015

25 Klein, J Z (2010) [accessed 7 September 2015] Curse Of The Nike World Cup Commercial, Confirmed, *New York Times*, 30 June [Online] http://goal.blogs.nytimes.com/2010/06/30/curse-of-the-nike-world-cup-commerical-confirmed/?_r=1

26 BBC (2012) [accessed 5 November 2015] London 2012 Olympic Games – Trailer, BBC Sport [Online] https://www.youtube.com/watch?v=4ViLiXA0E70

27 Philip Almond, director of marketing and audiences, BBC, interview 14 September 2015

28 Nudd, T (2012) [accessed 7 September 2015] The Spot: ESPN's Perfect Game, *Adweek*, 31 January [Online] http://www.adweek.com/news/advertising-branding/spot-espns-perfect-game-137850

29 Funny sportcenter commercials (2009) [accessed 7 September 2015] This Is Sportscenter Maria Sharapova [Online] https://www.youtube.com/watch?v=Y5dbpG4IoYk. Also: ESPN (2011) [accessed 7 September 2015] Alexander Ovechkin – This Is SportsCenter (Russian Spy) [Online] https://www.youtube.com/watch?v=HjfTWbDUrow. Also: ESPN (2009) [accessed 7 September 2015] Arnold Palmer – This Is Sports Center [Online] https://www.youtube.com/watch?v=cBHMomSR9_E

30 Aaron Taylor, former senior vice president of marketing at ESPN, interview, 23 September 2015

31 GenY Television (2009) [accessed 7 September 2015] NFL Pick Me Reebok Campaign [Online] https://www.youtube.com/watch?v=adG34woMVs4

32 Ezer, A and Friend, B (2015) [accessed 7 September 2015] FA Cup Demon [Online] http://antonandben.com/projects/fa_cup/fa_cup_tv.php

33 Hall of Advertising (2013) [accessed 7 September 2015] BBC FA Cup – Don King (2003, UK) [Online] https://www.youtube.com/watch?v=r3EcUdFCUSU

34 White, P (2014) [accessed 7 September 2015] Premium Sports Rights To Hit £17bn In 2015, *Broadcast Now*, 15 September [Online] http://www.broadcastnow.co.uk/news/international/premium-sports-rights-to-hit-17bn-in-2015/5077554.article

35 Kantar Media (2014) [accessed 5 November 2015] Kantar Media Takes Historical Look At Winter Olympics Ad Spending, Press Release, 22 January [Online] http://kantarmedia.us/press/kantar-media-takes-historical-look-winter-olympics-ad-spending

36 Futterman, M (2014) [accessed 5 November 2015] NBC Gets Olympic-Size Deal, *Wall Street Journal*, 11 May [Online] http://www.wsj.com/articles/SB10001424052702304655304579552292070830078

37 Perlberg, S (2015) [accessed 7 September 2015] How NBCUniversal Is Marketing The Rio Olympics One Year Out, *Wall Street Journal*, 31 July [Online] http://blogs.wsj.com/cmo/2015/07/31/how-nbcu-is-marketing-the-rio-olympics-one-year-out/

38 NBC (2008) [accessed 7 September 2015] The Office Olympics Promo Dwight's Centathlon [Online] https://www.youtube.com/watch?v=-3LvVX_rJEg

39 McDonald, J (2012) [accessed 7 September 2015] Does Channel 4's Paralympics Campaign Take Gold? [Blog] Red Bee Media, 28 August [Online] http://www.redbeecreative.tv/insights/blog/does-channel-4s-paralympics-campaign-take-gold

40 Harris, S (2012) [accessed 7 September 2015] Channel 4's Paralympics Trailer Is A Superhuman Effort, *Telegraph*, 19 July [Online] http://blogs.telegraph.co.uk/culture/scottharris/100065124/channel-4s-paralympics-trailer-is-a-superhuman-effort/

41 Harris, S (2012) [accessed 5 November 2015] Channel 4's Paralympic Trailer Is A Superhuman Effort, *Telegraph*, 19 July [Online] http://blogs.telegraph.co.uk/culture/scottharris/100065124/channel-4s-paralympics-trailer-is-a-superhuman-effort/

42 Dan Brooke, chief marketing and communications officer, Channel 4, interview 26 June 2015

43 James Walker, head of marketing, Channel 4 Television, interview 25 May 2015

44 Welsh Rugby Forum (2012) [accessed 7 September 2015] BBC Wales 6 Nations Rugby 2012 – History In The making 'England' [Online] http://welshrugbyblog.co.uk/forum/showthread.php?tid=897

45 Olivier Schaack, director, Creative Services, CANAL+, interview 11 June 2015

46 Robert Tansey, brand director, content products, Sky, interview 26 June 2015

47 Deighj01 (2009) [accessed 5 November 2015] Five Live – 8 Mile [Online] https://www.youtube.com/watch?v=XPvKddHlehc

48 TimeSlice ® Films (2014) [accessed 7 September 2015] BBC Sporting Anthems 1999 [Online] https://vimeo.com/111111986

49 NBC Sports (2015) [accessed 7 September 2015] America Start Your Engines: NASCAR On NBC Featuring Nick Offerman [Online] https://www.youtube.com/watch?v=wi68a0LsLDA

50 McCarthy, M (2015) [accessed 7 September 2015] Nick Offerman Will Hilariously Pitch NASCAR Right After The Superbowl's Final Whistle, *Adweek*, 26 January [Online] http://www.adweek.com/news/advertising-branding/nick-offerman-will-hilariously-pitch-nascar-right-after-super-bowls-final-whistle-162540

51 Markus Schmidt, founder, United Senses, interview 1 September 2015

CHAPTER THIRTEEN

MARKETING TO CHILDREN
Nailing jelly to a moving train

*Yes, use all new Tudor Sugar-Paste toothpaste on your teeth
and you too could have teeth just like Queen Elizabeth's!*

VOICE-OVER, *HORRIBLE HISTORIES*[1]

– STORIES AND CHARACTERS –

Curiously, out of all the channels we work with and talk to, children's brands were the most reluctant to discuss publicly their strategies. This could be because there is still an inherent tension between those whose job it is to secure the biggest possible audience of child viewers, and society's broad frowning on the targeting of and advertising to minors. Or it is just because reputational damage for any deemed breach is so much greater for channels entrusted by the world's parents with their children's education and entertainment?

Whatever the reason, it is important that we as an industry share openly the creative tactics we employ, not least because children's TV channels are at the greatest risk of collapsing into irrelevance in an era of universal access to internet streaming. Broadcasters still have the upper hand in terms of long form, truly immersive televisual storytelling. As we will see later in the chapter, stories and characters remain the trump card in the battle with gaming vloggers, farting cat videos and pirated Peppa Pig loops on YouTube, Twitch and beyond.

Successful children's television marketing relies on a mixture of the techniques that we explore elsewhere in relation to the industry as a whole: storytelling across media, innovation in reach and scheduling, forming relationships with characters and building compelling brands. One area, however, that we would suggest is dramatically more important is the need to build two-way relationships.

– INVOLVE ME AND I'LL UNDERSTAND –

From the earliest age the viewers of *Sesame Street* – perhaps one of the world's greatest enduring TV brands – are involved in the programme. They shout out answers to Big Bird, stand on one leg and touch their noses when encouraged to and count along with the count. *Sesame Street* also knows that for this preschool audience repetition and familiarity are important. Child psychologists talk about the need for established patterns of behaviour at this age in all aspects of their life. Malcolm Gladwell, in his book *The Tipping Point*, analysed exactly why children responded so positively to James Earl Jones repeating letters of the alphabet:

> After a couple of repetitions, they would respond to the appearance of the letter before he did, in the long pause. Then, with enough repetitions, they would anticipate the letter before it appeared. They were sequencing themselves through the piece; first they learned the name of the letter, then they learned to associate the name of the letter with its appearance, then they learned the sequence of letters.[2]

From this call-and-response form of involvement comes the importance of sound mnemonics for preschool brands. For example, the sing-song CBeebies of the BBC's channel, or the 'Eh-Oh' of *Teletubbies*. As Gladwell remarks:

> An adult considers constant repetition boring, because it requires reliving the same experience over and again. But to preschoolers repetition isn't boring, because each time they watch something they are experiencing it in a completely different way.[3]

There is then more direct involvement – active participation in either content or marketing. This can be divided into two broad areas. That of putting the audience on screen, and then the more multiplatform world of interactivity that we also look at in Chapter 14.

– KIDS ON SCREEN –

Putting the audience on screen refers both to the filming of children in interstitial material, and also the co-creation of parts of the brand. For Ketnet, the Belgian children's channel, our creative director Ian Wormleighton led an on-air branding solution that was designed with an active kit of parts that could be constantly updated with children's submissions, for example. So the background to our seamless junctions, or indeed the starring characters, could be animated from a child's drawing.[4]

Interstitial content for Belgium's Ketnet channel, complete with children's submissions   Source: Reproduced by permission of Ketnet (VRT)

Nick Jr's 'I Love Art' campaign placed the audience firmly at the heart of the brand promotion, with brilliantly cast children explaining how galleries work and, in one memorable example, bringing to life and interacting with Pierre Auguste Renoir's *The Umbrellas*.[5] Seeing a peer wandering through the actual rainy road inside the gilt frame demonstrates an understanding of a child's eye view of the world.

– PLAYING ALONG AT HOME –

Surprisingly few marketing campaigns for children's broadcasters involve genuine multiplatform interaction. The reasons for this are diverse: sometimes the cost would be deemed prohibitive, any social participation with minors needs careful procedures for monitoring and responding, and sometimes it is because of structural divisions within broadcasters – the digital and web teams being fractured from the marketing and channel management themselves.

When done well it can produce results that no straightforward trailers will ever do. Lesli Rotenberg, the SVP of marketing and communication for PBS Kids and charged with overall responsibility for Children's Media for PBS, remarks that they don't even talk to producers about new programming concepts...:

> ...unless they have a plan for developing a complete suite of transmedia products. This includes immersive and interactive web games, mobile apps, classroom white board applications, and more. This is not just a matter of branding. Studies show that children can make more educational gains if they are exposed to new concepts across different platforms.[6]

Perhaps the poster boy for this sort of marketing is CBBC's break-out comedy hit *Horrible Histories*. Born out of a successful series of books written by Terry Deary, the TV version is a sketch show that manages to hide instructive factual history within comedy written and performed by some of the UK's top comedic talent. Gruesome, scatological and focusing on deaths, illnesses and general weirdness, it also managed to teach the

Encouraging kids to get involved with Horrible Histories *on the CBBC website*
Source: Reproduced by permission of BBC

children of the UK 1,100 years of kings and queens in one ridiculously catchy song. The BBC quickly identified it as a potential 'super brand', which both commercially and critically overdelivered for them – informing and entertaining a hard-to-reach audience. So they twice invested in major participative marketing campaigns. In the first, 'CBBC Yourself', we treated viewers to a spoof beauty campaign brilliantly performed by the cast with Mathew Baynton, in particular, showing the comic timing that would lead him to starring roles in future feature films. The trailer sent the kids to an interactive site where, once they had uploaded a photo of themselves, they could be transformed into several looks from different eras: Georgian, Viking or Egyptian. On the first day it went live the microsite had 35,000 unique visitors, or 25 per cent of all visitors to CBBC; 180,000 viewers represented the second-highest viewing figures for the time slot.[7]

Two years later and a spoof *X Factor*-style show reached out to discover a 'Horrible Hero'. Contestant Aztec ('I've made so many sacrifices to be here') competed with Victorian Pauper and Queen Elizabeth I. Again kids could select their choice for hero and create personalized albums with uploads of their own photos. There were over 100,000 requests for online content driven by the campaign, and the carefully tracked marketing dials for 'fun and involving' moved dramatically for the CBBC brand, along with correct association of the show with its commissioning home.[8]

Even more immersive is a chance to get properly hands-on with characters or scenes from a show. *Doc McStuffins* is a Disney TV show about a six-year-old girl who heals toys out of her imaginary clinic. To promote the second series, and again with an eye on secondary merchandise sales, Disney re-created the Doc's clinic in Tesco, Smyths and Toys R Us in the UK.[9]

Children were allowed into the clinic for a 10-minute experience where they took the role of Doc and diagnosed what was wrong with Big Ted before treating his 'ouchie symptoms'. Nearly 8,000 children took part, leading to a significant 5 per cent upswing in merchandise sales.

While the level of investment needed to build a microsite or stunt is rarely available for individual programme promotion, particularly for cable and satellite companies, interactivity can still be present in the spirit of the marketing. Indeed, given the challenge presented to broadcasters from the growing influence of gaming, it is essential.

– TRACKING DOWN KIDS AWAY FROM TV –

An emerging challenge for children's marketers lies in the changing behaviour of the target audience. The UK media regulator Ofcom's latest research shows a 12.4 per cent decrease in numbers of minutes watching television – in just one year.[10]

So on top of the problem of a proliferation of channels aimed at this audience, and the move to on-demand content across all ages, there is a more worrying trend for broadcasters. Children increasingly prefer other things to linear television.

The corollary of this is that marketing budgets and creative resources need to be spent 'off channel' to reach a broader audience. Traditional campaign structures to launch new programmes – billboards, press and TV buys – clearly involve a huge degree of wastage. The upside is that when you can target them, they are a discrete audience. Hence the BBC spending its rare and precious off-air budgets on cinema commercials to promote CBBC.

When Cartoon Network began a dramatic process of network reinvention in 2013, Scott Thomas, the VP of consumer marketing for the brand, told *Profile* magazine they felt that in order to drive reappraisal they needed to be found as a brand in more surprising spaces: 'I needed kids to know this was something different from their regular expectations.' Their initiatives again included cinema buys, and sponsorship with Six Flags theme parks (giving sampling opportunities to kids waiting in queues), but the biggest hit according to Thomas was a deal with the Atlantis resort in the Bahamas:

> Over 80 per cent of guests who check in are US passport holders, and most have kids between age 6 and 13. We are in our third year of a fully integrated brand experience. We are on their key cards, in the family restaurant, have movie premieres in the pool, host concerts, and have games and prizes. It's an amazing partnership.[11]

The logical extension of this drive to find new ways of reaching prospective audiences has also seen Nickelodeon, Disney and DreamWorks launch their own cruise ships – or partnerships with cruise companies. So now on Royal Caribbean cruises you can sit at dinner with Princess Fiona or Hiccup, or with Norwegian Cruises you can explore with Dora and enjoy Slime Time.[12]

In many ways, though, whilst off-air print media, experiential and event partnerships all serve to broaden reach, perhaps they miss the 'elephant in the room'. Returning to that Ofcom report, the answer really lies in finding where the children have gone:

> Previous Ofcom research has shown that among people who watch short online video clips such as those found on YouTube and social media sites, 6- to 15-year-olds spend the most time, racking up an average of 64 minutes a day.[13]

Children are not spending less time engaged in audio-visual pursuits, it is just that our definition of them has changed. The rise of YouTube stars such as Stampy Cat, PewDiePie, and the Minecraft vlogger phenomenon are perhaps more responsible for the drop in TV viewing than even gaming itself. The upside of this for television brands is that if they harness these new video outlets in engaging ways, they can and should still retain those hearts and minds for their brands. But to do that involves a dramatic shift in broadcaster behaviour – tackling thorny issues like geo-blocking, rights boundaries, shorter form storytelling and open source commissioning. To examine Cartoon Network again, its UK YouTube site has 20,000 subscribers at the time of writing (compared with Stampy Cat's 6.5 million), and it almost solely consists of bits of content that are available on the linear channel or on demand, not material discretely created for this new platform. CBBC with 70,000 subscribers and Disney UK with 160,000 are improvements, but still have yet to adopt the publishing habits of the YouTube channels that are raiding their viewers so effectively. Perhaps this is ultimately because traditional broadcasters are used to controlling and steering their viewers in a way that is the antithesis of YouTube. The reason kids love YouTube is because of the limitless possibilities that search provides, the very absence of guide rails. In 2014 youth research companies Dubit and Sherbert commissioned a survey amongst 5,000 parents and children in the United States and the UK.[14] Peter Robinson, Dubit's head of research, told the *Guardian*:

> Kids still love channels but YouTube gives them the opportunity to forge their own path and discover content in a way that other services don't allow.[15]

– THE INVENTORS OF MASH-UP –

The irony is that Cartoon Network as a brand virtually created what we now consider a 'YouTube editing' style, a joyous mash-up of characters and properties. For years their trailers won countless awards around the world for whip-smart cutting and a gloriously childish disregard for their 'brands'. In direct contrast with the reverence of Disney, complete with brand bibles and scrupulous control of properties, Cartoon Network behaved like a 10-year-old kid. The creative director (now elevated to chief marketing officer), Michael Ouweleen, told *Ad Age* in an article celebrating the network's 20th anniversary that the initial work was partly born out of a practical need to fill airtime. The other more traditional role was deliberate attention grabbing to make viewers pester their parents to phone up cable operators and ask them to add Cartoon Network. He described it as creating a psychographic feel for the channel:

> There were mash-ups that brought classic cartoon characters into contact with each other, minivideos that used classic characters with modern music and longer on-air promos that took a tongue-in-cheek look at the business of running a cartoon channel. The content was topical and hilarious. The *Scooby-Doo* gang appeared in a parody of *The Blair Witch Project*. The CN 'Crisis Center' offered advice to cartoon characters in precarious situations.[16]

– AN EVER-CHANGING AUDIENCE –

For most children's channels writing to hit exactly the right age profile is like nailing jelly to a moving train. Children's attitudes, tastes and maturity almost change faster than broadcasters can commission. Ally to that the huge changes that kids undergo between seemingly tightly targeted brackets such as 5-8, or 8-11, and you begin to see the challenges facing broadcasters. Broadly, most channels have aligned themselves into two groupings: 'preschool', targeting from babies up to four-year-olds (Nick Jr, CBeebies, Disney Junior are examples here), and then a second much more complex sector attempting to draw in 5- to 11-year-olds. They are aware that past the age of nine they are probably losing a large section of the demograph to YouTube, but simultaneously are needing to target those aged 10+ with their brand tone of voice – in order to appear aspirational to the 6- to 8-year-olds who are really their core. This particular tone of voice has always been Cartoon Network's strength.

The owners of these channels or networks have attempted different branding techniques for moving viewers seamlessly from preschool through to 'main channel', though they could principally be defined as two techniques: 1) zoning and signposting a single channel; 2) running two discrete channel brands.

Let's examine them in turn.

– ALL THE WAY THROUGH CHILDHOOD –

We have just helped to launch the first channel for DreamWorks Animation, the Hollywood studio and producer of such modern children's classics as *Kung Fu Panda*, *Shrek*, *Madagascar* and *Home*. You would think that their franchises would be capable of appealing to children from 2 to 13 quite easily. Yet we produced a very defined and signposted preschool zone within the channel. Why? First, for practical reasons, the programme supply deals for DreamWorks mean that alongside their broader film-inspired programming they had bought a library of unquestionably preschool programming. Second, because emotionally eight-year-olds don't want to think that they are watching something that could be enjoyed by their babyish former self. They need to see that *Raa Raa The Noisy Lion* and *Guess with Jess* are housed in a distinctive state of 'not for them'. So whilst the main channel idents feature *Puss in Boots*, *Po* and *Penguins of Madagascar*, creating the very fabric of the channel with their movements, the preschool zone branding is free from DreamWorks characters and inhabits a neutral world of pastel colours and rounded shapes. Jennifer Lawlor, head of distribution services for DreamWorks Animation, explains further:

As we had to build our preschool offering into the channel, we devised DreamWorks Junior as clear signposting through the channel to establish which day parts were scheduled with preschool content. Rather than launching a separate channel, DreamWorks Junior as a distinct area with its own colour scheme, logo and presentation environment lets parents know when to tune in for age-appropriate shows for their kids whilst not impacting on the core brand values and targeting of the DreamWorks channel.[17]

Using graphic design to create age-appropriate programming zones for DreamWorks
Source: *Reproduced by permission of DreamWorks Animation*

– KEEPING THE WORLDS APART –

The second approach is followed in two examples from central Eastern Europe and the UK. Minimax is one of the best-loved preschool channels currently running in 13 countries from Hungary to Slovenia. Launched in 1999 with an editorial positioning of 'edutainment' and non-violent programming it has been owned by a variety of conglomerates and was most recently sold by Chellomedia to AMC Networks International.

Inevitably the challenge of trying to keep older children in an environment where Babar, Elmo and Fireman Sam were staples of the schedule became increasingly difficult. So in 2011 we were invited to introduce a new partner brand to the market. Aimed purely at 8- to 12-year-old boys, Megamax provides an edgy destination for those who have outgrown Minimax. Our core idea defined Megamax as a beacon brand reflecting the key stage of childhood that is all about the emerging role of friendship. From this thought came two hero characters, 'Spark-e and I-ron', robots from another dimension who live in the Megamax transmission station. Spark-e and I-ron represent everything the channel stands for: action, adventure, magic, fantasy, humour and excitement, all blended with a cool and credible edge.[18]

The BBC have long believed, unlike their commercial rival ITV (who maintain one brand for children, CITV) that 0–5 and 6–12 are stages of development so fundamentally different that they deserve entirely separate channels. So CBeebies for preschool and CBBC for school-age children were launched in 2002. As of 2016 a new brand is planned to enter that equation, provisionally referred to as iPlay. This initiative, developed again with an eye to changing audience behaviour, will create an online walled garden of children's content that parents can trust entirely. It will provide children with the capacity to search that the Dubit and Sherbert research found so valuable, but in a safer environment. As Philip Almond, the BBC's director of marketing and audiences, explains:

> There's something really strong that the BBC stands for and CBBC stands for in that market, which you then take pan-media. It's the trust and the quality of the content, saying that we can do this for you in this world where your child is not just going to be sitting down watching telly.[19]

– TALKING TO THE GROWN-UPS –

For most marketers this more formal division of brands between audiences seems essential. The principal audience for CBeebies (or Minimax, or Nick Jr) is parents. Ultimately they control the remote, with varying degrees of pester power in play. For CBBC, Megamax, Nickelodeon and Cartoon Network, the audience will be almost exclusively the children themselves. The role of the brands is crucial in determining the tone of voice therein. For example, CBeebies will regularly make two trailers to launch a show, one that is content driven and playfully encouraging the repetition and delight in the familiar of its junior audience, and an entirely different trailer to talk to the parents, underlining the developmental aspects of the same programme. There is acute sensitivity, particularly amongst public service broadcasters, or those governed by strict legislative codes of conduct, around how preschool television could be promoted almost as a pacifier. While every parent knows that sticking a fractious toddler in front of an hour of *In the Night Garden* or *Curious George* is all about a priceless hour of freedom, simultaneously they like to be reassured that all the content their children are consuming is carefully structured to be as developmentally nutritious as possible. The promos are often specially and delightfully shot to illustrate what 'the little ones' will be learning. A whole campaign examining the youthful genius of Tiger Woods, Jodie Foster and Mozart may have been a deliberately tongue-in-cheek association with the stimulus of shows such as *Tweenies*, but it was certainly built on the insight that every parent expects their toddler to be a baby Einstein.[20]

– KIDS VERSUS PARENTS –

A brand that from its very launch has been 'marketing led' is Nickelodeon and, in contrast to the above examples, they set out from that very launch to be more about 'kids versus adults'. This sense of siding with the natural messy boundary testing in kids led directly to the green splat logo, as TV strategist Lee Hunt remarked to us:

> Nickelodeon – when they decided to adopt the positioning 'Us versus Them' – the marketing went forward and it took about 18 months for the programming to catch up. The very first show that did that was *You Can't Do That on Television*, which introduced the green slime that made Nickelodeon so famous. In those early days you never saw kids get slimed, it was just adults, parents and teachers. And that was the whole perspective of the channel. It was kids versus adults, parents and teachers – and that's what made it so successful.[21]

– PAST AND FUTURE GENERATIONS –

Perhaps the greatest children's promotional film ever produced was, in fact, firmly targeted at parents. Designed as part of a campaign to demonstrate the BBC's value for money in 1999, producer Sarah Caddy and director Chris Palmer stunningly wove one child's journey through decades of BBC children's programmes in the multi-award-winning spot 'Future Generations' (written by agency Leagas Delaney). A five-year-old boy – the brilliantly cast Scott Chisholm – interacts with puppets, presenters and animals from *Bill and Ben* and *Bagpuss* to *The Lion, The Witch and The Wardrobe*, while explaining how 'one day a big corporation decided to make programmes for little people'.[22] Justin Bairamian, then an executive at Leagas Delaney and now director of BBC Creative, remembers that the film actually came from a brief to follow the musical 'Perfect Day' trailer with an equally emotional example of the universal benefit gained from the unique way the BBC is funded. The trailer dramatically showed the golden seam running through British childhood, a sense of shared memory and experiences born out of a nation sitting down collectively at 4.20 pm to watch the same programme on the same day of the week.

Maybe the film's real strength, however, is that the characters and narratives involved were so much stronger than those generated by the vloggers, game players and cat animators of YouTube today.[23]

– REBELS WITH A CAUSE –

Talking to the dual audience of children and parents may not simply be for reasons of balancing educational reassurance against high-energy promotion. Disney XD explained, while outlining their *Star Wars Rebels* campaign to the PromaxBDA conference in Los Angeles in 2015, that one audience brought with it a lifetime of experiences and expectations to a brand like *Star Wars*, whereas a six-year-old will see the series as his or her first interaction with a franchise. Disney XD's creative director, Vincent Aricco, outlined how they felt they had one audience who it was vital to reassure that this new series would not trample incorrectly on the Lucas storyworld. So they created a 'Generation Dad' spot, which placed 'Rebels' within the Star Wars timeline, simultaneously hoping that for any watching six-, seven- or eight-year-olds it would sell how the show fits into the Empire legacy, with such a light touch that it wouldn't make them feel like they have to do hours of homework: 'Where did the rebels come from? Let's start from the beginning, there was a boy named Anakin, a Jedi named Obe-Wan Kenobi, a master named Yoda, a war with clones, Anakin becomes Darth Vader'... and so on in accelerating and breathless tones.[24]

What the trailer also did was something rare for children's shows: it set it within a wider story arc. The vast majority of kids' programming is highly episodic, designed for 24-minute attention spans and programmes being heavily rotated and watched out of sequence. *Rebels* has a sense of dynasty and narrative that Disney hoped would elevate it above other animated science fiction fare. This fed into their whole approach to the marketing, with reverence given to the source material at all times. Aricco and the art director Lon Moeller talked of visiting Lucas Ranch and holding in white-gloved hands the films' original concept art and accessories by famed designer Ralph McQuarrie. McQuarrie's use of colour, and his line quality (the heaviness and lightness of the strokes), became the inspiration for the *Rebels* campaign's overall art directional look and feel. The trip was also important, Aricco told the conference, so that they could reassure the Lucas content team that 'we weren't going to put Mickey Mouse ears on their characters'.[25]

A critical element of the Disney thinking when both commissioning and launching *Rebels* was the need for strong female characters. So, as we have seen with the drama campaigns in Chapter 7 with adult audiences, a children's campaign can feature multiple discrete pieces of creative with distinctive roles. One *Rebels* trailer starred almost exclusively the droid Chopper, whose deadpan grumpiness highlighted the comedy within the show, while Sabine, the female weapons expert and graffiti tagger, gets a two-minute introduction all to herself with the intention of broadening the audience to a girl demographic.[26]

Sabine and Chopper were important to Disney in a marketing role far beyond that of initial viewership, that of their plastic figurines retailing for $20 in stores across the United States.

– MERCHANDISE AS MARKETING –

Inevitably the value in many children's TV properties lies beyond the format rights and the advertising revenue generated around linear screenings, and can be found in the much wider world of merchandise. Fortunately this is a virtuous circle for marketers, because every Chopper droid in a child's bedroom, every *In the Night Garden* pyjama set and every *Bob the Builder* lunch box is a trailer for the founder show. The first person to realize the marketing power of merchandise was of course Walt Disney himself. As the Disney museum expert Keith Gluck explains in a blog post:

> The real spark for Disney marketing came thanks to a chance meeting Walt had in a New York hotel lobby in 1929. A man approached Walt and offered him $300 in cash for the right to feature Mickey Mouse on a children's pencil tablet he was about to produce.[27]

This reliance on merchandise as the economic fulcrum brings with it new problems for broadcasters, though. Anne Wood, the creative genius whose Ragdoll company lies behind so many worldwide preschool hits, from *Teletubbies* to *In the Night Garden*, explained to *Broadcast* magazine that retailers are obsessed with the new. This can lead to tension with the model that production companies work to, where to monetize the development of a show you need to run for several years:

> The toy and publishing industries have been very much more influenced by character-led properties, and the retailers are looking for the next thing very quickly. So even if people want Paddington Bear, and many do, it's very hard to find it in the shops now. Unfortunately it has something to do with the marketing of these things, not with the things themselves.[28]

– A TRUSTED FRIEND –

The structure of children's channel junctions and ad breaks can be markedly different from those of more adult-targeted brands, and nowhere more so than in the use of in-vision presenters as the glue to the channel – trusted friends who virtually sit with the viewer on the sofa enjoying the shows with you, and providing a point of interactivity. Pioneered initially by the BBC as part of the Presentation Department we described in Chapter 1, the remit includes literally pressing play on video vision mixers, as much as reading out birthday messages and showing viewers' fan artwork. The Broom Cupboard to host children's programmes was a significant innovation in television presentation (while simultaneously being a throwback to the 1950s and 1960s era of live in-vision continuity – something that still persists in a wide variety of European countries). The double acts of presenters and puppets that anchored the hours of coverage became a potent timeline of childhood. Were you a 'Phillip Schofield and Gordon the Gopher child', or an 'Andi Peters and Edd the Duck' or 'Ed Petrie and Oucho T. Cactus', or 'Iain Stirling and Hacker the Dog'? Thirty years have now passed where the BBC Children's brand has arguably been defined more by these voices than by any design work, trailers or marketing initiatives. What was powerful in each of the puppets listed here was the ability to generate so much character within relatively unsophisticated puppetry.[29]

– SHOWING CHARACTER –

Characters have always been a shorthand to children's brands from the day that Walt Disney first sketched a pair of circular ears on top of a cartoon mouse. The Magic Kingdom castle may well be the Walt Disney brand emblem, but Mickey Mouse is Disney. The ears have become the motif for every Disney channel, globally surviving content shifts as generational as *Hannah Montana* and *The Suite Life of Zack and Cody*.

Tom and Jerry, Road Runner and Wile E Coyote, Hiccup and Toothless, *Grange Hill*'s Zammo and Roly – whether two-dimensional and trapped in perpetual comedic hero's journeys like Jerry, or textured, complex and nuanced as with *Grange Hill*, tackling subjects from drug abuse to disability, children are drawn to narrative and character, just as much as their parents.

One of the biggest global hits in children's television this century has been the *High School Musical* franchise, Disney Channel's series of television films. The first film launched with nearly 8 million viewers in the United States, and the follow-up became the most watched basic cable programme ever.[30]

Clearly the originality of the format – it was the first TV musical written for a tween audience – was a part of this success, but to many the scale of the marketing triumph was a genuine surprise. Adam Bonnett, SVP of the original series for Disney Channel and Jetix, speaking to the Animation World Network, said:

A lot of people talk about the success of the music, and you can see how successful the music has been, but what gets overlooked is the relationship between the audience and these characters. You can't underestimate that. That's what's driving the tween appeal.[31]

Disney has developed an intricate way of developing and growing the relationship between viewers and characters, often by seeding those characters across established shows. Ashley Tisdale, one of the stars of *High School Musical*, was already known to fans of *Zack and Cody*. (Disney repeated the formula with *Wizards of Waverly Place* star Selena Gomez, who was known to the *Hannah Montana* audience.) 'That cross-pollination is really, really important,' explained Bonnett in the same interview.

High School Musical had also benefited from the range and breadth of Disney's promotional campaign, treating the soundtrack to the film as a simultaneous major album launch. Pop videos played across the network as interstitials in the weeks leading up to the premiere, and viewers were pushed to the channel's website to download lyrics to the songs in preparation for a karaoke screening the day after. As *Slate* magazine reported, this insight into demographic behaviour anticipated the effect of the pyjama-clad, singalong cultural phenomenon:

> Radio Disney played the soundtrack on heavy rotation, and it became the top-selling album on iTunes and Amazon. To encourage repeat viewings, subsequent telecasts offered free downloads and dance-alongs, ready-made for slumber parties.[32]

– REWARDING THE VIEWERS –

Returning to the enduring threats posed by the gaming industry, social media and video search engines to traditional children's channels, we have outlined some of the strategies that are key to survival. A final lesson lies in one of the world's oldest continual children's television programmes.

The BBC's *Blue Peter* is a remarkably enduring brand. The marketing campaign our team created to promote it in 2015 points to a key reason behind that lasting appeal. It focuses on extraordinary pets, such as a remarkably skilful hamster, a musical tabby and an athletic tortoise, but the trailer ends with a focused message, 'Get Your Badge', and a close-up of just that tangible end user benefit. The *Blue Peter* badge.

Blue Peter is a programme that has both requested and rewarded children's participation, decades before 'user-generated content' became the *phrase du jour*. Founding producer Biddy Baxter said that at one point around three-quarters of the programme's content came from viewers' suggestions.[33] Any contributor to the show was awarded a *Blue Peter* badge... and with it the membership of a club with undiminished kudos amongst peer groups

The tortoise who channelled Usain Bolt gets his reward. A Blue Peter *badge*
Source: Reproduced by permission of BBC

through the decades. If you need any proof of the enduring appeal of the coveted reward, then watch Sir Jonathan Ive, the legendary Apple designer, being presented with his own gold *Blue Peter* badge, and witness his genuine emotional response (see: **https://www.youtube.com/watch?v=FLUn7xCuQx o#t=342**).[34] The ownership of a *Blue Peter* badge now brings with it actual returns, such as free entry to over 200 attractions in the UK, but research continues to show it is the recognition itself that is a huge driver towards participation and thus viewing too. The badge scheme has evolved to include even more collectable items – green badges for environmental ideas, purple badges for reviewers, and so on.

Overall it appears that if you can reward children for their attention with enduring characters, interactivity and co-creation, merchandise and brand partnerships, great storytelling, and perhaps a tangible, physical form of recognition, then children's television can survive for generations.

NEXT
★ *Defiance*'s Comic-Con takeover.
★ The back story of Robin Sparkles.
★ 'The Day of the Doctor'.
★ Roasting Joffrey.
★ New York's 'Draper bench'.
★ The flagship store for synthetic humans.

LATER
★ Fright night in the asylum.
★ Why Adrianne Curry was the #Luckiestgalonearth.
★ A walled garden strategy.

NOTES

1 *Horrible Histories*, 'Sugar Paste Tooth Fairy' (2011) season 3, episode 11, CBBC, 5 July

2 Quote from Sam Gibbon in Gladwell, M (2002) *The Tipping Point: How little things can make a big difference*, Abacus, Boston

3 Gladwell, M (2002) *The Tipping Point: How little things can make a big difference*, Abacus, Boston

4 http://www.redbeecreative.tv/work/ketnet

5 Nick Jr (2015) [accessed 23 September 2015] I Love Art – Umbrellas [Online] http://www.nickjr.co.uk/watch/nick-jr-shorts/umbrellas#

6 Loria, K (2012) [accessed 23 September 2015] The CMO.com Interview: PBS Senior Vice President Lesli Rotenberg. CMO, 5 November [Online] http://www.cmo.com/articles/2012/11/5/the-cmocom-interview-pbs-svp-lesli-rotenberg.html

7 https://www.youtube.com/watch?v=oRBg4f7SFsA

8 https://www.youtube.com/watch?v=VqK1_rOqFzo

9 Disney (2015) [accessed 23 September 2015] Disney: Doc McStuffins' Check Up Clinic [Online] http://www.hotcow.co.uk/portfolio/disney-doc-mcstuffins-check-up-clinic.htm

10 Ofcom (2015) [accessed 23 September 2015] The Communications Market Report [Online] http://stakeholders.ofcom.org.uk/binaries/research/cmr/cmr15/CMR_UK_2015.pdf

11 Baliva, Z (2013) [accessed 23 September 2015] The Reign Of Scott Thomas, *Profile Magazine* [Online] http://profilemagazine.com/2013/cartoon-network/

12 Heptinstall, S (2011) [accessed 23 September 2015] Cruises For Children: The Best Family Friendly Voyages With Spongebob And Shrek, *Daily Mail*, 30 October [Online] http://www.dailymail.co.uk/travel/article-2055330/The-best-family-cruises-Voyages-SpongeBob-Shrek.html

13 Jackson, J (2015) [accessed 23 September 2015] Children Spending Less Time In Front Of TV As They Turn To Online Media, *Guardian*, 6 August [Online] http://www.theguardian.com/media/2015/aug/06/children-spending-less-time-in-front-of-tv-ofcom

14 Dubit (2014) [accessed 23 September 2015] How Young Early Adopters Share New Entertainment [Online] http://www.dubitlimited.com/blog/2014/07/07/how-young-early-adopters-share-new-entertainment/

15 Robinson, P quoted in Dredge, S (2014) [accessed 23 September 2015] YouTube Is Already Big For Kids, But It Wants To Be Even Bigger, *Guardian*, 7 October [Online] http://www.theguardian.com/technology/2014/oct/07/youtube-makes-its-move-into-childrens-tv-heres-why

16 Ouweleen, M (2012) [accessed 23 September 2015] Cartoon Network 20th Birthday Celebration, *Ad Age*, 1 October [Online] http://brandedcontent.adage.com/pdf/Cartoon-Network-Turns-20.pdf

17 Jennifer Lawlor, head of distribution services, DreamWorks Animation, interview 6 November 2015

18 https://www.youtube.com/watch?v=AE1FicEjlpU

19 Philip Almond, director of marketing and audiences, BBC, interview 14 September 2015

20 King, A (2015) [accessed 23 September 2015] CBeebies [Online] http://www.akingcreative.co.uk/aking/Cbeebies.html

21 Lee Hunt, managing partner, Lee Hunt LLC, interview 24 March 2015

22 IMDB (2015) [accessed 24 September 2015] Scott Chisholm [Online] http://www.imdb.com/name/nm0158264/

23 Holywell-Walker, N (2013) [accessed 23 September 2015] BBC Future Generations Promo 1998 [Online] https://vimeo.com/52295008

24 Star Wars (2014) [accessed 23 September 2015] Timeline – TV Spot, Star Wars Rebels [Online] https://www.youtube.com/watch?v=Jh_U2wnA98I

25 Sanders, J W (2015) [accessed 23 September 2015] How 'Star Wars Rebels' Spread Across The Galaxy, *Promax BDA*, 6 November [Online] http://brief.promaxbda.org/content/how-star-wars-rebels-spread-across-the-galaxy

26 Star Wars (2014) [accessed 6 November 2015] Meet Sabine, The Explosive Artist – Star Wars Rebels [Online] https://www.youtube.com/watch?v=-_0A2-YDexw

27 Storyboard (2012) [accessed 23 September 2015] Selling Mickey: The Rise Of Disney Marketing [Blog] Walt Disney Family Museum, 8 June [Online] http://www.waltdisney.org/blog/selling-mickey-rise-disney-marketing

28 Woods, A (2003) [accessed 23 September 2015] Interview – In The Silly Money, *Broadcast Now*, 14 April [Online] http://www.broadcastnow.co.uk/interview-in-the-silly-money/1115302.article

29 Webb, C (2015) [accessed 23 September 2015] Secrets Of The Children's BBC Broom Cupboard, *Radio Times*, 9 September [Online] http://www.radiotimes.com/news/2015-09-09/secrets-of-the-childrens-bbc-broom-cupboard

30 The Associated Press (2007) [accessed 23 September 2015] High School Musical 2 Sets Ratings Record, *Today*, 20 August [Online] http://www.today.com/id/20360800/ns/today-today_entertainment/t/high-school-musical-sets-ratings-record/#.VgKwb99VhBd

31 Raugust, K (2007) [accessed 23 September 2015] Tween Power: How High School Musical Has Affected Animation, *Animation World Network*, 26 October [Online] http://www.awn.com/animationworld/tween-power-how-high-school-musical-has-affected-animation

32 Meltzer, M (2006) [accessed 23 September 2015] We're Soaring! We're Flying! *Slate*, 31 March [Online] http://www.slate.com/articles/arts/music_box/2006/03/were_soaring_were_flying.html

33 Martinson, J (2013) [accessed 23 September 2015] Blue Peter's Biddy Baxter: I Never Wanted To Do Anything Else, *Guardian* 24 November [Online] http://www.theguardian.com/media/2013/nov/24/blue-peter-biddy-baxter-bbc

34 Davenport, T (2013) [accessed 23 September 2015] Jonathan Ive On Blue Peter (Full Version) [Online] https://www.youtube.com/watch?v=FLUn7xCuQxo#t=342

PART FOUR

BUILDING BRANDS IN THE AGE OF ONLINE TV

CHAPTER FOURTEEN

STORYWORLDS
Blurring the lines between content and marketing

My world does not end with these four walls, Slough's a big place.
And when I've finished with Slough, there's Reading, Aldershot, Bracknell...

DAVID BRENT, *THE OFFICE*[1]

– A 'FATAL' FALL –

The season two finale of BBC drama *Sherlock*, titled 'The Reichenbach Fall', ended with a bang or, more accurately, a thud. The detective Sherlock Holmes (Benedict Cumberbatch) leapt to his death from a London rooftop. His friend, Dr Watson (Martin Freeman), found him in a bloody mess on the pavement. We ended on Watson at Sherlock's graveside, as the detective (very much alive) watched from a distance.

As fans of TV shows go, 'Sherlockians' are amongst the most obsessive, and what followed was a mountain of speculation across social media about the ending and what might happen next. As entertainment website Den of Geek put it:

> The tragedy of Sherlock's flappy coat seeming to have flapped its last flap in 'The Reichenbach Fall' was of such personal importance to so many people that, unwilling to wait 18 months or longer for an explanation, the web's hive mind set about doing some deducing of its own.[2]

So when, 18 months later, people started spotting a hearse driving past London landmarks bearing mysterious messages written in flowers – a date (01/01/14), a TV channel (BBC One) and a Twitter hashtag (#sherlocklives) – social media lit up in anticipation. Eager fans quickly traced the hearse to a parking space outside Speedy's Cafe in Baker Street, a familiar location below the fictional detective's lodgings. Later, outside St Bart's Hospital, fans could find a chalk outline on the pavement to mark the spot of Sherlock's 'fatal' fall, again tagged #sherlocklives.

A hearse driving past London landmarks to intrigue Sherlock *fans*
Source: Reproduced by permission of Red Bee

These were just a couple of elements of a 'transmedia' marketing campaign that our team created to reward Sherlock's superfans and excite them ahead of the launch of season three on New Year's Day 2014, with the opening episode appropriately titled 'The Empty Hearse'. They formed a small part of the *Sherlock* 'storyworld', which marketing has helped to build.

– OCEANIC 815, THE SERIAL HUNTRESS AND BICYCLE GIRL –

We're certainly not the first to use the phrase 'transmedia storytelling'. It has been a familiar theme for TV producers and commissioners around the globe in recent years as they have seized the opportunities presented by new technology and changing consumer behaviour to create 'cross-platform narrative experiences'.[3]

There are many books, academic studies and online resources covering this subject in relation to creators and producers, so there is no need for us to go over the same ground. Our focus is TV marketing. However, a brief potted history of transmedia storytelling would be helpful to set the scene.

Its 'Godfather' is Henry Jenkins, currently Provost Professor at the University of Southern California. It is generally accepted that he coined the phrase transmedia storytelling. Writing in MIT's *Technology Review* (of all places) in 2003, he predicted that:

> What is variously called transmedia, multiplatform or enhanced storytelling represents the future of entertainment.[4]

So, it is fair to say that Jenkins was ahead of his time. Three years later his influential book *Convergence Culture: Where old and new media collide* explored, in particular, *The Matrix* franchise and the way the story was built up with overlapping narrative strands across the movies, the video games and the animated short films. He famously wrote:

> A transmedia story unfolds across multiple media platforms, with each new text making a distinctive and valuable contribution to the whole.[5]

It is hard to imagine that, back in 2006 when *Convergence Culture* was first published, there was no such thing as an iPhone or iPad; Facebook only had around 12 million users; Twitter was in its early launch phase; we would have to wait another two years for BBC iPlayer; and Netflix was primarily a DVD rental business.

In recent years there have been several celebrated case studies of transmedia storytelling for major US dramas. Three examples stand out. In 2006 ABC's *Lost*, which traced the story of the survivors of crashed passenger jet Oceanic 815, started experimenting with alternate reality games (ARGs) between seasons.[6] A five-month interactive game, The Lost Experience, built a complex narrative to explore parts of the *Lost* mythology beyond the TV episodes.[7] In 2010, in the run-up to the season five premiere of *Dexter*, Showtime also launched a multilayered alternate-reality game involving crowdsourced crime solving, centred on an ex-FBI agent known as 'The Serial Huntress'. That same year, AMC launched possibly the best transmedia case study to date in *The Walking Dead*, which started life as a comic book and then became a TV drama, a video game and much more besides.[8] *The Walking Dead*'s innovative webisodes, which told the back stories of zombie characters such as Bicycle Girl, worked together with second screen apps, social media content, video games and a live after-show TV programme to build a multidimensional storyworld.

– IS IT CONTENT OR IS IT MARKETING? –

The three examples – *Lost*, *Dexter* and *The Walking Dead* – are explored extensively in a number of articles and blogs, and the extent to which each of them was faithful to Henry Jenkins's original definition could be debated at length. However, one question that has rarely been discussed is this: where was the dividing line between the storytelling and the marketing? The Lost Experience expanded a number of themes from the *Lost* universe, for example via the creation of a number of fictional websites, including one for the Hanso Foundation, a corporation referred to in the TV episodes. It is notable that ABC Entertainment's then senior VP of marketing, Mike Benson, was quoted as saying:

> It's a hybrid between content and marketing.[9]

The Dexter ARG featuring 'The Serial Huntress' and her crowdsourced efforts to track down 'The Infinity Killer' was most definitely a marketing initiative to drive a big audience to the new season. The diverse components of the case study of *The Walking Dead* include a number that could be classified as marketing.

The producer and media strategist Anne Zeiser has written one of the only books we are aware of to tackle the specific subject of transmedia marketing (across movies and games as well as television). In her words, 'entertainment content and content marketing have become a single storytelling enterprise', and she goes on to say:

> Transmedia marketing... is the holistic discipline of making media and marketing media across multiple platforms – on air, online and on the go – through engaging storytelling, rich story worlds and interactive audience experiences... Developing and marketing media projects simultaneously across multiple media platforms creates an integrated transmedia project with multiple pathways for audience engagement – spawning loyal, participatory fans.[10]

The term 'storyworld' has become a familiar way to denote the fictional universe in which a transmedia narrative takes place: the mythology, the characters, the settings, the events and the back stories. And TV marketers and creatives are now playing an increasingly important role in shaping these storyworlds. The boundaries between content and marketing are blurring all the time.

If we look at the best recent illustrations of this and explore the techniques that marketers are using to build and enhance these storyworlds, they can be grouped under six headings:

★ Start building early.
★ Create immersive experiences.

★ Develop the characters.
★ Send 'love letters' to the audience.
★ Keep the storyworld alive between seasons.
★ Take the story into the real world.

Actually, there is a seventh heading. One of the most prevalent ways in which storyworlds are being built is by harnessing social media. This is the subject of Chapter 15, so to avoid unnecessary duplication we will hold our best examples of social media activation until then (although we can't talk about storyworlds without coming across social media throughout: as with content and marketing, many of the themes of this book tend to overlap too).

Let's look at each of the other six headings in turn.

– BUILDING EARLY: THE LAUNCH OF *DEFIANCE* –

The multilayered launch campaign (dubbed 'The Maester's Path') for the first season of HBO's *Game of Thrones* started a couple of months ahead of the TV premiere. HBO built anticipation, for example, by despatching boxes of scents, scrolls and maps to key TV critics and bloggers and sending food trucks out on the streets of New York and Los Angeles with *Game of Thrones*-themed dishes.[11] Going back a few years, that was the way that marketing campaigns for major dramas were typically phased, even those involving multiple components and media.

These days, the promotional media options are so diverse and the competitive stakes so high that marketing activity is starting much further out from the TV airdate, especially for brand new franchises not benefiting from several previous seasons (as with *Dexter*) or an existing fan base (as with *Game of Thrones*).

The annual Comic-Con fan convention in San Diego is becoming a familiar location for the major US TV networks to attempt to whip up excitement for a new show (with the 2015 event featuring world premiere screenings of new shows including *Scream Queens*, *Into the Badlands* and *Supergirl*). Visitors to the 2012 event could not have failed to notice the huge promotional push behind a new TV series called *Defiance*. Or was it a video game? Actually it was both: a joint venture between NBCUniversal's Syfy channel and video-game developer Trion, described by Syfy as:

> The most ambitious transmedia project the world has seen, uniting scripted drama and online gaming in one convergent world.[12]

Visitors arriving at San Diego's Lindbergh Field Airport were confronted with giant billboards for *Defiance*, and they soon became aware of 'a total Comic-Con takeover',[13] with huge *Defiance* building wraps, branded buses, cast appearances and celebrity parties. Part of this 'all-out assault' was to transform the Hard Rock Hotel restaurant Maryjane's into Defiance Café, where fans were invited to 'Watch. Play. Eat' and immerse themselves completely in the *Defiance* storyworld, which united a 'massive multiplayer online game' (MMOG) with a TV drama for the first time.[14]

Comic-Con 2012 happened in mid-July. The first TV airdate of *Defiance* was 15 April 2013: a full nine months later (the game had launched simultaneously across PC, PlayStation 3 and Xbox 360 platforms on 2 April). This was an unprecedented gap between a promotional campaign launch and a TV premiere, and planned by the Syfy marketing team to kick-start a project the like of which had never been seen before, as Syfy's former marketing chief, Michael Engleman, describes:

> In a landscape where social recommendations from peers have become critical markers for success, we aim to make any and all of our shows a part of the cultural conversation. That said, *Defiance* was a unique property – a first of its kind – and needed to be handled as such. As marketers we weren't just selling a compelling storyline, we were selling a new way to engage in entertainment.[15]

To make the budget work as hard as possible during such an extended promotional period, the Comic-Con takeover led into a multilayered social campaign, including Facebook, Twitter and a stand-alone *Defiance* website, into which the Syfy team drip-fed content including 'making of' videos to start building the *Defiance* storyworld. At the centre of all this activity was what the Syfy team called a Cultural Momentum Map: a calendar that plotted each stage in the campaign against key moments in popular culture, including major sports events and premieres of other big TV shows. Based on that map, advertising was scheduled to coincide tactically with other relevant TV shows such as season finales of *The Walking Dead* and *American Horror Story*, the launch of the movie *The Hobbit* and coverage of the entertainment awards season. The showrunners, game developers and marketers worked hand in hand to develop a huge 'wiki' of mythology for *Defiance*. New roles on the team were created to pull the whole thing together and help to align the development of the storyworld with events on the cultural map. Michael Engleman explains why this approach was important:

> The complexity of the world was so deep, we hired a dedicated internal team – part writer, part producer, part digital librarian... All of us working on the project – from every discipline imaginable – aligned around a single set of story rules.[16]

Having conquered Comic-Con, Syfy didn't hold back from capitalizing on other events of cultural significance. In February 2013, a TED talk by David Peterson on developing the Dothraki language for *Game of Thrones* gave

Syfy an opportunity for another cultural 'moment', since David was at that time alien language and culture consultant for *Defiance*.[17] Then, the following month, a presence for *Defiance* was also created at the South by Southwest (SXSW) Interactive Festival (another convention that has grown rapidly in popularity amongst TV marketers). In the parking lot of the event in Austin, Texas, Syfy built what they described as a 'concierge-style container village' – three shipping containers with 24/7 concierge service and bathroom facilities – in which they installed a *Defiance* cast member (Jesse Rath), a Forbes columnist (Jeff Bercovici) and a blogger with an influential following (Curt Johnson), all of whom continued to spread the word about *Defiance* across social media, still a full month before its TV premiere. By the time the big day came around, *Defiance* already had 250,000 Facebook fans, an extraordinary number for a TV show that had yet to air – and reward for the Syfy marketing team's painstaking efforts to introduce the drama and maintain the buzz for a full nine months.

– CREATING IMMERSIVE EXPERIENCES –

The alternate reality games that helped to build the mythology of *Lost* and *Dexter* were early examples of innovative and immersive content created by marketers to draw in the audience and keep them hooked. Some of the most successful storyworlds have been enriched with the help of experiences such as complex and absorbing microsites, online treasure hunts and interactive trailers.

When CANAL+ in France prepared to launch the Anglo-French crime drama *Tunnel* (a remake of the Swedish-Danish co-production *Broen*, or *The Bridge*), rather than challenging potential viewers to track down a killer in the manner of *Dexter*'s Serial Huntress, they invited them into the world of the villain, known as the Truth Terrorist. A stand-alone website, with a hauntingly eerie soundtrack, allowed visitors to navigate around the Truth Terrorist's lair and search for clues on a bank of surveillance screens and a giant pinboard of cuttings and photos that *Homeland*'s obsessive agent Carrie Mathison would be proud of. People were encouraged to share clues on Twitter or post on the Truth Terrorist's own Facebook profile (with an average of three shares or actions per visitor, according to the creators, digital agency ESV),[18] all of which helped to build *Tunnel*'s atmospheric storyworld and increase visibility of the new drama ahead of its TV premiere.

The Truth Terrorist website was created to introduce a new programme concept, but when a storyworld already exists, with an established fan base, there is invariably a rich stock of material with which to build immersive experiences. The UK launch of season three of the BBC's *Sherlock* gave our team a lot to work with. The fact that the detective drama had been off our screens for nearly two years, following the intriguing ending of season two, had primed fans to seek out any fragments of news about the impending arrival of a new series that might unravel the mystery of the lead character's fake death.

The secret of creating promotional campaigns that will truly involve viewers and encourage them to spend time decoding clues, playing simple online games or sharing snippets on social media is to be true to the content. *Sherlock* fans love to immerse themselves in the world of the 'high-functioning sociopath' (in the detective's own words), so we wanted our campaign for season three to be intriguing enough to foster a degree of obsessive amateur detective work.

By the time we drove our hearse with its flower messages through central London towards Baker Street we had already unveiled on-air teaser promos to launch the hashtag #sherlocklives and drip-feed fans news of *Sherlock*'s return. As the day of the season premiere approached, an on-air promotional campaign was accompanied by an interactive trailer built with the help of video tagging technology. This allowed the addition of clickable 'hotspots' throughout the trailer that fans could search for and click to access new pieces of exclusive *Sherlock* content. To add to the intrigue we also built in a hidden hotspot, requiring a code to unlock it (if you're wondering, it was the date of Guy Fawkes Night, 051113). It took the most committed fans less than 30 minutes to crack the code and open up exclusive behind-the-scenes interviews with the cast and writers before sharing and bragging about their discovery on social media using #sherlocklives.

The interactive *Sherlock* trailer was viewed over 500,000 times in its first 48 hours, with fans spending, on average, over five minutes enjoying the hidden content, in time generating over 1.5 million hotspot interactions. On the day of the premiere episode, images of the body outline on the pavement outside St Bart's Hospital were shared thousands of times on social media. Correlating marketing data like this with viewing figures is notoriously difficult, but nearly 10 million viewers tuned in to the season premiere of *Sherlock*: the biggest audience on that New Year's Day, to the delight of everyone involved. The season three marketing campaign undoubtedly added to the mythology and strengthened the bond between *Sherlock* and its fans with immersive transmedia storytelling.[19]

Another drama benefiting from an established base of superfans has been *Game of Thrones*, with its sprawling world of kingdoms, cities, islands and gods providing rich material with which to encourage active participation in online experiences. The digital marketing team at CANAL+ in Spain (since merged by its owner Telefónica into the Movistar+ brand) has been particularly prolific in its creation of content aimed at getting fans to take part. A second screen app built for season three was the first of its kind in Spain – a live interactive experience for smartphones and tablets, which also included a game layer that allowed fans to unlock rewards depending on the extent of their participation. Grito de Guerra (Battle Cry), which CANAL+ described as a curated online experience, was an interactive game that allowed fans to role-play in the *Game of Thrones* universe, submit their own insignia and fan art, and compete with other players in a series of challenges. This interaction between fans allowed them to add to the richness of the mythology of the storyworld between them.

Sabrina Caluori, HBO's SVP of digital media and marketing in the United States, describes the immersive nature of *Game of Thrones*, which influences HBO's own transmedia marketing:

> One of the defining characteristics of *Game of Thrones* is that the world is so incredibly detailed and complete. So much of what drives our transmedia and digital work is allowing viewers to better understand that world and to ultimately participate in it – to feel like they're a part of it. Many of our fans would live in it if they could!![20]

CANAL+ Spain took participation in the storyworld to another level when they offered fans a chance to star in their launch campaign for season four. They issued an invitation via Facebook and the winning fans got their chance to recite the Oath of the Night's Watch (the well-known pledge of the show's ice-wall guardians) in their promotional trailer for the season premiere, which ended with the words 'Si Lo Vives, Es Verdad' (If You Live It, It Is True).[21]

An invitation from CANAL+ in Spain to take part in their next promotional campaign for Game of Thrones *Source: Reproduced by permission of CANAL+ Spain/ Telefónica. CANAL+ is a registered trademark of GROUPE CANAL+*

– DEVELOPING CHARACTERS: 'LET'S GO TO THE MALL' –

It is probably no coincidence that all the examples we have mentioned so far in this chapter have been drawn from the crime/fantasy/sci-fi genres. As the academic Jason Mittell explains:

> Fantasy and science fiction shows can use transmedia to create more expansive and detailed versions of their storyworlds, which typically are a core appeal within the genre – the emphasis on world building through paratexts is a time-honoured strategy for narratives set in universes with their own scientific or magical properties that beg further investigation and exploration.[22]

We mentioned that word 'paratexts' in Chapter 6 in relation to channel idents. It is not a word you hear often in the corridors of our humble creative agency but, to continue this academic thread just a little longer, Mittell does helpfully add:

> For comedies, transmedia can be a site to develop additional gags or highlight throwaway plotlines for secondary characters without disrupting the plot and character arcs of the television mothership.[23]

Marketers are increasingly finding creative ways to develop the characters in a storyworld: creating additional content beyond the show itself with the specific goal of telling the characters' back stories or extending the audience's appreciation of their personalities, with the ultimate goal of strengthening fans' loyalty to the show.

One of the best examples of this is the long-running CBS comedy *How I Met Your Mother*, the story of five friends from New York recounted in 2030 via flashbacks by a father to his children. From the very early days the production and marketing teams have created a lot of additional assets to help deepen viewers' engagement with the characters.

Two running themes in the show illustrate this, the first of which is the way that CBS has carried through plot points in the TV show to the production of real websites based on those storylines or gags. There are many examples, the best of which build on the character of Barney Stinson, a womanizing banker. In season seven, episode four mentioned websites for Stinson Breast Reduction and Linson Breast Lawsuit, and the CBS team created these websites for real. They were both deliberately crude and amateurish, which is all part of the conceit. Another spoof website, notafathersday.com, built on a storyline in which one of the characters was ecstatic about a negative pregnancy test and celebrated Barney's single, child-free life ('... remember that it is better to change partners than diapers, that the only thing in a bottle should be beer, and that the only reason to be up at 6 am is because you haven't gone to sleep the night before') comes complete with downloadable 'Happy Not A Fathers Day' postcards.[24]

The second illustration is the gentle ribbing of one of the characters – the Canadian would-be news anchor Robin – by her four American friends, which proved to be an ongoing source of laughs at the expense of Canadians throughout nine seasons. Early in season two we discovered that Robin had been a teenage popstar in her native land, with the stage name 'Robin Sparkles' and a video posted on MySpace. CBS created a cheesy song 'Let's Go To The Mall' and produced a full-length music video for real, to carry the gag beyond the TV show itself. This spoof video, which was really just part of the back story of the show, took on its own life in the real world and, for example, appeared on the Wii game Just Dance 3 as an authentic music video. Nearly 10 years on, the joke has endured, with the video having gathered over 3 million views on YouTube and Robin Sparkles MySpace and Facebook pages still going strong.[25]

CBS tied together the Canada theme and the Barney character with another spoof website, canadiansexacts.org, when we learned in the show that Barney had bookmarked this site as the source of all his knowledge of the subject. After nervously entering our age verification details in a 'not safe for work' office environment and clicking on a list of 'Canadian sex acts' including, intriguingly, Sneaky Snowplow, Newfoundland Lobster Trap and Saskatoon Totem Pole, we discovered a series of images of Canadian actor Alan Thicke with increasingly apologetic excuses for the site being 'temporarily unavailable'.[26] When we asked Beth Haiken, vice president of communications at CBS, to help us understand the distinctions between content created by the show's producers and by the CBS marketing team, she made it clear just how intertwined those processes had become at CBS:

It's all marketing and it all comes from the story.[27]

– SENDING 'LOVE LETTERS' TO THE AUDIENCE –

Andrea Phillips is one of the true pioneers of transmedia storytelling: both a writer and a game designer specializing in creating interactive stories that span multiple platforms. She worked as a copywriter on 'The Maester's Path' campaign that launched Game of Thrones in the United States and wrote A Creator's Guide to Transmedia Storytelling, a practical guide for creative people across the publishing, TV, games and movie industries. Interviewed by the Wharton School, Phillips described how an early transmedia marketing campaign for the movie A.I. made her feel:

We loved it so deeply and so passionately – because it didn't feel like we were being marketed to. I talk a lot about love letters to the audience. It felt like a love letter to us. It was rewarding us with content just for showing up.[28]

One of the most powerful ways that marketers are enriching storyworlds is by creating rewarding content for fans to enjoy in a way that doesn't really feel like marketing, at both ends of the budget scale. When our team was given the task of launching the 50th anniversary episode of the BBC family sci-fi drama *Doctor Who*, we realized that the core fans already had a deep appreciation of the storyworld. Over its 50-year lifespan, a total of 11 actors had played the lead character of Doctor Who (in the unlikely event that you don't know the show, we refer you back to Chapter 7), and we knew that fans had an amazing capacity to recall detailed storylines and iconic images throughout the seasons. So we created a trailer for the anniversary episode ('The Day of the Doctor') that brought back all the different Doctor characters throughout its history – and filled it with visual references to key plot points.

With the magic of CGI and the mastery of a special effects team Matt Losasso, the director, brought a number of deceased Doctors to life, including the very first Timelord from 1963, William Hartnell, making his high-definition colour debut. Only black-and-white stills of Hartnell remained, so the team painstakingly layered in skin tones until we felt we had captured a lifelike Hartnell for the first time in living colour.

As the camera flies through scenes recognizable from past series (Dalek saucers invading London from 1964, the Himalayas from 1967, the Golden Gate Bridge from 1996), fans could spot over 100 'Easter eggs': objects and props on shelves (a Roboform helmet, a Yeti sculpture, the Masque of Mandragora), on the ground (Bessie – the third Doctor's yellow vintage car, the giant arachnid Empress of the Racnoss) or simply floating in space (a spade-shaped TARDIS key, a Gallifreyan fob watch and, of course, a sonic screwdriver). One clue spotted and never unlocked was etched into the mountain face that Matt Smith's Doctor stood atop. Written in Gallifreyan symbols it read... well, let's leave it for you to work out, shall we? (See: **https://www.youtube.com/watch?v=loGm3vT8EAQ**)[29]

For any marketing campaign seeking to build on a storyworld, it is of course vital to understand even the smallest nuance of every creative decision made. Clearly there was a huge amount of discussion with showrunner Steven Moffat but, in the end, we were largely entrusted to make the right creative decisions about who to include. This was most telling in the scene where we transition from past companion Sarah Jane Smith examining a snowglobe containing Patrick Troughton to the current companion Clara. The trailer aired not long after the death of actress Elisabeth Sladen, who had played Sarah Jane, and the acknowledgement of her central role in the show's mythology was viewed as a hugely touching moment.

Central to hiding Easter eggs was the involvement of *Doctor Who* archivist and prop expert Andrew Beech, who brought a huge number of items from his personal collection, including an electrician's tool box that opened up to reveal a treasure trove of sonic screwdrivers from each of the 11 Doctors.

A trailer full of rewarding details for the 50th anniversary of Doctor Who
Source: Reproduced by permission of BBC

The whole set became a playground for the largely 'Whovian' crew, although the mysterious and seemingly slow and unaided movement down from the rafters of a Weeping Angel throughout the two-day shoot was a terrifying coda. Even the score wove in key passages and nods to past themes.

No one understands *Doctor Who* fans better than the writer and producer Steven Moffat, and his reaction to the trailer gave us confidence that we had cracked it:

Actually that is AWESOME. That will set people on ACTUAL FIRE.[30]

The trailer was launched immediately after *Strictly Come Dancing* on BBC One and released simultaneously on YouTube. Within 24 hours it became the most viewed video on YouTube globally and quickly exceeded 1 million views. As we had hoped, *Doctor Who* fans immediately started blogging and sharing tiny details from the trailer. Even national newspapers got involved in trying to decode every single reference. This was unashamedly a promotional campaign on a big scale for a blockbuster event, but at the same time we were keen to cram it full of content to reward the superfans.

The test of a really rich storyworld is when people don't just want to star in your trailers (like our Spanish *Game of Thrones* fans), they actually want to make their own. In the vacuum that awaited the *Doctor Who* launch trailer, fans had ingeniously created their own versions of a 50th anniversary trailer using archive footage. Now they had our 'love letters' to play with themselves, and perhaps the greatest tribute to the success of the campaign was the number of remakes that it spawned – a Minecraft version, a Lego version, even one starring a young seven-year-old version of Matt Smith with a bedroom full of toys.

The creation of 'love letters' does not have to lead automatically to video content. Marketers are also finding ways to reward fans with bitesize, 'snackable' content that they can enjoy online or on mobile devices. HBO's US marketing team really understands the importance of keeping fans engaged with rewarding content that doesn't feel like marketing, and they have done this particularly well with *Game of Thrones*. In the words of Sabrina Caluori:

> The overall digital strategic framework for season three centred around the concept of bringing our fans into the world of *Game of Thrones* – getting them to 'Join the Realm'.[31]

One of the most successful elements of the 'Join the Realm' campaign was a global mobile app, built in HTML5, with full social media integration. This

HBO's global mobile app, Join the Realm, to promote season three of Game of Thrones   Source: *Photograph courtesy HBO®. HBO® is a service mark of Home Box Office, Inc*

simple app enabled viewers to create their own family arms – called 'sigils' (medieval symbols believed to have magic powers) – with over 100 icons for personalization and translation into 24 languages. Example sigils encouraged people to have fun with the app (House Simpson, house words 'D'oh!', or House Oreo, house words 'Been there, dunked that'). Within a few weeks the Join the Realm app attracted over 1.2 million visits, with fans creating over 750,000 personalized sigils and sharing them on social media.[32]

In the run-up to the *Game of Thrones* season four premiere HBO created a simple paid post with BuzzFeed, inviting fans to find out how they would die in *Game of Thrones* ('What, you think you'd actually survive in the world of Westeros?'). A set of multiple-choice questions (for example, pick your spirit animal, specify your weapon of choice and choose which character you would rather sleep with) led to your most likely cause of death (for example, by dragon fire, by falling through the Moon Door or by decapitation – killed by a backwards system of justice, which turned out to be our collective fate). Within days this became BuzzFeed's most successful paid post – ever – and a good example of the kind of rewarding content that Andrea Phillips would classify as 'love letters to the audience'.

– KEEPING THE STORYWORLD ALIVE –

In an interview, Phillips underlined the importance of continuing to build the mythology of a storyworld even during the gaps between episodes and seasons:

> We're reaching an era where just having a TV show isn't going to be enough to keep someone's attention. We're entering a period where if I let you forget about my show for seven days until I air again, that gives you seven days to find something else to care about more.[33]

Michael Engleman emphasizes this in relation to the learning gained by the Syfy team from the *Defiance* experience:

> Today's non-linear world is one of a ton of instantly available, high-quality choice... From the moment you release new IP, from then on, every day is premiere day for someone new... It means adjusting how we think and behave. In addition to creating great stories, we need to create easy access – easy access to our messaging through data-informed targeting, easy access to our content through extra-linear access, and more ways to learn and go deeper into the story through smart, shareable transmedia and social content. *Defiance*...in many ways, helped us write the road maps we use today for launching content of all kinds – it taught us the significance of being always on and always authentic.[34]

There is no such thing as 'going dark' any more. It is vital to keep fans continually engaged. A great example is *#lovemilla*, a multiplatform drama for tweens and teens from Yle, Finland's national public broadcaster. #*lovemilla* tells the story of 17-year-old Milla, who works at Café Robot in a small Finnish town. It started as a pilot project, appearing first on Yle's video-on-demand service, Areena. The pilot set out to discuss the problems of teenage life in the audience's own language and attract younger viewers via an experiment in transmedia storytelling. Yle wanted to create content that could be watched in non-chronological order on various devices, so each episode was only five minutes long and self-contained.

The key to #*lovemilla*'s success was the way the viewers' relationship with Milla was built up by the marketing team on Facebook and Instagram, even during the gaps between the episodes. The five-minute instalments were only part of the storyworld and a significant amount of the audience's engagement was generated by the additional marketing content on social platforms. Central to this was Milla's picture and illustration blog on Instagram: a window into the character's world. The Yle team found this a very powerful way to carry the themes of the video episodes further and encourage the young audience to interact. In the words of Yle producer Riikka Takila:

> We were painfully aware of the fact that since the young audiences won't come to us, we'd have to go to them. We had to take our content to the platform they already use on a daily basis.[35]

Importantly, Milla's storyworld was developed daily even during the hiatus between seasons, for example by challenging fans via Instagram to submit daily photos or illustrations on set themes. This generated a lot of images and fan art, the best of which were awarded personalized illustrations and prizes as if coming from Milla herself.

To keep the *Game of Thrones* storyworld alive between seasons three and four, the HBO team launched what they claimed to be the first-ever 'internet roast': a campaign, not linked with any plot points in the show, focused on a character that digital agency 360i had discovered to be the most reviled on social media. With the help of the Sysomos Map Social Listening Tool, they calculated that over a period of nearly a year there were 30,000 mentions of the creepy young king Joffrey Baratheon connected with the word 'hate', which was much higher than any other TV character, even Walter White from *Breaking Bad*. To build on this, HBO created a YouTube intro video and tweeted a snarling image of the loathsome Joffrey, with the line 'Payback's a wench' accompanied by the hashtag #RoastJoffrey. Content seeded on social media included short videos featuring *Game of Thrones* actors who were particularly active on social media, including Maisie Williams and Kristian Nairn. This between-seasons digital campaign created a lot of buzz amongst fans, and many celebrities and well-known brands got in on the act on Twitter, from Charmin ('There are some people so crappy even we won't go near them. #RoastJoffrey') to the recruitment site Monster ('Being king might not be your calling. We'd be happy to help you find a better job. #RoastJoffrey'), from Oreo ('Send the king to bed without his cookies. #RoastJoffrey') to NBC's rival show *Hannibal* (#RoastJoffrey? Sounds delicious').[36]

Announcing the Game of Thrones *internet roast*
Source: *Photograph courtesy HBO®. HBO® is a service mark of Home Box Office, Inc*

HBO's 'always on' approach to the *Game of Thrones* storyworld was summed up by Sabrina Caluori: 'As much as possible we try to beat the drum for *Game of Thrones* all year round.'[37]

– TAKING THE STORY INTO THE REAL WORLD –

One of the shows that has been most successful in translating its mythology into live experiences is AMC's zombie drama *The Walking Dead*. It has become a celebrated case study of transmedia storytelling, partly due to the rich variety of events and experiences that the production team and marketers have created for fans. For example, there was already a tradition of Zombie Walks predating the launch of the drama: organized groups or flash mobs of people dressed as zombies and roaming erratically around cities or conventions. Early zombie gatherings were reported in Milwaukee in 2000 and Sacramento in 2001. *The Walking Dead* has built on these foundations by setting up 'official' Zombie Walks, frequently promoted on social media (providing copious opportunities for posting cast images, trailers and other promotional material) and linked to charitable activities such as food drives. The annual Comic-Con fan convention now stages 'The Walking Dead Escape', which is a real-life obstacle course that simulates the setting of the TV show, complete with marauding zombies (more commonly referred to as 'Walkers') and other hazards. There's even a Zombie Academy to train the best amateurs and get them match-fit to audition to appear as a Walker in the forthcoming TV series.

An important role in AMC's support of the final season of *Mad Men* was played by experiential marketing initiatives. As mentioned in Chapter 7, a major exhibition was staged at the Museum of the Moving Image in New York as well as the Smithsonian National Museum of American History in Washington DC, as if giving the show an official stamp of approval for its part in contemporary US culture. A 'Draper bench' was also installed outside the Time & Life Building in midtown Manhattan: the fictional home of ad agency Sterling Cooper Draper Pryce. The black bench featured the iconic silhouette of the legendary adman Don Draper, made famous in the show's opening titles (see image on page 138). AMC's EVP of marketing, Linda Schupack, explains the effect of this real-world presence:

> It felt like from the middle of March through the middle of May you couldn't open the *New York Times* without seeing some sort of reference to *Mad Men*, either in passing or a feature on *Mad Men*. Pop cultural currency and being talked about, being written about, having a presence in the pop cultural landscape – that is important to us.[38]

If this experiential marketing for *Mad Men* was created to celebrate the finale of a long-running and successful show, Channel 4 in the UK proved that viewers can also be drawn towards a brand new programme by taking the story into the real world. Their launch campaign[39] for the drama *Humans*, which explores the theme of artificial intelligence, involved an initial phase with no Channel 4 branding, as head of marketing, James Walker, explains:

> If the premise of the show is that you're almost in a near-term present where you can buy synthetic humans, why don't we actually launch our campaign as a campaign for the company that makes synthetic humans? The brand in the show is Persona Synthetics, so we launched an ad campaign for Persona Synthetics, not for the drama *Humans*... we put it out on Gogglebox and other shows on Friday night and people were going 'Is this real?'[40]

To add to a sense of authenticity the end frame of the ad stated 'Regent Street Store Opening Soon'. The Channel 4 team had found an empty shopfront in London's prime shopping district and turned it into Persona Synthetics' flagship 'store' via a high-tech cover wrap equipped with Microsoft Kinect technology. Its motion-sensing devices enabled passers-by to interact with the 'synthetic humans'.

The Persona Synthetics 'flagship store' promoting Channel 4's Humans
Source: © Channel 4 Television

The brand was also promoted in print ads and then two 'synths' were listed for sale on eBay: the first time a fictional brand has been allowed to sell items on the site.

It was only after this Persona Synthetics campaign had generated millions of impressions on Twitter and Facebook, with the brand trending number one on both Twitter and Google, that Channel 4 launched a more conventional promotional campaign and branded website for the show *Humans*. It became Channel 4's biggest original drama hit in over 20 years.[41]

– SO WHERE NEXT? –

We have looked at the increasingly inventive ways in which content creators and TV marketers are building storyworlds and the extent to which the distinctions between content and marketing are blurring. Can we predict the next stage of evolution (apart from the fact that synthetic humans are unlikely to be on sale in Regent Street any time soon)? Well, maybe we can't, but two global storytelling giants, Steven Spielberg and George Lucas, looked into their crystal balls when speaking on a panel at the USC School of Cinematic Arts in June 2013. For Spielberg it was about total immersion of the viewer in the story itself:

> We're never going to be totally immersive as long as we're looking at a square, whether it's a movie screen or whether it's a computer screen. We've got to get rid of that and we've got to put the player inside the experience, where no matter where you look you're surrounded by a three-dimensional experience. That's the future.[42]

Lucas went even further and talked about the kind of brain implants that are already being used to control artificial limbs:

> The next step is to be able to control your dreams. You'll just tap into a different part of your brain. You're just going to put a hat on or plug into the computer and create your own world... We'll be able to do the dream thing 10, 15 years from now. It's not some pie-in-the-sky thing.[43]

So maybe that's the next step for all of us working in the world of TV marketing. We all need to become experts in deploying motion sensor devices and brain implants to create a new breed of experience that takes our storyworlds into a state of hyperreality.

NEXT
★ The water cooler on steroids.

★ A murder mystery for 'Psych-Os'.

★ *Top Chef*'s Instagram quickfire challenge.

★ Joe Carroll's anonymous stalker.

★ The social TARDIS.

★ 'WTF is truTV?'

LATER
★ Driving credit back.

★ Far, far away from your parents.

★ 'TV Is Good'.

NOTES

1 *The Office*, 'The Interview' (2002) season two, episode six, BBC, 4 November

2 Mellor, L (2012) [accessed 28 September 2015] Explaining The Ending Of Sherlock Season 2 , *Den Of Geek*, 17 January [Online] http://www.denofgeek.com/tv/sherlock/21050/explaining-the-ending-of-sherlock-series-2#ixzz3OglbZbD2

3 Evans, E (2011) *Transmedia Television: Audiences, new media and daily life*, Routledge, Abingdon

4 Jenkins, H (2003) [accessed 11 December 2015] Transmedia Storytelling, *MIT Technology Review* [Online] http://www.technologyreview.com/news/401760/transmedia-storytelling/

5   Jenkins, H (2008) *Convergence Culture: Where old and new media collide*, 2nd edn, NYU Press, New York
6   Ramos-Serrano, M and Lozano, Delmar, J (nd) [accessed 28 September 2015] Promoting Lost: New Strategies And Tools Of Commercial Communication, *Nuevas Estrategias Publicitarias* [Online] http://www.academia.edu/1148126/Promoting_LOST._New_Strategies_and_Tools_of_Commercial_Communication_Promocionando_Perdidos_._Nuevas_estrategias_publicitarias_
7   Smith, A (2009) [accessed 28 September 2015] Expanding The Lost Universe Part 2 [Online] http://sites.middlebury.edu/mediacp/2009/07/05/expanding-the-lost-universe-part-2/
8   Trans Media Lab (nd) [accessed 28 September 2015] The Walking Dead: A Tentacular Transmedia Success [Blog] [Online] http://www.transmedialab.org/en/the-blog-en/case-study-en/the-walking-dead-a-tentacular-transmedia-success/2
9   Stanley, T (20016) [accessed 28 September 2015] Product-Placement-Free 'Lost' TV Show Gets Viral Integration Partners, *Advertising Age*, 24 May [Online] http://adage.com/article/madisonvine-news/product-placement-free-lost-tv-show-viral-integration-partners/109427/
10 Zeiser, A (2015) *Transmedia Marketing: From film and TV to games and digital media*, Focal Press, Burlington
11 Transmedialab (2012) [accessed 29 September 2015] Game of Thrones – Transmedia Experience Around 5 Senses – Case Study [Online] http://www.dailymotion.com/video/xqqwhs_game-of-thrones-transmedia-experiences-around-5-senses-case-study_creation
12 Syfy (2013) Defiance Multi-Platform Awards Case Study Video. Provided by Syfy
13 Syfy (2013) Defiance Multi-Platform Awards Case Study Video. Provided by Syfy
14 Hollinger, A (2012) [accessed 28 September 2015] SYFY Imagines Greater... Cars, Yachts And Buildings, Oh My... *Hollywood Today*, 7 October [Online] http://www.hollywoodtoday.net/2012/07/10/syfy-assaults-comic-con-2012-with-defiance/
15 Michael Engleman, former executive vice president of marketing, digital and global brand strategy, Syfy and Chiller, interview 12 October 2015
16 Michael Engleman, former executive vice president of marketing, digital and global brand strategy, Syfy and Chiller, interview 12 October 2015
17 TED Blog video (2013) [accessed 29 September 2015] David Peterson On Developing Dothraki [Online] https://www.youtube.com/watch?v=rl3Wc5yhIuI
18 Canal+ (2014) [accessed 5 November 2015] Light At The End Of The Tunnel [Online] http://www.esvdigital.co.uk/case-study/canal/
19 Red Bee (2014) [accessed 29 September 2015] Sherlock Lives Campaign [Online] http://www.redbeecreative.tv/work/bbc-one-sherlock-lives?service=entertainment-marketing
20 Sabrina Caluori, senior vice president, digital media and marketing, HBO, interview, 1 March 2014
21 Movistar+ (2014) [accessed 29 September 2015] Juego De Tronos TV: Invocación [Online] https://www.youtube.com/watch?v=ajyK8B2MToE

22 Mittell, J (2014) *Strategies of Storytelling on Transmedia Television*, University of Nebraska Press, Lincoln NE

23 Mittell, J (2014) *Strategies of Storytelling on Transmedia Television*, University of Nebraska Press, Lincoln NE

24 GNB (2015) [accessed 29 September 2015] Not A Father's Day [Online] http://www.notafathersday.com/

25 Imawesomeandbea (2011) [accessed 29 September 2015] Robin Sparkles – Let's Go To The Mall [Online] https://www.youtube.com/watch?v=9mJAsgIIfN M&list=PL625072DDF8DB9A87

26 Canadian Sex Acts (nd) [accessed 29 September 2015] www.canadiansexacts.org

27 Beth Haiken, vice president, CBS Entertainment Communications, interview 25 February 2014

28 Phillips, A (2012) [accessed 29 September 2015] Transmedia Storytelling, Fan Culture And The Future Of Marketing, Knowledge @ Wharton, 3 July [Online] http://knowledge.wharton.upenn.edu/article/transmedia-storytelling-fan-culture-and-the-future-of-marketing/

29 BBC (2013) [accessed 29 September 2015] 'Doctor Who: 50 Years' Trailer – The Day Of The Doctor – Doctor Who 50th Anniversary – BBC One [Online] https://www.youtube.com/watch?v=loGm3vT8EAQ; see also http://www.redbeecreative.tv/work/bbc-one-doctor-who-50th-anniversary?service=entertainment-marketing

30 Moffat, S (2013) E-mail from Steven Moffat to executive producer Brian Minchin, 1 October

31 Sabrina Caluori, senior vice president, digital media and marketing, HBO, interview 1 March 2014

32 Join the Realm Campaign [accessed 5 November 2015] [Online] http://industry.shortyawards.com/nominee/6th_annual/Mb/join-the-realm-campaign?category=viral_campaign

33 Phillips, A (2012) [accessed 29 September 2015] Transmedia Storytelling, Fan Culture And The Future Of Marketing, Knowledge @ Wharton, 3 July [Online] http://knowledge.wharton.upenn.edu/article/transmedia-storytelling-fan-culture-and-the-future-of-marketing/

34 Michael Engleman, former executive vice president of marketing, digital and global brand strategy, Syfy and Chiller, interview 12 October 2015

35 Riikka Takila, producer, Yle, interview 28 February 2014

36 Diaz, A (2013) [accessed 29 September 2015] UPDATE: HBO Invites You To Burn 'Game Of Thrones' Creepy King Joffrey In Internet Roast, *Advertising Age*, 12 December [Online] http://adage.com/article/news/hbo-launches-internet-roast-game-thrones/245650/

37 Sabrina Caluori, senior vice president, digital media and marketing, HBO, interview 1 March 2014

38 Linda Schupack, executive vice president of marketing, AMC, interview 11 June 2015

39 Persona Synthetics (2015) [accessed 29 September 2015] Personal Synthetics TV Commercial: The New Generation [Online] https://www.youtube.com/watch?v=vc7k-DwrITI

40 James Walker, head of marketing, Channel 4 Television, interview 25 June 2015

41 Plunkett, J (2015) [accessed 5 November 2015] Humans Becomes Channel 4's Biggest Drama Hit In 20 Years, *The Guardian*, 22 June [Online] http://www.theguardian.com/media/2015/jun/22/humans-becomes-channel-4s-biggest-drama-hit-in-20-years

42 Cohen, D (2013) [accessed 29 September 2015] George Lucas And Steven Spielberg: Studios Will Implode, VOD Is The Future, *Variety*, 12 June [Online] http://variety.com/2013/digital/news/lucas-spielberg-on-future-of-entertainment-1200496241/

43 Cohen, D (2013) [accessed 29 September 2015] George Lucas And Steven Spielberg: Studios Will Implode, VOD Is The Future, *Variety*, 12 June [Online] http://variety.com/2013/digital/news/lucas-spielberg-on-future-of-entertainment-1200496241/

CHAPTER FIFTEEN

SOCIAL MEDIA
From viewers to fans to friends

Moss: 'My mum's on Friendface! My mum! I've opened up another
line of communication with her!'
Roy: 'Isn't that a good thing?'
Moss: 'She's listed her 'current mood' as 'sensual'!'
Roy: 'Why didn't you just not accept her friend request?'
Moss: 'What are you, an animal?'

THE IT CROWD[1]

– TWO ESSENTIAL TRUTHS –

At the risk of stating the obvious again, the TV industry is in a state of constant flux. There is no bigger disruptive force than the internet and no bigger influence on TV marketing than the dynamic growth of social media. Even for the so-called digital natives (as a generalization, let's say all those born after 1990), it is not easy to keep up with the almost daily evolution of the major social platforms. Several of our interviewees mentioned the growing influence amongst millennials of platforms such as WhatsApp, Snapchat and an application that was only released in late 2014, Dubsmash.

So, for these reasons, we are not going to attempt a detailed up-to-the-minute analysis of each of the current social platforms – their strengths and weaknesses, their audience reach and demographics and the best ways that TV marketers can use them. We refer you instead to specialist resources such as the largest industry site dedicated to social TV coverage and analysis, *Adweek*'s Lost Remote (see: **http://www.adweek.com/lostremote/**). However, it is worth saying that a general trend is the extent to which social media activity is becoming driven by video, which is an obvious benefit for TV marketers.

Having established that, in this chapter we focus on the underlying themes that we believe will continue to be important for TV marketers using social media, however the available platforms evolve further. It is helpful to approach the whole subject with two very simple and related points in mind:

1 TV has always been social.

2 Social media is, at heart, a form of good old-fashioned word of mouth.

– THE WATER COOLER ON STEROIDS –

We're not sure who was the first to point out that television has always been social. It may have been Mike Proulx and Stacey Shepatin in the opening words of their excellent book *Social TV* (more recommended reading).[2] As we emphasized in Chapter 1, the great advantage that TV marketers have over those in most other sectors is that people find the content inherently interesting, and over many decades it is no exaggeration to say that the big TV moments have had the capacity to unite whole nations in speculation and conversation. From the infamous episode of *Dallas* in 1980 that led to months of global speculation about 'Who shot J R?' to the more recent UK debate about who killed Danny Latimer in *Broadchurch* and even the 'bingate' saga of the melted baked Alaska in *The Great British Bake Off*, people simply love to talk about television. This is a boon for TV marketers. As Linda Schupack, EVP of marketing for AMC Networks, says:

> When we are at our best our shows are talkworthy... There is no better marketing tool... than a show that people want to talk about... A big piece of our responsibility as marketers is to marshal this conversation, to fuel the conversation, to give people elements that continue to further the conversation, which is what we're doing both digitally and on our social platforms.[3]

Given that millions of these conversations about TV are happening anyway, with or without the intervention of marketers, the opportunity is there to build on them and, as Linda says, fuel them. Walter Levitt, CMO of Comedy Central, puts it like this:

> For years as television marketers we talked about people talking about stuff at the water cooler. Social media is really the water cooler on steroids and the beautiful part is that we can be part of the water cooler conversation and we can feed the conversation.[4]

In Chapter 14 we looked at a number of examples of content created to do just that, from our hearse with its floral hashtag #sherlocklives to the *Game of Thrones* internet roast, from Milla's Instagram challenges to the 'Easter eggs' in our Day of the Doctor trailer. In this chapter we cover many more.

– WORD OF MOUTH AMPLIFIED –

For several years marketers in all sectors, not just television, have become familiar with the phrase 'paid, owned and earned media'. In particular, the potential impact of earned media (shares, reviews, mentions) has increased dramatically. However, we prefer Proulx and Shepatin's view. For them, 'paid, owned and earned' is not the way that consumers experience media. Rather, 'media impressions are either choice or nonchoice-based'.[5] Choice-based impressions, whether we decide to view a video, click on a paid ad on Google or enter a hashtag on Twitter, for example, result from content that we choose to engage with or even seek out. A subset of this, they say, is social impressions, which if they come from someone we trust, influence us the most.

It is in this way that social media content can have a word-of-mouth effect. This is how the marketing team at FX Networks approaches it, as their leader Stephanie Gibbons explains:

> We like to look at social media in a technical world as a basic thing –
> it's human beings talking. Regardless of what media we have, the most
> powerful form of marketing still and possibly always will be like being a
> child and going to a playground and having a friend tell you what they
> did last night, what they listened to and what they watched... For us social
> media is simply word of mouth amplified.[6]

If a person whose opinion you value tells you that a new TV show is worth watching, the chances are you will give it a go. Liz Dolan, CMO of Fox International Channels, sums this up perfectly:

> You don't need an algorithm when you have friends.[7]

– IT'S ALL ABOUT THE FANS –

The best and most obvious place to start in creating content that will generate choice-based impressions, for an existing show at least, is the show's core fans. AMC understood this when putting together their multilayered activity to promote the final season ('7B') of *Mad Men*. To celebrate the love affair that fans had built up with the Madison Avenue advertising drama, AMC created *Mad Men*: The Fan Cut, an online project in which the original pilot episode was cut up into sequences from 8 to 38 seconds and then offered to fans to 'claim' them, shoot their own home-made versions and upload them to YouTube. The result was a lovingly crafted cut of the first episode, created by – and, in many cases, starring – *Mad Men* fans. The episode, 'Smoke Gets in Your Eyes', was stitched together scene by scene, in 'a quilt of fan experience'.[8] (You may find the full-length version geo-blocked in your region but enter *Mad Men* Fan Cut in the YouTube search bar and you will find many fans' interpretations of individual scenes.)[9]

A second initiative, *Mad Men* Carousel, was a Facebook app that recalled Don Draper's iconic pitch to Kodak in the first season ('This device isn't a spaceship. It's a time machine. It goes backwards, forwards. It takes us to a place where we ache to go again. It's not called the Wheel. It's called a Carousel.')[10] The app allowed fans to upload their own pictures from their Facebook profile into the carousel and share the results with their network. AMC's Linda Schupack summarizes the roles played by this social media activation in the overall launch campaign for the final season:

> One of the things we say at AMC is that our mandate is to turn viewers into fans and fans into evangelists. Evangelizing is a big piece of what social media is about because it is about conversation and it is about sharing and it is about expressing affection and affinity for a property in a somewhat tangible way. The Fan Cut allows people to personalize their relationship with *Mad Men* and to enter the world of *Mad Men* by re-creating scenes, while the Carousel allows the world of *Mad Men* to enter into a fan's world by pulling pictures from their Facebook page and the worlds are blurred that way. They did slightly different things, but ultimately it was a blurring of the world of *Mad Men* and the fans' own personal world.[11]

One of the most celebrated social TV case studies is USA Network's Emmy-nominated #HashTagKiller project for the detective comedy-drama series *Psych*. This was a social game centred on a murder-mystery storyline created specifically for the game. Fans were invited to solve the case and, over a seven-week period, could immerse themselves in online messages, picture clues and video content shot with the cast in an authentic *Psych* style, generating 455,000 Facebook shares in the process.[12] Although a few years old, it is an enduring example of understanding and engaging with a show's core fan base. In fact, *Psych* was one of the first truly social TV shows: loved by a young adult audience that was becoming increasingly familiar with social platforms and tools, as USA Network's Alexandra Shapiro described to us:

> Our fans were as important as the characters on the show... They identified themselves as 'Psych-Os'... We really made the fans part of the creative process, by identifying a tagline, choosing key art, or creating transmedia experiences where they became characters in the narrative themselves.[13]

Another social TV landmark was the work done by TNT in the United States, and its agency R/GA, to engage fans during the run-up to the season three premiere of *Falling Skies*, a post-apocalyptic sci-fi drama centred on a battle between humans and aliens. During the reruns of the first two seasons, and then into the season three premiere, TNT launched on Twitter what they called the 'Battle for the Handle', in which they invited fans to declare their allegiance to the forces of either the alien invaders (using #aliens) or the humans (using #resistance). TNT went to the trouble of creating personalized recruitment images for the most engaged fans on Twitter: their profile pictures were transformed into graphic novel-style illustrations, some of which were included in a video that ran at the end of the new season premiere to declare the winners of the 'battle' (in case you're wondering, it was the humans).[14] *Falling Skies* is another brilliant example of using a social platform cleverly to create an experience for fans that deepened their engagement with the story.

One of the US networks best known for social media integration with its programming is Bravo, home of reality and competition shows such as *The Real Housewives* franchise and *Top Chef*. Ellen Stone, Bravo's EVP of marketing, says that a recent realization had a major influence on the way her team thinks about social media:

> Bravo has an incredibly engaged fan base. They are Bravo crazies and love everything about the brand. They want more and more and more, so... as we were developing the strategy to work with this fan base we realized that they're not just fans, they're really friends of the brand, and that's a huge distinction with how we market to them socially, when you talk to a fan versus when you're talking to your own friend.[15]

A simple post about making pancakes by Teresa Giudice, one of *The Real Housewives of New Jersey*, which went unexpectedly viral, confirmed for Ellen and her team that social media is not just a tool to be used for the big events like the launch of a new season. A friend 'wants to know everything, the big stuff, the little stuff and the in-between stuff' and this changed the way that Bravo looked at their social strategy.[16]

We know from our own experiences promoting shows like *Doctor Who* and *Sherlock* that if you demonstrate a real understanding of the most passionate fans and treat them as friends (sending them 'love letters', as we put it in Chapter 14), then highly successful campaigns can flow out to less obsessive viewers.

– A GAS IN YOUR SYSTEM –

Having stressed the importance of understanding a show's core fandom, it is just as important to recognize the extent to which a specific show, or programme genre, lends itself to social media engagement. Individual shows, even within the same genre, can vary enormously in this respect. Contrasting *American Horror Story*, a drama that is 'super social', with some other FX dramas, Stephanie Gibbons explains this eloquently:

In *American Horror Story*, in any given episode there are things that are titillating, shocking and provocative. Those are the things that people want to discuss because it's like a gas that expands in your system, it has to be released. There are other shows that are very internal... they're like smoke on your jacket that hangs with you well into the next day and beyond, that can't be screamed from the hilltops because what you have experienced has touched something personal within you. It's most likely something that you don't want to talk about, it's something that you want to savour and hold on to.[17]

Timing was tight ahead of the original launch of *American Horror Story* so social media content, aimed at existing online communities of horror fans, played a big role in the overall campaign. One of the signature features of the show is its title sequences and brief teaser trailers with fleeting glimpses of weirdness, hinting at horrific plot points.[18] FX have made a habit of releasing the opening titles a few days ahead of each season premiere, creating a lot of pre-launch social media buzz, and the *American Horror Story* Facebook fan page has become a rich source of exclusive content and behind-the-scenes clips.

Real-life stunts have also played a part. During the launch phase fans could sign up for a scary 'house call' from a character from the show. Then for season two fans could win a night of frights in a creepy old (authentic) asylum. Additional video content was shot from these real-life fan experiences and released online for other fans to enjoy. Currently in its fifth season, social media has made a big contribution to building and reinforcing the *American Horror Story* storyworld, but an identikit approach would not have been so successful for some other FX shows.

– BEFORE, DURING AND AFTER –

Depending on the genre of programme, it is not just about gauging the right level of activity, but also when to time it in line with the different stages of viewing. A significant percentage of TV watching amongst most viewers does not lend itself particularly well to social media engagement during the real-time broadcast. With dramas, for example, viewers tend to be engrossed in the plot and not inclined to divert their attention during the show itself. However, dramas that generate the most social media activity create a strong desire to share opinions, discuss storylines, read recaps and engage in extra content after watching the show and during the run-up to the next episode. The types of shows that naturally generate a lot of social media buzz during the live broadcast itself are those that involve the collective viewing of shared experiences, notably big sporting events, political debates, talent shows and live entertainment spectacles such as the Oscars. At times like this there is not only a lot to talk about but also plenty of pauses, timeouts and breaks during which to turn one's attention away from the main screen to a smartphone or iPad. As we saw with BBC One in Chapter 4, viewers still love shared viewing experiences and social media can help people to feel connected. Genres like reality dramas and factual programmes can also provide plenty of real-time social media opportunities, and with shows like these innovative marketing can encourage viewers to participate.

Proulx and Shepatin describe the core of social TV as the 'backchannel' – 'the millions of public conversations happening online while television programming airs'. The platform that currently works best in this respect is Twitter, which they compare to an electrocardiogram measuring 'television's heartbeat': raw, real-time social chat during the linear broadcast of a show that helps viewers feel part of a communal TV moment.[19] By demonstrating sensitivity to the audience's enjoyment of the show, TV marketers can create content that not only adds to this 'TV ECG' but also builds on it. Two examples from our own team illustrate this.

To enhance the social media buzz around the launch of season three of BBC Two's feel-good factual show *The Choir* (in which the charismatic Gareth Malone teaches groups of amateurs to sing and perform in harmony), we gathered a group of BBC singers in a studio to create short videos, using Vine, which became personalized 'singing tweets' sent to people who were commenting on the first episode during its live broadcast. When one viewer, for example, lamented that 'when I sing I sound like a crazed soprano chipmunk' our singers responded immediately on Twitter, to the familiar tune of Mozart's 'Eine Kleine Nachtmusik': 'Amanda, we love crazed soprano chipmunks.' Similar musical tweets were sent to other viewers,

Members of the BBC Singers sending 'singing tweets' to promote BBC Two's The Choir Source: Reproduced by permission of BBC

including an appreciative Ian Hyland (the *Daily Mirror* TV critic), and celebrities we knew were fans of the show (sample: 'Hey Gary Barlow, get yourself a brew, *The Choir* is starting very soon on BBC Two').[20]

With our social media campaign for BBC One's natural history epic *Africa* we tapped into the backchannel to help steer our on-air promotional support. The primary goal was to reach a younger, broader audience than would be expected for a nature documentary series. During the live broadcasts a team connected by Skype scouted for trending conversation themes and further fuelled the buzz, particularly by interacting with spontaneous comments from celebrities such as Radio 1 DJs Fearne Cotton and Sarah Cox. By tracking the most talked-about moments from each episode we were then able to create clip-based trailers for the following week acknowledging the fact that we were in tune with *Africa* viewers. Introduced simply by Sir David Attenborough saying: 'These were the moments you loved,' the trailers captured the scenes most popular on Twitter (a group of meerkats, a baby gorilla, a somewhat surreal giraffe fight...) and invited viewers to join Sir David the following week to discover more. Similar trailers directed people to the BBC's catch-up service, BBC iPlayer, where they could watch episodes they may have missed. Although our team had developed a detailed content calendar in advance, including behind-the-scenes footage and out-takes, they were highly responsive to the backchannel and adapted the plan as the series progressed. For example, noticing the craze for simple GIFs (ideal content for Twitter in particular) we created a set of them from the most popular moments (a sinister head turn from a shoebill, a dung beetle rolling down a sand dune...) and posted them on social media streams at the same time they appeared on TV, further encouraging sharing.[21]

Africa became the most socially discussed natural history series on record. Along with our work for *The Choir*, it demonstrates that a programme does not have to be a major sporting event or entertainment show finale to foster a high level of real-time social media interaction. Some industry commentators are even saying that the social backchannel is balancing the trend towards recorded, catch-up and on-demand viewing by encouraging people to tune in live. However, social media activity also has an increasingly important role to play in the gaps between airings of a show and its spikes of marketing support.

– BETWEEN THE TENT POLES –

One of the topics we looked at in Chapter 14 was the role of marketing in keeping a storyworld alive between seasons. We showed how marketers at Yle in Finland and HBO in the United States have been using social media to do this for shows as diverse as the teen drama *#lovemilla* and the fantasy epic *Game of Thrones*. Adam Zeller, Bravo's VP of social media, sets out the challenge:

One of the issues when you're working on a show that's not live, particularly a competition show, is how do you engage people socially while the show is still in production?[22]

Bravo's answer for *Top Chef*, for example, was to invite its foodie fans to take part in an Instagram quickfire challenge. In a short video, host Padma Lakshmi said 'Hey, I'm filming *Top Chef* and I need your help.' Fans were asked to check out a set of photos of dishes plated by the competing chefs and vote by 'liking' their favourite. They could tune in to the forthcoming season to see who won.[23] This Instagram challenge kept interest in *Top Chef* high while the show was off air.

Social is not really a campaign-led medium. There is a need for a heightened level of activity to support the so-called 'tent pole moments' (a season launch, a major plot point, a competition finale) but social media can maintain an ongoing relationship with viewers. TV brands with a committed fan base need to be 'always on'.

The most successful social activation does not feel forced. Social media ninja Kim Townend, who has collaborated with us on recent projects, cites the Comedy Central sitcom *Broad City* as a show with a social tone of voice that is almost always on point. She suggests that this is not surprising considering its stars, Abbi Jacobson and Ilana Glazer (who play twenty-something New Yorkers), both worked in search engine optimization (SEO), which helped them to develop the concept for the original *Broad City* online series:

> None of it feels like a marketing ploy dreamt up by a middle-aged man who doesn't get it... Their social strategy feels less 'put together' than HBO's for *Girls* (which caters to a similar demographic), where everything feels a little bit more corporate than it should. With *Broad City* it all manages to feel natural and effortless. And this in turn makes you really, really want to be their friend.[24]

(We'll let that comment about middle-aged men who don't get it pass...)

Part of this, according to Kim, is deploying the right form of content on each social channel: for example, longtail content on Tumblr, videos uploaded on Facebook and catchphrases turned into 'super hashtaggable moments, just ripe for the tweeting'.[25]

To build on the point that Ellen Stone of Bravo made about fans as friends, you don't talk to true friends only when you want something from them. It's about maintaining an authentic relationship based on mutual understanding. To achieve this, TV marketers have to learn to let go. As John Varvi of FX Networks says:

> At its best you can encourage and you can engage, but if you try to control and direct, social will eat you up.[26]

– BIG DATA –

At this point we should briefly mention social analytics. The better a TV marketer's audience insight, the deeper the engagement should be. Again, this is a subject that could fill a whole book, and we will return to the future promise of data and personalization in Chapter 16. Suffice it to say here that the increasingly sophisticated analytics tools offered by the major social platforms provide a wealth of information that marketers can draw on (as we did with our BBC One *Africa* campaign). Adam Zeller is typical amongst our interviewees in the way that he and his team at Bravo continually monitor and act upon social data:

> We look at content engagement in real time every week and then we determine what is resonating with the audience. We have weekly social sentiment reports, which outline the storylines and personalities – who is making the greatest impact? – and then we have reports for the production team and they make more informed decisions surrounding the production of the episodes. We also use social media, particularly Facebook analytics, to help us build our comms strategy.[27]

Stephanie Gibbons at FX adopts a similar approach:

> I have a dashboard where I follow all the streams and what people are saying and what's resonating and what's not and where the areas of interest lie, so then we say 'Okay, we're going to feed this fire and we're going to let this other one smoulder and essentially let it die.'[28]

Adam Zeller stresses that social analytics is a changing landscape, with the easy measurability of the big platforms such as Facebook and Twitter increasingly being offset by newer platforms favoured by millennials such as Snapchat and WhatsApp, which currently offer TV marketers limited data.

– LAUNCHING WITH SOCIAL –

Having talked about the role of social media before, during and after linear transmissions, between seasons of existing programmes and as a way to maintain an ongoing relationship with fans, how can it work for a brand new show or season premiere? In the words of Comedy Central's Walter Levitt:

> I don't believe you can launch a new piece of content today without social media being central to your plans... and so we approach every single launch with 'What's the thing we're going to do in social, what's the stuff we're going to do that's going to connect with fans... to promote this piece of content and that's going to create a ton of sharing?'[29]

A good starting point is recognizing the importance of the most influential bloggers and social media commentators. Ahead of the premiere of crime drama *Tunnel* the team at CANAL+ France staged a three-day campaign to create buzz amongst opinion formers with big social media followings. On day one, 15 carefully chosen bloggers were sent voice recorders with a note saying '*écoute moi*' (listen to me). The messages went like this: 'Hello [eg] Julien. Injustice, inequality, lies. The world we live in is no longer acceptable. It's time to change the rules.' Bloggers such as Golem13 (a commentator on advertising, video, art and general geekery) shared their intrigue on Instagram and Twitter. The following day they received an e-mail with a link to a mysterious video – grainy black-and-white footage of a man, bound and gagged, with the message 'Truth is near. #TruthTerror' (further encouragement to spread the word across their social networks). On day three they were all sent a link to the immersive website we described in Chapter 14.

Although not a brand new launch, HBO used a similar tactic during the build-up to *Game of Thrones* season three. They identified celebrity superfans, critics and pundits and delivered personalized sigil boxes including DVDs of the show and T-shirts with their personalized house names on. Celebrities including TV satirist Stephen Colbert, comedian Mindy Kaling and owner of pop-culture website Fred Entertainment, Ken Plume, tweeted or posted images of their sigil boxes on Instagram. Former *America's Next Top Model* Adrianne Curry got into the spirit by tweeting: 'I bend the knee & pledge my fealty... my House is forever yours @GameOfThrones #Luckiestgalonearth'. This celebrity buzz helped further enrich the *Game of Thrones* mythology amongst key opinion formers in the run-up to the season premiere.

– BUILDING A FOLLOWING –

We have emphasized how important it is for a show's core fans to be at the epicentre of social media marketing activity, but is it possible to *create* a fandom from scratch? That is what the marketing team at Fox in the United States set out to do with their campaign to launch *The Following*: the story of ex-FBI agent Ryan Hardy (Kevin Bacon) and his attempts to catch notorious yet charismatic serial killer Joe Carroll (James Purefoy), who has built a mysterious cult of like-minded followers.

Fox created a complex and immersive social media experience, with a home base on Tumblr, which mirrored the way in which the fictional serial killer Carroll collected his followers (the character had amassed '47 dedicated websites, over 1,000 blogs, chat rooms, online forums'). Well ahead of the premiere, Fox created a multiplatform storyline delivered from the point of view of an anonymous character stalking Carroll, introducing viewers to the storyworld. As the Fox team described it:

Our hub on Tumblr replicated Carroll's world wide web of followers by linking to countless sites, maps, boards and postings. The content began to slowly reveal the nefarious plans of nine cult members through disturbing vocals, haunting audio and hidden conversations, all building to the shocking events of the pilot.[30]

At this point in the launch campaign there was no overt marketing: Fox wanted viewers to discover the multilayered story and dig deeper as the debut season of *The Following* progressed. With each episode, Fox began to unlock the true identities of the nine mysterious characters (with names like Lenore, The Knight and Prince Prospero) by spreading the storyworld to other platforms and applications including Twitter, Facebook, Soundcloud and Vine. A series of clues unveiled during key episodes led fans to reveal the fact that the digital characters were in fact actual characters in the show.

Robin Benty from the Fox Digital team said this about the social media storytelling experience they created for *The Following*:

Instead of straightforward marketing, we wanted fans to find the content organically and spread the word. This allowed them to become immersed in a more multilayered story than was seen on air. Our social media plan continually created doorways for anyone to enter the world and we created content specifically for each digital platform so that fans could engage in all sorts of ways.[31]

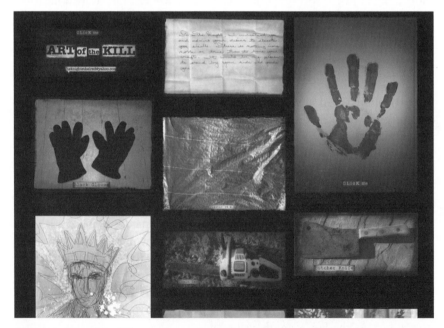

The sinister world of The Knight – one of the mysterious monikers created to promote The Following *in social media*   Source: *Reproduced by permission of Fox*

– BEING THE FIRST –

Whether for the launch of a completely new show or the run-up to a returning series, one of the keys to social media success is creating buzz that people want to be part of. One of the classic case studies from the UK is E4's launch of the youth drama *Skins*, about the lives and loves of a group of Bristol teenagers. Launch activity for the first season was centred on a custom profile on MySpace via which users could download music from the show, subscribe to blogs, read cast profiles and download backgrounds and icons. The first episode of *Skins* was then available to view exclusively on MySpace ahead of its linear transmission on E4. Building on the success of the launch, season two activity was based on the theme of a house party. An actual party was staged, with fans invited to join cast members at a secret location, and the events were filmed for a 10-minute special, again broadcast first on MySpace.

Wild goings-on at the Skins *party*   Source: © *Channel 4 Television*

A social media marketing technique that we are seeing more frequently now enjoys its own buzz phrase: 'flock to unlock'. What this means underneath the jargon is simply holding back exclusive content and inviting fans to 'unlock' it through their social media participation.

Our Day of the Doctor trailer for the 50th anniversary episode of *Doctor Who* (see Chapter 14) carried this call to action: #savetheday. It was an invitation for fans to mark the date of the global simulcast (94 countries, with 3D cinema screenings) firmly in their diaries, but also a strong suggestion that on that epic day the Doctor would yet again be compelled to save the human race from another alien threat. We encouraged fans to use the hashtag to show their support by adding to the content on a stand-alone website, doctorwhosavetheday.com, built by the digital agency Zag. The centrepiece of the site was the Social TARDIS (the TARDIS is the Doctor's time machine, in the form of an old-fashioned London police phone box). The more that fans added content on Twitter, Facebook and Instagram, and tagged it with #savetheday, the more the TARDIS image built up. Fans could zoom in and out and possibly even see their own tweet or picture as one of the tiny pulses that made up the image. Special sneak preview content was unlocked stage by stage as the Social TARDIS got completed. One excited fan tweeted: 'Please be aware that Twitter will break down this weekend.' Well, it didn't, but The Day of the Doctor did turn out to be, at the time, the most tweeted-about drama in Twitter's history.[32]

Ahead of the launch of a new season of a very different show, season three of *Dynamo: Magician Impossible* on UKTV's channel Watch, we knew how much *Dynamo* fans love to be the first to see his new magic. Our team built a second screen app that invited fans to watch a run of season two repeats, look out for 'hidden' playing cards and then enter them on the app to unlock an exclusive online premiere of the entire first episode of season three. Social comments were gathered under the hashtag #DynamoUnlock (as with *Doctor Who*, promoted in on-air trailers) with the best played out on air. The pre-launch awareness created by the app and its social media integration helped Watch to become the number one pay channel in the UK on the launch night of the new season, achieving its highest audience of the year.[33]

'Flock to unlock' worked particularly well for *Doctor Who* and *Dynamo* because they both have a base of very committed fans. If there is already a high level of anticipation ahead of a new season launch, fans will rush to unlock preview content, as they did when ITV launched their campaign for season two of the hugely popular crime drama *Broadchurch*. Tony Pipes of ITV explains:

> The first series had so much social interaction... everyone was talking about it on social. So we always wanted to start off series two with something big

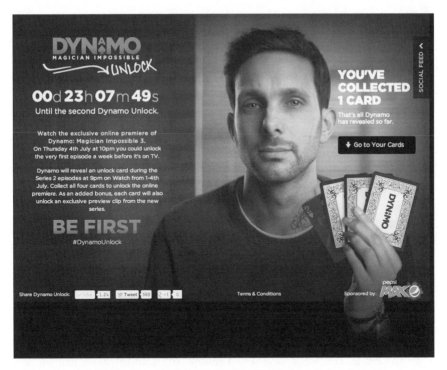

The Dynamo Unlock app invited fans to collect hidden cards to release an exclusive online premiere Source: *Reproduced by permission of UKTV Media Limited*

socially, and it was led by the fact that we really couldn't show anything. Chris (Chibnall) the writer was so, so protective of it, he didn't want anyone to know any plot details, so how do you market something like that, when you can't show or say anything?[34]

Having managed to tease out of Chris Chibnall the fact that the new season picked up the story immediately following the end of season one, in the same fictional seaside town of Broadchurch, the ITV marketing team were able to shoot a teaser trailer in the original location with the line: The End Is Where it Begins. Encouraging fans to tweet with the hashtag #BroadchurchReturns, as the volume of tweets increased a trailer for season two was revealed, stage by stage, on YouTube. Tony continues:

The biggest buzz we could make was the reveal of the trailer for the first time. It felt like the right thing to do – 'We can't show you anything except this trailer.' It was a really effective device because it builds anticipation and makes the trailer seem much bigger than it is because you've been waiting all day to see it.[35]

ITV's 'flock to unlock' campaign for season two of crime drama Broadchurch
Source: Reproduced by permission of ITV plc

Another way to create buzz ahead of the launch of a new show, as discussed earlier in relation to *American Horror Story* and in Chapter 14 with Channel 4's *Humans*, is via experiential marketing. Staging stunts can demand higher levels of investment than most social activity but can pay off in terms of the awareness and media coverage they generate. When Bravo launched their first scripted programme, *Girlfriends' Guide To Divorce*, they spray-painted three luxury sports cars with messages written by seemingly scorned women ('We're Over', 'You Suck' and 'I'm Leaving You') and drove them on tow trucks round Manhattan with the hashtag #GG2D. According to Bravo's EVP of marketing, Ellen Stone:

> A lot of the experiential marketing that we do gains so much more when you add a social component to it... The social amplification of that was insane.[36]

Reaction to Bravo's Girlfriends' Guide To Divorce *launch stunt*
Source: Reproduced by permission of Bravo Media

– BEING RESPONSIVE –

Returning to the point made by John Varvi of FX that TV marketers can engage with fans on social media but should not try to control it, the smartest teams keep a close eye on what is being said about their brand and respond in the same spirit. truTV did just that in recognition of years of tweets from basketball fans expressing their frustration at not knowing where to find the channel during its coverage of the NCAA March Madness college championship. 'But really like what even is truTV?' was one of the more polite examples.[37] So, in 2015, the channel decided to launch a pre-emptive strike by introducing the hashtag #HaveUFoundtruTV and setting up a social war room during the first week of March Madness to craft over 1,200 responses to people commenting on the network's relative obscurity. For example, when one user with the handle @PoopKisses tweeted: 'It's that time of year when I have to figure out which channel something called truTV is on'[38] @ truTV replied swiftly: 'It's also the time of year when we have to talk to fully grown adults who call themselves "Poop Kisses".'[39] Along with an online hub (truTVisHere.com) that helped viewers to locate the channel by entering their postcode, promoted by the stars of some of their biggest shows such as *Impractical Jokers*, truTV created a huge amount of visibility and a Twitter best-practice case study by accepting and responding to the good-natured jokes being made at their expense. With the help of a Twitter Promoted Trend (a product offered by Twitter for a promoted message to appear at the top of the trending topics list) truTV gained over 270 million conversation impressions and reached over 32 million people: not bad for an 'obscure' TV channel. Puja Vohra, EVP, marketing and digital, attributes the success to a knowing tone of voice, in tune with the channel positioning we described in Chapter 3:

> It was snarky and funny – a mixture of self-deprecation and swagger that demonstrated self-awareness of our history, evolution and reputation. We tapped into an organic meme that occurred every year on social media ('WTF is truTV?') and turned it on its head by responding to detractors and taking ownership of the conversation in a playful manner. And it worked: there was a palpable change in how we were perceived and a new energy around the brand. We took a lot of chances and it really paid dividends.[40]

– FORGING NEW BONDS –

If we think about many of the examples we have described, from the *Mad Men* Fan Cut to our singing tweets for *The Choir*, from the Tumblr created by Fox for *The Following* to the *Top Chef* internet challenge, we come back to the central theme of Chapter 14. The boundaries between content and marketing are inexorably blurring.

Self-awareness from truTV on Twitter: helping viewers to find them during March Madness   *Source: Reproduced by permission of truTV*

Ellen Stone of Bravo is very clear on this. Stressing that 'with the advent of social we need so much more content', she says:

> Marketing is about content creation at this point and anything that you do that isn't the core show, that enhances it, that makes it just that much more interesting and to bring people to the core show, is marketing.[41]

This has had the unintended consequence of encouraging much closer working relationships between programme makers and marketing. In Chapter 1 we looked at the unofficial hierarchies that have tended to exist within broadcasting organizations, with marketing being seen in the past as a low-status 'programme support' function. The need to embrace social media has led to new attitudes and ways of working. Jacob Shwirtz of Viacom (interviewed by Proulx and Shepatin) put it like this:

> Social TV breaks down the barriers between the TV people and the marketing people who are working much more collaboratively with show producers, creators and talent. Consumers and fans have a growing desire to be a part of the show... so the closer that digital folks and linear TV folks start to work, the cooler the experiences we'll be able to create.[42]

Carsten Lakner supports that view. Carsten is the head of marketing at Discovery Networks Denmark and previously held a senior marketing role at DR, the Danish national public service broadcaster and home of such internationally renowned dramas as *The Killing*, *The Bridge* and *The Legacy*. He talked to us about the increasing role of social media in expanding what he calls the 'metastory' of a drama. A good example was *The Legacy*. Season one had prompted many Danes to contact solicitors to discuss their wills. Building on the understanding that a powerful and evocative drama can encourage wider conversations, beyond the specific plot points and characters, DR created social media content for season two to explore the theme of 'family': what does the concept of family mean today? Crucially, this process resulted in closer working relationships between DR's production and marketing teams:

> Unless those two departments work together then social is a complete waste of time. When we were doing traditional trails and radio spots and whatever, that could work okay if they just handed us the finished product and said 'Can you cut a trail and make the radio spot out of this?' Yeah, we can. We weren't forced to work together. But with social, it doesn't make any sense if you're not working together. Social is starting to open the doors to something that should have happened a long time ago.[43]

– KEEP IT IN PERSPECTIVE –

So, after over 70 years of evolution in television it has taken the emergence of a new communication medium involving 140 character messages, 'Like' buttons and short looping animations to forge a closer bond between programme makers and marketers. These new working relationships will continue to develop in response to the rapid changes in the social media landscape that lie ahead. Between now and the time you read this book we feel sure there will be at least one other well-funded start-up in New York, London, Berlin, Stockholm or Silicon Valley producing a new social app with millions of global downloads. The demand for social assets will grow and grow. As we have described, social activation can turn fans into friends, keep storyworlds 'always on', launch new shows and foster real-time conversations.

However, amidst all this it is important to keep the role of social media in perspective and to remember that, at heart, it is simply word of mouth amplified. Liz Dolan of Fox sums this up beautifully:

> I had five senior executives sitting around the table in my office trying to craft one tweet... and I thought 'This is insane!' I worry about the trivialization of marketing... People don't love Twitter, per se. They love their shows and talking about them on Twitter. Twitter is just a tool to connect them with the shows they love.[44]

NEXT

★ A medium of value.   ★ Netflix adultery.

★ 'What shall we search for, kids?'   ★ A hybrid future.

★ TV should love you back.   ★ A plot worth following.

NOTES

1 *The IT Crowd*, 'Friendface' (2008) season three, episode five, Channel 4, 19 December

2 Proulx, M and Shepatin, S (2012) *Social TV: How marketers can reach and engage audiences by connecting television to the web, social media and mobile*, John Wiley & Sons, Hoboken, New Jersey

3 Linda Schupack, executive vice president of marketing, AMC, interview 11 June 2015

4 Walter Levitt, executive vice president, chief marketing officer, Comedy Central, interview 25 August 2015

5 Proulx, M and Shepatin, S (2012) *Social TV: How marketers can reach and engage audiences by connecting television to the web, social media and mobile*, John Wiley & Sons, Hoboken, New Jersey

6 Stephanie Gibbons, president of marketing, digital media marketing and on-air promotions, FX Networks, interview 26 June 2015

7 Liz Dolan, chief marketing officer, Fox International Channels, interview 11 June 2015

8 Greene, A (2015) [accessed 24 September 2015] AMC Bids Fond Farewell to 'Mad Men', *PromaxBDA*, 4 February [Online] http://brief.promaxbda.org/content/amc-bids-a-fond-farewell-to-mad-men

9 AMC (2015) [accessed 24 September 2015] Mad Men: The Fan Cut [Online] http://www.madmenfancut.com/

10 *Mad Men*, 'The Wheel' (2007) season one, episode 13, AMC, 18 October

11 Linda Schupack, executive vice president of marketing, AMC, interview 11 June 2015

12 https://www.youtube.com/watch?v=fSnneKba6Ks

13 Alexandra Shapiro, executive vice president, marketing and digital, USA Network, interview 26 May 15

14 TNT (2013) [accessed 24 September 2015] The Battle For The Handle: Twitter Credits Video, Falling Skies, TNT [Online] https://www.youtube.com/watch?v=HCPUIQt4z4s

15 Ellen Stone, executive vice president of marketing, Bravo and Oxygen Media, interview 9 September 2015

16 Ellen Stone, executive vice president of marketing, Bravo and Oxygen Media, interview

17 Stephanie Gibbons, president of marketing, digital media marketing and on-air promotions, FX Networks, interview 26 June 2015

18 Samy B (2013) [accessed 24 September 2015] American Horror Story: Opening Credits Of All 3 Seasons [Online] https://www.youtube.com/watch?v=omu0lDUcMP4

19 Proulx, M and Shepatin, S (2012) *Social TV: How marketers can reach and engage audiences by connecting television to the web, social media and mobile*, John Wiley & Sons, Hoboken, New Jersey

20 Red Bee (2011) [accessed 19 November 2015] The Choir [Online] https://www.youtube.com/watch?v=H3IUQsellnc

21 https://www.youtube.com/watch?v=yKAmDwU_VC0

22 Adam Zeller, vice president, social media, Bravo and Oxygen, interview 9 September 2015

23 BravoTV (2015) [accessed 24 September 2015] Vote In The Top Chef Instagram Quick Fire Challenge [Online] https://instagram.com/p/3M5Ea4RP1I/

24 Townend, K (2015) [accessed 24 September 2015] How Broad City's Social Media Strategy Delivers, As Well As Being MASSIVELY FUN [Blog] Kim Townend, 12 March [Online] http://kimtownend.com/how-broad-citys-social-media-strategy-delivers-as-well-as-being-massively-fun/

25 Townend, K (2015) [accessed 24 September 2015] How Broad City's Social Media Strategy Delivers, As Well As Being MASSIVELY FUN [Blog] Kim Townend, 12 March [Online] http://kimtownend.com/how-broad-citys-social-media-strategy-delivers-as-well-as-being-massively-fun/

26 John Varvi, executive vice president, on-air promotions, FX Networks (FX, FXX, FXM, FXNOW), interview 26 June 2015

27 Adam Zeller, vice president, social media, Bravo and Oxygen, interview 9 September 2015

28 Stephanie Gibbons, president of marketing, digital media marketing and on-air promotions, FX Networks, interview 26 June 2015

29 Walter Levitt, executive vice president, chief marketing officer, Comedy Central, interview 25 August 2015

30 Fox (2014) Fox Case Study, video

31 Robin Benty, senior director of digital brand, Fox, interview 7 October 2015

32 Red Bee (2013) [accessed 19 November 2015] Doctor Who 50th Anniversary [Online] http://www.redbeecreative.tv/work/bbc-one-doctor-who-50th-anniversary?service=entertainment-marketing

33 Red Bee (2013) Dynamo Season 3 [Online] http://www.redbeecreative.tv/work/watch-dynamo-unlock?service=entertainment-marketing

34 Tony Pipes, executive creative director, ITV Creative, interview 16 September 2015

35 Tony Pipes, executive creative director, ITV Creative, interview 16 September 2015

36 Ellen Stone, executive vice president of marketing, Bravo and Oxygen Media, interview 9 September 2015

37 Donohue, R (2013) [accessed 24 September 2015] But Really Like What Even Is truTV [Twitter] 21March [Online] https://twitter.com/RealRyanDonohue

38 PoopKisses (2015) [accessed 24 September 2015] It's That Time Of Year When I Have To Figure Out Which Channel Something Called truTV is on [Twitter] 17 March [Online] https://twitter.com/PoopKisses

39 truTV (2015) [accessed 24 September 2015] It's Also The Time Of The Year When We Have To Talk To Fully Grown Adults Who Call Themselves 'Poop Kisses' [Twitter] [Online] https://twitter.com/truTV

40 Puja Vohra, executive vice president, marketing and digital, truTV, interview 8 July 2015

41 Ellen Stone, executive vice president of marketing, Bravo and Oxygen Media, interview 9 September 2015

42 Schwirtz, J, quoted in Proulx, M and Shepatin, S (2012) *Social TV: How marketers can reach and engage audiences by connecting television to the web, social media and mobile*, John Wiley & Sons, Hoboken, New Jersey

43 Carsten Lakner, head of marketing, Discovery Networks Denmark, interview 24 March 2015

44 Liz Dolan, chief marketing officer, Fox International Channels, interview 11 June 2015

CHAPTER SIXTEEN

THE FUTURE OF TV MARKETING

Seismic change, timeless principles

We're all stories, in the end. Just make it a good one, eh?

THE DOCTOR, *DOCTOR WHO*[1]

– THE ENDURING POWER OF HITS –

Former *New York Times* TV reporter Bill Carter, in his entertaining book about the giants of US television, *Desperate Networks*, wrote about the then chairman of NBC, Bob Wright, who was anxious about the success of rival network ABC:

> As much as he was convinced that the future of television would be ruled by unpredictable, sweeping change, Wright knew one thing had not changed and would not change. No matter how they viewed television – on their computer monitors, on their mobile phones, or on TV screens as big as medieval tapestries – people would still want to see hit shows. If you had hits, it would not matter where and how the revenue came in; you would always be in business.[2]

Today's TV marketers could be forgiven for thinking that 'unpredictable, sweeping change' bringing new ways to watch television has been a relatively recent phenomenon, but Carter was writing back in 2006.

With the rise and rise of online media, a surefire way to grab attention and attract clicks has been to write headlines and soundbites about the disruptive forces in the TV industry. We opened Chapter 2 with predictions of doom for TV channels. In September 2015 Apple CEO Tim Cook proclaimed that 'the future of TV is apps',[3] followed within days by Netflix chairman and CEO Reed Hastings confidently predicting that cable networks will die for good and all TV will be on the internet.[4] It is much less fashionable to talk about the features of the industry that will endure in the face of tech-driven upheaval, not least, as Bob Wright knew in the middle of the 2000s, the fact that successful television organizations have always been and will continue to be driven by programmes that people love to watch.

As we have shown throughout this book, there have been many new hit shows since Carter wrote *Desperate Networks* and innovative marketing has been influential in building their success. In some cases this has been through the extraordinarily creative application of traditional methods such as on-air promotional campaigns, title sequences and print ads: HBO's spellbinding launch trailer for *True Detective* and the layered approach of Fox's *Empire*; the iconic 'falling man' in *Mad Men*'s opening titles; the striking key art for FX shows such as *American Horror Story*. In other cases it has been by harnessing social media and interactive technology to promote titles as diverse as *Game of Thrones*, *How I Met Your Mother*, CBBC's *Horrible Histories* and Bravo's *Real Housewives*. And throughout the 2010s viewing decisions and content discovery have been aided by clearly positioned channel brands with distinctive visual identities: the fearless storytelling of FX, the witty banter of Dave, the characters of USA Network or the alternative voices and risk taking of Channel 4. As the US essayist and journalist Michael Wolff wrote in his book *Television Is the New Television*, far from being trampled by digital challengers TV has become one of the fastest-growing business sectors, where consumers and advertisers are prepared to pay for 'the influential, the prestigious, the culturally significant, a business and medium of value, need, originality, and exclusivity'.[5] And marketing has played a big part in creating this value.

So, what of the next decade or so? How are hit shows going to be driven in an industry in which the distribution of wealth is undoubtedly shifting and traditional ad-supported TV models are being shaken? How are valuable TV brands going to be built?

We'll say right here that we're not taking on the responsibility of predicting the future of the entire TV industry. Expert consultants and analysts earn big fees for doing that. Our focus is TV marketing. But we felt we couldn't end this book without suggesting a number of themes that we believe will influence our part of the industry over the coming years. We asked many of our interviewees about the things that are keeping them awake at night and, from Los Angeles to London, from Sydney to Brooklyn, they had forthright and consistent views about the role of brand building in an age of internet television. So, in the midst of seismic change, what are the key themes and essential truths?

– LONG LIVE TV CHANNEL BRANDS –

If this book was called *The TV Tech Builders* it might well assert that in the near future all TV content will be set free in a world of universal search. But the denizens of Silicon Valley sometimes overlook the basics of human behaviour, emotions and decision making, particularly when it comes to TV watching. As we described in Chapter 2, it is a leisure activity and most of the time people don't want to make much effort. Robert Tansey of Sky puts it like this:

> TV is often a shared experience. You come to it with your partner or with your family, and you say 'Right, what are we going to watch?' That's not search engine behaviour. You don't go to Google and say 'Right, what shall we search for kids?'[6]

Magnus Willis, one of the founding partners of insight and strategy consultancy Sparkler, spends a lot of his time researching the way people behave in relation to entertainment choices, and he stresses the fact that, compared with markets in which optimizing one's decision making is important (say, when buying a car), when it comes to TV for much of the time 'good enough is good enough'. Viewers will continue to be quite happy to settle for a programme that just happens to be on one of the channels that is most familiar or habitual:

> TV's just TV... The idea of people investing loads of time to try and find the perfect piece of family entertainment – it doesn't really work that way... there's nothing really to be gained from investing loads and loads of time finding the perfect telly because life's too short.[7]

In Chapter 2 we looked at heuristics: mental shortcuts that help us to make decisions. The role of TV channel brands in this respect will remain important. For many people, busy jobs and demanding families mean there is only an hour or two in a typical evening for TV watching. As Magnus points out, 'the architecture of people's lives is still pretty similar to what it was 50 years ago, getting home at a certain time, going to bed at a certain time', and in this context he says:

> It's not just 'What are you about?' but 'Where do you fit in the context of the accepted architecture of an evening?'... In the modern world, where you can have access to anything at any time, in practice most people don't. They can watch whenever they want to but they actually don't, there's a classic arc... it's not about infinite choice, you can do these things any time, any place, anywhere, the 'Martini strategy' – actually, no.[8]

As sources of content continue to proliferate with the launch of more and more new platforms and online streaming options, for many of us the evening will continue to be a time for going into 'standby', to make little effort and minimize risk in our TV choices. Unless we are currently gripped by a box set and we know exactly where to go to call up the next episode on demand, we will still frequently rely on the security of a channel brand to guide us. In the words of ITV's Rufus Radcliffe:

> We write off channel brands at our peril. What viewers have is different need states where they're looking for different experiences and different things. There is definitely a very strong need state, which is 'I don't want to be the scheduler here and I would like to enjoy a live experience with millions of other people through a channel brand.'[9]

– THE EVOLUTION OF CURATORIAL TV BRANDS –

We don't want to give the impression that our TV brand builders are barricading themselves behind their reels of idents or trying, Canute-like, to turn back the online streaming tide. There was a clear recognition amongst our interviewees that the ecology of TV brands is changing, that new brands are emerging to help viewers navigate portfolios of content, and that fresh approaches are required to maintain the role of brands as shorthand for trust and quality as they travel across multiple platforms.

It is particularly important to look at the TV watching behaviour of today's teenagers and young adults – the millennials that marketers have become so obsessed with and the so-called Generation Z that is succeeding them. There are no prizes for making this observation but what needs to be stressed is the speed at which their TV viewing patterns are changing, as we described in Chapter 13 with the challenges of the YouTube generation. Data from our parent company Ericsson's ConsumerLab (a global TV and media study representative of over 680 million people) shows that while linear TV is still highly valued in families as the 'household campfire' only 60 per cent of millennials watch it on a daily basis. In comparison, nearly 8 out of 10 teenagers now say they watch on-demand TV and video daily (with a lot of this viewing happening on smartphones, laptops and tablets).[10] Ellen Stone, Bravo's EVP of marketing, is acutely aware of the need to develop new brand models to guide viewer decision making amongst this demographic group in particular:

> This new millennial audience, this tempestuous audience. They're fickle but once they dig in they really dig in... What we need to do is find out what that core model is for the millennials and once we do I... believe we'll be able to create a brand that stays true to the audience. Do I think that it's absolutely going to be a TV network? I don't know, but I do know that we can create content that's curated and that can be distributed in some way and relevant to millennials.[11]

We cannot offer a magic formula for connecting with this target group. The marketing challenge of reaching young consumers is nothing new, but there are rich rewards for brands that can do it successfully. In Chapter 9, for example, we looked at the strong appeal of Vice News to millennials and in Chapter 6 we talked about MTV's new co-created brand identity. The key point for this chapter, though, is the way that the behaviour of younger audiences is driving the rapid overall increase in streamed on-demand viewing and the impact this is having on brands. Confounding the predictions of many pundits a decade or so ago, TV has not been decimated by online media. Rather, online has become 'TV'.

One of the biggest debates in television marketing these days is about the ways that brand portfolios and hierarchies work best in the on-demand space. This challenge is occupying the minds of the marketers we talked to at both the BBC and Channel 4, for example. Let's take the popular drama, *Indian Summers*. An epic series set in 1930s colonial India and starring Julie Walters, it was originally commissioned to run on Channel 4 in the UK. Now available to view on Channel 4's video on-demand service All 4, it is preceded by an All 4 branded sting (not a Channel 4 ident). However, for viewers in Australia (for example) it appears on subscription channel BBC First: a brand created by BBC Worldwide as 'the home of premium, original British drama'.[12] And in the United States, *Indian Summers* airs as part of PBS's drama anthology sub-brand 'Masterpiece'. Another example is the BBC gangster drama *Peaky Blinders*: originally aired in the UK on BBC Two but launched in the United States as a 'Netflix Original'. Maybe, separated by the Atlantic Ocean, this is simply a commercial arrangement that suits all parties with no serious brand consequences, but in some markets this issue is much closer to home, and nowhere more so than in the United States. Take the Fox comedy-horror series *Scream Queens*, another Ryan Murphy creation, which premiered in September 2015. Viewers can watch the show live on Fox, stream it on the online catch-up app FOX NOW or, alternatively, watch it on demand if they are subscribers to the premium streaming service Hulu.

As we mentioned in our Introduction, FX Networks CEO John Landgraf rattled the industry when he talked about the glut of good TV shows, which he said is making it harder than ever to 'cut through the clutter and create real buzz'.[13] From his vantage point as leader of the TV marketing community PromaxBDA, Steve Kazanjian is only too aware of the challenges:

> The existing OTT environment makes finding content very difficult cross-app. Multiple products, multiple platforms, similar content and poor UX creates non-intuitive navigation and confusion across the entire space. Ultimately, the technology combined with the glut of material makes searching, sampling and exploring new content very difficult. Consumers

are finally saying that there's too much work involved with finding what I want to watch across all these different apps.[14]

In this context, viewers need help and that is the enduring role of curatorial brands with clear identities, as Alexandra Shapiro of USA Network says:

> The halo effect of a strong brand in a highly fragmented, cluttered marketplace can be the seal of approval that people need for sampling.[15]

In an increasingly global entertainment industry, which brands 'own' *Indian Summers*, *Peaky Blinders* and *Scream Queens*? Who plays the editorial role that viewers will trust the most in providing the decision-making shortcuts and guiding their viewing choices (beyond their own social networks, of course)? Will the primary brand be a channel with an established reputation for bringing viewers new programmes of guaranteed quality (Channel 4, BBC Two, Fox)? Will it be a genre-focused sub-brand such as BBC First or Masterpiece? Could the curatorial role of on-demand brands such as All 4 or Hulu become dominant? Or is the TV brand landscape simply set to get much more complex, with only the most distinctive, relevant and clearly positioned brands surviving?

We believe there are three implications for TV brand builders: producer brands need to assert themselves, the role of TV masterbrands will become more important and on-demand brands will need to work harder to develop consumer affinity. Let's look at each of these points in turn.

– ASSERTIVE PRODUCER BRANDS –

One of the phrases we hear often amongst our BBC clients is the need to 'drive credit back'. That is understandable for a public service broadcaster that is constantly aware of the importance of associating its most popular and/or critically acclaimed content with the creative decisions and risks it takes on behalf of its licence fee payers. In a global TV market in which it is tempting to sell IP to the highest bidder, particularly if that means generating funds to reinvest in the next season or next new show, it will be increasingly vital for originators and commissioners to maintain their brand associations with that content. If a BAFTA-nominated series such as *Peaky Blinders* is allowed to appear in the United States as a Netflix Original, then however compelling the commercial argument, it's a missed opportunity for the BBC to drive credit back to its reputation as the creator of some of the world's best TV dramas. Contrast this with the way Sky Atlantic was launched in the UK as 'the home of HBO'.[16]

We worked with ABC Studios back in 2011 when they were making three of the top five most watched shows in world television: *Lost*, *Desperate Housewives* and *Grey's Anatomy*. Our observation at the time was that in a typical store you could see a whole DVD stand just for HBO shows while ABC's were scattered to the four winds. That's the power of a producer brand investing in itself.

Several of our interviewees stressed the strength of their focus on this issue and none more so than Linda Schupack of AMC:

> That is our challenge. We are always trying to associate our properties with the AMC brand. We want people to know that it is AMC and that we're trying to use one show to introduce or to flow into another. The future is going to be about figuring out the choreography between the power of a show and the power of a brand as a navigational tool or a curatorial tool.[17]

– FEWER, BIGGER, BETTER –

While we have made the case for the continued role of channel brands, especially in the traditional linear TV environment, for the branded houses in particular we believe it will be increasingly challenging for individual numerically delineated channels (say, BBC Two or ITV4) to act as curators online. Take BBC Two, for example. British TV viewers may well agree with the BBC's own definition of its role as 'a mixed-genre channel with programmes of depth and substance',[18] but in an online world the simplest solution may be to reassure viewers that, say, *Peaky Blinders*, is a drama brought to them by 'the BBC' (just as *True Detective* is from HBO and *Mad Men* from AMC). The plethora of 'Go' and 'Play(er)' sub-brands do not reflect the ways that viewers think of TV brands online. Rather than continuing to invest in establishing brands like this in a disintermediated landscape, it seems more important to us for TV marketers to ensure that their masterbrands are positioned as strongly and distinctively as possible.

We can learn a lot here from FX Networks. As industry guru Lee Hunt observed in his New Best Practices 2015 conference presentation, with the launch of FXX, FX Networks established what he described as 'a walled garden strategy' to connect the FX, FXX, FXM and FXNOW brands, for example with the TV channels and their OTT service sharing promo end pages, and with the whole portfolio underpinned by the 'Fearless' proposition.[19]

As we heard from John Varvi in Chapter 5, the marketers at FX Networks see the network holistically, with a shared philosophy and with the individual differences determined primarily by demographic skews. The marketers at Channel 4 look at their brand portfolio in a similar way.

As masterbrands grow in importance it is likely that there will be 'fewer, bigger, better' TV brands. Echoing Steve Kazanjian's comments about the hard work involved in making online TV choices, NBCUniversal

International's Lee Raftery suggests that the antidote to 'trawling through thousands of programmes' will be a reduction in the number of brands on offer:

> In the boom years of pay-TV growth, it was all about niche offerings. I think that's already beginning to shake out. We're coming down to fewer brands and it's even more important to be clearly positioned in that top tier.[20]

— BUILDING AN ON-DEMAND BRAND —

Talking with Channel 4 CEO David Abraham, who is firmly in the 'channel brands will live on' camp, we discussed the extent to which the new breed of over-the-top brands will develop their own curatorial role. In David's words:

> That voice of the channel is very important. It raises an interesting question, because what is the voice of an on-demand service and does it have an editorial voice?[21]

Hulu in the United States is a good example of a brand that recognizes the need to be much more than a commodity subscription service offering access to a vast library of content. Marketing head Jenny Wall emphasizes that 'it is imperative in this world that you create a brand'. She says:

> There's a lot of great content out there and more and more places to watch that content. We know that people have incredibly strong and personal relationships with their shows. We want to build a brand that imparts some value to watching their favourite shows on our service – whether it's shows we license or shows we make. We need to have a deeper, emotional relationship with our viewers. Otherwise it will just become an arms race of who has what show, not about the total experience we can create for the viewer.[22]

Jenny's words echo the conclusions of PwC's global entertainment and media outlook 2015–19, which looks at the key industry themes for the years ahead. PwC emphasizes the fact that 'consumers see no significant divide between digital and traditional media' and signs off with a definitive statement: 'It's time to embrace the fact that mastering the user experience is critical to success in this industry.'[23]

Returning to Hulu, although, as we will come on to talk about, they are working hard to apply data analytics in continually smarter ways, Jenny and her team believe with a passion that a premium streaming service needs to connect with consumers on an emotional level to build 'loyalty beyond reason' and to apply lessons learned from other brands that have achieved this:

The best brands out there like Apple and Nike start with a brand belief and they live that brand belief. Our brand belief is that TV should love you back. For decades people have loved TV. They've spent so much time with TV; it's a big part of their lives. We believe that it's time for TV to return that love. Whether it's through the content that we make or buy, our product experience, or simply connecting fans with the shows they love.[24]

Hulu promotional campaigns have captured this sentiment. For example, when all 180 episodes of classic comedy *Seinfeld* became available for streaming on Hulu they created an animated campaign featuring some of its most iconic lines: 'double dipped', 'I can't spare a square', 'yada yada yada' and so on. It was a quirky and affectionate tribute demonstrating that Hulu loves TV as much as its subscribers.[25]

Iconic lines from Seinfeld – *'now streaming on Hulu'*
Source: Reproduced by permission of Sony Pictures Television and Hulu

Recent research by Hulu underlined the deeply personal relationship people have with television and this led to a new tagline: Come TV With Us.

According to Jenny Wall:

> It's an open invitation to a community of TV lovers. It shows that we love TV as much as you do. We're using TV as a verb that has an exciting tension in it. It aligns to our corporate mission to redefine TV.[26]

Beyond marketing communications, on-demand services can also build consumer affinity by adopting a curatorial approach to the way they present content from their libraries. Jenny Wall talked to us about the way Hulu tries to bring a personal touch, much like the way, many years ago, the manager of a local video store would select 'picks of the week': curating 'trays' of content to encourage sampling and creating targeted 'stories of the week' from clips from a number of shows, all demonstrating that 'there's a human behind the machine'.[27]

Similarly, US consultant Lee Hunt describes the way Verizon's Fios TV, a service he subscribes to, applies creativity to the way it categorizes content:

> Sometimes it's thematic, based on what's going on, so February is a Valentine's Day thing, lots of love stories, but they'll also come up with unusual groupings. For example, if there's going to be a new *Marvel* film released they'll put together a category of superhero films and television shows, trying to capture the cultural zeitgeist of media and entertainment.[28]

In this way, we predict that television is likely to see more 'pop-up brands', mirroring the trend for temporary sub-branded restaurants, fashion outlets, artisan stores and nightclubs, for example. And these new branded formats would not have to stem from traditional TV sources: the likes of Red Bull, Hasbro and Burberry, in three very different sectors, are showing how non-media brands with ambition and creativity are increasingly becoming more video-centric. Similarly, could Glastonbury keep more of its own rights and create a pop-up music TV channel during its festival period? Or what about Net-a-Porter during London Fashion Week? This is a big opportunity for on-demand TV streaming services, in particular, learning from the success that some linear TV channels have had in creating themed seasons of programming.

In fact, it seems inevitable that streaming brands will take on more of the characteristics of successful TV channels. It is notable that in August 2015 Sony Pictures Television's online entertainment service Crackle introduced a new identity that looks and feels more like a traditional linear TV experience. With an 'always on' interface looking a bit like a conventional cable channel, its promise is: 'Spend less time browsing and more time watching.'[29]

– THE RISE OF USAGE-BASED PROMOTION –

One way that on-demand brands are seeking to build consumer affinity is via promotional campaigns that focus not so much on the programme content itself but the changing ways people can view it.

HBO's Awkward Family Viewing campaign, created by the agency SS&K, is a great example. A young adult brother and sister are shown watching racy, explicit content from HBO shows, including *Game of Thrones* and *Girls*, while their seemingly oblivious parents heighten their discomfort with inappropriate comments. The voice-over directs the young people to a feature of HBO's on-demand service that they might appreciate: 'HBO Go. The best of HBO on all your favourite devices. Far, far away from your parents.'[30]

Over at Netflix, when chief content officer Ted Sarandos made the fateful decision in early 2012 to release simultaneously all eight episodes of their first original commission, comedy crime drama *Lilyhammer*, a new phenomenon was born: binge viewing.[31] A year later, following the success of season one of *House of Cards* (which had the same release pattern), Netflix research identified a new form of infidelity: 'Netflix adultery'. Many subscribers confessed to covertly viewing episodes of TV shows ahead of their partners and Netflix created a promotional campaign to highlight this new form of 'stream cheating', which their research claimed was affecting half of subscriber relationships.[32] The campaign line was 'Watch Responsibly': a seemingly counter-intuitive injunction for a campaign promoting an 'eight bucks a month' service, yet a clever way to reflect the fact that Netflix had created a new, addictive way to watch TV.[33] In the words of strategist Lee Hunt:

> 'Watch Responsibly' is a way of saying 'We're beyond just trying to get you to buy in: we're part of the social fabric and we're very much a part of your day-to-day life.' It's part of understanding that it's a lifestyle brand... a recognition that the way they present television changed behaviour and has changed the culture.[34]

On 1 April 2015 (surely no coincidence) Netflix released a series of 'public information' films within their service featuring artists including Michael Kelly (*House of Cards*) and Taylor Schilling (*Orange Is the New Black*) advising viewers of the 'dangers' of watching too many episodes back-to-back and suggesting they go outside, breathe some fresh air and make a proper meal. The tagline 'Binge Responsibly' served as further recognition that Netflix understands its subscribers. This is impressively confident advertising for such a relatively new brand in the TV landscape.[35]

We are starting to see UK brands adopt a similar approach, notably Sky. Idris Elba welcomes us to 'the four stages of box sets':

Stage 1: Just one more.

Stage 2: The preacher (when we all bore anyone who will listen about, for example, 'that bit in *True Detective*').

Stage 3: The void (when it is over).

Stage 4: Here we go again (when we start a fresh new series).[36]

All box-set addicts would recognize these stages and we predict that we will see more and more promotional campaigns for TV brands and services creating differentiation by reflecting new forms of viewing behaviour and demonstrating, in different ways, that 'our brand loves TV as much as you do'.

(Incidentally, it is worth noting in a 'what goes around comes around' sense that there may have been a subliminal influence here from one of the most iconic advertising campaigns of all time for a TV network. In the late 1990s ABC in the United States ran a campaign with a simple line: TV is good. With its vibrant use of yellow and lines such as 'Don't just sit there. Okay, just sit there' and 'It's a beautiful day. What are you doing outside?' it was an honest celebration of the role that TV plays in our lives.)[37]

– GETTING PERSONAL –

Another way that TV service providers are set to build stronger bonds with their subscribers and viewers is by applying the increasingly rich amount of data they are collecting to deliver content recommendations their consumers will truly value. PromaxBDA's Steve Kazanjian (who experienced the power of data when working as a design expert in the consumer packaged goods sector) describes its potential for TV marketing:

> Our industry has always been over-indexed in the creative side of marketing. Why is that the case? Because until recently we have never had hard-core analytics. We have never been able to get to a one-to-one level of understanding consumer behaviour, understanding patterns, understanding the unique individual. We're still not totally there but over the last three years we have made incredibly significant strides in understanding, down to an actual one-to-one relationship... As we are starting to get a better understanding of consumer behaviour, entertainment is performing more like a consumer product than ever before. That's incredibly exciting because it is affording us opportunities to connect with our viewers in ways that we have never been able to before, truly understanding empirical data now.[38]

So personalization (along with its close relatives 'programmatic' and 'addressable') is a word we are set to hear much more frequently in TV marketing. The online world of video content on tablets, smartphones and apps will be influenced by general consumer expectations (access to what they want, when they want it, with a seamless experience across screens delivering genuine help in finding content to watch and connections with their social networks). Despite Magnus Willis's earlier point that most viewers don't want 'Martini media' for much of the time, there is no doubt that it is a fast-growing phenomenon, particularly among younger audiences. More sophisticated data analysis holds the promise for TV service providers to deliver a smart and trusted experience, based on behaviour, taste and social media and always to be ready with an answer to the familiar question: What shall I watch next? Netflix has been at the leading edge of developments in personalization, and *Wired* magazine in February 2015, talking to chief product officer Neil Hunt, described the iterative experimentation that the firm carries out to help make 'if this then that' type conclusions. (These are complicated things that sound a long way from TV as we know it: Markov chain models, matrix factorization, machine learning tools and intensive A/B testing.)[39] The ultimate outcome of an approach like this could be a new form of curatorial brand: not curating content for a demographic or attitudinal grouping of viewers but for an individual: 'My channel'.

However, as Steve Kazanjian says, we're not there just yet. Research from the Ericsson ConsumerLab reveals that 50 per cent of consumers are unable to find anything to watch on their linear TV service at least once a day, and we can all recognize the current frustrations caused by the still somewhat crude technology employed by on-demand services.[40] Shared accounts with family or friends can easily lead to inappropriate or random recommendations for an individual, and suggestions based on accurate interpretations of viewing habits are not always received positively:

> Netflix's suggestion of category based on my viewing 'Violent Supernatural Movies from 1980s'. What does that say about me?[41]

The Ericsson research goes on to show that one in four TV/video consumers are open to providing personal data to get more accurate recommendations. Personal data in this context means online and in-service behavioural tracking, actively providing data and volunteering information when opting in to the service. We believe the brands and service providers that will achieve the most success in this area will be those that establish a genuine two-way dialogue based on mutual value and respect. Hulu's Jenny Wall expresses this beautifully:

> We have a tremendous amount of data that we use to try to provide a personal experience for every individual. There is so much great content to choose from, viewers want help discovering new shows to fall in love with. Today, consumers have come to expect recommendations and curation with everything, whether it's watching shows or buying shoes. The key is

to make sure the recommendations are meaningful and valuable; so it's not just about the data, it's how we look at the data – how we connect the dots – and apply it real-time.[42]

As we described in Chapter 7, this new data-enabled relationship is an exciting prospect for TV marketers because it offers the opportunity for 'programmatic' promotion: put simply, using data to serve messages that will be more relevant and valuable for consumers. ESPN is a good example of a TV organization that is adopting this approach with enthusiasm, hiring an SVP of global data and using information in more sophisticated ways, as former SVP of marketing, Aaron Taylor, describes:

> Having first party data on our fans, having them register with ESPN.com or on the ESPN app and state their preferences for teams, for athletes, for sports personalities and for journalists across the ESPN platforms, helps us to better understand the content they want to consume, helps us better serve it to them and market to them based on their preferences. We have a relatively robust first party data set and we are trying to grow that all the time... so we are better serving our fans and better at monetizing the data we have.[43]

Even bigger opportunities will be possible when further tech developments enable more effective blending of online user data with social networks and fan sites. For example, a recommendation to try a new show is likely to be received more favourably if it comes with a meaningful star rating derived from sources you trust. As we observed in Chapter 15, via Stephanie Gibbons of FX Networks, the most powerful form of marketing is word of mouth, and social media is word of mouth amplified.

New learning will be possible when more TV brands live purely in the online space, as the BBC is poised to experience when the BBC Three channel, which exists 'to provoke thought and to entertain audiences from 16-year-olds to thirtysomethings' moves fully online, as it is set to do in 2016.[44] In this situation an even more intense audience focus will be essential, as the BBC's director of marketing and audiences, Philip Almond, stresses:

> In a world where you don't have that captive audience and where you're really trying to have a permanent relationship it's much more like 'Who are you, what are you interested in and what am I going to serve you to keep you loyal and keep you in BBC Three?', so it is... a much more audience-centred approach rather than a channel- or a content-centred approach.[45]

Talking more generally about the BBC's attitude to using data, Philip describes a very balanced approach:

> At the BBC we have always talked about a combination of what we can learn from data with editorial curation combined... Data is extremely

useful in marketing and targeting and understanding your audience and can generate new audience insight to help with commissioning, but it will never be a replacement for editorial judgement. This is still going to be an industry where, say, you get *Happy Valley* [the crime drama] because you say to Sally Wainwright, 'We really loved what you did with *Last Tango in Halifax*, can we have your next project please, what do you want it to be?' That's driven by talent. It's always going to be a mixture.[46]

– A HYBRID FUTURE –

For all the reasons stated, we believe that the future of TV and therefore TV marketing – in the near term at least – is going to be (to use Philip's words) 'a mixture'. We will use viewer data in increasingly smart and sophisticated ways to understand the tastes and preferences of individual viewers and serve them more personalized promotional messages. Yet there will still be an important role for distinctive channel brands positioned with collective appeal to large audiences. TV watching will become increasingly fragmented, with more content streamed on demand on a variety of devices. Yet the social power of TV will endure. We are social beings and the desire to watch what others are watching, at roughly the same time, and then talk about 'last night's TV' will not go away any time soon. This hybrid situation will increasingly drive the ways that TV organizations distribute and promote their content. For example, Channel 4 CEO David Abraham describes their approach:

> The future is... not an either/or future. I don't see a future in which **all** consumption is going to be on demand, which is why we focused on our hybridization strategy. The linear schedule used to be fairly fixed. It has now become a 'flexi-linear' schedule where the first TX of a new show, let's say a show like *Glue* on E4, is still the biggest hit that you get but it's driving all those other windows... Without the linear window the energy and the oxygen behind launching new shows is greatly diminished... so there's something about the economics of television that requires this hybridization of the linear and non-linear rather than a move from A to B.[47]

David goes on to talk about how these innovations in different parts of the TV industry are leading to mutual learning and development. As we have seen with Hulu, tech-driven brands are experimenting with original commissioning and editorial voices while traditional broadcasters are rapidly adopting new technology to make their content available in different ways: 'Everything in a sense is complementing itself. I don't see this as a zero sum game at all.'[48]

What will this hybrid future mean for the way audience behaviour will change? Lee Hunt captures this neatly by comparing the new TV landscape with the way we listen to music in our cars:

> When you want somebody to make choices for you... you go to the radio and you hit different stations based on the kind of music they have and the relationship you have with them, and that's going to be like linear television. Or you plug in your iPod and that's on demand and you choose what you want. Or you go to Spotify or Pandora and it's very much like a Netflix, it helps you choose the content you want. So I think where we're going to be in the future, it's not going to be just on-demand, it's not going to be just linear, it's not just going to be streaming or downloading, hopefully it's going to be a healthy mix of all those. Just like in your car, your mood determines how you use that sound system.[49]

In this world, the ecology of TV brands will evolve and new relationships will develop. On our next generation smart TVs and hand-held devices we will see, for example: the 'Fearless' FX brands next to the Hulu brand that shares your love of TV; the Discovery brand that helps to 'Make Your World Bigger' next to the democratizing voice of the Vice Media brand; the authentic sports fandom of the ESPN brand next to the Netflix brand that recognizes your changing behaviour and encourages you to 'Binge Responsibly'. New brands will emerge, new propositions will be developed; the most creatively driven brands will thrive and the weakest brands will disappear. Rafael Sandor of Vice Media has a vision of how this is going to play out:

> I can see a clear evolution of this business to this multiplication of media attacking the big guys but at the same time the big guys having bigger budgets, they can come with bigger productions, bigger marketing budgets, so it's going to be an evolution... You're going to have, from the democratic online world, some rising stars who are going to become part of the big guys, and some of the big guys will fall because they'll become too clumsy or slow, so this is a revolution we're going through and revolutions are ruthless.[50]

There is no need for TV marketers to fear this revolution, though. It will be a time of huge creative potential. Steve Kazanjian, on behalf of the entertainment design and promotion community that his organization represents, takes an optimistic view:

> If you look across any creative field, technology has always led the way to creative explosion... All the way back to the printing press, technology allowed more people in a creative field to express themselves more than ever before. We are at the same space now, so it's not about access to

technology, it's about distribution, aggregation and marketing. There's such a revolution going on right now, it's incredibly exciting and... over the next five years we are going to see such an explosion of creativity that we're going to look back at this new golden era and be so happy that we had the opportunity not just to exist during that time, but thrive and help mould that time.[51]

– OUR MANIFESTO REDUX... –

In his book *Television Is the New Television* Michael Wolff captures the essence of the value of TV: ie what, ultimately, advertisers are buying and audiences are paying for:

An imaginative moment or mood or relationship or leave-taking from everyday life... a plot worth following, characters worth knowing, a world worth being part of.[52]

Essentially, what Wolff is talking about is stories. Throughout this book we have tried to describe the ways that skilled TV marketers lead us to plots worth following, introduce us to characters worth knowing and amplify worlds worth being part of.

If there has to be an invisible hierarchy in television organizations (as we described in Chapter 1 in relation to the BBC), the creative people who invent and produce the content are still, rightly, at the top: David Chase, J J Abrams, Sally Wainwright, Ryan Murphy, Matt Groening and Jim Brooks, to mention just six names we have come across in the preceding chapters. But long into the future they will depend totally on talented marketers creating curatorial brands to help audiences find their content, and compelling campaigns to promote their shows: in the words of the manifesto in our Introduction, to bring their stories to people.

The future belongs to popular and valuable TV franchises – the hits that Bill Carter described a decade ago – and to distinctive and powerful TV brands. An exciting and dazzling future lies ahead for marketers and creatives with the talent and skill to build them.

NOTES

1 *Doctor Who*, 'The Big Bang' (2010) season five, episode 13, BBC, 26 June
2 Carter, B (2006) *Desperate Networks*, Doubleday Books, Random House, New York
3 Zakrzewski, C (2015) [accessed 23 October 2015] Apple's Tim Cook: 'We Believe The Future Of TV Is Apps' [Blog] WSJ, 9 September [Online] http://blogs.wsj.com/personal-technology/2015/09/09/apples-tim-cook-we-believe-the-future-of-tv-is-apps/

4 McAlone, N (2015) [accessed 23 October 2015] Netflix CEO Reed Hastings Predicts When Cable TV Will Die For Good, *Tech Insider*, 21 September [Online] http://www.techinsider.io/netflix-ceo-says-all-tv-will-be-on-internet-in-10-to-20-years-2015-9

5 Wolff, M and Nelson, E (2015) *Television Is the New Television: The unexpected triumph of old media in the digital age*, Portfolio Penguin, New York

6 Robert Tansey, brand director, content products, Sky, interview 26 June 2015

7 Magnus Willis, founding partner and joint chairman, Sparkler, interview 27 May 2015

8 Magnus Willis, founding partner and joint chairman, Sparkler, interview 27 May 2015

9 Rufus Radcliffe, group marketing and research director, ITV, interview 14 April 2015

10 Ericsson (2015) [accessed 25 February 2016] Ericsson Consumer Lab, TV And Media 2015 Report [Online] http://www.ericsson.com/res/docs/2015/consumerlab/ericsson-consumerlab-tv-media-2015-presentation.pdf

11 Ellen Stone, executive vice president of marketing, Bravo and Oxygen Media, interview 9 September 2015

12 BBC (2015) [accessed 23 October 2015] Babylon: Law, Disorder And Damage Control [Online] http://www.bbcaustralia.com/channels/first

13 Koblin, J (2015) [accessed 23 October 2015] Soul-Searching In TV Land Over The Challenges Of A New Golden Age, *New York Times*, 30 August [Online] http://www.nytimes.com/2015/08/31/business/fx-chief-ignites-soul-searching-about-the-boom-in-scripted-tv.html?_r=0

14 Steve Kazanjian, president and CEO, PromaxBDA, interview 12 August 2015

15 Alexandra Shapiro, executive vice president, marketing and digital, USA Network, interview 26 May 2015

16 Sky Atlantic (2011) [accessed 23 October 2015] Sky Atlantic HD: Let The Stories Begin [Online] https://www.youtube.com/watch?v=XlYrkhSUPyA

17 Linda Schupack, executive vice president of marketing, AMC, interview 11 June 2015

18 BBC (2015) [accessed 23 October 2015] BBC Annual Report and Accounts 2014/2015 [Online] http://downloads.bbc.co.uk/annualreport/pdf/2014-15/bbc-annualreport-201415.pdf

19 Hunt, L (2015) [accessed 23 October 2015] New Best Practices [Conference Presentation] [Online] http://www.leehunt.com/articles/LeeHunt_BestPractices2015_video.pdf

20 Lee Raftery, executive vice president of marketing and communications, NBC Universal International, interview 8 May 2015

21 David Abraham, CEO, Channel 4, interview 26 June 2015

22 Jenny Wall, senior vice president, head of marketing, Hulu, interview 9 October 2015

23 PwC (2015) [accessed 6 November 2015] Key Industry Themes [Online] http://www.pwc.com/gx/en/industries/entertainment-media/outlook/key-industry-themes.html

24 Jenny Wall, senior vice president, head of marketing, Hulu, interview 9 October 2015

25 Hulu (2015) Seinfeld Now Streaming On Hulu [Online] https://www.youtube.com/watch?v=FSuyHMnmdlg

26 Jenny Wall, senior vice president, head of marketing, Hulu, interview 9 October 2015

27 Jenny Wall, senior vice president, head of marketing, Hulu, interview 9 October 2015

28 Lee Hunt, managing partner, Lee Hunt LLC, interview 24 March 2015

29 Littleton, C (2015) [accessed 23 October 2015] Sony's Crackle Tries To Look And Feel More Like Traditional TV, *Variety*, 5 August [Online] http://variety.com/2015/digital/news/crackle-dennis-quaid-art-of-more-1201557493/

30 HBO (2015) [accessed 23 October 2015] Stop Awkward Family Viewing With HBO Go [Blog] SS+K Blog, 11 May [Online] http://blog.ssk.com/stop-awkward-family-viewing-with-hbo-go/#.Vin_kberSUm

31 Fritz, B (2012) [accessed 23 October 2015] Netflix To Premiere All Eight Episodes Of 'Lilyhammer' Simultaneously, *LA Times*, 3 January [Online] http://latimesblogs.latimes.com/entertainmentnewsbuzz/2012/01/netflix-to-premiere-all-eight-episodes-of-lilyhammer-simutaneously.html

32 O'Conner, M (2013) [accessed 23 October 2015] Netflix Adultery Afflicts Half Of Relationships, Says Netflix, *NY Magazine*, 16 May [Online] http://nymag.com/thecut/2013/05/netflix-adultery-afflicts-half-of-relationships.html#

33 MultiVu Video (2012) [accessed 11 December 2015] Netflix – Watch Responsibly [Online] https://vimeo.com/66341459

34 Lee Hunt, managing partner, Lee Hunt LLC, interview 24 March 2015

35 Jackson, D (2015) [accessed 23 October 2015] Netflix: Binge Responsibly [Online] https://www.youtube.com/watch?v=HSVjIU6fzeE

36 Sky (2015) [accessed 23 October 2015] The 4 Stages Of Box Sets With Idris Elba [Online] https://www.youtube.com/watch?v=Ll0n_7hKnro

37 http://www.adteachings.com/post/35645685729/actual-headlines-more-selections-from-abcs

38 Steve Kazanjian, president and CEO, PromaxBDA, interview 12 August 2015

39 Silver, J (2015) [accessed 23 October 2015] Meet Netflix Founder Reed Hastings, *Wired*, 5 February [Online] http://www.wired.co.uk/magazine/archive/2015/02/features/do-adjust-your-set/viewall

40 Ericsson (2015) [accessed 25 February 2016] Ericsson ConsumerLab Report [Online] http://www.ericsson.com/res/docs/2015/consumerlab/ericsson-consumerlab-tv-media-2015-presentation.pdf

41 Ericsson (2015) [accessed 25 February 2016] Ericsson ConsumerLab Report [Online] http://www.ericsson.com/res/docs/2015/consumerlab/ericsson-consumerlab-tv-media-2015-presentation.pdf

42 Jenny Wall, senior vice president, head of marketing, Hulu, interview 9 October 2015

43 Aaron Taylor, former senior vice president of marketing, ESPN, interview, 23 September 2015

44 BBC (2015) [accessed 23 October 2015] BBC Annual Report And Accounts 2014/2015 [Online] http://downloads.bbc.co.uk/annualreport/pdf/2014-15/bbc-annualreport-201415.pdf

45 Philip Almond, director of marketing and audiences, BBC, interview 14 September 2015

46 Philip Almond, director of marketing and audiences, BBC, interview 14 September 2015

47 David Abraham, CEO, Channel 4, interview 26 June 2015

48 David Abraham, CEO, Channel 4, interview 26 June 2015

49 Lee Hunt, managing partner, Lee Hunt LLC, interview 24 March 2015

50 Rafael Sandor, head of TV marketing and creative, Vice Media, interview 11 June 2015

51 Steve Kazanjian, president and CEO, PromaxBDA, interview 12 August 2015

52 Wolff, M and Nelson, E (2015) *Television Is the New Television: The unexpected triumph of old media in the digital age*, Portfolio Penguin, New York

ABOUT THE AUTHORS

ANDY BRYANT

Andy is managing director of Red Bee, a London-based, internationally acclaimed creative agency specializing in marketing and design for entertainment and media companies. He is a member of the leadership team of parent business Ericsson Broadcast & Media Services. He joined Red Bee in 2002, when it was originally established as a BBC commercial division, after a 20-year career in advertising working for highly regarded agencies in London and Sydney. Since then he has led the business to independence from the BBC and to become recognized as a global leader in its field, awarded Europe's Agency of the Year multiple times by PromaxBDA, the association representing creative and marketing professionals in broadcast media worldwide.

Andy has led many high-profile, transformational creative projects for clients including the ITV Network, the BBC, UKTV and CCTV (China's state broadcaster). He has pioneered the development of Red Bee's business in new areas including digital marketing across multiple platforms, user experience design for televisual brands including Virgin Media and new forms of content for a multiscreen world.

A keen social media commentator and blogger on the entertainment industry, Andy is also a frequent speaker at leading industry conferences including the Guardian Edinburgh International Television Festival, European Broadcasting Union and PromaxBDA, having presented on TV brand strategy, marketing and creativity across Europe, the United States, Asia and Australia. A member of the British Academy of Film and Television Arts, he also has a keen interest in the education sector and is honorary professor in film and media at the University of Nottingham and an independent member of the governing Council of the University of Sussex.

CHARLIE MAWER

Charlie is executive creative director of Red Bee, responsible for their global creative output. A graduate of Lady Margaret Hall, Oxford, he began his career in advertising with JWT before joining the BBC promotions team in 1994, where he held a variety of creative director roles. Part of the founding management team of Red Bee, he has led the creative team across a multitude of disciplines including motion design, content for brands and cross-platform storytelling. He is most widely known for his work branding BBC channels, including creating 'the hippos' for BBC One, after which he was selected as one of *Broadcast* magazine's 'Hot 100' faces of the television industry.

He has overseen complex channel rebrands for UKTV, Virgin Media, BT Sport, DreamWorks and NBCUniversal, and entertainment marketing campaigns including Doctor Who 50, World Cups, Olympics, RTÉ2, Universal Channel, BBC America and Comic Relief. Red Bee's digital and UX specialism has led to Cannes Lions-winning work for *The Walking Dead* (Fox International) and decorated campaigns for *Sherlock*, *Horrible Histories* and *Dynamo: Magician Impossible*.

Charlie has won countless creative awards including PromaxBDA, Creative Circle, BTAA and D&AD, as well as a BAFTA nomination. A former chair of industry body Promax UK, he has spoken widely on conference platforms around the world. He has delivered lectures for TEDx, D&AD, the BFI, EBU and Visuelt. He has also contributed to several books on TV marketing. Away from the world of television, Charlie has won several awards for poetry including a Tennyson Anniversary Prize. He is a governor of the digital media specialist Hammersmith Academy and a trustee of Riverside Studios in London.

INDEX

Note: The index is arranged in alphabetical, word-by-word order. Numbers in headings are filed as spelt out in full. Page numbers in *italics* indicate an image or its source.

Aaker, David   44, *45*, 50
ABC   121, 185, 301, 306–07, 312
    Lost   257
Abraham, David   2, 23, 51, 77, 87, 89, 308,
    315
Abrams, J J   23
Adalian, Josef   39
Ainsworth, Peter   172
Al Jazeera   169
Allison, John   91, 113
Almond, Philip   105–06, 183, 222, 244,
    314–15
AMC   21, 307
    Mad Men   129, 130, 136, 138, 272,
        281–82
    The Walking Dead   257, 272–73
Ashgar, Musharaf   90
Aston, John   69
Attenborough, Sir David   71, 200, 286
Australian Broadcasting Corporation (ABC)
    73–75
    Idents   74
    The Chaser's War on Everything   158–59

Bairamian, Justin   3, 20, 76–77, 81, 185,
    245–46
Balmond, Chris   217
Batey Kazoo   74
Batten, Alan   12
Bazalgette, Peter   180
BBC   31, 44, 68, 174, 191–92, 216
    Blue Peter   249–50
    branding   68–73, 75–78, 84, 204
    Casualty   130
    Doctor Who   123–25, 136, 266–68, 292
    EastEnders   14, 21, 130
    'For' campaign   77–78
    Holby City   130
    House of Saddam   142
    idents   70–72, 73, 104
    Luther   139
    marketing and   11–13
    News 24   165, 166
    Only Fools and Horses   150
    Panorama   170
    Peaky Blinders   305, 306

'Perfect Day' promotional film   75–76
Sherlock   255–56, 261–62
Strictly Come Dancing   183, 190–91
The Choir   285–86
The Mighty Boosh   152
The Virgin Queen   133
The Voice   185–86
Top Gear   181
Torchwood   131
'Up the Junction' report   1, 2, 11–12
visual identity   71
Walking with Dinosaurs   197–199
Warriors   134–35
BBC Four   204–05
BBC Three   92, 156, 314
BBC Two   106–09, 307
    comedy   155–56
    50th anniversary   109
    idents   107, 108
    W1A   159
BBC Wales   228–29
BBC World   164
Bean, Sean   215
Beech, Andrew   266–67
Berry, Mary   186
Birt, John   76
Bonnett, Adam   248–49
Booth, Andy   186, 201
Bovill, Chris   91, 113, 114
box sets   311–12
brand positioning   48–49
Brand Relationship Spectrum   44, 45
brands   *see* channel brands
Bravo   283, 286–87, 288, 294, 296
Brill, Steven   55
Brody, Neville   114
Brooke, Dan   88, 91, 92, 170, 173, 175,
    228
Brooker, Charlie   156
Brooks, Jim   6, 153
Burnett, Mark   182

Caddy, Sarah   245
CANAL+ (in France)   44, *45*, 91–92, 217,
    219, 229,
    Tunnel   261, 289

CANAL+ (in Spain) 262, 263
Carter, Bill 301, 317
Cartoon Network 240, 241
CBBC 238, 240, 244
    Horrible Histories 238–39
CBeebies 244, 244
CBS 30, 191
    How I Met Your Mother 264–65
    Survivor 182, 184, 185
channel brands 29–42, 103, 303–04
    competition for 'eyeballs' 2–3
    conduit to programmes 31–32
    masterbrands 307–08
    multiple touchpoints 35–36
    on-demand 308–10
    'pop-up brands' 310
    relaunching 43–65
    taglines 35–37
    USA Network case study 33–40
    viewer data 314, 315
    viewers' expectations 30–31
Channel 5 181
Channel 4 23, 44, 87–92, 112–16, 121,
        130, 302
    Big Brother 180–81, 182
    'Born Risky' campaign 88, 89, 90, 202
    Dispatches 170
    4Creative 112, 152, 203
    Friends 160
    Humans 272–73
    idents 101, 102, 103, 114
    Indian Summers 305
    NewsWall 175
    Skins 132, 291
    The Million Pound Drop 190
    2012 Paralympics 227–28
    Viktoria Modesta video 91
Chibnall, Chris 293
children's programmes 235–52
    audience behaviour 239–43
    channel brands 242–43
    importance of characters 248–49
    involving viewers 236–39
    marketing and 235
    mash-ups 241
    merchandise as marketing 247
    parents and 244–46
    presenters 247–48
    rewarding viewers 249–50
    YouTube 240–41
Cisco 29
CNN 165, 167, 174–75
comedy 147–62
    channel brand and 154–57
    live shows and 159–60
    problems with 149
    trailing shows 147–54

Comedy Central 151, 287, 288
    Workaholics 151
Comic-Con fan convention 259–60
Conway, Sean 209
Cook, Tim 301–02
Corden, James 187–88
Costantini, Diana 74–75
Court TV 43, 54–55
Cowell, Simon 184, 185
Cox, Brian 200
Cronkite, Walter 168
Crozier, Adam 2

Dalai Lama 167
Daley, Paul 75
Dancing with the Stars 184–85, 191
Darroch, Jeremy 68
Dave 43, 46–54, 156, 302
    brand identity 50
    relaunch 53–54
    tagline 50
    'World of Dave' 52
Davie, Tim 2
Davies, Russell T 124
de Zoete, James 156, 201
Desperate Housewives 125
Discovery Channel 196, 198, 200, 201,
        206, 209
    Deadliest Catch 200–01, 205
    'Save Snuffy' campaign 206
Disney Channel 30, 248, 249
    Doc McStuffins 239
    High School Musical 248–49
Disney, Walt 247
documentaries 195–212
    as a thriller 207–08
    channel brand communication 204–05
    'landmark factual' 197–200
    presenters 200–202
    reasons for watching 195–97
    schools 202–03
    scores 208
    season strategy 206–07
    type of storyteller 203–05
Dolan, Liz 13, 21, 140, 197, 198–99, 281,
        298
Dörnemann, Daniel 57–58
drama 121–45
    branding 136–38
    channel branding 132–34
    different strategies 134–36
    emotional engagement of audience 123
    follow-up series 139–42
    three-act structure 130–32
    trailers 128–29
    universal themes 126–28
    use of music 132

DreamWorks   105, 242–43
Drucker, Peter   49
Dubit and Sherbert   241, 244
Duncan, Andy   2
Dyke, Greg   67

EastEnders   14, 21
Eatock, Daniel   180
Eccleston, Christopher   124–25
E4   291
Eiserman, Rick   19–20
Elba, Idris   125, 139, 311–12
Elliott, Yan   147–48
Endemol   180
Engleman, Michael   260, 269
Engine   83
Emin, Tracey   73
entertainment shows   179–94
    audience participation   184–85
    channels and   191–92
    creating an event   182–83
    hosts   185–89
    lasting brands   180–82
    live shows   190–91
    role of hosts   185–89
    social media   183, 189–90
ESPN   214, 216, 218, 220, 314
    'This is SportsCenter'   224, 225, 229
Evans, Ceri   170, 171, 228
Ezer, Anton   204, 225

Fallon   32
Feldwick, Paul   18
Fielder, Jane   53
Fincham, Peter   70–71, 72, 184
'flag channel'   47, 51, 54
Foraker, Brett   102
4Creative   112–13
Fox   13, 21, 140, 302
    Cosmos: A Spacetime Odyssey
        197–200
    Empire   134–35
    Scream Queens   305
    The Following   289–90
    24   137
    Wayward Pines   140
Fox News   163
Fox Sports   219
'frame channel'   68
Friend, Ben   204, 225
FX Networks   4, 92–97, 122, 126, 133,
        281, 287, 288, 295, 302, 307
    American Horror Story   22, 95, 126,
        127, 128, 283–84
    'Fearless'   95, 96 , 97
    Sons of Anarchy   95, 141
    The Simpsons   153–54

Gardner, Julie   124
Garnett, Robin   196, 201–02, 209–10
Garvey, Guy   221–22
Generation Z   304
Gibbons, Stephanie   4–5, 93, 95, 96, 122,
        126, 133, 281, 283–84, 288
Gilbert, Grant   113
Giles, Tom   170
Giusti, Marco   60
Gladwell, Malcolm   236
Glazer, Jonathan   114–15
Gorringe, Neil   132
Gran, Maurice   147
Gray, Jonathan   104
Green, Laurence   32
Green, Robson   195
Groening, Matt   6, 153
Grylls, Bear   200

Haiken, Beth   265
Haines, Tim   198
Hall, Tony   77, 172
Harnett, Oliver   204
Hastings, Reed   302
HBO   97, 125–26, 302
    Awkward Family Viewing campaign   311
    Game of Thrones   259, 262–63,
        268–69, 270–71, 286, 289, 311
    The Sopranos   139–40
    True Detective   131, 132, 136
Heggessey, Lorraine   70, 124
Hewlett, Steve   172
Hicks, Bill   157–58
Hill, Kevin   52
Holzman, Jason   38
Horrocks, Peter   166
hot switching   103
Howe, Dave   2
Hulu   308–10, 315
    Seinfeld   309
Hunt, Jay   90
Hunt, Lee   34, 59, 95, 96, 197, 307, 310,
        311, 313
Hunt, Neil   313

idents   70–72, 73, 101–18
    as brand statements   105
Illuminas   31
Irwin, Steve   200
Isaacs, Jeremy   101
ITV   1, 44, 67, 121, 216
    Ant and Dec   186–87
    brand purpose   83
    brand revitalization   78–83
    Britain's Got Talent   191
    Broadchurch   292–93
    idents   81

ITV *continued*
   logo 80
   The X Factor 184, 189–90
ITV News 165
Ive, Sir Jonathan 250

Jenkins, Henry 257, 258
Joachimsthaler, Erich 44, *45*, 50
Johnson, Cathy 78, 104, 106

Kazanjian, Steve 305–06, 307, 312, 313,
   316–17
Keane, Fergal 170
Kemble, Stephen 171
Ketnet channel 236–37
'key art' 21
Knight, Phil 13
Koonin, Steven R 155
Kosminsky, Peter 134, 135

Lakner, Carsten 297
Lambert, Verity 123
Lambie-Nairn, Martin 69, 101–02, 106,
   107, 113
Landgraf, John 4, 93, 97, 305
LaPointe, Michael 14–15
Lawlor, Jennifer 242–43
Lawrence, Bill 159–60
Lee, Joe 133
Levitt, Walter 148, 150, 280, 288
'Lighthouse identity' 48, 52
Lingham, Jane 13, 17, 77–78, 109
Linn, Chris *55–56*
'living hold' 104
Losasso, Matt 266
Lucas, George 273–74

MakeUseOf 29
Malone, Gareth 285–86
marketing in TV 1–25, 255–77
   advertising revenue 3
   content 13–14, 296
   future of 301–19
   influence of social media 279–300
   navigation role in TV 5
   pace of 19–20
   personalization 312–15
   role of creative in 14–15
   skills 16
   Tao of 16–18
   telling the story 18
   transmedia storytelling 256–57
   see also channel brands, children's
      programmes, drama, documentaries,
      news, sports

Marks, Laurence 147
Masters, Pam 69, 101
Mawer, Charlie 6
McCumber, Chris 1, 33–34
McDonald, John 227
McDowell, Walter 12
McKee, Robert 128
McKenney, Clara 136–37
McKeown, John-Paul 204
Megamax 244
Michaelides, Simon 16–17, 18, 47–48,
   53–54
millennials 279, 304
Minimax 243–44
Mitchell, David 213, 231
Moffatt, Steven 6, 266, 267
'monstering' 168
Moran, Caitlin 14
Morgan, Adam 47–48
Morgan, John 228
MTV 110–11, *112*, 305
Murphy, Ryan 6, 21, 128
Murray, Susan 202
Murrow, Ed 175
Myerson, Jeremy 101

National Geographic Channel 197, 198,
   206
   Cosmos: A Spacetime Odyssey 198
NBCUniversal 1–2, 30, 33, 44, 45–46, 60,
   61
   logo 62
   100% Characters 60–61, *106*
Netflix 301–02, 306, 311, 313
news/current affairs 163–78
   anchorman 168–69
   editorial balance 163–64
   ethics of recreating 172
   fight to be first 165–67
   future challenges 173–76
   making people care 169–71
   online viewing 173
   use of social media 174–75
   viewer loyalty 169
Nickelodeon 245
Nike 13
North, Steve 51, 148

Obama, Barack 199
Ouweleen, Michael 241

Palin, Michael 201
Palmer, Chris 245
'paratexts' 264
Patel, Mina 142

PBS Kids 238
Perera, Rafaela 188
Phillips, Andrea 265, 269
Phillips, Clare 90, 110
Pipes, Tony 136, 179, 185, 187, 203–04, 292–93
Price, Stephen 142
Probst, Jeff 184, 185
producer brands 306–07
PromaxBDA 11, 312
'proof of performance' (POP) 167–68
Proulx, Mike 280

Radcliffe, Rufus 1, 12, 16, 23–24, 78–79, 80, 304
Raftery, Lee 59, 63, 308
R/GA 282–83
Rhodes, Matt 136
Robinson, Mike 172
Robinson, Peter 241
Rotenberg, Lesli 238
RTÉ2 105
Rudd, Matt 80
RKCR/Y&R 77, 222

Saatchi & Saatchi 2
Sandor, Rafael 173, 316
Saunders, Jennifer 148
Scalpello, Ron 229
Scarff, Matt 124
Schaack, Olivier 92, 217, 229
Schmidt, Markus 231
Schupack, Linda 3–4, 21, 129, 280, 282, 307
Schwartz, Barry 32
    The Paradox of Choice 32–33
Schwirtz, Jacob 297
Senior, Richard 124, 157
Shabi, Ruth 52
Shapiro, Alexandra 38, 39, 282, 306
Shepatin, Stacey 280
Showtime
    Dexter 257
    House of Lies 133–34
Sigur Ros 208
Silverman, Evan 210
Skolnick, Barry 215
Sky 17, 44, 83, 220, 311
    Believe in Better tagline 83–84
Sky Atlantic 121, 306
    Boardwalk Empire 128–29, 141
Sky News 165–67, 168, 174
Sky Sports 215–16
Snow, Jon 88
social analytics 288

social media 183, 189–90, 279–300
    building a following 289–90
    influence on TV marketing 279–88
    launch campaigns 288–89
Sparkler 47, 303
Spielberg, Steven 273–74
Spencer, Chris 125–26, 139
sports 213–34
    animation 222–23
    avoid clichéd imagery 220–21
    creating shared memories 228–29
    football 216–17
    global rights 225–26
    humour 218–20
    marketing 213–14, 223–25
    pundits 229
    6 Nations 217–18
    Super Bowl 230–31
    tribalism 216–18
    2012 Paralympics 227–28
    understand the fans 215–16
    use of humour 218–20
    use of music 221–22
Star Wars 246
Stone, Ellen 283, 294, 296, 304
storyworld 258–59
    characters 264–65
    Defiance 259–61, 269
    Doctor Who 266–68, 292
    Game of Thrones 262–63, 268–69, 270–71, 289
    Humans Persona Synthetics 272–73
    immersive experiences 261–63
    launch campaigns 259–61
    'love letters' to the audience 265–69
    Sherlock 255–56, 261–62
    The Choir 285–86
Stotsky, Adam 2
Stun Creative 23, 57, 97, 187, 202
Sugar, Sir Alan 186
Sullivan, John 150
Sutherland, Rory 32
Swadley, Margo 31, 32

taglines 35–37, 50, 103
Takila, Riikka 270
Tansey, Robert 17–18, 83–84, 166, 168, 174, 220, 229, 303
Taylor, Aaron 214, 217, 220, 314
Taylor, Kerry 110, 111, 116
TBS 154–55
Theroux, Louis 195
Thinkbox 31
Thomas, Scott 240
Thompson, Mark 76, 173

TNT   282–83
Tonge, Alice   114
Townend, Kim   287
Trailer Park   19
transmedia storytelling   256–74
    see also storyworld
Tranter, Jane   124
truTV   55–58, 295, 296
Turner Broadcasting   30, 55, 56, 155

UK Gold   150 , 157
UKTV   18, 43, 45
    invisibility   46–47
United Senses   231
Universal Channel   105
    see also   NBC Universal
USA Network   33–40, 49, 59, 103, 302, 306
    brand personality   37–38
    Characters Welcome   36–39, 49, 59
    #HashTagKiller project   282
    logo   35, 37
    Modern Family   155
    Mr Robot   39–40
    Psych   282
    The Dead Zone   33, 36

Vamosy, Michael   57, 97, 202
Varvi, John   93, 94, 96, 97, 141, 153–54,
    287, 295, 307

Viacom   30, 297
Vice Media   316
Vice News   173
Virgin   44
Vohra, Puja   56–57, 58, 295

Wainwright, Sally   315
Walker, James   90, 92, 104, 228, 272
Wall, Jenny   308–09, 310, 313–14
Watch   292
    Dynamo: Magician Impossible
        292
Weiner, Matthew   6, 129, 137
Willis, Magnus   47, 54, 68–69, 303, 313
Winston, Ben   189
Wolff, Michael   302, 317
Wood, Anne   247
Woollen, Mark   131–32
Wormleighton, Ian   236
Wright, Bob   301, 302

Yentob, Alan   106–07, 172
Yesterday   204
Yle   270, 286
Yorke, John   21, 142
Young, Mal   21, 130
YouTube   240–41, 304

Zeller, Adam   286–87, 288